TOURISM DEVELOPMENT
Impacts and Strategies

TOURISM DEVELOPMENT
Impacts and Strategies

Edited by
Dr. Manjula Chaudhary • Dr. K.K. Kamra
Dr. S.S. Boora • Dr. Ravi Bhushan Kumar
Dr. Mohinder Chand • Dr. R.H. Taxak

ANMOL PUBLICATIONS PVT. LTD.
NEW DELHI - 110 002 (INDIA)

ANMOL PUBLICATIONS PVT. LTD.
H.O.: 4374/4B, Ansari Road, Darya Ganj,
New Delhi-110 002 (India)
Ph.: 23278000, 23261597

B.O.: No. 1015, Ist Main Road, BSK IIIrd Stage
IIIrd Phase, IIIrd Block
Bangalore - 560 085 (India)
Visit us at: www.anmolpublications.com

Tourism Development: Impacts and Strategies

First Published, 2007

ISBN 978-81-261-3207-2

PRINTED IN INDIA

Printed at Mehra Offset Press, Delhi

Contents

SECTION III
Strategies and Sustainability

SECTION IV
Information Technology and Tourism

Foreword

The present volume of research articles titled ***Tourism Development: Impacts and Strategies,*** collectively edited by the faculty of the Department of Tourism and Hotel Management of Kurukshetra University is a commendable venture, especially as its publication and release synchronize with the national seminar on the same theme from February 23 - 24, 2007. The book, as it is laid out, seeks to cover a wide range of topics devoted to exploring various important aspects of tourism industry at the national and international levels.

The significance of the book lies in that a multitude of perspectives on the challenges of tourism industry, the strategies to cope with them, and the future trends of growth coalesce into a single volume. Thereby, it readily offers a wide critical scholarship to a large clientele of readership on the subject. Such holistic endeavour will certainly prove useful and productive as much for the students and research scholars as for the personnel engaged in tourism industry in various capacities.

It is no denying the fact that tourism is an important economic activity that, along with other travel related services, accounts for 11.5 per cent of world GDP, 7.9 per cent of world export earnings, and 7.8 per cent of global employment. Its impacts are so far-reaching that in any academic composition on the subject two important concerns are always highlighted. The first, how tourism and the second have propelled development of nations and societies is the feasibility of sustainable approach to tourism development.

Tourism came into being as an alternate to other forms of economic development as it was considered an eco-friendly option but soon its polluting effects not only on environment but on society and culture, alarmed its advocates. Ecotourism was quickly offered as an effective alternative and was adopted in enclaves, though not on a mass scale.

Like other developing nations India too is facing the problem, of negligible share of 0.36 per cent in international tourism traffic. Despite this, tourism accounts for 5.3 per cent of GDP, 10.3 per cent of exports, and 6 per cent of employment. It has a huge domestic base of 300 million tourists that provides confidence to the industry to stand in the international market with greater vitality. It is a happy development that of late, Incredible India has conjured the imagination of world wanderers and the nation suddenly finds itself among top preferences around the globe.

In such a fast changing scenario in the tourism sector the world over as also in India, there is a dire need for scholars and experts to exploit every possible fora and address the issues of current relevance so as to generate such knowledge inputs as can help the industry tide over the roadblocks and open up in new vistas of growth.

It is in this context, I believe, that the present volume of critical essays assumes a special significance. I believe the perceptions and insights gained into the various issues of tourism industry by the scholars on the subject will prove highly valuable to the academicians as well as practitioners engaged in the field of this fast emerging economic activity.

Whereas, I felicitate the faculty of our Tourism Department for their concerted efforts to bring out this volume, I also express the hope that it will make a quality contribution to the existing body of scholarship on the subject.

R.P. HOODA
Vice-Chancellor
Kurukshetra University
Kurukshetra

Preface

Tourism in the developing countries is making a significant headway by focusing on the issues in development and future growth. India is no more an exception to these practices. The tourism record of India, so far, has been a dismal one when compared with her international compatriots but have a reason to derive solace when seen in the context of growth rate of tourism in India in the recent years. India attracted 3.92 million foreign tourists in 2005 registering a growth rate of 13.2 per cent over the previous year. The feat is recommendable in the sense that the world growth rate for the same year was around 5 per cent. The magnitude of growth is more discernible in case of domestic tourism which, according to World Tourism Organisation (WTO), is considered as 10 per cent higher than the international tourism inflows. In 2004, the number of domestic tourists in India was 366 million - a rise of almost 30 per cent over 2003. The World Travel & Tourism Council (WTTC) projections puts the growth of tourism sector in India to grow at 9.7 per cent, which will create nearly 7 million jobs in ten years.

This is the beginning for a long travel. The juncture requires a careful and planned movement into the future. Tourism possesses immense potential — economic, socio-cultural, environmental—provided a right model for development has been adopted. Tourism has led to social, cultural and economic devastation wherever narrow interests and unsustainable practices have taken the lead over the sane ones. It is in this context that serious deliberations are the need of the hour.

Tourism is viewed as a means of achieving both 'economic and social development and progress' and that too through the increase in earnings from tourism. Tourism generated wealth to the tune of US $ 622.7 billion in 2004. The amount goes in trillions when international and domestic tourism are combined. The developed countries are the major beneficiaries of tourism development since they act as major tourists producing markets and covers majority of the destinations. Moreover, the regulatory mechanisms and legal provisions in the developed countries have made tourism to serve the interests of the stakeholders in tourism. The developing countries are in the process of evolving of such mechanism and provisions.

The present book is a modest effort to assess and analyze the nature of development of tourism in the developing countries and to explore the strategies to contain the existing ills in the name of development. Tourism, as is shown in the articles in the book, has provided immediate relief to the communities at the destinations but the long-term consequences are full of side-effects. These impacts are a serious cause of concern for the developing countries. The book presents all such concerns in four major sections. The first section carries the article on the theme tourism development. Since tourism development is the outcome of interplay between various forces and factors, it will require great diligence to explain the role of each and every factor that has influenced tourism development. The second section deals primarily with the impacts of tourism—environmental and socio-cultural. The third section comes in the form of strategies-needed to tackle the negative impacts of tourism and to seek future growth. The fourth section speaks about the role of information technology in tourism that looks into the IT needs of the industry.

Overall, the book intends to provide a wider coverage and discussion to the issues in tourism precisely that of development and sustainability. The issues dealt with in the book may appear to be diverse one but unanimous in their orientation that focuses on the theme 'TOURISM DEVELOPMENT, IMPACTS AND STRATEGIES'.

The Department of Tourism & Hotel Management at Kurukshetra University, Kurukshetra feels grateful to the publishers for their active cooperation and professional expediency to ensure the early publication of the book.

Editors

Section I
Tourism Development

1

The Challenges of EU Integration for Tourism Development—The Hungarian Perspective

Dr. Tamara Ratz
K. J. University College
Székesfehérvár, Hungary

Dr. Laszlo Puczko
Xellum Consulting
Budapest, Hungary

INTRODUCTION

Although tourism has been a major economic activity in Hungary since the 1970's, the industry's structure and characteristics have undergone significant changes in the last decades. Similarly to the impacts of the political transition in 1989-1990, the country's recent EU accession has also considerably influenced the Hungarian tourist industry.

Since the beginning of the preparation period for EU accession, the country received substantial EU funds that were allocated to development projects in various fields including conference tourism as well as spa and health tourism development. As part of the accession process itself, the Hungarian tourism industry gradually adopted the relevant body of European legislation in order to be in harmony with the EU's legal framework.

The paper discusses the major practical and strategic consequences of the EU integration process for Hungarian tourism, and analyses the adaptation measures implemented at national and regional levels. Special consideration is given to the most significant impact to date, notably the expansion of the low cost airline market, and the subsequent changes in the spatial distribution of the country's tourist supply and demand.

1. European Integration and Tourism

The European integration process that led to the enlargement of the European Union in 2004 has affected tourism development in both the 'old' and the 'new' EU states, although the extent of the integration's impacts have obviously been different. The 25-member European Union is faced with challenges arising from the presence of a new diversity of societies and environments, and changing geographical and structural patterns of European tourism development (Hall, Smith and Marciszewska 2006).

In order to facilitate economic, political and legal integration into the European Union, pre-accession funding – through EU development assistance frameworks such as Phare, Sapard or Ispa – has been available for the new member states since 2000 (Hall and Danta 2000). However, due to the heterogeneity of the accession states, the new EU countries are likely to benefit from their Union membership to a different extent. It is expected that there will be winners and losers in the short and medium term, both spatially, from community levels to global relationships, and structurally, in terms of policy priorities and interdependencies (Hall, Smith and Marciszewska 2006).

One of the key challenges for the new member states is to develop the range and quality of their tourist attractions and products, and to communicate them with greater visibility in the dynamic European tourist market, in order to overcome the existing prejudices tourists from the 'old' EU states (NIT 2004). Although EU-membership could, in principle, increase the new entrants' chances of building their overseas image on the Union's already established brand, the currently dominant trend of individual promotional activities as opposed to co-operation in marketing renders this possibility rather unfeasible (Anastasiadou 2006). A similar problem exists on regional level as well: most countries in East Central Europe also desire to promote national diversity and uniqueness rather than offering a common image based on Central European heritage.

As a result of both the long transition process since 1989-90 and the enlargement of the EU in 2004, the countries of East Central Europe experienced a significant development in the range and quality of tourism services and attractions (Michalkó 2001). Although the initial attraction of having "a glimpse behind the Iron Curtain" has begun to wane due to the increased cosmopolitanism of the region's major cities, culture and heritage continue to play a significant role in the new member states tourism product. Critical issues of further tourism development include the improvement of existing facilities, product-based and geographical diversification of markets, and the creation of creative, contemporary attractions in order to satisfy the needs of experience-oriented tourists (Michalkó and Rátz 2005).

2. Hungary

Hungary is situated in the centre of East Central Europe (Figure 1) and, due to its rich variety of cultural and natural resources, relatively high level of economic development, political stability, and good accessibility, it has been a popular tourist destination for decades: following the political changes of 1989-1990, Hungary has been listed by WTO among the 15 most visited countries in the world each year (HNTO 2005).

In Hungary, EU accession represented an extension of an already ongoing process of political and social transition (Smith and Hall 2006). In addition to adopting Western-style regulations and legislation, one of the country's major challenges was to re-assert its pre-socialist European identity and emphasise its individuality and difference within the East Central European region.

Source: http://www.jencons.co.uk/hungary.html

Figure: Hungary in the European Union

According to the marketing strategy of the Hungarian National Tourist Office, the country's major tourism products targeted mainly at international, predominantly EU visitors may be categorised into the following four groups:

- *Health tourism*: medical-oriented and wellness-oriented services provided throughout the country.
- *MICE (Meetings, Incentives, Conferences and Incentives) tourism*: concentrated in Budapest, although the last few years have seen the opening of high quality conference facilities in the country's other major cities.
- *Cultural tourism*: based on Hungary's 1000-year-old heritage (including 8 UNESCO World Heritage sites) and its contemporary culture, as well as historic cities, gastronomy and wine or rural tourism.
- *"Active tourism", an umbrella concept of tourism products based on activities requiring the travellers' physical involvement*: this type of tourism product is built on the existing youth, sport, green and recreational tourism facilities available around

the country's major lakes (Balaton, Velence, Fertõ, Tisza), rivers (Danube, Tisza) and mountains.

3. The main impacts of EU accession on Hungarian tourism

Although a relatively short period has passed since Hungary's EU accession on 1 May 2004, the country was an associate member for ten years prior to that, so the EU integration process has influenced Hungarian tourism development for more than a decade. In preparation for Hungary's EU accession, the tourism industry underwent a step-by-step harmonisation with the EU's legal framework. The country adopted the common body of EU law that governs areas such as foreign policy, movement of goods, persons and capital, transport and the environment. Although integration into the EU seemed to proceed smoothly during the first year of accession, the magnitude of future changes could not be fully anticipated (Puczkó and Rátz 2006).

According to recently published WTTC (2004) industry-supported research data, Hungary and Poland have the highest latent potential for tourism growth among the new EU member states. The prospective additional travel and tourism resulting from structural changes to Hungary's economy following EU accession is estimated at an additional US$22.8bn in GDP and 901,000 jobs. As a direct positive impact of EU accession, Hungary's image among EU members is expected to improve, leading to an increase in the number of visitors from both old and new member countries. This is particularly notable because EU nationals generally perceive other EU destinations as posing less risk, particularly in relation to laws, standards and access to health services (Blake, Sinclair and Sugiyarto 2003).

During the preparation period for EU accession, Hungary received European aid within the framework of the Phare programme. Between 1995-2003, Phare CBC programmes contributed €135mn to the establishment of cross-border co-operation projects in the fields of tourism, infrastructure and transport development, human resources and environmental protection (VÁTI, 2003). As a result of the latest regional development Phare programme for the period of 2002-2003, a total of €54.12mn EU funds were allocated to projects that included: conference tourism development, rural tourism training, spa and health tourism development, transformation of heritage buildings into tourism facilities and urban rehabilitation (VÁTI 2005).

By joining the EU, Hungary has obtained the right to benefit from the Community's Structural Funds which aim to support less developed regions in order to achieve economic and social cohesion between the different member states. Although the key objectives of the Structural Funds do not include the development of tourism explicitly, the tourism industry and tourism destinations may become direct or indirect beneficiaries of all the objectives (adjustment and development of regions where GDP per capita is less than 75 per cent of EU average (European Commission 2004); development of areas undergoing industrial conversion; economic diversification of rural areas; reduction of long-term unemployment and vocational training for young people). In addition to the Structural Funds, Hungary also receives aid from the EU's Cohesion Fund for infrastructural development in the fields of environment and transportation. The country's participation in Community Initiatives such as INTERREG and Equal may also assist cross-border and inter-regional tourism co-operation, and the development of human resources in the tourism industry, respectively (Puczkó and Rátz 2006).

Altogether, as the whole territory of Hungary belongs to the Objective 1 area, during 2004-2006 the country will receive €3.21bn structural aid from the EU (European Commission 2004). However, in this period, EU experts estimate that Hungary will only absorb 30 per cent of funding at most. Specific programmes supported by the Structural Funds include the encouragement of a more diverse rural development and the growth of complementary activities such as rural tourism, as well as the exploitation of natural and cultural heritage resources in the least favoured regions through the development of tourism services.

4. The Immediate Consequences of EU Accession for Hungarian Tourism

Following EU enlargement, Hungary borders four non-EU nations and accounts for 15 per cent of the EU's external land border. In order to comply with the far more stringent EU border control regulations, Hungary spent €40mn to strengthen its eastern and southern borders over the decade prior to accession. Another €150mn EU funding is expected in the following years to further improve border infrastructure, equipment and information technology and to organise training to enable Hungary to join the Schengen Treaty (NFH 2005). However, the fact that Hungary's frontiers coincide with the external frontiers of the EU, at least until the next enlargement, unfavourably affects VFR tourism from the country's eastern and southern neighbours, as Hungarian minority members living in Ukraine, Romania, Croatia and Serbia are now subject to more stringent visa requirements.

One of the major direct impacts of EU accession is the growing number of budget airlines entering the Hungarian market (Puczkó and Rátz 2006). As the new member states are becoming more popular among European customers, accessibility to Central Europe is a key to international success, both for destinations and for airlines. Changes in the regulatory environment following EU accession, particularly the liberalisation of air traffic, opened up the market for several European budget airlines that were ready to seize the opportunity. While in 2003 only two low-cost carriers operated from Budapest, the number of budget airlines grew to eight by the end of 2004, and by October 2006 the number serving Hungary had increased to ten, with new companies continuing to appear.

Low-cost airlines have contributed significantly to the growth of international passenger traffic at Budapest: between March 2005 and February 2006, a record number of 8.174 million travellers were registered at the capital's Ferihegy International Airport, an over 22 per cent increase over the previous 12 months, which made Ferihegy the third busiest Central European airport after Vienna and Prague. Although this growth can also be attributed to the global rebound of air travel after the global depression following 11 September, the rising number of both incoming and outgoing budget airline passengers is a major factor of change in the overall increase of demand. While in 2004 every seventh customer travelled by budget airlines, in the first three months of 2005 already every third passenger was transported by low-cost carriers, and the ratio has remained the same ever since. Comparing the absolute volumes of budget demand, Budapest Airport registered 445,420 customers between January and March 2005, as opposed to 51,667 in the same period of 2004, representing a more than eight-fold increase in the year following the country's EU accession (Budapest Airport 2005, 2006).

Certainly the growth of budget airlines serving Hungary has helped to increase international tourism revenues. In 2004, low-cost airlines brought around 340,000 tourists to the country, increasing direct revenues from tourism by an estimated €90mn and generating an additional €13mn in tax receipts (Galla 2004). In addition to attracting recognised budget airlines such as easyJet or Air Berlin, the significant market demand for low-fare air travel from and to Central and Eastern Europe, together with the elimination of administrative boundaries with EU accession, have also led to the establishment of new low-cost carriers with a regional hub such as WizzAir and SkyEurope (Puczkó and Rátz 2006).

Furthermore, as the EU accession is expected to result in growing incoming demand, the Hungarian government considers the development of regional airports as an economic priority. During 2004, €4.5mn was spent to improve the infrastructure of six regional airports, including FlyBalaton Airport in Sármellék, the gateway to Lake Balaton and to the renowned spa destination Hévíz, and Airport Debrecen in the country's second largest city, which received €1.460mn and €0.880mn respectively (Galla 2004). In 2005, the project continued on a similar scale as the development of regional airports was expected to reduce the spatial concentration of tourism demand and to extend the tourist season. Since the opening of the region's first international airport in May 2006, the country's largest holiday destination, Lake Balaton, has also experienced an increase in foreign interest. Besides visitors, international investors have also noticed the potential of the area; expected economic and social impacts include the development of new resorts, employment creation, and the rise of real estate prices.

In the field of air transport, a potential negative consequence of enlargement is the likely future consolidation process that will particularly affect the Central Eastern European airlines, including the Hungarian national carrier Malév, because of their fragile financial situation (Puczkó and Rátz 2006).

5. Hungarian Tourism in the European Union

Since 2003, in order to become more successful in the European tourism market, Hungary has developed stronger links in the field of marketing with the other members of the Visegrád Group: the Czech Republic, Slovakia and Poland. Experiences show that both intra-European and overseas tourists tend to see the Visegrád countries as one region (e.g. 'East Central Europe'), such that, although all participants joined the EU in 2004, further tourism co-operation within the region is both a necessity and an opportunity. The lessons learnt from the Visegrád project may also help Hungary to become fully integrated into the enlarged EU's international tourism activities (Rátz 2005).

Obviously, in addition to being potential partners in regional tourism marketing, all Central and Eastern European countries are also Hungary's competitors in the European market. Throughout the region, one of the greatest challenges of EU accession is to meet the increased standards and expectations of European customers and to provide the same service quality that they are accustomed to in any other EU destination. Although the quality and the range of the Hungarian tourism supply have improved significantly in the past decade, the country's high 20 per cent VAT rates levied on hotel and catering services may potentially prove a competitive disadvantage (HHA - KPMG 2004). Since VAT rates are generally more favourable elsewhere within the EU (e.g. the Czech Republic boasts a 5 per cent VAT rate on tourism, as does France at 5.5 per cent and Spain at 7 per cent, and even next-door Slovakia's 19 per cent is lower), Hungary as a holiday destination may compare less positively among price-conscious leisure tourists. This therefore suggests a future strategy emphasising higher quality, higher yielding tourism experiences.

Vienna and Prague have long been traditional competitors of the Hungarian capital, Budapest, and although they remain so following EU enlargement, the integration process has opened up further co-operation opportunities as well. With Vienna being the most successful of the three Central European capital cities, in international tourism Prague has been more popular than Budapest over the past decade (Puczkó and Rátz 2006). Although, in the short term, EU enlargement does not seem to threaten Prague's current position as the leading CEE heritage city, Budapest has the geographical advantage of being closer to both Vienna and Bratislava. Following Hungary's and Slovakia's EU accession, visits to the three cities may easily be combined, which, in the medium term, may put geographically more separated Prague in a less competitive position. Co-operation between the national tourist offices of the Czech Republic, Austria and Hungary is aimed especially at the US and Japanese markets, particularly promoting the three capitals to likely visitors to Europe.

A significant future impact of EU accession is the introduction of the single European currency (Rátz 2004). To join the EMU, the country must meet the Maastricht convergence criteria in terms of price stability, long-term interest rate, budget deficit, government debt and exchange rate stability (Rátz and Puczkó 1999). The past few years' economic policy has been characterised by considerable budget and current account deficits, rising inflation and exchange rate volatility. In the country's 2004 convergence programme, the target date for adopting the euro was set at 2010, although today it is unlikely that the country would meet the Maastricht criteria by before 2012. Although both these targets seem to be relatively late after the country's EU accession, the euro is in fact already penetrating the Hungarian private sector. The country's service industry, particularly the hospitality sector, is taking its own steps towards euro integration, with many restaurants and retailers in tourist destinations accepting payment in euros. Hungarian tourists, on the other hand, seem to be relatively unaffected by the single currency: as the results of a recent survey suggested, adoption of the euro in member states does not seem to have influenced significantly the travel behaviour of Hungarian tourists, although there is a significant awareness as well as a favourable perception of the lower transaction costs brought about by the euro (Rátz and Hinek 2005).

CONCLUSIONS

In the relatively short period since EU accession, practical changes have proved to be the most important immediate impacts of EU membership: the expansion of the low cost airline market, the improvement of the border control system in order to meet the Union's criteria, . Budget airlines have played a major role in stimulating both incoming and outgoing traffic, making Hungary a more accessible destination for foreign visitors and a more attractive market for investors. But the low-income yielding end of the market that such visitors may represent, and potential issues of dependence on price-sensitive markets and operators, may require a reappraisal of the role of such airlines in the future.

REFERENCES

- Anastasiadou, C. (2006): Tourism and the European Union. In: D. Hall, M. Smith and B. Marciszewska eds.: *Tourism in the New Europe: The Challenges and Opportunities of EU Enlargement.* CABI Publishing, Wallingford, pp.20-31.
- Blake, A., Sinclair, M.T. and Sugiyarto, G. (2003): Tourism and EU Accession in Malta and Cyprus, Discussion Paper 2003/7. University of Nottingham Tourism and Travel Research Institute (TTRI), Nottingham, http://www.nottingham.ac.uk/ttri/pdf/2003_7.pdf (last accessed 14 November 2005).
- Budapest Airport (2006): Számok - adatok. http://www.bud.hu/szamok_adatok (last accessed 28.10.2006).
- Budapest Airport (2005): Duplázhatnak a Diszkontok Ferihegyen. Budapest Airport, Budapest, http://www.bud.hu/sajtoszoba/kozlemenyek/?article_hid=86 (last accessed 6 May 2005).
- European Commission (2004): The European Structural Funds (2004-2006), Magyarország (Hungary). European Commission, Brussels http://europa.eu.int/comm/regional_policy/atlas/hungary/factsheets/pdf/fact_hu_en.pdf (last accessed 15 May 2005).
- Galla, G. (2004): Két év alatt másfélmilliárd forint regionális repterekre. http://www.magyarorszag. hu/hirek/gazdasag/repterek20041209.html (last accessed 14 November 2005).
- GKM (Gazdasági és Kõzlekedési Minisztérium) (2003) A Széchenyi Terv Hatásai. Budapest: Gazdasági és Kõzlekedési Minisztérium (Ministry of the Economy and Transport).
- Hall, D. and Danta, D. (2000): Enlargement. In: D. Hall and D. Danta eds.: Europe Goes East: EU Enlargement, Diversity and Uncertainty. The Stationery Office, London, pp.377-393.
- Hall, D., Smith, M. and Marciszewska, B. (2006): Introduction. In: D. Hall, M. Smith and B. Marciszewska eds.: *Tourism in the New Europe: The Challenges and Opportunities of EU Enlargement.* CABI Publishing, Wallingford, pp.3-19.

- HHA - KPMG (2004): A szállodaipart érintõ Áfa-kulcs emelésének várható gazdasági hatásai Magyarországon. Hungarian Hotel Association and KPMG, Budapest.
- HNTO (Hungarian National Tourism Office) (2005): *Tourism in Hungary 1990-2004*. HNTO, Budapest.
- Michalkó G. (2001): Beyond the Iron Curtain - Some Aspects of Hungarian Tourism before Integration to European Union. *Integra* 1(1):21-23.
- Michalkó, G and Rátz, T. (2005): A kulturális turizmus élmény-gazdaságtani szempontjai. In: Gy. Enyedi and K. Keresztély eds.: A magyar városok kulturális gazdasága. MTA Társadalomkutató Központ, Budapest, pp.123-141.
- NFH (National Development Office) (2005): The National Institution System of the Schengen Fund and the Use of Funding. NFH, Budapest http://www.nfh.hu/angol/xindex2.htm?t=3&i=28&ci=61 (last accessed 14 November 2005).
- NIT (Institut für Tourismus- und Bäderforschung in Nordeuropa GmBH) (2004): *Impacts of EU-enlargement on Tourism. Report from the International Conference ,A New Tourism for a New Europe'*, http://www.tourism.org.mt/uploads/1453/Report_New_Europe.pdf (last accessed 28.10.2006)
- Puczkó, L. and Rátz, T. (2006): Product Development and Diversification in Hungary. In: D. Hall, M. Smith and B. Marciszewska eds.: *Tourism in the New Europe: The Challenges and Opportunities of EU Enlargement*. CABI Publishing, Wallingford, pp.116-126
- Rátz, T. (2005): The Development of Tourism as a Catalyst in European Integration. *Proceedings of the 1st International Conference on "Challenges of Regional and Market Integration for Tourist Destinations"*, Giza, Egypt, 14-16 November 2005. October 6 University, Giza, pp.61-70.
- Rátz, T. (2004): *European Tourism*. Kodolányi János University College, Székesfehérvár.
- Rátz, T. and M. Hinek (2005): The Implications of the Single European Currency for Hungarian Tourism. In: *Proceedings of the First International Scientific Conference 'Theoretical Advances in Tourism Economics'*, Évora, Portugal, 18-19 March 2005. Évora, Portugal: Urban and Regional Analysis and Research Laboratory, University of Évora, CD-ROM, File Tamara Ratz P.
- Rátz, T. and Puczkó, L. (1999): The Future of Tourism in the European Monetary Union. Paper presented at the IV CEMS Academic Conference, Barcelona, Spain, 23-26 March 1999.
- Smith, M. and Hall, D. (2006): Enlargement Implications for European Tourism. In: D. Hall, M. Smith and B. Marciszewska eds.: *Tourism in the New Europe: The Challenges and Opportunities of EU Enlargement*. CABI Publishing, Wallingford, pp.32-43.

- VÁTI (2005): Phare 2002-2003. Promotion of Integrated Local Development Actions Programme, Granted Projects. VÁTI Kht Hungarian Regional Development and Town Planning Non Profit Company, Budapest.
- WTTC (2004): Latent Potential of Travel & Tourism in New EU Accession Countries Totals an Additional US$54.6bn GDP and 2 Million Jobs. WTTC, London, http://www.wttc.org/news50pdf.pdf (last accessed 6 May 2005)

2

Perception of Selected Dimensions of Ecotourism: A Comparative Study of Tourists and Locals in Amphawa Community, Samutsongkram Province

Panrawee Na Lamphoon and Adarsh Batra, Ph.D
Graduate School of Business, Assumption University

ABSTRACT

The overall objective of this research was to investigate the difference in the perception of tourists and locals towards the selected dimensions of ecotourism. A sample survey method was used, with a structured questionnaire as the research instrument, at Amphawa Community Samut-songkram Province. Primary data from 200 locals and 200 tourists, as the respondents, was used for statistical analysis.

Key findings showed that there were significant differences in the perception of tourists and locals toward the 'natural environment', 'learning experience' and 'responsible action' whereas there was no difference in the perception of tourists and locals toward 'participation' as the selected dimension of ecotourism. The research also indicated that ecotourism can provide contributions and incentives for nature conservation as well as providing opportunities for both community livelihoods and tourists.

Keywords: Ecotourism, Community, Perception, Sustainable tourism, Tourists, Locals

INTRODUCTION

The Tourism industry has been developed into a large industry as a result of the development of transportation, telecommunication, infrastructure and superstructure. The number of international tourists has grown rapidly from 1950 to 1990, increasing from 25 million people to 565.4 millions over the period (WTO, 2000). The industry is accepted internationally and provides a major boost to the economy of the country as Thailand, a driver of development and in reduction of unemployment.

With the emergence of ecotourism globally, Thailand has attempted to promote this type of tourism by setting up guidelines for sustainable tourism development. The Tourism Authority of Thailand (TAT) aims to preserve the culture, tourism resources and natural environment of the country so as to maintain its uniqueness and heritage, and to engage all stakeholders.

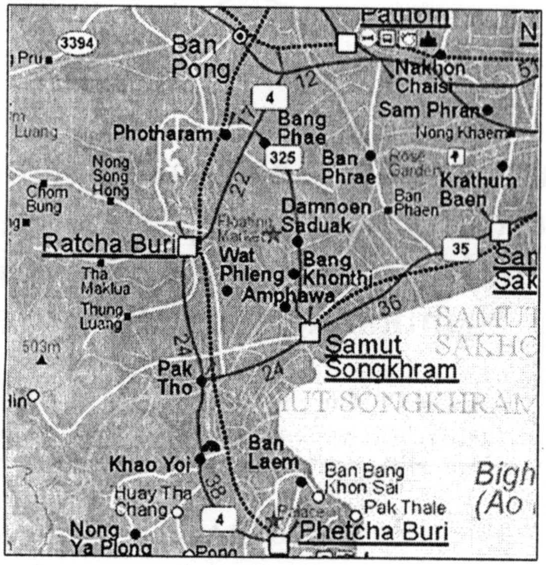

Source: www.thailandguidebook.com (2005)

On the other hand, it also focuses on maximizing the number of tourists in order to encourage economic development, and promote internal tourism to national attractions (TAT, 2003). Ecotourism goes hand in hand with sustainable tourism and TAT encourages local authorities to develop this form of tourism as a means of maintaining the social, cultural and conserving the natural environment of the community. It also aims to increase awareness and understanding of local cultures and local environment through the participation of local people.

The Study Area

The Amphawa community in this study covers the sub-districts of Amphawa, Suanluang, Bangchang, Bangkae, Bangnanglii, Taka and Plaipongpang in Samutsongkram Province. This area has started to attract both Thais and foreigners with ecotourism being the main focus. Besides the outstanding classic lifestyles, the historical, traditional and cultural attractions, scenery and natural atmosphere of Amphawa community, Samutsongkram is both amazingly and fascinating. So it is necessary for the government to set appropriate guidelines to regulate the groups working to operate the businesses in the region including home-stay and sight seeing areas. The well being and standard of life of the locals is also a function to be taken into account. Therefore, regulations need to be implemented as guidelines in every area and enforced so the local people follow the regulations, and damage to the environment is minimized.

Many misconceptions about ecotourism persist. The widespread misuse of the term has led to skepticism, especially among local communities and visitors. Many of Thailand's natural areas continue to be threatened with rapid degradation due to illegal hunting, and the extraction of trees, bamboo and other plants from the forest. Encroachment by neighboring landowners and uncontrolled fires are also threats. Much of the destruction is driven by local poverty and the absence of more lucrative pursuits. Visitors are often left with little understanding of local natural history and the linkages necessary to generate conservation incentives for local communities are lacking. Therefore, ascertaining the similarities and differences in the perception of tourists and locals—that is how they sense and know the rich and varied world of things and people that surrounds them may help in future planning for effective sustainable tourism. This leads to the basic question: "Whether there are any differences in the perceptions of tourists and locals towards selected dimension of Ecotourism in the Amphawa community, in Samutsongkram province?"

LITERATURE REVIEW

Weber (1991) stated that perception is usually taken to mean the final, organized and meaningful experience of sensory information. Halonen and Santrock (1999) clarified that perception is the process of organizing and interpreting sensory information to give it meaning. The International Ecotourism Society defined ecotourism as - "Responsible travel to natural areas which conserves the environment and improves the welfare of local people".

Lindberg and Hawkins (1999) stated that Ecotourism areas often include local communities, especially of traditional people, and therefore, ecotourism plans must be holistic in approach and consider ways to conserve local culture traditions and identities and how to bring benefit to them. Local populations are usually the first to be affected by any change in activities in their locations. Pragmatically managed, ecotourism can play a significant role in provisioning for livelihood as an integral component of an ecosystem. However, meeting such conservation objectives requires careful and appropriate planning and design.

Bhattacharya, et al., (2003), attempted to explore a few aspects of community based ecotourism of an essentially local area, in close proximity to Bhopal, the capital of Madhya Pradesh, India. This research presented a general consensus on the basic elements of ecotourism that "Ecotourism contributes to biodiversity conservation; sustains well-being of local people; includes an interpretation/learning experience; involves responsible action on the part of tourists and the tourism industry; stresses local participation and ownership of business opportunities". It showed that while there is appreciation by tourists, there is a strong resentment towards the non-environmental tourist behavior.

Goodwin (1996) defined ecotourism as low-impact nature tourism which contributes to the maintenances of species and habitats either directly through a contribution to conservation and/or indirectly by providing revenue to the local community sufficient for local people to value, and therefore protect, their wildlife heritage area as a source of income.

RESEARCH FRAMWORK

In this study, the researchers compare the difference in the perceptions of Locals and Tourists on the selected dimensions of ecotourism. The four selected dimensions include natural environment, learning experience, responsible action and participation.

The independent variables were the locals and Tourists both domestic tourist and international. The researcher used the word 'locals' instead of 'resident'. The definition of 'resident' given by TAT (2003) is used to explain the word 'locals' in this research as: a person considered to be resident in a country (place) if that person has lived in that country (place) for at least twelve (six) consecutive months prior to his/her arrival in another country (place) for a period not exceeding one year (six months).

The dependent variables were (1) *Natural Environment*: surroundings, especially those affecting people's lives, all the conditions and influences affecting the development of an organism (Theingburanathum, 1995). (2) Learning experience: To become aware by information or from actual observation of facts or events, training and personal participation (Theingburanathum, 1995). (3) *Responsible action*: having to account for one's act, behavior, and physical movement (Theingburanathum, 1995). (4) Participation: The act of providing input into such decision and it has become part of the conventional wisdom in planning as a whole, as well as in much tourism development (Stone and Wall, 2003).

RESEARCH METHODOLOGY

Questionnaire

The research instrument used was a structured questionnaire. There were two parts. In 'Part I', there were 20 statements concerned with selected dimensions of ecotourism that included natural environment, learning experience, responsible action and participation, that used the five points Likert scale to measure the perception with 1 for "strongly disagree", 2 "disagree", 3 "neutral", 4 "agree", and 5 "strongly agree". In 'Part II', questions were asked about the respondents' personal data.

Hypotheses

There were four hypotheses and twenty sub-hypotheses in this research which tested whether significant differences exist in the perception of tourists and locals in relation to ecotourism.

Method

The methodology used in this research was a sample survey. Convenience sampling was used as the survey technique, with the target respondents comprising tourists and locals in the area of Amphawa community, Samutsongkram province. The sample size for this study was 400 comprising 200 tourists and 200 locals as respondents. Tourists were selected based on the purpose of their visit and length of stay in Amphawa, and whether they had stayed at least one night. Locals were asked how long they have been living in Amphawa, and the questionnaires were given to those who had lived for more than five years in the province. The questionnaires were distributed in May 2005.

Method of Analysis

The collected data was analysed using the Statistical Package for Social Sciences (SPSS). First of all demographic variables were summarized by using frequency and percentage distributions. Then the paired sample t-test was used to test four main hypotheses. P value of 0.05 or less was used as the criterion to determine the significance of observed differences.

RESULTS

Respondents' Profile

Table one reports the respondents' demographic characteristics: the majority of the respondents were female (both tourists 56.5% and locals 52.0%), in the age range of 21 to 30 years (both tourists 36% and locals 29.5%), with monthly average income in the range of 5,001-15,000 bahts (both tourists 36.5% and locals 46.0%) respectively. Most of tourists had bachelor's degree (46%) in comparison to most of locals (36.5%) having high school or equivalent.

Table 1: Description of the Participants (N = 400)

Profile variables	Tourists' Majority	Percentage	Locals	Percentage Majority
Gender	Female	56.5	Female	52.0
Age (years)	21-30	36.0	21-30	29.5
Educatio-nal level	Bachelor's	46.0	High school or equivalent	36.5
Income level (Bahts)	5,001-15,000	36.5	5,001-15,000	47.0
Occupation	Private sector	44.5	Public sector	28.0

Respondents' Perception of the Dimensions of Ecotourism

The first perception of ecotourism considers natural environment. The average mean for natural environment, for locals and tourists was (m_l = 4.05 and m_t = 3.84) respectively. The average mean for learning experience were valued at (m_l = 4.08) specified to locals and while the tourists' (m_t = 3.89). The average mean of perception of ecotourism toward responsible action was (m_l = 4.08) for locals and (m_t = 3.79) for tourists. And the average mean score for participation was (m_l = 4.18) for locals and (m_t = 4.06) for tourists' respectively (see figure two and table two).

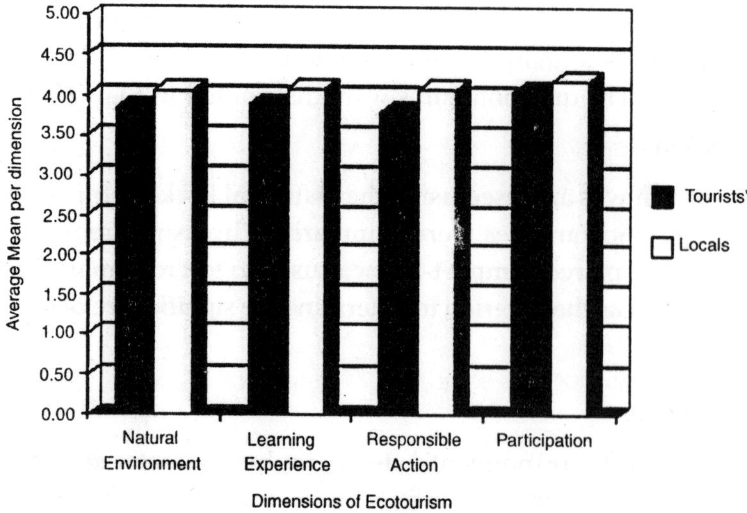

Figure 2

Table 2.

Dimensions of Sustainability	Respondent	N	Mean[a]	SD	t	df	Sig. (2 tailed)
Natural	Tourists	200	3.84	0.572	-3.355	199	.001*
environment	Locals	200	4.05	0.636			
Learning environment	Tourists	200	3.89	0.681	-3.505	199	.001*
	Locals	200	4.08	0.538			
Responsible action	Tourists	200	4.08	0.553	-4.138	199	.000*
	Locals	200	3.79	0.734			
Participation	Tourists	200	4.18	0.585	-1.870	199	0.63
	Locals	200	4.06	0.647			

[a] all responses is based upon a five-point strongly disagree (1) to strongly agree (5) scale

* Significant at 0.05

DISCUSSION

1. Respondents' Perception of Natural Environment

This research revealed that the tourists and the locals have significant differences in perception, when taking natural environment, as the main dimension of ecotourism in the Amphawa community. Most of the local respondents agreed that ecotourism in Amphawa community encourage long-term viability of the region, even they somewhat agreed that ecotourism helps in minimizing environmental stress. In contrast, most of the tourist respondents agreed that ecotourism in Amphawa community conserves the natural resources and improve habitat protection, but they somewhat think that ecotourism can encourage long-term viability of the region.

Environmental preservation and resource conservation plans should be set up, implemented and regularly monitored by all stakeholders. Training and education programmes should cover subjects such as the environment and socio-cultural impacts of ecotourism and national flora and fauna etc. An immediate need is to improve empowerment situation so locals can control resources and decisions affecting their lives as locals are the end users. Tourists should support any activities encouraging ecotourism, and refrain from indulging in activities that may harm the environment.

2. Respondents' Perception of Learning Experience

This research also revealed that the tourists and the locals have significant differences in perception with respect to the learning experience, the second main dimension of ecotourism in Amphawa community. Local respondents believed that ecotourism in Amphawa provide opportunities to experience nature in ways to gain greater understanding. Tourists experienced nature and highly appreciated nature as an important resource but expressed concerned that most tourist activities or the tourist attractions do not have much educational value.

All stakeholders need to be well educated about ecotourism. Some training courses should be arranged to educate or brief the locals, to foster a clearer understanding and appreciation of the value of the land and its effective contribution as a capital resource. Hence there is a need to inform them of the impacts of tourism clearly and this should be articulated through campaigns, information exchange and proactive educational programs. When the locals are completely clear of the concept of ecotourism, they can transfer the right "messages" to tourists, so tourists can experience nature in ways that give them greater understanding, and they will behave accordingly. It should be ensured that tourists have the opportunity to learn from local people to create a close relationship which respects the attainments made through community efforts.

3. Respondents' Perception of Responsible Action

This research indicated that tourists and the locals have different perceptions, when taking responsible action; the third main dimension of ecotourism in the Amphawa community. While most of local respondents agreed that ecotourism in the Amphawa community helps protect the community's economy and avoids environmental damage, tourist respondents do not share this perception. Tourists perceived that, the locals perform their economic activities without taking environmental costs and values into account.

Empowerment comes with responsibility. When power is delegated to locals, they can reclaim self-determined development. Some courses, seminars, and discussions about ecotourism should be arranged to raise awareness of locals about ecotourism and this may stimulate responsible action.

4. Respondents' Perception of Participation

This research also indicated that tourists and locals share no different perceptions about participation; the fourth main dimension of ecotourism in Amphawa community. Both tourists and locals are willing to promote ecotourism of Amphawa community. Both were willing to donate money to support ecotourism in the Amphawa community. Locals have shown more willingness to get more education about ecotourism in the area and agreed that ecotourism in the Amphawa community provides social interaction between visitors and locals. Tourists have shown moderate willingness to purchase local products and services while locals have also shown moderate willingness to produce local products.

Both tourists and locals may need to view ecotourism from a broad prospective, hence there could be a need for measures geared to emphasize the meaningful participation of all the actors involved in promoting sustainability. The challenge that lies ahead therefore consists of establishing cooperation between tourists and locals.

Limitations and Scope for Further Research

The main limitations of this study are: Firstly, the number of dimensions selected for this study was limited to only four topics—natural environment, learning experience, responsible action and participation. Secondly, the design of the study was for tourist and local respondents who were in the Amphawa community at the specific time; therefore, the findings cannot be generalized for other time periods. Thirdly, because this study was conducted in Amphawa community, Samutsongkram province, the findings may not be generalized to other areas within Thailand or elsewhere.

It is possible through further studies to investigate other related dimensions of ecotourism such as economic factors, and the cultural environment. Investigating other kinds of tourism such as agro-tourism, waterway tourism, home-stay, could be conducted as well. Further studies could be conducted in another community, or the other areas where there are the similar ecological issues.

BIBLIOGRAPHY

Balmer, M. (2004). *Questionnaires* Volume I. SAGE, London.

Besculides, A., Lee, E., Matha., and McCormick J., P. (2002). Residents'. Perceptions of the Cultural Benefits of Tourism. *Annals of Tourism Research,* A. Social Sciences Journal. 29(2), 303-319.

Benjapinya, M. (2002). *Residents' perception of impacts to tourism development on national and build environments on Koh Chang.* Unpublished Master of Arts tourism management thesis, Assumption University, Bangkok, Thailand.

Bhattacharya, A.K., Banerjee, S., and Saksena, V. (2003). Local Initiatives to Localize Ecotourism: An Exploratory Study in Kerwa, Van Vihar National ParkCatchments. *Tourism Recreation Research,* 28(1), 97-102.

Blake, R. and Sekuler, R. (1990). *Perception.* McGraw-HILL. New York.

Boyd W., S. & Butler W., Richard (1996). Managing ecotourism: an opportunity spectrum approach, *Tourism Management,* 17(8), 557-566.

Buckley, R. (2003). *Case studies in Ecotourism.* CABI.

Crouch, I. G., Ritche, J.R., Brent (2003). *The competitive Destination: A Sustainable tourism perspective.* CABI.

Davidoff, S., Doris CTC, Davidoff G. Philip CTC, and Eyre, Douglas J., (1995). *Tourism Geography.* Prentice Hall. New Jersey.

Dowling, K. R. and Fennell, A. D. (2003). *Ecotourism Policy and Planning,* CABI.

Dowling, K. R. and Page, J. S. (2001). *Ecotourism.* Prentice-Hall. Essex, UK.

Dowling, K. R., Singh, S., and Timothy J., D. (2003). *Tourism in Destination Communities.* CABI.

Garrod, B. (2003). Local Participation in the Planning and Management of Ecotourism: A Revised Model Approach, *Journal of Ecotourism,* 33-53.

Goodwin, H. (1996) In pursuit of ecotourism. *Biodiversity and Conservation.* 5(3), 277-291.

Griffin, T., Harris, R., and Williams, P. (2002). *Sustainable Tourism: A global perspective.* Butterworth-Heinemann.

Hawkins, R., and Middleton T.C. V. (1998). *Sustainable Tourism: A Marketing Perspective.* Butterworth-Heinemann.

Hawkins, E., Donald (2001). Ecotourism opportunities for developing countries. *Ecotourism Development in the Third Millennium Sustainable Tourism and Community Development.* The 5th International Conference, Srinakarinvirot University, Bangkok.

Hockberg, J. (1969). *Perception.* Prentice-Hall of India. New Delhi.

Holden, A. (2000). *Environment.* Routledge, London

Kerlinger, N. F. (1964). *Foundations of Behavioral Research: Educational and Psychological Inquiry.* Holt, Rinehart and Winstons, Inc. New York.

Lennon J., John (2003). *Tourism Statistics: International Perspectives and Current Issues.* Continuum.

Lindberg, k. and Hawkins, D. (eds) (1999). *Ecotourism: A Guide for planners and Managers.* Vol. 1, Dehradun, Natraj Publishers.

Mcclaren, F. T. (2002). Report International Year of Ecotourism in Review. *Journal of Sustainable Tourism,* 10(5).

Milne, S.S. (2000). *Tourism and sustainable development: exploring the Global-local nexus.* Addison Wesley Longman, New York.

Neil, J., and Wearing, S. (1999). *Ecotourism: Impacts, Potentials and Possibilities.* Butterworth-Heinemann.

Orams, B. M. (1995). Towards a more desirable form of ecotourism. *Tourism Managemen,* 16(1), 3-8.

Proyrungroi, R. (2002). Tourism Development and Environmental Concerns in Thailand. *Christian University Journal*, 8(3), 19-28.

Puczko, L. and Ratz, T. (2000). Tourist and Residents Perceptions of the Physical Impacts of Tourism at Lake Balaton, Hungary: Issues for Sustainable Tourism Management, *Journal of Sustainable Tourism*, 8(6), 458-478.

Ross, W. (2003). Sustainable Tourism in Thailand: Can Ecotourism Protect The Natural and Cultural Environment? *Second Meeting of the Academic Forum for Sustainable Development.*

Shaw, G. and Williams, M. A. (2002). *Critical Issues in Tourism: A Geographical Perspective*, Blackwell Publishers. Oxford, UK.

Stone, M. and Wall, G. (2003). Ecotourism and Community development: Case studies from Hainan, China. *Environmental Management* 33(1), 12-24.

Swarbrooke, J. (1999). *Sustainable Tourism Management*, CABI Publishing, Oxon, UK.

Theigburanathum (1995) Thai English dictionary on-line document.

Weaver, B. D. (2001). *Ecotourism.* WILEY

Weaver, B. D. (1998). *Ecotourism in the Less Developed World.* CABI.

Weaver, B. D. (2003). *The Encyclopedia of Ecotourism.* CABI.

Weber (1991)Zikmund, W.G. (1994). *Business Research Methods.* The Dryden Press: Orlando.

Online Sources

http://www.world-tourism.org on 10th December 2004.

http://www.tourismthailand.org on 15th December 2004.

http://www.wttc.org on 22nd August 2005

http://www.maeklongtoday.com on 22nd August 2005

3

Active Tourism in Hungary –Local Development Patterns in a Global Market

Dr. Tamara Ratz
Professor of Tourism
Head of Tourism Department
Kodolányi János University College
Székesfehérvár, Hungary

Mr. István Vizi
Associate Professor
Head of Institute of Economic Sciences and Tourism
K.J. University College
Székesfehérvár, Hungary

INTRODUCTION

Hungary is situated in the centre of East Central Europe and, due to its rich variety of cultural and natural resources, relatively high level of economic development, political stability, and good accessibility, it has been a popular tourist destination for decades.

Active tourism as a tourist product has been in the forefront of Hungarian national tourism policy throughout the last decade. The active tourism product, however, exists as a specifically Hungarian notion (the international tourism literature sources mainly refer to 'adventure tourism', 'sport tourism' or 'active holidays'): as an umbrella concept, it incorporates a wide range of highly different tourism products with consumers' physical activity as their single common feature.

The Concept of Active Tourism

By definition, the concept of active tourism in Hungary includes all forms of tourism that require the active physical involvement of tourists in the consumption process while providing an experience outside their normal residence or workplace (Michalkó 2004, Vizi 2005). The products and activities offered within the umbrella concept of active tourism may be categorised into three major groups depending on the type of resource providing the basis for product development (Table 1).

Table 1: Main Types of Active Tourism Products

Air-dependent	Earth-dependent	Water-dependent
Hang gliding	Hiking, walking	Diving, snorkelling
Hot air ballooning	Orienteering	Swimming
Parachuting	Rock climbing	Surfing
Skydiving	Cycling, mountain biking	Canoeing, rowing
Ultralighting or microlighting	Horse riding	Rafting
	Golf	Canyoning
	Hunting	Fishing
	Skiing, snowboarding	Angling
	Snowmobiling	Sailing
	Quad driving	
	Paintball	
	Archery	

However, there is a conceptual vagueness characterising the definition of active tourism in the tourism literature. 'Active tourism' as such is a relatively infrequently used term by researchers, probably due to its complexity and the inherent difficulties arising from classifying such a wide variety of activities as one single product. Although practitioners – particularly marketing officers, tourism developers, and other local and regional decision makers – tend to refer to 'active tourism development' more regularly (e.g. Wieczorek 1999), the concept often overlaps with ecotourism (Furlan et al 2004), rural tourism (Breda et al 2006), nature tourism (Cazes 1989, Lennon et al 2006), health tourism (Steward 2005) or sport tourism (e.g. De Knop 1990, Standeven and De Knop 1999).

Marketing Active Tourism in Hungary

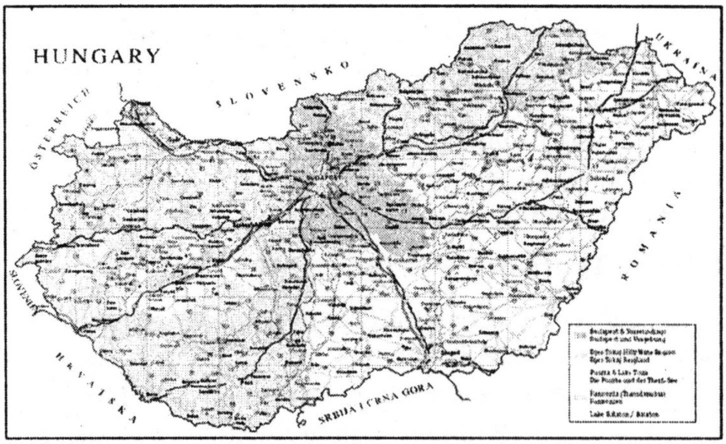

Source: HNTO 2006

Figure 1: The main tourist regions of Hungary

Active tourism development in Hungary is based on the country's physical features such as the River Danube and Tisza, the lakes of Balaton, Tisza, Velence and Fertõ, the relatively low mountain ranges, the Eastern and Western plains as well as the abundant flora and fauna (Figure 1). Active tourism products are distributed relatively evenly throughout the country, with a concentration of water-based activities around the lakes, particularly around Lake Balaton, the largest freshwater lake of Central Europe and the most significant holiday resort of Hungary (Rátz and Vizi 2005).

In the annual marketing strategy of the Hungarian National Tourist Board (HNTO) as well as in the organisation's recent international marketing campaigns, active tourism has been defined as a priority product. As the following excerpt from the introduction of the 'Active Holiday' brochure illustrates, product development in active tourism is mainly based on water and earth, with a special emphasis on the freedom offered by the country for Western tourists, thus turning Hungary's relative underdevelopment into an advantage:

> *"If you're a devotee of water sports or fishing, you'll be met by sunshine, clean air, an undisturbed countryside, numerous rivers, lakes and streams as well as Central Europe's largest lake and river. Lovers of the hunt will be tempted by territories rich in game and enormous trophies, while there are professional courses for golfers. If it's hills and woods that you're after, then there are hundreds of kilometres of nature trails through spectacular countryside, while for passionate cyclists and equestrians there are flat and hilly terrains, marked routes and unspoilt nature, free of restraints, forbidding signs and fences "* (HNTO 2006).

Research Methodology

The main aim of the research was to investigate Hungarian travellers' attitudes towards and participation in active tourism activities. Attitudes and participation in active tourism were analysed on the basis of a structured questionnaire survey with a sample size of 1296. Based on the HNTO's marketing strategy, a pre-determined set of active tourist activities were assessed within the framework of the survey, including horse riding, water sports, cycling, hiking, golf, angling, hunting, skiing and aviation sports.

The survey was conducted during May and June 2005. Due to financial limits and the lack of necessary data, convenience sampling was used which limits the representativity of the research findings to the attitudes and activities of the respondents. Table 2 summarised the survey participants' characteristics.

Table 2: Characteristics of the sample

Age Distribution (%)					
Under 18	18-25 years	26-35 years	36-49 years	50-59 years	N/A
19.2	45.8	14.7	10.9	8.2	1.3

Education level (%)			
Primary	Secondary	Higher	N/A
20.2	61.1	18.5	0.8

Occupation (%)							
White collar	Blue collar	Self-employed	Inactive	Student	Military	Other	N/A
26.4	5.8	5.2	3.4	56.5	0.2	0.6	1.9

Income (%)						
Well under average	Slightly under average	Average	Slightly over average	Well over average	Refused response	N/A
7.2	9.3	31.0	15.0	3.1	30.1	4.3

Research Findings

Table 3 provides an overview on respondents' interest in various active tourist offers. As the Table indicates, the socio-demographic characteristics of respondents only played a significant role in a few cases (marked by bold).

Table 3: Respondents' interest in active tourism (mean*)

Gender			
Activity	**Male**	**Female**	**Total**
Horse riding	2.43	3.08	2.81
Water sports	3.33	3.05	3.17
Cycling	3.18	3.23	3.21
Hiking	3.61	4.00	3.84
Golf	2.19	1.81	1.97
Angling	2.99	1.87	2.34
Hunting	2.49	1.54	1.94
Skiing	3.10	2.94	3.00
Aviation sports	3.00	2.80	2.88

Age						
Activity	**Under 18**	**18-25**	**26-35**	**36-49**	**50-59**	**Total**
Horse riding	2.91	2.84	2.88	2.77	2.47	2.82
Water sports	3.21	3.34	3.28	2.77*	2.51*	3.17
Cycling	3.11	3.17	3.50*	3.28	3.07	3.21
Hiking	3.32	3.79	4.09*	4.29*	4.34*	3.85
Golf	2.00	2.10	1.92	1.65	1.69	1.97
Angling	2.29	2.34	2.52	2.13	2.30	2.33
Hunting	2.15	1.94	1.96	1.57	1.84	1.94
Skiing	3.17*	3.18*	2.99	2.56	2.37	3.01
Aviation sports	3.31*	3.04*	2.86*	2.24	1.95	2.89

Education level

Activity	Primary	Secondary	Higher	Total
Horse riding	2.84	2.82	2.78	2.81
Water sports	3.11	3.17	3.21	3.17
Cycling	3.11	3.20	3.34	3.21
Hiking	3.41	3.90*	4.09*	3.84
Golf	2.02	1.99	1.85	1.97
Angling	2.31	2.38	2.24	2.34
Hunting	2.03	1.90	1.96	1.94
Skiing	3.06	3.00	2.98	3.01
Aviation sports	3.15*	2.85	2.71	2.88

Income

Activity	**Well under average**	**Slightly under average**	**Average**	**Slightly over average**	**Well over average**	**Refused response**	**Total**
Horse riding	2.94	2.81	2.77	2.80	2.53	2.86	2.81
Water sports	3.08	3.03	3.15	3.26	3.18	3.22	3.17
Cycling	3.10	3.46	3.23	3.06	3.37	3.18	3.20
Hiking	3.88	4.34*	3.96	3.76	3.58	3.61	3.84
Golf	1.78	1.89	1.96	2.06	2.03	1.98	1.96
Angling	2.22	2.32	2.36	2.49	2.40	2.29	2.35
Hunting	1.93	1.92	1.88	2.06	1.92	1.95	1.94
Skiing	2.61	3.04	3.01	3.06	3.36	3.02	3.01
Aviation sports	2.53	2.87	2.90	2.80	3.03	3.00	2.89

* Measured on a 1-5 scale, with 1=not interested at all, 5=very interested

Means typed in bold are significantly higher than the mean of other groups formed from the sample. In the case of means marked with an asterisk, we carried out a Tukey post-hoc analysis at a 95% significance level.

Examining the individual respondent groups, the data indicate relatively limited differences between genders:

- Women proved to be more interested in horse riding, cycling than men, and they were definitely attracted to hiking in nature (though the attraction of nature was also relatively high with males).

- Men were slightly more interested in golf, angling, hunting and skiing, but the attraction of several of these falls in the rejection zone even with males. These differences are also significant based on the ANOVA variance analysis[1].

Concerning the relevance of age as a factor of interest, it can be stated that significant differences exist in the case of all but three active tourist activities:

- Based on the post-hoc test, in water sports the preferences of elder age groups, 36-49 and 49-59 differ significantly from the mean of the other groups. According to the data, water sports fall lower in the preference rank as compared to younger age groups, where the mean preference tends to be positive.
- In the case of cycling, the preferences of the 26-35 age group differ significantly from the rest of the sample.
- A higher interest in hiking is typical to persons over 26, where the mean of the age groups is over 4.00 indicating a clearly positive attitude.
- Interest in golf is more typical to the younger generation (under 26), i.e. they are less uninterested. Interest in golf as an active tourism product was generally very low throughout the sample.
- Also angling meets a lack of interest (mean: 2.33) with no significant difference among the responses of different age groups.
- Hunting did not prove to be attractive either - it is the second least interesting active tourism programme according to the sample. Based on the responses the younger generation seems to be less indifferent, however the post-hoc analysis did not support differences among the responses.
- Skiing is definitely more interesting for the younger generation, since the mean responses given by the age groups over 36 are significantly less positive.

In aviation sports (parachuting, paragliding, gliding), while the mean indicating the younger generation's interest is slightly over the neutral value (3.15), the age groups over 36 definitely rejected these activities.

At the same time, on evaluating the results one must note that despite the differences indicated by the post-hoc analysis, there is no such activity where the intensity of interest in any age group would significantly differ from the others..

Concerning the education level of the respondents, there is no difference in the interest in active tourism services between respondents in any but two variables.

- In the case of hiking, the interest of those with primary education is significantly lower than those with secondary or higher education, though the index is over 3.00 (neutral) even in the former group. This result is worth our attention because

[1]In conducting the ANOVA variance analysis, significant difference meant that the probability of no difference (H0 hypothesis) among the means of responses given by individual groups is under 5%. (Reversely: the probability of any difference (H1 hypothesis) among the means of responses given by respondent groups is over 95%)

the age group under 18, with only primary education completed, constitutes one fifth of our sample, and they proved to be less attracted to hiking.

- Extreme aviation sports indicate a reverse situation, where only those with primary education (that is mainly respondents under 18 years of age) show a slightly stronger interest. .

The results of the variance analysis explore no definite differences in groups formed around the financial situation, except hiking, where the interest of those with incomes slightly under the average is significantly higher than the means of all the other groups.

In addition to respondents' stated interest in various active tourism services, we also analysed their participation in active tourism during international and domestic holidays. Figure 2 provides an overview of the role of active tourism in the survey participants' travel experience

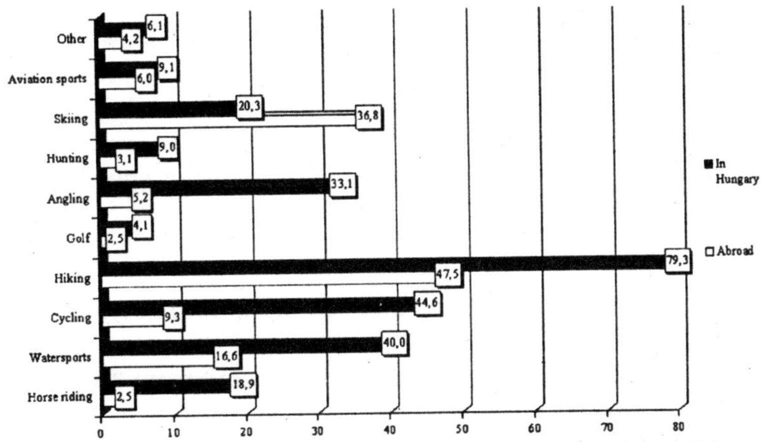

Figure 2: Participation in active tourism during holiday (%)

As Figure 2 illustrates, among the selected activities, hiking – which proved to be the most attractive leisure activity among respondents (Table 3) – was most likely to be included in a holiday, particularly within Hungary, followed by cycling, water sports, skiing and angling. The results justify the assumption that the characteristics of everyday leisure patterns affect the individual's tourist behaviour as well, and those who are generally more active in their leisure time will consciously seek out active tourism programmes and opportunities during their travels.

Skiing was the only active tourism product that featured much more strongly in respondents' international holiday experiences than in their domestic travels. Obviously, this marked difference is explained by Hungary's lack of high mountain ranges (the country's highest peak is only 1015 m), the uncertainty of sufficient precipitation in winter, as well as the accessibility of high quality ski resorts in the neighbouring countries, particularly in Austria and Slovenia, but also in Slovakia.

The ANOVA variance analysis showed significant differences by gender in the case of domestic travel: water sports, angling and hunting proved to be pursued mostly by male travellers. The tendency is similarly in the case of foreign travel, with cycling and ski tourism joining water sports, angling and hunting.

According to the age group analysis, horse riding is definitely more attractive for the younger generation. Based on the data of our sample, one fourth of those under 18 had travelled a distance from home with the specific aim of horse riding. At the same time, less than 15% of all the other age groups (over 26) were motivated to participate in horse riding tourism. Water sports show similar participation patterns, where nearly half of those under 18, while less than a third of those over 36 had travelled domestically for the purpose of participating in water sports. In the case travel abroad, there is a significant difference among hikers, but this time to the elder generation's advantage (the difference is 10-15% between the activity measured in the youngest and the eldest group; 60% of 36-49-year-olds had already travelled abroad as hiking tourists). The other difference – favouring the younger generation – appears in the case of ski tourism.

The ANOVA variance analysis proved a significant relationship between income levels and domestic participation in golf, angling and hunting tourism, and aviation sports, with the higher income groups being more likely to travel within Hungary in order to pursue these activities. In the case of international travel, wealthier respondents were more likely to have travelled abroad with the aim of participating in water sports and aviation sports, hiking, golf, hunting and ski tourism.

CONCLUSIONS

The research results suggest that the currently accepted Hungarian concept of active tourism is not viable in the global market, due to the inherent variety of the products' components, and the conceptual misunderstandings arising from this variety. The various individual activities incorporated in the notion of 'active tourism' attract significantly different market segments, with gender, age, income and education level all playing a major role in determining both interest and participation in certain forms of active holidays.

In addition, the natural and economic preconditions of the individual activities are also highly diverse. Hiking, for example, is a relatively low-budget, not particularly seasonal, moderately climate-dependent activity: it only requires the maintenance of hiking trails and signposting in an attractive natural environment, as well as a range of interesting sights within walking distance from each other. Golf or sailing, on the other hand are based on significant financial investments leading to generally high prices associated with these activities; consequently, both products are relatively exclusive and inaccessible for all social strata. Sailing also depends on wind characteristics, while the operating costs of a golf course are influenced by the given destination's precipitation levels.

Although active tourism is marketed as one product by the Hungarian National Tourist Office, it is advisable in the future to differentiate among the various components of the product and develop individual marketing and communication strategies for each component, in order to reach the country's potential visitors with offers that are more tailored to their needs and expectations.

REFERENCES

- Cazes, G.H. (1989): Alternative Tourism: Reflections on an Ambiguous Concept. In: Singh, T.V., Thevas, H.L. and Go, F.M. eds.: *Towards Appropriate Tourism: The Case of Developing Countries.* Peter Lang, Frankfurt am Main, Germany, pp.117-126.
- De Knop, P. (1990): Sport for All and Active Tourism. *World Leisure and Recreation* 35(3):30-36.
- Breda, Z., Costa, R. and Costa, C. (2006): Do Clusters and Networks Make Small Places Beautiful? The Case of Caramulo (Portugal). In: Lazzeretti, L. and Petrillo, C.S. eds.: *Tourism Local Systems and Networking.* Elsevier, Oxford, UK, pp.67-82.
- Furlan, M.C., Meneghello, S. and Minghetti, V. (2004): From "Predatory" to "Experience Tourism: Estimating Tourist Fruition for a Greenway. In: Weiermair, K. and Mathies, C. eds.: *The Tourism and Leisure Industry: Shaping the Future.* The Haworth Hospitality Press, Binghamton, NY, USA, pp.271-282.
- HNTO (2006): *Active Holiday. Active Tourism.* http://www.hungary.com/main.php? folderID=857&articleID (last accessed 31 October 2006)
- Lennon, J.J., Smith, H., Cockerell, N. and Trew, J. (2006): *Benchmarking National Tourism Organisations and Agencies. Understanding Best Practice.* Elsevier, Oxford, UK.
- Michalkó, G. (2004): *A turizmuselmélet alapjai.* Kodolányi János Fõiskola, Székesfehérvár, Hungary.
- Rátz, T. and Vizi, I. (2005): Travel Behaviour Influenced by Climatic Factors - The Case of Lake Balaton, Hungary. *Annalen der Meteorologie* 41(2):612-615.
- Standeven, J. and De Knop, P. (1999): *Sport Tourism.* Human Kinetics, Champaign, IL, USA.
- Steward, J. (2005): 'How and Where to Go?': The Role of Travel Journalism in Britain and the Evolution of Foreign Tourism, 1840-1914. In: Walton, J.K. ed.: *Histories of Tourism: Representation, Identity and Conflict.* Channel View Publications, Clevedon, UK, pp.39-54.
- Vizi, I. (2005): A magyar lakosság aktív turizmussal kapcsolatos preferenciái és az aktív turisztikai tevékenységek intenzitása. *Turizmus Bulletin* 9(4):30-40
- Wieczorek, E. (1999): *The Silesian Voivodship Invites: Active Tourism.* Silesian Voivodship Tourist and Promotion Office, Katowice, Poland.

4

Development of Eco-friendly Tourism in the Roopkund area of Nanda Devi Biosphere Reserve of Garhwal Himalaya (Uttaranchal) India

Laxmi Rawat, H.B. Vashistha and Deepak Kholiya
Forest Ecology and Environment Division;
Forest Research Institute, Dehradun

ABSTRACT

The fascination for mountains, breathtaking natural beauty, rich cultural diversity, socio-economic traditions, history and life style attract mountaineers, trekkers, naturalists, explorers and cultural tourists from all over the world to Nanda Devi Biosphere Reserve (NDBR). In order to promote Eco-tourism (environment friendly tourism) in any region it is required to conduct studies on the impacts of tourism on natural resources as well as on socio-economic conditions of the area. Keeping this in view the present study was conducted in the famous tourist place i.e. Roopkund Lake of NDBR in Uttaranchal. The area comes in Nandakini Block of Nandprayag Range of Badrinath Forest Division, situated at an altitude of 5,029m in the interior of the Chamoli district in Garhwal Himalaya. Roopkund is famous for the mysterious shallow lake of about 2 meters, with the edges covered with snow almost throughout the year. The lake is nestled amidst panoramic mountain scenery. After the snow melts, number of skeletal remains can be seen laying here. There is a lot of controversy about the mystery of Roopkund.

Roopkund Lake, Bedni and Ali Bugyals are the important tourist places of NDBR where number of tourists visit for different purposes. In Roopkund the tourists visit mainly the area for its mysterious skeletons, picturesque snow clad Himalayan beauty, bugyals/ grasslands and for Nanda Devi Raj-Jat, a religious function attended by visitors along with local people after every 12 years, while celebrate Raj-Jat per year. The most commonly trek route followed by visitor's starts from Wan village (2010-2436 m) the last road head, to Chopal (Gharoli) towards Bedni Bugyal (3354-3650 m) with a total of 12 km trek. For night halt at Bedni Bugyal there is a Forest Rest House for 4 to 5 men's capacity while pitching of tents are allowed on normal Forest Department charges. The next trek starts from Bedni Bugyal to Patanchanya - Ghoralothana (3950 m) - Kaluwabinayak (4200 m) - Bhaguawasa (4778 m). From Bedni to reach Bhaguawasa it is a total 10 km trek. Then the next trek starts from Bhaguawasa - Garbhpatanya - Ballpasuladiya - Hudiyathal - Chiyanal to reach final destination point Roopkund lake (5025 - 5029 m). It is a 5 km trek from Bhaguawasa to reach Roopkund lake. Thus the total trekking consists of 27 km one way to reach Roopkund from Wan village.

In the present study trends of tourists visiting the areas, the frequency of their visits, transport and accommodation, characterization of their activities, how these activities are affecting the natural resources of the area particularly local flora, soil and landscape, socio-economic status of the villagers enroute and their involvement in the tourism are some of the point covered under study.

Key words: Eco-friendly development, NDBR, controversy, sustainable management, strategies, natural resources etc.

GENERAL INTRODUCTION

Tourism is a multidimensional, multi-faceted activity. It is a phenomenon arising out of the temporary movement of the people from their normal place of work and residence to some other interesting destination for varied reasons like rejuvenation, appetite for sightseeing, relaxation etc. Tourism has gained much relevance and plays a major role in the global socio-economic scenario today. The second half of the last century witnessed tremendous developments in the tourism sector. Now, tourism industry enjoys one of the topmost positions in the overall business scenario worldwide. The International tourist arrivals increased from 25 million in the year 1950 to 67 million in 2000, registering an annual growth rate of 7%. It is accepted world over that tourism is a major force in the world economy, an activity of global importance and significance. This most rapidly expanding industry is contributing over 10% to global GDP and generating employment for 200 million people. The WTO's tourism vision 2020 forecasts the International arrivals to cross 1.56 billion by the year 2020. Among that, 1.18 billion will be intra regional and 0.371 billion will be long haul travelers.

Eco-tourism has become the 'buzzword' in tourism today. The widespread environment menace of mass tourism and the growing concern for environment has facilitated the growth of nature-based tourism globally. Many destinations in the world have already promoted eco-tourism on a big scale. Ecotourism, according to The International Ecotourism Society (TIES) is: -"*Responsible travel that promotes the conservation of nature and sustains the well-being of local people*". Eco-tourism is a growing niche market within the larger travel industry, with the potential of being an important sustainable development tool. With billions of dollar in annual sales, ecotourism is an industry that seeks to take advantage of market rends. At the same time, it frequently operates quite differently than other segments of the tourism industry, because ecotourism is defined by its sustainable development results: -

conserving natural areas, educating visitors about sustainability and benefiting local people. It is a form of nature based tourism in the market place and is a sustainable tool of development, while including rural & cultural tourism elements. The planning and development of ecotourism focus on environmental, social, cultural and economic sustainability criteria.

India being a vast and diverse country has always something to offer to everyone. Its glorious traditions and rich culture are linked with the development of tourism. In India the concept of ecotourism is a new trend and in spite of such bounties of nature and varieties of religion, culture and ethnicity, India accounts for only 0.4% of the global tourism market. Both the Ministry of tourism and the Ministry of Environment & Forest have respond to the development in the field of ecotourism with policy initiatives. Department of Tourism issued policy and guidelines on Ecotourism in July, 1998. The policy lays down the objectives for ecotourism and contains operational guidelines for major stakeholders. During 2000, ecotourism in protected areas and territorial forest divisions was recognized as on of the 15 thrust areas of the Ministry of Environment & Forests. The Indian chapter of the Pacific Asia Travel Association (PATA) has formulated an action plan for National Ecotourism Policy, which has been forwarded by Ministry of Tourism to State Governments for review.

The beauty of the Himalayan forest, alpine meadow and snow-clad mountains are the main sources of tourist attraction of Uttaranchal. Tourism in the Himalayan region of Uttaranchal has a long, uninterrupted history. In older times, it was essentially 'Pilgrimage', embodying simplicity, morality, ecological purity and self-imposed discipline. It helped in preserving Himalayan heritage by participation of local populace and did not have any adverse effects on environment of these areas. Only a few people used to undertake the long and arduous journey to the holy shrines and being strong devout, the pilgrims never exploited the local people and natural resources. Thus, pilgrimage was good for the region against the minimum social and ecological/environmental crisis. The great Himalayas, which have always been a continuous rays of good hopes and new life coupled with the challenge to unreval the mysteries, still shroud in their flora and fauna, are also.

A natural abode of medicinal plants. Roopkund Lake, a place of mythological episode, lies in the lap of Garhwal Himalayas at an elevation of 4,850 - 5029 m above mean sea level, and intersection of 79° 45′ E longitude and 30° 18′ N latitude. The region is a natural heritage of medicinal herbs and their uses in disease remedy are as old as man himself. In India the earliest mentioned use of medicinal plants is found in Rigveda. Thomas Hardwick (1757 - 1835) was the first European to collect the plants from North-West Himalaya, including the Alakananda Valley. William Spencer Webb, Hyder Jung Hearsay and Felix Vincant Raper, who were members of and expedition during 1802-1803 collected plants from Gangotri and Yamunotri area. (as Burkill, 1965). Gupta (1956, 57,62); Roa (1959, 60), Naithani (1967), Semwal and Gaur (1981), Kala and Gaur (1982), Bhattacharyya and Malhotra (1982) and Negi et al. (1985). The study of Indian indigenous drugs was first begun in the early part of the last century. Dutt (1877), Watt (1889-93), Dey (1986), Kirtikar and Basu (1935), Chopra and Chopra (1955), Biswas (1956), Dastur (1970), Usher (19470 and Jain (1975) have described the medicinal properties of Indian medicinal plants.

REVIEW OF LITERATURE

A few of the impact researches conducted in the developing countries and island nations reveal that their fore runners of the 60's had exaggerated tourism's economic gains by assuming tourist dollar to say where it was first spent. They told that 'leakages' might benefit other parts of the country and least the indigenous society (Bosselman, 1978).

In many cases, tourism often takes away what it gives, leaving ugly scars that are hard to efface. Weaker economies suffer the most. Economic tangibles are more to be seen on macro level; the micro world, more often than not, finds itself disillusioned at the grassroots. Quite a good literature exists on the non-economic side effects of tourism (Nunez, 1963; Greenwood, 1972; Cohen, 1972; Jafari, 1974; Thompson, 1974; Doxey, 1975; Smith, 1977; Mings, 1978; Pizam and Milman, 1986).

The state of the art has been reviewed by Noronha (1976), Van Hout (1979), Williams (1982), Jafari (1982), Travis (1984) and Singh (1984), Madan and Rawat (2000). Most of these studies point more to negative and adverse consequences of tourism.

Tourism is held responsible for transformation of societies by introducing undesirable changes in their value system, tradition and morals, collective lifestyle, creative expression, language and individual behaviour (Pizam and Milman, 1986). Ranging from demonstration effects to accumulation, tourism and tourist sin by promoting moral laxity, drug addiction, crime and prostitution, seasonal unattractive jobs, price rise are some of many sufferance and sorrows of the indigenous population.

Ecologists and Environmentalists lament the loss of flora and fauna, spoliation of scenery, litter and pollution (Echelberger, 1971; Edington and Edington, 1986; Kaur, 1980; Madan, 1998). Eutrophication of lake waters (Kant, 1983; Roza and Bano, 1989), degradation of mountain slope (Sinnhuber, 1982), pollution (Western, 1986; Lindsay, 1986), disregard of nature monuments (Mclellan, 1985) and damage of coral reefs (Salm, 1986) have been attributed to tourism.

'Leisure in nature' includes a lots of articles by various scientists/environmentalists etc., from different parts of Europe, viz. Pahr (1988), Secretary General of World Tourism Organization, is of the opinion that tourist carrying capacity and better seasonal and geographical distribution of tourists are important policy objectives. Hemele of Studienkreis Fur Tourismus reports 60% of the population of Federal Republic of Germany (FRG) takes holidays to get away from home, where the environment is in poor shape. He also reports tourist activities in FRG have caused a heavy burden to bear by the local population in tourist areas.

Saliba (1988) outlines the problems of the Mediterranean Coastal Zone and the steps being taken to solve them. Brogi highlights Coastal Zone that tourism in Switzerland and other Alpine regions has caused the well-known effects on environment. In Nordic countries (Norway, Sweden, Finland, Denmark, Iceland) stress on flora and fauna and pollution (air, water), deforestation and ski records, water based activities, sanitary, litter, waste disposal problems along with other environmental degradation caused by tourist activities are mentioned by Tuunanen (1988). Travis (1988) has studied impact of tourism in Denmark, remarks that tourism provides maximum direct economic benefit to the local residents in terms of income, jobs and minimum leakage from the local economy, least visual instruction in the landscape (by large unacceptable buildings) and minimum socio-cultural and ecological impacts.

So many case studies have been presented in the Encyclopedia of ecotourism, CABI Publishing, Wallington, UK (2000) by various authors, who have dealt with different aspect of tourism in different regions of the world. The current situation of policy and planning within ecotourism in major world regions (Australia, Asia, the Americas, Europe and Africa) are examined by Fennell et al. (2000) In order to create a sociocultural environment conducive to the ideals of ecotourism, the environment needs to be managed according to accepted standards. It is suggested that the features of the natural and cultural environment and supportive host communities are the foundations of a successful ecotourism industry (Wearing, 2000)).

Ahmed (1990) has worked on application of environmental impact assessment in the Himalayas for resource conservation and ecological sustainable development and highlighted the environmental problems associated with human activities in the Himalayas. Singh and Yadav (1980) made a study on impact of modernization with special reference to tourism. In the study, impacts of modernization of socio-economic, cultural and educational aspects were partially evaluated while assessing effects of the visiting communities on Srinagar on microscale. Kaur (1980) initiated a study dealing with assessment of scenic resource in a landscape and fixing a criterion for a long-term future use and meaningful organized development of tourism.

Rajwar (1981) reported ecological problems of Mussoorie hill and their solution. He reported that tourism, destruction of forests and indiscriminate exploitation of certain economically important species has caused ecological imbalance and this can be conserved by promulgation of law and by people's participation. A study (Anon, 1980) covers the pilgrim personality of Rishikesh town, concentration of tourists, and measures taken to meet this challenge, besides the resources it offers. Madan and Rawat (2000) have reported that the tourists visiting Mussoorie had direct or indirect impacts on different components of its environment. In recent years tourists have visited the area more than its carrying capacity. Singh and Kaur (1983) have presented case studies from the Himalayas on the problems on style and form of tourism, which could give more gainful and positive results obtained in different ecological, economic and socio-cultural environments.

While mapping the vegetation in Bedni and Ali Bugyals of Roopkund Jeet Ram et al. (1995) have mentioned that frequent grazing in these Bugyals by nearby villagers has caused degradation in the existing flora. Maikhuri et al. (2000) have emphasized that the ban on tourism in the core zone of the Reserve has created conflict between local people and Reserve authorities. The local people have severe concern about the significant income it provided. The paper deals with the history of expeditions and the impact on the local economy, identification of model eco-trekking / expedition routes and potential sites, and designing appropriate strategies/action plans for sustainable ecotourism. This will not only help to resolve the local people-policy conflicts and improve the local economy but will help to achieve the biodiversity conservation goal.

STUDY SITE

Roopkund situated at an altitude of 5029 m in the interior of the Chamoli district of Garhwal Himalaya, is famous for the mysterious shallow lake of about 2 mts., with the edges covered with snow almost throughout the year. The lake is nestled amidst panoramic mountain scenery. After the snow melts, number of skeletal remains can be seen. There is a lot of controversy about the mystery of Roopkund.

Roopkund is a important tourist places of Nanda Devi Biosphere Reserve (NDBR), where number of tourists visit for different purposes. The tourists visit the area for its mysterious skeletons, picturesque beauty and for Nanda Devi Raj-Jat, a religious function attended by visitors along with local people. In the present study; trends of tourists visiting the area, the frequency and intensity of their visits, the mode of their transport & accommodation; characterization of their activities, how these activities are affecting the natural resources of the area particularly local flora, soil and landscape, culture & livelihood of the local inhabitants will be studied. Strategies to minimize the impacts on natural resources of these areas are being suggested.

According to some as per the tradition, the Royal family of Garhwal conducted Nanda Raj Jat to please their isht-devi, so that their kingdom would be prosperous and the enemies would be defeated. According to another legend the royal family undertakes the pilgrimage along with their purohits to seek forgiveness from Nanda Devi and to offer 'tarpan' to one of their ancestors who died at Roopkund along with his pregnant wife and courtesans. Rajah Yashodhaval of Kannauj came on a pilgrimage to the dev bhoomi. His pregnant wife and women of the royal family accompanied him. He decided to go to Homkund along with his entourage. He didn't head to advice that women were not allowed beyond Bedni-Kund. He broke the tradition and went ahead. At Roopkund the Rajah and his entourage perished mysteriously, most probably in a snow-blizzard. Hundreds of skeletons still lie scattered in and around Roopkund. Another story says that they are the remains of the Dogra General Zorawar Singh's army from Jammu, who tried to invade Tibet in 1841, was beaten off & forced to find its way back home over the Himalayas. Along with bones of humans, bones of horses have also been found there. But this theory does not explain the presence of female skeletons. Carbon dating of the skeletons, done by Crane and Griffin in 1958 proves that the bones are indeed between 500 to 800 years old. During the Raj Jat even today, 'tarpan' is performed for Rajah Yashodhaval and his entourage.

Roopkund is visited not only for its mysterious skeletal remains but also for its picturesque beauty and the famous Nanda Devi Raj-Jat. The approximate number of tourists other than religious (Nanda Devi-Jat) visiting the area is 700 Indians and 250 Foreigners per year. The popular route followed by the tourists starts from Mandoli to Loharjung then to Wan (2,433m), which is the last village in this route. There is FRH and GMVN rest house at Wan. Visitors have to travel to Gharoli Patal, Bedni Bugyal, to Pathar Nachoni and finally

Roopkund at 5,029m. At Bedni Bugyal there are two snow huts of Forest Department and a small rest house of District Panchayat. After Bedni Bugyal tourists have to use tents.

The Nanda Devi Raj Jat, dating back to the 9th century, is mostly held in intervals of 12 years, when a four-horned Ram is born in one of the villages in the area. The pilgrimage starts from Nauti village in Chamoli district and takes several days of trekking through the hilly terrain to reach the final destination of Homkund.

The following map shows routes to Roopkund with altitudes of some of the places in Feet.

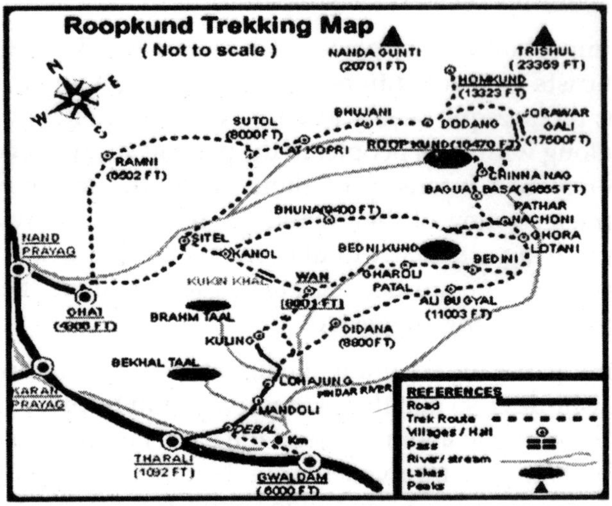

The stoppage sites are at/nearby Mandoli, Loharjung, Wan, Gharoti Pathar, Bedni Bugyal, Ali Bugyal and Pathar Nachoni/ Roopkund. The area comes in Nandakini Block, Nandprayag Range under Badrinath Forest Division.

In recent years tourist Deptt. is organising a three days Roopkund Mahotsav on the day of Nanda Devi Jat (yearly Jat, Raj Jat comes after 12 years). During Nanda Devi Jat / Raj Jat, thousands of Bramhakamal flowers (Saussurea obvallata) are offered to the deity 'Nanda', which are plucked from nearby areas like Bedni Bugyal, Ali Bugyal etc. This flower can grow in this type of climatic conditions only. Plucking of these flowers without any conservation measure has made the plant rare in these areas.

The study specially focused on the exploitation of plant species, which may be due to tourist activities like camping, trampling / plucking of plant parts, use of wood for warming / fire etc. and the strategies for protection and measures to conserve the flora in their natural habitat will be worked out.

The Nanda Devi Raj Jat, dating back to the 9th century, is mostly held in intervals of 12 years, when a four-horned Ram is borne in one of the villages in the area. The pilgrimage starts from Nauti village in Chamoli district on Tuesday and takes several days of trekking through the hilly terrain to reach the final destination of Homkund.

In the present study, trends of tourists visiting the areas, the frequency of their visits, transport and accommodation, characterization of their activities, i.e. how their activities are affecting the natural resources of the area particularly local flora, soil and landscape, socio-economic status of the villagers enroute and their involvement in the tourism are some of the point to be covered under study.

Bedni and Ali Bugyals are on the way to Roopkund, although there are several worth-seeing places through which the famous religious Nanda Devi Raj Jat Yatra passes and ends at Homkund. Some strategies for eco-friendly trekking in these areas have also been suggested

Roopkund Major Tourist Attractions

Roopkund is visited not only for its mysterious skeletal remains but also for its picturesque beauty and the famous Nanda Devi Raj Jat. The approximate number of tourists other than religious (Nanda Devi Jat) visiting the area is average 700 Indians and 250 foreigners per year. The popular route followed by the tourists will be taken for present study, which starts from Mandoli to Loharjung then to Wan (2433m), which is the last village in this route. There is FRH and GMVN rest house at Wan. Then visitors halt at Gharoli Patal then at Bedni, then comes Pathar Nachoni then Roopkund at 5029m. At Bedni there are two snow huts of Forest Deptt and a small rest house of Distt. Panchayat. After Bedni tourists have to use tents.

The glacial lake of Roopkund (4778 - 5029m) in Chamoli District is in the jurisdiction of Badrinath Forest Division, Garhwal Circle and is famous for the mysterious shallow lake of 200 meter in circumference with a catchments area of nearly 2 sq. km. The edges are covered with snow mostly throughout the year. After the snow melts, one can see human skeleton remains, believed to be 500 - 800 years old well preserved under snow.

The way to Roopkund starts from Tharali to Debal (13 km), Debal to Wan village (39 Km). The trek starts from Wan → Chopal (Gharoli) → Bedni Bugyal (13 Km trek) → Patanchanya → Bhaguwasa → Hudiyathal → Chiyanal → Roopkund (15 km). Wan is the last village/ road head for visiting Roopkund. Thus from Wan to Roopkund lake it is a 28 km trek one-way.

Geography and Climate

Roopkund lake, lies at the longitudinal and latitudinal intersection of 79° 45′ E and 30° 18′ N and has an area of hardly one acre with a diameter of nearly 50 m. The lake is situated at an elevation of ± 4,850 m high above mean sea level, within the southern outer fringes of the Nanda Devi sanctuary and just at the base of Trishul Massif. The approach of the lake begins from Goaldam, the border town of district Chamoli adjacent to the district Bageshwar and round about 150 km from nearest railhead, Kathgodam. Though, the possible approaches are from Joshimath via Tapovan and Buhna by trekking but Goaldam to Wan and then via Bedni Bugyal is comparatively easier to approach. The distance from Goaldam to Roopkund lake is round about 80 km. The lake is situated at snow line zone.

The principal climatic factors influencing the alpine zone, are high rainfall, high relative humidity and low temperature, showing light ice piece floating at the water surface. Above the lake, there are steep mountainous slopes with permanent snow.

General Vegetation

The vegetation of Roopkund lake is characterised by an alpine flora represented by temperate and high altitudinal Himalayan plants. The vegetation, right from the subtropical terraced fields of Kumaon hills, spotted with the bushes of Rosa brunonii and Berberis chitria leads to the alpine zone terminating in ever persisting snow line through a timber line with the Quercus semecarpifolia and Rhododendron arboreum as a dominating tree flora.

The route on way to this high altitude lake crosses an area having almost all diversities of floristic composition, which are rarely met within other areas of Garhwal Himalayas. The last forest of Quercus-Rhododendron, just below to the Bedni Bugyal is rich in under growth vegetation consisting of species such as Anaphalis busua, Bupleurum candollii, Epilobium royleanum, Lactuca violoefolia, Lychnis indica, Polygonum amplexicaule, Salix elegans, Solidago virgaurea, Saxifraga diversifolia, Schizandra grandiflora, Hydrangea heterophylla, Rosa brunonii, Clematis connata, etc.

The Bedni and Ali bugyals (alpine grassland) composed mainly of Danthonia schneideri, Stipa roylei, Kobresia duthiei, K. nepalensis, Corydalis ramosa, Saxifraga diversifolia, Ranunculus hirtellus, Swertia cuneata and Delphinium vestitum.

Roopkund Trek Details

Roopkund is situated at an altitude of ca 4850 m within the Southern outer fringes of Nanda devi Biosphere Reserve and is just at the base of Trisul massif. The enchanting landscapes of the high Himalayas have attracted many tourists since time immemorial. Among the Nanda Devi group of mountains, the beautiful peaks of Nandakot (6872 m), Dunagiri (7025 m), Nandaghunti and others, including Trisul being in the neighborhood of the area, attract many mountaineers also.

Roopkund can be approached from many places. The most popular route is from Karan Prayag via Tharali, Debal, Mandoli, Wan, Bedni Bugyal, Kalu Abhinayak and Bhaguawasa. The other route is from Nandprayag via Ghat, Sital, Sital, Bhainswara, Latakpuri, Bhunjari and Hemkundi, From Sital, Rupkund can also be approached via Talkapor along the Rupkund nala. The vegetation along Roopkund Nala is not disturbed and more or less virgin as there is no human interference. There is dense forest of Quercus-Acer-Rhododendron with rich undergrowth of herbaceous and shrubby plants along with high altitude bamboos. They are replaced by Betula-Rhododendron forests. Beyond this type of forest there are alpine meadows as the route joins the main Bedni Bugyal. Wan the last village on way to Rupkund from Loharjung is approached through a crooked forest of Quercus leucotricophora and Rhododendron arboreum. The main track within the forest offers an interesting assemblage of temperate species with good number of epiphytes.

Some of the herbaceous plants along the route are Anaphalis triplinervis, Corydalis heterophylla, Elsholzia fruticosa, Gentiana sp., Geranium spp., Polygomum sp., etc.

Some of the common plants near Wan are Indigofera heterantha, Salix elegans, Viburnum erubescens, Hippophae salicifolia, etc. Surrounding mountains in the neighborhood of Wan have a dense forest of Quercus semecarpifolia and Rhododendron arboreum. Besides these groves of Cedrus deodara, Cupressus torulosa with scattered trees of Picea smithiana are also seen.

Vegetation near Vedini Ganga valley is of mixed forest of Acer acuminatum, Quercus semecarpifolia, Rhododendron arboreum, Taxus wallichiana and occasionally Picea smithiana. The dense forest of Rhododendron, Quercus is replaced by alpine bugyals at Vedini where only herbaceous plants like Gentiana argentea, Ranunculus etc, can be seen. Danthonia cachenyiana, Stipa roylei, Kobresia duthiei, K. nepalensis are some of the common grasses and sedges on the alpine slopes. Delphinium vestium, Swertia cuneata and Gaultheria trichophylla are also found scattered all around. Shrubs like Rhododendron lepidotum, R anthopogon are common in the alpine region.

AIMS AND OBJECTIVES

1. Developing strategies for eco-friendly trekking.
2. To develop management strategies for reducing environmental impact and ensure involvement of stakeholders.

Tourism in India has been growing for the last several years and the 'Incredible India' campaign has catapulted the growth. Eco-tourism developments have already begun in India. But still there is a long way to go and plenty of resources are yet to be tapped. Also, some issues have been reported in relation to the development of eco-tourism in India. Efforts have to be there from all the stakeholders in eco-tourism sector to think about the sustainability of tourism.

METHODOLOGY

1. Impacts on Natural Resources: Tourist trends were studied and activities identified for specific impacts on following Natural Resources;
   a) Impact on vegetation; vegetational studies at different altitudinal zones enrouting the track done by quadrate / transect sampling methods. Vegetation survey done along the gradient including undisturbed site also. Rare, endangered and medicinal plants were also identified / enlisted.
   b) Impact on soil: Soil samples collected at 0-20 cm depth from the sites and analysed for some parameters like pH. Organic Carbon etc.
   c) Impact on landscape: wrappers, cans, packing materials, bottles etc. collected, from the core zone, weighed and shown to local people, made them aware of their environmental effects and also told them their proper collection and disposal.
2. Impact on socio-economic status: Socio-economic status of local inhabitants studied by surveying the villages already indicated as study points or nearest villages to

the study points. Survey was done using questionnaires. Villages having less than 20 households sampled as whole, otherwise 20% of total households sampled.

3. Awareness programmes / meetings done with villagers enroute to the areas to develop management strategies to reduce the impacts on natural resources and to ensure their involvement in tourism /environmental programmes

Socio-economic studies: were carried out in Wan and Mandoli villages. The survey shows that the villagers are very poor. They are dependent on subsistence agriculture from their rain fed lands. About 10-30% people are involved in tourism related activities like guides, ponies owners, small dhabas, hotels etc in these villages. Education rate is very low, girl education is abysmal low, the reason being poor parents, lesser number of schools and far away situated colleges (minimum distance 7 km) for intermediate education. There is only one degree college at Bageshwar in the whole area. Some more villages are yet to be surveyed, only then the whole area could be described.

Table 1: Halting/Camping sites along trek route to Roopkund along with the altitudes

S. No.	Camping sites	Altitude (m)
1	Loharjung	2133
2	(a) Wan (b) Dedina	2436-
3	Bedni Bugyal	3354
4	Bhaguawasa	4778
5	Roopkund	5029

Table 2: Route allowed for Roopkund Trek.

S. No.	From	To	Distance (Km)
1	Loharjung	Wan (FRH)	13
2	Wan*	Bedni Bugyal	13
3	Bedni Bugyal	Bhaguawasa	10
4	Bhaguawasa	Roopkund	5
5	Bhaguawasa	Ali Bugyal – Dedina	12
6	Dedina	Loharjung*	12

*Loharjung and *Wan villages are the two different nearest road heads from where the trekking route starts for Roopkund.

Table 3: Total No. of Tourists visited Roopkund from January – December 2005

Total Tourists	Indians	Foreign	Males	Females	Children's	Guides/ Potters	Mules/ Horses	Total Govt. Revenue earned
536	313	223	151	366	19	291	281	Rs. 53,010/=

(*Source*: Forest Check post Bedni)

Table 4: Number of Tourists to Roopkund during 29.03.06 to 14.06.06.

Date	Total Visitors	Male	Female	Children upto 12 years age	Indian	Foreigner	Guide	Potter	Mule
29.03	3	1	1	-	2	1	-	-	.06
3.04	20	7	7	-	14		2	4	4
16.04	21	6	5	-		11	1	9	9
24.04	2	1	1	-		2	-	-	-
April Total									
1.05	6	2	-	-	2		1	3	-
6.05	2	1	1	-		2	-	-	-
7.05	2	2	-	-		2	-	-	-
7.05	23	15	5	-	3	17	1	2	10
7.05	7	3	-	-	3		1	3	-
10.05	3	1	-	-	1		1	1	-
10.05	27	14	5	-		19	2	6	12
11.05	3	2	-	-	2		1	-	-
12.05	15	9	1	-		10	1	4	3
16.05	16	4	4	-		8	2	6	4
16.05	11	2	3	-	5		1	5	4
16.05	6	-	2	-		2	2	2	4
17.05	11	1	2	-		3	1	7	8
19.05	10	2	3	2	7		1	2	2
21.05	10	8	-	-	8		1	1	1
21.05	8	-	3	-	1	2	1	4	5
25.05	7	2	1	-	3	1	3	4	
25.05	9	5	-	-	5		-	4	-
27.05	9	-	6	-	6		1	2	2
27.05	5	2	-	-	2		1	2	-
28.05	10	3	-	-		3	2	5	4
28.05	30	11	4	-		15	3	12	22
29.05	2	1	-	-	1		1	-	-
30.05	6	1	-	-		1	2	3	-
May Total									
1.06	19	2	4	-		6	2	11	1
1.06	6	4	-	-	4		1	1	-
2.06	23	3	7	-	10	3	10	19	
4.06	6	1	1	-		2	1	3	2
6.06	4	2	-	-	2		1	1	-
6.06	7	1	1	-		2	1	4	3
7.06	2	2	-	-	2	-	-	-	
10.06	10	6	1	-	7		1	2	4
11.06	5	4	-	-	4		1	-	-
13.06	9	4	1	-	5		1	3	1
13.06	16	11	-	-	11		1	4	1
13.06	6	4	-	-	4		1	1	-
14.06.	7	4	-	-	4	2	1	3	06
Upto 14th June 06									
Total	**404**	**154**	**69**	**2**	**101**	**124**	**48**	**131**	**132**

Table 5: Facilities Available in the Block of Debal /nearby villages

S.No.	Particulars	Areas/Locations
1.	Hospitals with Allopathic medicines/ facilities - 3	a. Jain Bist b. Boragarh c. Debal
2.	Hospitals with Ayurvedic medicines - 5	a. Mundoli b. Debal c. Wan d. Ghass e. Manmati
3.	Family welfare Sub- Centers - 6	a. Mundoli b. Wan c. Boragarh d. Nand kesri e. Ghass f. Harmal
4.	Veterinary Hospitals - 2, Animal Welfare Center - 3	a. Debal b. Mundoli c. Boragarh d. Nuldhura e. Balarh
5.	Preliminary Agricultural Societies - 4	a. Debal b. Nuldhura c. Ghass d. Mundoli
6.	Commercial Bank - 3	a. SBI, Debal b. (Alaknanda Gramin Bank), Mundoli c. (Distt. Coop. Bank), Debal
7.	Sheep Development Center - 5	
8.	Seed and Fertilizers Sales Center - 2	

Table 6: General information in Block of Debal /nearby villages

S.No.	Debal Block Area Particulars	Number
1.	Total Geographical Area	
	(i) Forest Area	51100 (ha)
	(ii) Agriculture Land	40247.7(ha)
	(iii) Irrigated Land Area	2188.0(ha)
	(iv) Altitude (msl)	184.0(ha) 1218 (meters)

2.	Total Population (Census1991)	20432
	(i) S. Caste	3979
	(ii) S. Tribes	32
	(iii) O.B.C.	41
	Total Population (Census 2001)	23110
	(i) S. Caste	4939
	(ii) S. Tribes	39
	(iii) O.B.C.	184
3.	Total Village Panchyat	44
4.	Judicial Panchyat	03
5.	Rajashwa villages	74
6.	Abaad villages	68
7.	Non Abaad Villages	06
8.	Panchyat Home	25
9.	District Meeting Center	09
10.	Inter Colleges	03
11.	High Schools	03
12.	Higher Primary School	18
13.	Primary Schools	79
14.	Sub Post office	01
15.	Branch Post office	18
16.	Control (Govt. subsidy) shops	48
17.	BPL (Below Poverty Line) Card Holders Numbers	1358
18.	Aanpurna Card Holders Numbers	125
19.	Prime Minister's Annthodhya Aan Scheme Beneficiaries	490
20.	Village Panchyat Development Officers (BDO) Areas	07
21.	Electrified Villages	46
22.	Non Electrified Villages	28
23.	Total Villages enroute to Roopkund	9

Name of Villages	Forest Area (ha)
(i) Kandai	51
(ii) Ulangra	-
(iii) Haat kalyani	100
(iv) Echolilaga Sailkhola	38.058
(v) Mundoli	469.081
(vi) Kuling	-
(vii) Wan	59.124
(viii) Wank	38.015
(ix) Lwani	22.664

Table 7: Populations Census of Development Block Debal (Year 1991)

S. No.	Name of Village	Area of Village (ha)	No. of household	No. of Family	Total Population	Male	Female	S. Cast		S. Tribes		Literates Persons		Children's : (0 – 6) years			*Agricultural land (ha)
								Male	Female	Male	Female	Male	Female	Total	Male	Female	
1	Kandai	203.68	67	67	383	181	202	66	58	-	-	92	60	86	41	45	69.688
2	Ulangra	67.31	48	48	267	119	148	5	4	-	-	80	48	56	28	28	33.093
3	Losre	229.334	80	111	365	167	198	39	44	-	-	88	33	86	39	47	46.893
4	Haat Kalyani	224.14	82	122	664	327	337	109	106	-	-	219	101	142	57	85	62.308
5	Echolilaga Sailkhola	71.71	232	256	882	594	288	42	16	5	6	459	162	117	65	52	13.168
6	Mundoli	412.69	131	131	495	261	234	50	32	-	-	200	41	62	32	30	102.323
7	Kuling	57.89	33	43	172	82	90	1	-	-	-	44	23	31	40	17	12.878
8	Wan	554.0	200	200	1015	524	491	72	69	-	-	231	33	208	105	103	162.313
9	Wank	339.47	85	85	445	218	227	53	66	-	-	148	63	85	38	47	53.038
10	Lwani	326.39	108	108	563	310	253	8	6	1	-	209	43	104	56	48	36.706
11	Harini	244.636	60	60	368	176	192	-	-	-	-	85	32	90	46	44	59.589

*Agricultural land (ha) is total unirrigated land (Rain fed agriculture)

Table 8: Socioeconomic survey details of the area

S. No	Name of Vill.	Area of Village (ha)	No. of household	No. of Family	Total Population	Male	Female	S. Cast		S. Tribes		Literates Persons		Children's : (0 – 6) years			*Agricultural land (ha)
								Male	Female	Male	Female	Male	Female	Total	Male	Female	
1	Kandai	203.68	67	67	383	181	202	66	58	-	-	92	60	86	41	45	69.688
2	Ulangra	67.31	48	48	267	119	148	5	4	-	-	80	48	56	28	28	33.093
3	Losre	229.334	80	111	365	167	198	39	44	-	-	88	33	86	39	47	46.893
4	Haat Kalyani	224.14	82	122	664	327	337	109	106	-	-	219	101	142	57	85	62.308
5	Echoli laga Sailkhola	71.71	232	256	882	594	288	42	16	5	6	459	162	117	65	52	13.168
6	Mundoli	412.69	131	131	495	261	234	50	32	-	-	200	41	62	32	30	102.323
7	Kuling	57.89	33	43	172	82	90	1	-	-	-	44	23	31	40	17	12.878
8	Wan	554.0	200	200	1015	524	491	72	69	-	-	231	33	208	105	103	162.313
9	Wank	339.47	85	85	445	218	227	53	66	-	-	148	63	85	38	47	53.038
10	Lwani	326.39	108	108	563	310	253	8	6	1	-	209	43	104	56	48	36.706
11	Harini	244.636	60	60	368	176	192	-	-	-	-	85	32	90	46	44	59.589

Table 9: Populations Census of Development Block Debal (Year 2005 – 2006)

S. No.	Village Panchayat Name	Villages	Total household Family	Total population of village	Male	Fem.	Scheduled Cast Tot.	Scheduled Cast Male	Scheduled Cast Fema.	Scheduled Tribes Tot.	Scheduled Tribes Male	Scheduled Tribes Fema.	Literate persons Tot.	Literate persons Male	Literate persons Female	Illiterate Persons Tot.	Illiterate Persons Male	Illiterate Persons Fem.
1	Sailkhola	Sailkhola	296	1166	701	465	113	63	50	-	-	-	916	586	330	250	115	135
		Echoli	35	141	72	69	-	-	-	-	-	-	104	61	43	37	11	26
2	Haat Kalyani	Haat Kalyani	119	602	276	326	203	105	98	-	-	-	378	205	173	224	71	153
3	Ulangra	Ulangra	70	331	142	189	70	10	07	-	-	-	192	100	92	139	42	97
		Pothilaga Ulangra	-	-	-	-	-	-	-	-	-	-	-	-	-	-	-	-
		Mudhawaliyar	25	118	53	65	85	38	47	-	-	-	68	42	26	50	11	39
4	Kandai	Kandai	74	427	202	225	130	68	62	19	09	10	296	160	136	131	42	89
		Bamanbara	40	197	87	110	8	3	5	-	-	-	136	76	60	61	11	50
5	Mundoli	Mundoli	150	864	429	435	172	95	77	2	-	2	506	316	190	358	113	245
		Melacheck Mundoli	2	8	5	3	8	5	3	-	-	-	4	4	0	4	1	3
6	Lwani	Lwani	116	591	281	310	21	10	11	4	2	2	331	198	133	260	83	117
7	Tajpur	Tajpur	44	274	135	139	119	65	54	-	-	-	160	105	55	114	30	84
8	Wank	Wank	109	647	315	332	182	87	95	-	-	-	381	221	100	266	94	172
9	Kuling	Kuling	46	244	152	92	1	1	-	-	-	-	137	101	36	107	51	56
		Dadiyanacheck	02	11	7	4	-	-	-	-	-	-	7	5	2	4	2	2
10	Wan	Wan	228	1286	678	608	165	82	83	-	-	-	626	423	203	660	265	405

Table 10: Type and number of livestock per family

		Livestock population								
Sl. No.	Villages	Cow	Bu-ffalo	Goat	Sheep	Oxen	Mule	Horse	Donkey	Total
1	Mundoli	289	162	186	75	320	18	23	2	
2	Banuri	82	75	26	-	104	-	-	-	
3	Wank	192	152	55	76	226	15	7	-	
4	Kuling	51	25	77	84	44	5	2	-	
5	Wan	431	187	700	2570	361	38	7	-	
6	Harni	106	125	50	47	124	17	18	-	
7	Tajpur	73	61	17	34	97	-	18	-	
8	Lwani	202	116	327	-	192	-	18	-	
9	Kandai	101	105	51	-	102	3	1	-	
10	Ulangra	73	57	68	-	79	-	-	-	
11	Haat Kalyani	178	105	64	-	145	-	-	-	

Rules and Regulation of Trekking in Roopkund area as mentioned by forest department

1. Camping Site Fees: -

   (a) Rs. 1000/= per small tent per night for more than 6 nights.

   (b) Rs. 300/= per small tent per night for 4 to 6 nights.

   (c) Rs. 200/= per small tent per night for 1 to 3 nights.

Note: - Small tent 2 to 4 persons, the rates as fixed above shall be double for large sized tent for more than 4 persons.

2. Trial Management Fee: -

   (a) Rs. 60/= per visitor for 7 days.

   (b) Rs. 100/= per visitor for more than 7 days.

   (c) Rs. 20/= per guide/potter for more than 7 days.

3. Mule/Horse Fee: -

   (a) Rs. 20/= per mule per round.

   (b) Rs. 5/= per pair mule per camp.

UTILITARIAN ASPECT OF THE FLORA

The area is very rich in medicinal, ornamental and other economic plants. Over and above there is crop diversity in different altitudinal zones. Certain commonly grown crops are Allium, Cucurbits, chenopods etc. Other are extensively cultivated, e.g. buck wheat, amaranths, beans, potato, pseudocereals and millets. Several species of Amaranthus are cultivated by the villagers, both for leaves and for grain. Similarly Chenopodium album is cultivated for leaves and grain. There is a great diversity in grain types with variation in inflorescence, colour, size of the plant. Buck wheat or Fagopyrum esculentum and F. tataricum are grown in the high altitude zone at Malari, Milam, Wan, etc. there are several local types available for F. esculentum which is extensively grow in almost all places in the proposed recreational zone. Panicum miliaceum and Secale cereals (Ura) are also cultivated mainly for grains.

Vegetables

Among vegetables, potato (Solanum ruberosum is widely cultivated along with cucumber (Cucumis sativus); radish (Raphanus sativus)chilly . (Capsicum annuum); fresh bean (Phaseolus vulgaris); cabbage (Brassica oleracea var. capitata); cauliflower (Brassica oleracea var. botrytis); cabbage leaved mustard (Brassica juncea var. rugosa); sweet belladonna - Matazor, Sarangum - Hindi (Phytolacca acinosa), chuhva (Amaranthus caudatus), marsha (A. paniculatus), etc.

Fruits

The villagers around the Biosphere Reserve also cultivate some of the common fruit trees of the hills for example, apple (Malus pumila), peach (Prunun persica), common plum (Prunus domestica), pear (Pyrus pyrifolia var. culta) common apricot (Prunus armeniaca) etc.

Medicinal plants

The area is very rich in medicinal plants. Following are some of the important medicinal plants which are found in the area. As the uses are mentioned in most of the literature of medicinal plants, only names of plants are mentioned below:

Aconitum balfourii Stapf (Gobari-Nepali), A. falconeri Stapf (Bikh Garhwal), A. violaceum Jacq. Ex Stapf. Actaea spicata L., Anemone obtusiloba D. Don, Delphinum brunonianum Royle (Musk larkspur), D. denudatum Wallich {(Apavisha-Sans-Vishalakarori, Jadivar, (Nirbisi)}, Thalictrum alpinum L., T. elegans Wallich ex Royle (Id-Salap), Berberis aristata DC., (Kingor) Podophyllum hexandrum Royle (Papra), Meconopsis aculeate Royle, Arabidopsis thaliana (L.) Heynh., Capsella bursa-pastoris (L.) Medik. (Shepherd's purse), Geranium wallichianum D. Don ex Sw. (Laljhari, Liljelhri), Acer acuminatum Wallich ex D.Don, Rhus punjabensis Stewart (Allara, Dosmila), Thermopsis barbata Royle, Princepia utilis Royle (Bekkra, Bhekol), Hedera nepalensis K. Koch, Viburnu continifolium D. Don, Galium aparine L., Nardostachys grandiflora DC. (Balchhar, Jatamansi), Valteriana hardwickii Wallich, Artemisia maritima L. (Kirmola), Saussurea costus (Flac.) Lipsch. (kut), Rhododendron arboreum Sm. (Burans), Rhododendron campanulatum D. Don (Cherailu), Jasminum humile L. (Peeli chameli), Syringa emodi Wallich ex Royle (Kmalayan lilac), Arnebia benthamii (Wallich ex G. Don) Johnston (Balchar), Arnebia euchroma (Royle) Johnston, Picrorhiza scrophulariflora Royle ex Benth. (Katki, Karu), Dactylorhiza hatagirea L, (Salam).

Important Timber Plants

Pinus Wallichiana A.B. Jackson - Blue Pine (Kail-Hindi), wood is of commercial importance, Cedrus deodara (Roxb,) Loud. (Deodar-Hindi) - Himalayan Cedar, strongest of Indian Coniferaceae woods used for door and window frames, Picea smithiana Boiss. West Himalayan Spruce (Ragha Garhwal) - wood is used for planking, rough furniture, etc., Taxus wallichiana Zucc. Himalayan yew (Thuner, Thano-Hindi)-wood is used for cabinet work and other fancy articles. Abies spectabilis (D.Don) Spach - East Himalayan Silver Fir, A. pindrow Royle- Himalayan silver fir, yields light wood used for packing cases, planking, Cupressus torulosa (Surai) etc.

SOME OBSERVATIONS /ACHIEVEMENTS

- No sheds for resting on the way are built up from Wan to Bedni.
- Girls education is very poor, reasons being

  Parents are poor & not motivated

  The Schools / colleges are far away from villages.
- The packaged tours are being operated by rich people at Delhi. They have direct contacts with Foreigners or rich tourists, they arrange their stay in star hotels at Ranikhet/ Almora. They have their own guides, they bring tinned food with them. So they don't have any link with local people. Thus local people are not getting any benefit from such tourism
- One man at Wan has Stone -wooden house (Pathar shed) where tourists stay, they don't stay at Forest Rest House (FRH) or GMVN rest houses. Local people's provide accommodation as rural hotels - as they don't have all the basic infrastructure facilities or they are not well maintained.
- To encourage the sale of the indigenous items villagers should display these items along the route e.g local pulses like Rajma, cereals like china, kauni, madua, phaphad, Ringal handicraft items with proper name/ price tags etc.
- The area has rich forest with some highly valued trees like Betula, Taxus spp. Are needed to be conserved and not to be exploited along with endangered spp. which local people do not have idea about their conservation / importance.
- Motivation of local people for conservation of natural resources flora. fauna, rivers, falls, glaciers etc. and their participation in Eco- tourism.
- Water conservation Local people have traditional thinking of "Let it flow" - we emphasized to use stopper on running tap water to stop wastage, so that people living in the higher elevations may get proper water supply .
- Solid waste disposal - Locals were made aware of solid waste disposal, how dangerous these could be if not managed properly. We collected about 250 gms waste materials including wrappers of Toffee, Chocolate, Chips, Namkeen, Plastic polybags, bottles of drinks water and beer canes etc. The immediate effect of our

awareness programme was seen when villagers started collecting these in bins instead of spreading them here or there.

- More participation of local people as porters, guides, restaurants/hotel owners etc. is suggested.

Strategies for Promotion of Eco-Tourism in Roopkund area

Based on the survey / discussion / meetings with villagers, tourists and our personal observations, following actions can be taken for promoting eco tourism in the areas:

- Registered association of local guides, porters, and ponywallas be formed to avoid cheating and burgling of tourists.
- There should be a Permanent check post at the entry points (Wan and Bedni for Roopkund) to maintain the number of tourists and income generated through entry fees.
- To maintain safe and comfortable stay and to increase the number of tourists, Tourist Rest Houses, PWD Rest Houses need to be renovated and maintained properly.
- Signboards indicating proper disposal of solid wastes along the tracks be displayed.
- Hoteliers, PWD rest houses and TRC officials on the way should be properly instructed about the proper disposal of garbage / solid waste / non-degradable wastes in their hotels / bungalows etc.
- Training about how to behave the tourists be given to the hoteliers, chowkidar of rest houses / bungalows etc.
- Awareness need to be developed among shepherds about destruction of vegetation in Bugyals. There should be rotational grazing to avoid overgrazing of one area.
- Tourists at the base camp should clearly be instructed about maintaining the sensitivity / fragility of the area.
- Unauthorized construction should be prohibited in the core zone of NDBR area.
- Basic facilities like telecommunication, electricity, toilet facilities on the route be provided.
- Tourists must be encouraged to stay with the local people as paying guests, for which local people should provide them all facilities.

Practical relevance/utility of the trekking as promoting Eco-tourism in Hills

In the developing countries like India there is an absence of general public pressure on the state to take strong measures on environmental protection. The awareness among the people is low and the tourism and environment groups that exist are very particularistic and lack a mass base unless people feel individually threatened by environmental degradation. Unregulated tourism can cause manifold problems – unbalanced social change, and unplanned economic development, social tensions and environmental pollution, distortion of life style and cultural decay. Thus, the present study will highlight the impact of tourist activities on the environment of these areas and suggestions could be made for scientific and sustainable development of mountain tourism by assessing the carrying capacity of the areas to regulate tourist activities in a sustainable way.

The continuous flow of tourists, mountaineers, trekkers etc. is likely to have positive as well as negative impacts on the natural resources to a certain extent. Mythological beliefs and tradition that are prevalent in the Himalayan regions are also responsible for adverse effects on the flora. Religious tourists habitually collect flowers and colourful herbs to offer to temples like Gangotri, Yamunotri, Badrinath, Kedarnath etc. Consequently, many species, which are part of our cultural and religious heritage, are beginning to get wiped out. e g. In Badrinath temple Tulasi (Santalum album) is offered to lord Badrinath Ji. At Roopkund Brahmkamal (Saussurea obvallata) is offered to Goddess Nanda Devi. A study (Trivedi, 2003) reports that at Surkunda Devi (25 km from Mussoorie to Tehri), which is situated at a most picturesque spot in the highest (2750m) peak of outer Himalayan range, about 10,000 people gather for a week on the occasion of Dushera and everyone offers few flowers / twigs of Ronsli (Abies pindrow) to Goddess Surkunda. Every visitor roughly plucks 10 flowers and 2 twigs. In this way about 10,000 flowers and 20,000 twigs are lost annually. This has resulted total degradation of Abies pindrow forest in the nearby areas with its associated shrubs and herbs. Some of the scrub species like Primula denticulata, Anemone vitifolia etc. have started growing there.

MY VIEWS AND THOUGHTS FOR BEING ECO-FRIENDLY IN THE UTTARANCHAL HILLS: (PROMOTE ECO-TOURISM)

Awesome scenes and inspiring snow bounded Kumaon-Himalayas of Uttaranchal are one of the nature's most beautiful gifts to mankind. As a visitor, all please make sure to respect local tradition and culture, help to maintain local harmony and protect the majestic natural environment.

Please observe the following:

Do's:

1. Use of polythene and plastics is unhealthy for the environment of the Himalayas, kindly avoid it.
2. Carry away all non-degradable litter, empty bottles, tins, polythene bags etc and throw then in municipal dustbin's .So that they can be disposed off properly or recycled.
3. Observe the sanctity of holy sites. In case of any offerings contact the staff of the temple committee only.
4. Respect local traditions when taking photographs, respect privacy, ask for prior permission and use restraint.
5. In case temporary toilets are set up near camp site, after defecation cover with mud or sand. Ensure that the spot is at least 30mt. far from a water source.

DON'TS

1. Taking away of cuttings, seeds and roots is illegal in the Himalayas. Allow the flora and fauna to flourish in their natural environment.
2. Avoid using pollutants, such as detergents in stream or springs.
3. Do not use wood as fuel to cook food at the camp site and do not destroy the forest wealth of the Himalayas which are our heritage.
4. Do not throw lit cigarettes or make open fires in the forests.
5. Do not consume alcohol, drugs or any other intoxicant.
6. Do not tempt the local children by offering them food stuff or sweets.
7. Do not listen to musical entertaining instruments at high volume and avoid noise pollution.

While being a trekker in Hills please observe the following:-

Don't do

√ Trekking enthusiasts leave in their wake mounts of garbage and ecological destruction

√ While pitching temporary tent houses observe the land cleanness and not effect to surrounding wild life.

CONCLUSIONS

REFERENCES

- Adhikari, B.S., Tikhari, H.C., Rawat, Y.S. & Singh, S.P. 1991. High altitude forest: composition, diversity and profile structure in a part of Kumaun Himalaya. Tropical Ecology 32(1): 86-97.
- Ahmed, Afroz (1990. Application of Environmental Impact Assessment in the Himalaya for Resources, Conservation and Ecologically Sustainable Development. Energy Environment Monitor 6 (1): 23-26 March.
- Aitken, W.M. (1981) The Sad Saga of Nanda Devi, Indian Wildlife 1(4): 37-41.
- Aitken, W.M. (1983). Nanda Devi revisited 1982. Sanctuary Asia 3 (1): 44-48.
- Anonymous (1986). Rishikesh, A Doorway to Himalayan Resorts and Pilgrimages, U.G.C. Report. Journal of Himalayan Studies and Regional Development Vol. 9 & 10, P. 133-139.
- Bachkheti, N.D. (1986). The Valley of Flower. Indian Forester 112: 583-587.
- Badola, R. (1998). Nanda Devi Biosphere Reserve: a study on socio-econimic aspects for the sustainable development of dependent population. Final Report. WII, Dehradun.
- Balodi, B. (1993). Expedition to Nanda Devi: Floristic analysis. In Scientific and Ecological Expedition to Nanda Devi. Report, Army Head Quarters, New Delhi pp. 86-95.

- Bankoti, N.S. (1990). Woody Vegetation along elevational gradient (2,000-3,600 m) of upper Pindari catchment (Kumaun Himalaya). Ph. D Thesis, Kumaun University, Nainital.
- Bankoti, N.S., Rawal, R.S., Samant, S.S. &Pangtey, Y.P.S. (1992). Forest vegetation of Inner Hill Ranges in Kumaun, Central Himalaya. Tropical Ecology 33(1): 41-53.
- Bhattacharya, M.K. (1999). Fern flora along Saung-Pindari trek in the Kumaun Himalaya. Journal of Bombay Natural History Society 96(3): 444-446.
- Bhattacharyya, U.C. and Malhotra, C.L. 1982. A Botanical Exploration enroute Roopkund Lake (North-East Garhwal). In : The Vegetational Wealth of the Himalaya (Ed. G.S. Paliwal), 161-174.
- Biswas, K. 1956. Common Medicinal Plants of Darjeeling and the Sikkim Himalayas. Suplt. Govt. Printing Press, Calcutta.
- Bosselmon, Fred P. (1978). In the Woke of the Tourist: Managing special Places in Eight Countries. The Conservation Foundation. Washington, D.C.
- Burkill, I.H. 1965. Chapters on the History of Botany in India Calcutta.
- Champion, H.G. & Lambert, W.J. (1921). Notes on a visit to Pindari glacier, Kumaon. Indian Forester 47: 11-21.
- Champion, H.G. & Seth, S.K. (1968). A revised survey of forest types of India. Government of India Publication Division, New Delhi.
- Chatterjee, D. (1939). Studies on the endemic flora on India and Burma. Journal of Royal Asiatic Society Bengal 5: 19-67.
- Chopra, R.N. & Chopra, I.C. 1965. A Review of work on Indian Medicinal Plants I.C.M.R., New Delhi.
- Cohen, E. (1972). Towards Sociology of International Tourism. Social Research, 39, 164-82.
- Dastur, J.F. 1970. Medicinal Plants of India & Pakistan. D.B. Taraporevala Sons & Co. Pvt. Ltd, Bombay - I.
- Dey, K.L. 1896. The Indigenous Drugs of India. Thachei. Spink & Co., Calcutta.
- Dhar, U. (2000). Conservation implications of plant endemism in high altitude Himalaya. Current Science 82 (2): 181 –152.
- Dhar, U., Rawal, R.S. & Samant, S.S. (1997). Structural diversity and representative ness of forest vegetation in a protected area of Kumaun Himalaya India: implications for conservation. Biodiversity & Conservation 6: 1045-1062.
- Dhar, U., Rawal, R.S. & Samant, S.S. (1998). Endemic plant diversity in Indian Himalaya IV: Poorly Represented Primitive families. Biogeographica 74(1): 27-39.
- Dhar, U., Rawat, R.S. & Samant, S.S. (1996). Endemic plant diversity in Indian Himalaya III: Brassicaceae. Biogeographica 72(1): 19-32.

- Dutt, U.C. 1877. The Materia Medica of the Hindus Calcutta.
- Echelberger, H.E. (1971). Vegetative changes to Adirondak Campgrounds: 1964 to 1969. Forest Service Research Notes: 142.
- Edington, J.M. and Edington, A.M. (1986). Ecology, Recreation and Tourism, Cambridge University Press, London.
- Elton, C.S. (1958). The Ecology of Invasions by Plants and Animals. Methuen, London.
- Fennell, D.A. R.Buckley; D. B Weaver (2000). Policy and Planning the encylopedia of ecotourism. Editor DB Weaver, CABI Publishing, Wallingford, U.K.
- Garkoti, S.C. & Singh, S.P. (1997) Structure and function of herbaceous vegetation in high mountains of central Himalaya. Tropical Ecology 38(1): 153-156.
- Gaur, R.D. & Semwal J.K. (1983). Some little known wild edibles of Garhwal Himalaya. Man & Environment, 7: 161 - 165.
- Ghildyal, B.N. (1957). A Botanical trip to the Valley of Flowers. Journal of Bombay Natural History Society 54: 365 - 386.
- Ghildyal, B.N. 1957. A Botanical trip of valley of Flowers. J. Bomb nat. Hist Soc, 54: 365-386.
- Goel, A.K. & Bhattacharya, U.C. (1983). Rare flowering plants of Garhwal Himalaya. In S.K. Jain & R.R. Rao (eds.) An Assessment of Threatened Plants of India. Botanical Survey of India, Calcutta. pp. 13 - 17.
- Greenwood, D.J. (1972). Tourism as an Agent of change: A Spanish Basque Case. Ethnology, II, 80-91.
- Greig-Smith, P. (1957). Quantitative plant ecology. Academic Press, New York.
- Gupta, R.K. (1968). Flora Nainitalensis: A Handbook of the flowering plants of Nainital. Navayug Traders, New Delhi.
- Gupta, R.K. 1956. Botanical Exploration in the Bhillangana valley of the erstwhile Tehri Garhwal State. J. Bomb. nat Hist. Soc., 53: 581-594.
- Gupta, R.K. 1957. Botanical Exploration in the erstwhile Tehri Garhwal State II. J. Bomb. nat. Hist. Soc., 54:878-886.
- Gupta, R.K. 1962. Botanical Exploration in the erstwhile Tehri Garhwal State III. J. Bomb. nat. Hist. Soc., 59:486-512.
- Hajra, P.K & Balodi, B. (1995). Plant wealth of Nanda Devi Biosphere Reserve. Botanical survey of India, Calcutta.
- Hajra,P.K. & Dixit, R.D. (1984). Woodsia cycloba Hand - Mazz. (Woodsiaceae) a rare fern from Nanda Devi Nati
- Jafari, J. (1974). The Socio-Economic costs of Tourism to Developing Countries. Annals of Tourism Research (7): 227-262.

- Jafari, J. (1982). Understanding the structure of Tourism- An Avant Props to studying its costs and Benefit. A.I.E.S.T. 23.
- Jain, S.K. 1975. Medicinal Plants. National Book Trust, India.
- Kala, S.P. & Gaur, R.D. 1982. A contribution of the Flora of Gopeswar (Chamoli Garhwal). In: The Vegetational Wealth of Himalaya. (ed. G.S. Paliwal). 347 - 313.
- Kant, S. (1983). Limnology of the Himalayan Lakes. Problem of Resource use and Management. In Singh T.V. and Kaur, J Himalayas, Mountains and Men. Prints House India, Lucknow.
- Kaur, J. (1980). Re-Examining Tourist Capacity of Nainital: A case for Diffusion of Tourist Activity in the Kumaun Lake Basins. In Singh T.V., and Kaur, J. (eds.). Studies in Himalayan Ecology and Strategies for Development, the English Book Store, New Delhi.
- Kirtikar, K.R. & Basu, B.P. 1935. Indian Medicinal Plants Allahabad.
- Lindsay, J. J. (1986)..Carrying capacity for Tourism Development in National Parks of the United States. Industry and Environment, 9(1): 17-20.
- Madan, Sapna (1998). Consequences of tourist activities on environment of Mussoorie hills in the Garhwal Himalaya of U.P., India. Thesis submitted in Forest Research Institute Deemed University, Dehra Dun, 172 pp.
- Madan, Sapna and Laxmi Rawat (2000). The Impacts of tourism on the environment of Mussoorie Garhwal Himalaya, India. The Environmentalist, Vol. 20 (3): 249-255.
- Maikhuri, R.K., U. Rana, K.S. Rao, S. Nautiyal, K.G. Saxena (2000). Promoting ecotourism in the buffer zone areas of Nanda Devi Biosphere Reserve: an option to resolve people-policy conflict. Int. Jour. of sustainable Dev. & world Ecology, 7 (4): 333-342.
- Mclellan, R. (1985). Nature Monuments and Parks. Tourism Recreation Research special Issue: 10 (2).
- Mings, R. (1978). The Importance of More Research Impacts of Tourism. Annals of Tourism Research 5 (3): 340-43.
- Naithani, B.D. 1967. Plant Collection with Kedarnath Parvat Expedition. Bull bot Surv. India, 11:24.
- Negi, K.S; Tewari, J.K. and Gaur, R.D. 1985. A contribution to the flora of Dodial- A High Altitude Lake in Garhwal Himalaya (Uttarkashi),U.P., J. Bomb, nat. Hist. Soc., 82(2):258-270.
- Nunez, T.V. (1963). Tourism Studies in Anthropological Perspective . In smith v.l. (eds.) Hosts and Guests: The Anthropology of Tourism, Philadelphia, University Pennsylvania Press, 207-16.
- Osmoston, A.E. 1927. A. forest flora of Kumaun. Allahabad.

- Pahr, Willibald P. (1988). Leisure in Nature, Naturopa 59-1988.
- Piper, C.S. (1944). Soil and plant analysis interscience publication Inc. Australia.
- Pizam, A and Milman, A. (1986). The Social Impacts of Tourism. Tourism Recreation Research, 9(1): 29-32.
- R; Khari, H.C. , Negi G.C.S., Pant G.B. Rana B.S. and Singh S.P. (1992) Phytomass and productivity in several communities of a Central Himalaya Alpine Meadow, India. Aretic and Alpine Research (243): 344-351.
- Rajwar, G.S. (1981). Ecological Problem of Mussoorie Hills and their solution. Journal of Himalayan Studies and Regional Development Vol. 5-6.
- Ram, J., Singh S.P. and Singh J.S. (1989). Plant biomass, species diversity and net primary production in a Central Himalayan high altitude grassland. Journal of Ecology (77): 456-468.
- Ram, Jeet, GL Shah and SP Singh (195). Vegetation mapping in Higher Himalaya: Beidni - Alee Bugyal –A case. In: Glimpses of Central Himalaya - A Socio-Economic and Ecological Perspective. Part I (eds. BR Pant & MC Pant). Radha Publications New Delhi, pp 379-397.
- Rao, T.A. 1959. Report on Botanical Tour to Milam Glacier, Bull. Bot. Surv. India, I:97-120.
- Rao, T.A. 1960. A Botanical Tour to Pindari Glaciers and Kumaun Hill Station. Bull. Bot. Surv. India, 2:61-94.
- Rikhari, H.C., Negi G.C.S., Ram Jeet and Singh S.P. (1993). Human induced secondary succession in the alpine meadow of Central Himalaya, India. Arctic and Alpine Research (25): 8-14.
- Roza, M. and Bano, H. (1989). Anthropogenic factors in Lake Ecosystem conceptual and Ecological Parameters in Singh T.V. (ed.) Geography of the Mountains, Heritage, New Delhi.
- Saliba, Louis J. (1988). Leisure in Nature. Naturopa 59-1988.
- Salm, R.V. (1986). Coral Reefs and Tourist Carrying Capacity. The Indian Ocean Experience. Industry and Environment. 9 (1): 11-14.
- Saxena, A.K. and Singh J. S. (1980). Analysis of forest grazing and vegetation in Parts of Kumaun Himalaya. Indian Journal of Range Management (1): 13-32.
- Semwal, J.K. & Gaur, R.D. 1981. Alpine Flora of Tungnath in Garhwal Himalaya. J. bomb. nat Hist Soc., 78:498-512.
- Sharma C.E. and Weaver, W. (1963). The mathematical theory of communication. Urban: University of Illinois Press 117 pp.
- Singh S.P. (1991). Structure and function of the low and high altitude grazing land ecosystem and impact of the livestock component in the Central Himalaya, Final Report Submitted to MoEF, Govt. of India, New Delhi.

- Singh Y.P. and Rai J.P.N. (2000). Species diversity and phytomass production in response to grazing pressure in alpine meadows of Nanda Devi biosphere Reserve. Van Vigyan 38 (1-4) pp. 185-195.
- Singh, T.V. (1984). Tourism in the Himalayan: Case of Garhwal, Problem of Resource Use and Conservation". In Grotzbach, E. (ed). Beitrage Zur Verglichenden Kultur- Geographic der Hochgebrige, Veriage Friedrich Pustet Regensburg, Eischstatt: West Germany 169-184.
- Singh, T.V. and Yadav, D.B. (1980). A cross Road Pilgrim Tour in Garhwal: Studying Impact of Modernization with special Reference to Tourism. Journal of Himalayan Studies and Regional Development Vol.4.
- Singh, Tej Vir and Kaur, Jagdish (1983). Mountain Tourism, How Good and How Bad- case studies from the Himalaya. Journal of Himalayan Studies and Regional Development, Vol. 7&8.
- Sinnhuber, K.A. (1982). Recreation in the Mountains; Case of Alps in Reference to Elite Activities; In Singh T.V. (eds). Tourism wildlife Parks Conservation, Metropolitan, New Delhi: 88-113.
- Smith, V.L. (1977) (ed). Host and Guests. Anthropology of Tourism, Philadelphia University, Pennsylvania Press.
- Thompson, P, (1974). Some Real and Unreal Social Effects of Tourism in Fiji. Tourism in Fiji: Parkinson Memorial Lecture. The University of south Pacific, Suva, Fiji, 44-47.
- Travis, A.S. (1984). Social Cultural Aspects of Tourism" Industry and Environment (Special issue) UNEP, Paris 7 (1): 22-24.
- Trivedi, P.R. (2003). Study material, M Sc Ecology & Environment. Part III. Indian Institute of Ecology & Environment, New Delhi.
- Tuunanen, Pekka (1988). Leisure in Nature. Naturopa 59-1988.
- Usher, G. 1974. A Dictionary of plants used by man. Constable London.
- Van Hout, D. (1979). The Non-economic Impact of International Tourism in Developing Countries: A Review of Recent Literature. Travel Research Journal (1): 81-89.
- Walkley A. and Black I.A. (1965). An examination of the degtigarff method for determining soil organic matter and proposed modification of the chronic acid titration method. Soil Science (37): 29-38.
- Watt. G 1889-1893. A Dictionary of Economic Products of India. 6 Vols. Calcutta.
- Wearing, S. (2000). Exploring Socio cultural impacts on local communities. the encyclopedia of ecotourism. Editor D B Weaver. CABI Publishing, Wallingford, U.K.
- Western, D. (1986). Tourist Capacity in Eastern African Parks. In Industry and Environment 9(1): 14-16.

- Whittkar R.H. (1975). Dominance and Diversity in land plant community. Science (17): 1574 - 1582.
- Williams, A.T. (1982). Impacts of Domestic Tourism on Host Populations: The Evolution of a Model. In Singh, T.V. and Kaur, J. Studies in tourism wildlife Parks and Conservation, Metropolitan, New Delhi 214-223.

5

Promotion of Ecotourism in Kujapuri Hills of Garhwal Himalaya

Megha Rawat, H.B. Vasistha, Mridula Negi
Division of Ecology and Environment,
Forest Research Institute, Dehradun-248006

ABSTRACT

Eco-tourism is rapidly gaining importance in India in recent years, because nature has endowed India with all its beauty and resources. The Himalayan belt stretches in the north of the country has a unique potential for eco-tourism, being repository of various natural resources, including diverse vegetation, unique flora and fauna, perennial rivers, magnificent natural waterfalls, springs, varied landscape and more attracting the diversity, culture and tradition of the region.

Among various areas identified for the promotion of eco-tourism in Garhwal Himalaya, Kujapuri is one of them. It is situated in the Tehri district of Garhwal Himalaya embedded with multifaced glaring attractions benefiting towards the promotion of ecotourisim and is among one of the 52 Siddhapeeth in our country. It is located at about 35 km from Rishikesh and 7 km from Narendra Nagar. The Kujapuri hills provide various attractions such as undulating hills dominated by the lush green forest of Quercus leucotrichophora, panoramic view of river Ganga, Rishikesh, Shiwalik hills and Doon valley in the south, and snow clad Himalayan ranges in the north. The area is also surrounded by the clusters of villages having distinct culture and traditions. The site is also well suited for adventurous tourism like trekking, paragliding etc. The present paper discusses the major attractions, activities and strategy for the development of eco-tourism in the Kujapuri Hills.

Key words: Eco-tourism, landscape, Diversity, Siddhapeeth, Vegetation

INTRODUCTION

Eco-tourism both at conceptual and empirical levels is significant in a number of respects. Traditionally it encapsulates scientific, aesthetic, and philosophical approaches which reflect the structure and function of the society. Over the decades numerous changes have been observed both in the content and context of eco-tourism. With globalization the processes of these changes not only widened and multiplied, but also gained importance.

Ecotourism is perceived as a subset of alternative tourism, which places primary emphasis on the natural environment as the main motivation for travel (Weaver, 1991). The idea behind ecotourism is to preserve the natural and cultural environment and benefit the local community by conserving through development. It is not just an economic activity of importance to national development but also an important medium of cultural changes among nations. It posses a significant potential in realizing benefits in terms of the conservation of biodiversity and sustainable use of its components. Among the indirect benefits of ecotourism is the environmental ethos, which is fostered and reinforced through direct contact with the natural environment (Devall, 1988). Because of its relevance to local empowerment, conservation, education, sustainability, local employment, and ethics, ecotourism has emerged as an attractive and appropriate sustainable development option to many regions in the developing and developed worlds.

In India, the trends in tourism have shown variation in terms of both economic and socio-cultural values. With changing lifestyles, economy and paid vacations, there has been a change in the attitude and perception of people toward travel and tourism.

Himalaya has a great potential of ecotourism being a repository of natural resources, including diverse vegetation, unique flora and fauna, magnificent natural water falls, springs and more attracting the diversity, culture and tradition of the region that altogether make it a paradise on earth. Garhwal Himalaya occupies the most regal position in the Himalaya and is cherished by a natural environment full of cool weather and serene climate with scenic beauty (Chadha, 1989). The region is full of mountain, rivers, streams, lakes and glaciers. The gentle slopes and landscape above the timberline in higher Himalaya which have mainly *buggi* grasses locally called as *Bugiyals*, is enthralled by the tourists (Nigam, 2002). The region besides having natural scenic attractions, also have religious importance. These two factors in combination are adding the prospects of ecotourisim in Gasrhwal Himalaya.

Among various areas identified for the promotion of ecotourism in Garhwal Himalaya, Kujapuri is one of them, which has a great potential for the development of ecotourism. It is situated in the Tehri district of Garhwal Himalaya at an altitude of 1,676 mts and latitude 30°11′ N and longitude 78°28′E. It is located at about 35 km from Rishikesh on Rishikesh – Gangotri road. Kujapuri is a religious place and has been a hot spot of tourism due to its magnificently diverse landscapes, high biodiversity and rich cultural heritage, which can also be generated as a good source of income and employment to rural masses. It lies in the temperate region encompassing three major ecosystem i.e. forest, grassland and hill terraced ecosystem. Clusters of rural villages namely Pater, Badera, Khera and Sonigoan surround Kujapuri hill. These villages are directly influenced by the forest and grasslands in and around the temple. Agriculture and cattle rearing are their main source of livelihood.

The captivating site of Kujapuri is an alluring attraction for the pilgrims and tourists from all over the country and also from all over the world. About 150-200 pilgrims and 10-25 foreign tourists per day visit the temple. The religious fair is celebrated every year during

Navratras, over fifty thousand people gather here to participate in this celebration by indulging themselves into various activities. Pilgrims are the special tourists whose purpose is to visit the place where they become involved in the religious activities. Visitors can be religious, tourists, students, academicians, trekkers etc. depending on their exposure however, the first dominant impression of tourists about this place is the religious notion like one of the most sacred Siddhapeeth for Hindus. This paper looks into some of such issues related to development and management of ecotourism in Kujapuri hills of Garhwal Himalaya.

ATTRACTIONS / VALUES OF KUJAPURI

1. Location

Temple is located at the peak of the mountain and thus provides a picturesque view of the area, it lends a panoramic view of snow clad Himalayan range in the north (Chaukhamba ranges) and an exhilarating view of the sacred river Ganga, Rishikesh, Hardwar, Doon valley and Shiwalik hills in the south.

2. Topography

Topography of Kujapuri divides the area into two aspects i.e. Northern and Southern aspects. The north aspect is dominated by rich vegetation that helps in maintaining the aesthetic view of the area and provides cool, soothing and invigorating environment to the visitors visiting the area particularly during summers. South aspect has scattered bushy vegetation with various sunny faces where the tourists mass enjoy the full sunlight throughout the day particularly during winters.

3. Landscape

It encompasses three major ecosystem i.e. forest, grassland and hill terraced ecosystem. The forest ecosystem is dominated by lush green forest of *Quercus leucotrichophora*. The hill-terraced ecosystem has an eye-catching view of terraced cultivation containing agro forestry system of cultivation.

4. Habitation

Kujapuri hill is surrounded by clusters of rural villages namely Pater, Badera, Khera and Sonigoan. The forest and grasslands in and around the temple directly influence these villages. More than 150 households inhabit these villages. The human population of these villages is about 1,500 and livestock population is 800. Agriculture and cattle rearing are their main source of livelihood hence, they are totally dependant on the forest and grassland for their daily requirements like for fodder, fuel, timber and leaf litter etc. for organic manure.

5. Trekking

Kujapuri offers attractive destination for adventure tourism like trekking, it has the trekking route starting from Tapovan (Rishikesh) to Kujapuri and vice-versa. Taking all these points into consideration Uttaranchal Forest Department has planned to develop this place for ecotourism.

6. Paragliding

Kujapuri also offers an attractive destination for various aero sports like paragliding etc., foreign tourists besides enjoying the beauty of the place also indulge themselves into various adventure sports. Taking off from Kujapuri they glide down to Rishikesh enjoying the cool, invigorating climate and scenic beauty of the place.

APPROACHES

- The Forest Research Institute, Dehradun, carried out Restoration measures in Kujapuri in order to enhance plant diversity and general aesthetic view of the temple area. Various species of different categories such as forestry, fodder, horticulture, ornamental, commercial and plants of sacred importance were planted in forest and village community and private lands in and around Kujapuri temple.
- Trekking route of about 10-12 Km from Tapovan (Rishikesh) to Kujapuri has been developed by the Uttaranchal Forest Department.

FUTURE STRATEGY FOR THE PROMOTION OF ECOTOURISM

- The participation of local people is needed at all the stages of ecotourism evaluation, planning and implementation.
- To promote effective participation efforts should be made to enhance local people's appreciation and awareness of about the potential tourism values of their natural surroundings, i.e. the local people should be made aware of what their natural surrounding has including environmental, cultural and other attractions etc. to offer to the potential tourists.
- Outside institutions from provincial to national (egs. NGO's, National outreach groups, private sector firms and research and educational institutions) should be drawn upon to support tourism in Kujapuri.
- There is a need to popularize the trekking route from Tapovan (Rishikesh) to Kujapuri.
- There is also a need to popularize the sacred grove which is being developed by the Forest Research Institute, Dehradun so that people can know about the various important aspects of this area and about the work which is being carried out here in order to develop and maintain the beauty of this place.
- Basic features like electricity, telecommunication etc. and construction of tourists hut and rest houses should be provided to the people visiting this place.
- Besides this, some unique features like bird watching, model and telescopic display of the panoramic view of snow clad Himalayan peaks can be added to attract more tourists mob here.

- The information about Kujapuri and its importance should be made available in all the hotels, tourist bungalows and ashrams etc. in Rishikesh and Hardwar as these places are close to this place and are well known tourist spot.
- Incorporate Kujapuri in the tourist map of Garhwal Himalaya.

These strategies should be followed altogether to develop Kujapuri as a potential site for the ecotourisim. To be viable, ecotourism should be community based and the needs of the community, their ideas of conservation should be given prime importance. Local structures must receive patronage and promotion, so that ecotourism becomes a dynamic facet of economic development.

REFERENCES

- Chadha, S.K. (1989). *Himalayan Ecology*. Ashish Publishing House, New Delhi, pp. 102-126.
- Devall, B. (1988). *Simple in Means, Rich in Ends: Practicing Deep Ecology*. Peregrine Smith Books, Salt Lake City, USA.
- Nigam, D. (2002). *Tourism Environment and Development of Garhwal Himalaya*. Mittal Publication, New Delhi.
- Weaver, D.B. (1991). Alternative to mass tourism in Dominica. *Annals of Tourism Research* 18, 414-432.

6

Pilgrimage Tourism in Kashmir: A Case Study of Amarnath Yatra

S.K.Gupta Reader
Centre for Mountain Tourism and Hospitality Studies,
HNB Garhwal UniversitySrinagar Garhwal
Reyaz Ahmed Qurashi
Tourist Officer,Directorate ,
J & K Tourism, Srinagar,(Jammu & Kashmir)
Poonam Gupta
Research Scholar, Department of Sociology, HNB Garhwal University Srinagar Garhwal

Religion has been a powerful force, which has caused people to travel to religious centers in many parts of the world. From the very beginning even during prehistoric period pilgrimage has been one of the primary motives for travel. India has an age-old tradition of pilgrimages within her territories and across with her neighbors. Aesthetics, peaceful isolated land and environs of Kashmir have been providing an Ideal atmosphere for the men of god since ages. The valley of Kashmir has great culture of *Sufis, Rishis* and Mystics, and is identified with the name *'peer veer'*. It being a holy land, one comes across a network of Shrines, Mosques, and temples which are thronged by believers from within Kashmir and outside. Kashmir is receiving large chunks of domestic and International Pilgrim/Religious tourists. It is assumed that tourism has considerable physical, economic and socio-cultural significance throughout the world. It might be a powerful and beneficial agent of both economic and social transformation at the same time, it may rise questions concerning the social and environmental issues.

Therefore, for the sustainable tourism development there is need to give a thought towards these impacts of Tourism, keeping adverse impact in control and promoting the favorable impacts. Although tourism has emerged as a major socio-economic force and it has environmental implications too.

The Holy cave of Amarnath is situated at the farther end of the *Lidder* valley at an altitude of 3952meters. Hidden behind the snowy walls and far off from the dusty plains, the picturesque Amaranth has been called the temple of Gods. Among all Hindu Shrines in the valley of Kashmir, the cave of *Amaranathji* with its mysterious *Shiva lingam* is the most sacred spot.

Each year on the day of "*Sawan puran Mashi* (full moon night) in the month of "*Shravan*" thousands of Hindu pilgrims gather before the *Amarnathji* Shrine to offer their prayer to Lord Shiva. *Amarnathji* is a grand cave, the mouth of which is 150 feet with the same dimensions in length and breadth. In the interior of the cave is a mysterious self formed snow lingam of Shiva which waxes and wanes with moon. By its sides are fascinatingly, two more ice-lingams, that of *Parvati* and of their Son *Ganesha*.

Accessibility

Amarnath cave is approachable from Sonamarg via Baltal and from Pahalgam via Chandanwari. Sonamarg is 2740 meters above sea level and is situated on the Srinagar-Leh highway 83km north-east of Srinagar. Above 15kms ahead from Sonamarg lies the base camp Baltal, which is a small charming valley lying in the foothill of Zogilpass. The holy cave of Amarnathji is just a day's journey away from here by a trek of 14kms. Two Kms after Baltal is Domail and the trail from *Domail* to the holy cave lies along very steep hillsides. Therefore, great care needs to be taken while trekking along this route. Several snow bridges on the fast flowing streams have to be crossed over, while during the rains the road becomes slippery.

Sangam top from where the holy cave is quite near, the trail from Pahalgam meets the *Baltal* route. The traditional route to Amarnath cave is via Pahalgam, which are 96kms from *Srinagar*. From Pahalgam to the cave the distance is 46kms out of which 30kms is covered on foot from *Chadanwari* (2895meters) to Amarnath cave. The trek from *Chandanwari* to Amarnath cave is on an ancient route can be covered in fivedays. The 30km distance between *Chandanwari* and holy cave is covered in two days, with night halts at *Sheshnag* (3352meters) after 12km and *Panjtharni* (3657meters) after 24 kms. From *Panjtharni* to *Amarnath* is only 6 km.The distance from *Pahalgam* to *Chandanwari* (16kms) can be covered by vehicular transport.

From year 2003 Government of Jammu and Kashmir has started helicopter service between Srinagar and holy cave and now also from Baltal to holy cave. The nearest airport is at Srinagar 109kms and nearest railhead is at Jammu, which is 414kms. From the holy cave a large number of ponies both riding as well as pack ponies remain available during the yatra. For ill and physically handicapped *yatris* (pilgrims) dandies are available on approved government rates. During yatra only 1200 *yatries* are allowed to the holy cave via Baltal while 2700 *yatries* via Pahalgam.

Mythology

Many legends are associated with this sacred cave. From *Kalhana's RajtarangIni*, it is gathered that even before the 12th century, the cave was annually visited by thousands of pilgrims from all parts of the country. The famous book "*Brangish Sanhit*" says that the *chari* or the holy silver mace, was given by Lord Shiva to *Kashyap Rishi* for deliverance and the Lord commanded that this *Chari* be carried to his abode at Amarnath cave where he promised to uncover his blessings every year on the night of full moon in the month of August. Legend has it that Shiva recounted to Parvati the secret of creation in a cave in Amarnath. Unknown to them a pair of mating doves eaves-dropped on this conversation and having learned the secret, are reborn again and again and have made the cave their eternal abode. Many pilgrims' report seeing the doves-pair when they trek the arduous route to pay obeisance before the ice-*lingam.*

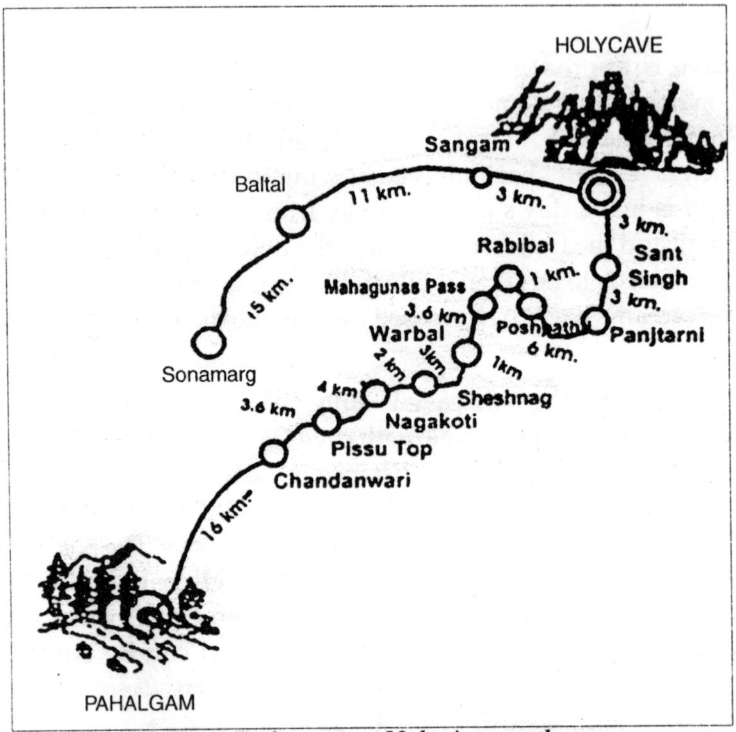

Figure 1: Trek route to Holy Amarnath cave

According to an ancient tale there was once a Muslim shepherd named Buta Malik who was given a sack of coal by a saint (*Sadhu*). Upon reaching home he discovered that the sack in fact contained gold. Overjoyed and overcame Buta Malik rushed back to look for the *sadhu* to thank him. But on the spot of their meeting he discovered a cave and eventually this becomes a place of pilgrimage for all believers. To date certain percentage of the donation made by pilgrims are given to the descendent of Malik , and the remaining to the Amarnath Shrine Board , which manages the Shrine.

Yet another legend has it that when *Kashyap Rishi* drained the kashmir valley of water, the cave and the *lingam* were discovered by *Brigu Rishi* while travelling through Himalayas. When people heard of *lingam,* Amarnath for them became Shiva's abode and a centre of pilgrimage.

Rituals and Performance

Before entering the holy cave for *Darshan* the pilgrims have a bath at Amarnath in a small stream near the cave. After bath the pilgrims sprinkle themselves with limestone dust and enter the cave, said to be the dwelling of *Shiva*. Entrance to the cave is a hasty affair and is regulated, as there are long queues of pilgrims waiting outside to pay homage before the awesome Shiva *Linga*. The devotees sing *bhajans*, Chant incantations and priests perform *aarti* and *puja* invoking the blessing of Shiva, the divine, the pure, the absolute. For those who journey with faith, these simple visitations to this cave shrine, the home of the greatest of the Hindu gods, who is both destroyer and healers a rewarding experience.

Facilities and Services

Shri Amarnath Shrine Board and State Government in collaboration with Jammu and Kashmir Tourism Department and other related organisations are making special arrangements for the convenience of Yatries during the whole Yatra period.

Accommodation is made available enroute to holy cave by Jammu and Kashmir Tourism Development Corporation and some other private agencies in tented camps at Baltal, Domail (Sonamarg) and at holy cave. Free *langer* facilities are provided by voluntary organizations for Yatris enroute to the Holy cave. From Baltal to holy cave and back ponies, dandies and porters are available on reasonable approved government rates. Telecom, Medical facilities, security arrangements are available round the clock during the yatra period. Yatra registration facilities are available at all the branches of Jammu and Kashmir Bank outside Jammu and Kashmir state for which the dates are being communicated on Radio, Television and leading National dailies. No pilgrims (*yatris*) are allowed without a registration card and shall be turned back from Jammu itself. Aged, infirm, ailing and insufficiently clothed persons are not allowed to proceed beyond Pahalgam.

Table 1: Rate List for Ponies, Labourers, *Dandies* for Amarnath Yatra for 2006

S.No.	Destination	Rate
I.	Riding/Pack Pony	
	1. Chandanwari to Holy Cave and back	Rs. 2650/-
	2. Baltal to Holy Cave and back	Rs. 1600/-
II.	Dandy	
	1. Chandanwari to Holy Cave and back	Rs. 10000/-
	2. Baltal to Holy Cave and back	Rs. 5500/-
III.	Labourers	
	1. Chandanwari to Holy Cave and back	Rs. 1000/-
	2. Baltal to Holy Cave and back	Rs. 1300/-

IV.	Labourers with *Pithoo*	
	1. Chandanwari to Holy Cave and back	Rs. 1400/-

Source: Director Tourism, Kashmir.

Do's and Don'ts For *Yatries* Visiting Shri Amarnath Shrine

Do's

1. One should be physically and mentally fit to perform the journey as the Yatra involves trekking at an altitude of 14,000ft and must be medically examined and certified fit for the journey.
2. One should carry sufficient heavy woolens including sweaters, (full as well as half-sleeved), drawers, woolen trousers, gloves, monkey caps etc. Other items to be carried include windcheater, light raincoat, a sleeping bag or blankets or a set of bedding items, waterproof tent, a torch with sufficient batteries, a walking stick with proper handgrip. Ladies are advised not to do the journey in Saris, instead pants or salwar suits with drawers should be used.
3. Some eatable like biscuits, candy, milk powder, sugar, assorted dry fruits, honey and some tinned food should be carried along with a water bottle, plastic plate, tumbler, spoons etc.
4. Ration and fire wood quota has been especially arranged for the pilgrim at all stations enroute, against payment.
5. One should ensure that the pony *walla*, the laborers, the *dandy walla* is properly registered and carried a token being allotted at fixed rates by competent authority at the base camps.
6. One should ensure that ponies carrying the luggage and eatables etc. remain with you all the time.
7. The pilgrim must observe discipline on the trek and keep on moving slowly and steadily and adhere to the instructions issued by the *Yatra* Officer from time to time. The officials of the Police, Tourism, Health, Food &Supplies and other Departments are there to help the pilgrims to perform the journey comfortably.
8. One must carry sufficient money to pay for the accommodation at Pahalgam and at other station en-route to the holy cave and for meeting other personal requirements.
9. All medical facilities during the *Yatra* are free, However one must carry own personal medical Kit also.

DON'TS

1. Pilgrims must not or throw anything on Holy Lingam.
2. Do not overstrain on steep gradients.
3. Do not relax at that points where there are warning notices.

4. Do not break traffic discipline or try to overtake others in difficult stretches of the route.
5. Do not pay more than the prices fixed for porters, ponies, dandies, rations, firewood, accommodation etc.
6. Do not use polythene, disposable plastic cups, saucers and glasses in and around the route.
7. Do not use polythene bags and plastic tents during *yatra.*

Tourist Traffic

As per the figures provided by Jammu and Kashmir Tourism Department and Shri Amarnath Shine Board, the flow of pilgrims to this cave has been increasing continuously over the period of time as demonstrated below in table. The table depicts certain ups and downs in the flow of pilgrims to this holy cave. Starting with arrival of 19578 in 1980, the number of arrivals reached to four Lakhs in 2004. The numbers how ever, dropped considerably in 1990 to a meager 4824. This decrease can be attributed to the turbulence in Kashmir which started in the same year. The subsequent years witnessed a gradual increase in the number of *yatries* indicating a positive trend. During the period of militancy a negative trend was observed only in 1994. In spite of the ban by some militants or outfits, the government dared to bring in a heavy number of pilgrims to the cave under heavy security arrangements. The increase in the numbers of pilgrims, is a testimony of the cooperation and benevolence of the Kashmiri Muslims towards their Hindu brothers.

Table 2: Arrival of Pilgrims at Holy Cave of Amarnath

Year	Number of Pilgrims / *Yatries*
1980	19572
1981	26000
1982	25000
1983	21021
1984	9483
1985	42000
1986	51000
1987	52000
1988	96055
1989	95238
1990	4824
1991	15599
1992	54638
1993	56000
1994	37000
1995	60000

1996	120000
1997	79035
1998	149920
1999	114366
2000	173334
2001	119037
2002	110793
2003	152000
2004	400000
2005	388000

Source: Directorate of tourism J&K Govt. Srinagar

Economic Impact

Tourism has major effect on the economy of Kashmir Valley. It often brings new and sometime necessary sources of capital and income that may supplement or replace traditional sources of earnings at destination .For that purpose tourism development has often received support from local residents and especially from government. In Valley of Kashmir, scope of large-scale industrialization is very limited and the potential of agricultural development is also scarce, especially in the area around Amarnath cave. The role of tourism is significant in the development of its economy. It has won considerable recognition as an activity generating economic benefits. Tourist spending generates considerable income both for the individual as well as state.

The tourism expenditure has both direct and indirect effects on the economy. Thousand of Hotel/House Boat Owners, Restaurant, pony *walas*, *Dandiwalas*, labors and guides earn their bread and butter from the yatris. The income generated by the Amarnath yatris can be worked out by the formula devised as under.

Income generated in the reference year.	= Per Capita Expenditure by the tourist in the reference year.	× No. of tourists reached the destination in the reference year.

Symbolically, it can be expressed as under: DI = PCE × NT

Where

DI = Direct Income

PCE = Per Capita Expenditure.

NT= No. of Tourist

Per capita expenditure by the tourist has been worked out by

PCE= PDE × AS

Where

PDE= Per Day Expenditure.

AS= Average stay in days.

Average expenditure and average stay of a tourist for this is based on the survey conducted by the scholar in 2005 regarding the expenditure/average stay of tourists. The average of the per capita tourist expenditure in respect of Amarnath *yatris* can give the income generated by the *yatris* in 2005.

1. Average of the per capita tourist expenditure = Rs.1187.75 (D).
2. Average duration of stay of tourist = 6.4 days.

Total numbers of pilgrims/tourists visited Amarnath in 2005 = 388000.

Therefore income generated

DI = PCE x NT

Where:

PCE = PDE x AS

PDE (Domestic) = Rs.1187.75

AS (Domestic) = 6.4

PCE = 1187.75 x 6.4 = Rs.7601.6

DI = 7601.6 x 3880000.00 = Rs 2950 million approx.

Environmental Impact

It is not just true that the thousands of pilgrims on the Amarnath Yatra are facing problems because of bad weather and other reasons, It is also true that they are equally responsible for the problems. The environment damage brought about by the large movement of pilgrims on fragile routes, passing through some of the most beautiful snow clad Himalayas, is assuming alarming proportions. The *yatra* in the years 2004,2005 and 2006, as perhaps never before, brought about the need for studies and action on subjects like sustainable tourism, impact, carrying capacities, good planning and implementation and most importantly social commitment and self discipline.

It is estimated that over three Lakhs mineral water bottles are dumped by the yatris to Amarnath each year, in addition to it an equal number of plastic packets of fast food like wafers etc. The plastic of bottles and food packets material is, unfortunately, not biodegradable. This means that once left behind in the hills, it stay there for ever, causing damages to the snow clad mountains.

Department of Tourism, Kashmir, are aware of the problem but admits that for a complete solution pilgrims and public participation is mandatory. As many as 140 laborer were engaged daily in the cleaning operation in 2005 which was also not adequate. Post-yatra clearance drive was taken by J & K Tourism in collaboration with local schools/ institutes to clear up the solid waste at Pahalgam, Chandanwari, Baltal and Sonmarg.

Government/Amarnath Shrine Board must provide filtered water facility enroute so that the pilgrims do not have to carry plastic water bottles and should make the provision for littering to avoid addition of night soil.

Socio-cultural issues (Lingam Row)

The Shrine attracts a large number of pilgrims during June-August every year when a *lingam* forms there naturally. But in the year 2006, media reports suggested that the shrine authorities had artificially installed the *Lingam*, as it did not form naturally. For this the governor in his capacity as chairman of the Shri Amaranth Shrine Board (SASB) had ordered the probe by the one-man inquiry by the Retired Justice of J&K High Court. The inquiry gave a clean chit to the temple board on the basis of his interaction with local people, security officials and a briefing on the SASB'S version of the entire issue. However, the *Martanc Purohit Sabha* an organisation that provides priests to the cave shrine during annua pilgrimage had rejected the probe report. They described it as "doctored" and alleged tha the shrine board was responsible for installing an artificial *lingam* at the shrine. A delegatior of Hindu pilgrim- the Amaranth Yatra Welfare Organization had met the President of India and sought his intervention in this sensitive matter and urged a CBI probe or inquiry by a sitting judge of Supreme Court to bring out truth.All this controversy resulted in a steep fall in the number of pilgrims to the shrine in the year 2006. Only 2,90,000 pilgrims arrived in the year 2006 during two month pilgrimage (June 11 to August 9), which was earlier of 45 days duration.

CONCLUSION

Sacred places like amaranth and Mount Kailash in Tibet are not centre for th propagation of religions ideas per se, because they are purely sacred foci without bein organization centers. The controversy of installation of artificial *Shivlingam* at the shrin has shaked the deep faith of millions of pilgrims. The shrine board should take adequat step so that this type of controversy will not arise in future. For the tourists visiting th holy cave of Amaranth, it requires major efforts and expenditure; which involves large scale deployment at receiving and transit points and facilities at Jammu ,Srinagar , enrout and at the base camps of Amaranth and near the holy cave. The threat of security to th pilgrims of Amaranth *Yatra* in between Jammu/Srinagar to the base camp is a majo challenge. Further the enroute places in the trek of Amaranth Yatra at high altitudes hav no infrastructure to meet the needs of great number of pilgrims. Health and safety probler arose in all the previous *yatras* due of bad weather.

Although number of pilgrims/*yatris* per day has been restricted officially from bo the base camps. But proper implementation was not done in previous years. Particular when the *yatra* was stopped/abandoned for a few days due to bad weather, an accumulation of pilgrim took place at base camps, and even at Jammu or Srinagar. Prope organization of the flow of pilgrim traffic from base camp to the holy cave and at the ca itself is very essential as the Amaranth trek route passes through extremely fragile high mountain area. More over sufficient tented accommodation with catering facilities should be made available enroute to holy cave. Keeping in view of the fragile ecology and environment of the area total ban must be imposed on the use of polythene bags

REFERENCES

- Ahamed, M.A. (2000), *Management of Tourism in J & K*, Dilpreet publishing house, New Delhi.
- Bagri S.C. & Gupta S.K. (2000), "Tourism in Garhwal Himalaya" in O.P. Kandari *et al* (Eds.) *Garhwal Himalaya: Nature, Culture & Society*,Trans Media, Srinagar Garhwal.
- Banskota, Kamal and Sharma, Bikash (1995), *Mountain Tourism for Local Community Development*. International Centre for Integrated Development in Nepal, Kathmandu.
- Directorate of Tourism, J & K Government, Srinagar.
- Farid, S.A. (2003), *Tourism in Kashmir*, Rajesh publication ,New Delhi.
- Gupta, S.K. 2002: *Tourism and Heritage Resources In Garhwal Himalaya*, Kaveri Books, New Delhi.
- Kaur, J. (1985), *Himalayan Pilgrimages and the New Tourism*, Himalayan Books, New Delhi.
- Lawrence, W.R. (1967) *The valley of Kashmir*, Kesar publisher, Delhi.
- Reddy, P.S. (1992) *Eco tourism and role of Industry in protection of environment, National Seminar Proceedings of Eco tourism*, New Delhi.
- Times Of India,"Lingam Row:Amarnath Board gets a clean chit,19th August,2006. P-6
- Yoel, M (1992) "Group Differentiated perceptions of social impacts of tourism". A Research article, *University of Haifa, Vol. 94 Nov. 4, 1992*. P- 376.

7

The Appraisal of Job Training Programmes in Indian Tourism Education

Dr. Mohit Vij (Lecturer)
Department of Tourism,
University College,
Kurukshetra University,
Kurukshetra

Surender Pal Singh (Lecturer)
Department of Tourism,
Government Post
Graduate College,
Ambala Cantt

ABSTRACT

The recent years have witnessed the demand and growth of tourism education in India at graduate and post graduate level. Training programs are the integral part of curriculum for tourism education aiming to the exposure of industry, to imply theory into practice, improving personal skills and settling job with the organization. The significance of industrial training is required to be recognized by the university/ institute as to improve the quality of their human resource since it been an important phase of education. Training supplements theory which makes it more productive and different from other conventional courses. It is imperative that university/institute review the training programs of the students in light of external dynamic environment, expectations of industry, problem and challenges of trainees in order to develop efficient and competent human resource and retain 'win-win' relations with industry key players. The present paper analyses different aspects of training programs in tourism industry and suggest remedies for the best practices of industrial training for developing efficient human resource.

INTRODUCTION

There is sudden surge in quality of human resource in tourism & hospitality sector being it world's largest service industry & utmost to meet customer's delight .The dynamic growth in the provision of tourism education since the late 1980 witness to the rising profile of tourism, primarily as an economic factor and the needs of those organizations involved in promoting & responding to the demand for tourism (Parsons & Cave, 1991; CNAA, 1993;Middleton & Ladkin,1996). Relatively new in India, tourism education is being offered by 18 universities and institutes at post graduate level comprising 1400 student, and 100 colleges providing tourism at graduate level. Job training as a part of formal education plays a crucial role in the provision of skilled & competent human resources. The last a few decade have observed the tremendous need & growth of tourism education world wide (Airey & Johenson, 1998; Johenson 1997). Training an important part of tourism education relies to update knowledge, skills in present day information technology & economic globalization that result in changing the traditional view towards education and training. Earlier it was believed that education is mainly provided by establishment like university/ institute while training is usually provided by employer (organizations). This distinctions, which is the cornerstone of the traditional view towards education and training, suggest Baum (1995) that education is for professionals training is for the artisan & the unskilled. However, at the end of 20th century it is widely recognized that education cannot be considered as a finite and terminal activity, while training cannot be considered as a strictly on-the-job, on going non–terminal process. There is need of understanding the gaps, disparity, weakness & direction for change in man power development and to describe the program of action which is being planned & implemented.

Overview of Tourism Education in India

Being a professional the subject curricula needs an industry input. There is a need for concerted effort of educational institutions and employers to secure the closest practicable e relationships between conceptual and vocational course contents (Rise 1994). Tourism course structure should be judicious mix of all areas of functional management as well as operational knowledge of different segment of tourism and travel industry (Gupta 1995).

Presently, tourism education is imparted in number of government and privately managed institutions. The directory of 'education and training institutes of tourism and travel in India 'released by Indian institute of tourism and travel management (IITTM) in may 2004 lists about fourty institutes which are imparting education and training programmes in tourism in the country. In 1983, the government started IITTM with the objectives to facilitate tourism education and research by designing courses and training programmes and promoting applied research in tourism. There are 9 chapters and one regional centre of this institute throughout in the country. The institute offers PG Diploma in Tourism Management ; PG Diploma in Travel and Tourism Industry Management; Bachelors in Tourism Management and MBA. One of the most pioneering institutes of tourism education in the country is the department of Tourism and Hotel Management at Kurukshetra University, Kurukshetra which started for the first time in the country two-years Masters progrmmes in Tourism Management (MTM) in 1990. The department now also runs a two-years Masters programmes in Hotel Management (MHM) besides conducting the doctoral level studies (Ph.D.). A number of other institute at the college and university level offer different courses-short term and long term. The courses offered by various institutes comprise of masters degree, one-year and two-year post-graduate diplomas, certificate courses, vocational courses, short-term crash courses of few months duration, training courses etc. the diverse contents and components are designated to cater to the needs of the industry at various levels.

Tourism was not seen as a separate field of education, till the 5th general assembly meet of W.T.O. held at New Delhi in 1983 which made us realizes the importance of tourism education promotion. Only then did the government thought of giving top priority to the tourism education and training at the university level.

It was after the formation of the national committee on tourism in 1988 that we came to know that the present systems of tourism training programmes suffer from several weaknesses both in the qualitative and quantitative dimensions. This was because tourism training is comparatively a new discipline in which curriculum developments of teaching has yet to take place. The biggest weakness was lack to capable and qualified faculty, as the teaching has to keep pace with the developments and innovations which take pace from time to time in tourism sector.

Evaluation of Job Training Programmes by Educational Institution

The self analysis of individual institutions will provide enough ideas and guidelines to meet the best learning practices for emerging competent human resource.

The institute can introspect their on the job-training programs on following basic questions:

(a) What is the level of research work being done at one's institute relating to the emerging challenges in job training programs of student?

(b) Do this work being new approaches, solutions in light of current issues in travel trade?

(c) To what extent the research is used for teaching, for training or for building perspective?

(d) To what extent the output of job training programs is used to develop curriculum, literature or course material?

(e) How much does the curriculum reflect the emerging challenges related to job-training programs? If so what extent?

(f) How much of the material used for teaching and training developed by the faculty rather than using ready made one? To what extent it reflects the above challenges? Does it differentiate between what is relevant?

(g) Is the faculty aware of the developments in job -training programmes of travel trade at macro level?

(h) Do the industry look up to the institute for help?

(i) The direction of feedback given by those organizations where students undergo training in relation to meet the objectives framed by educational institutes for job- training programmes of their students.

The Need of Job Training Programmes

The job training programmes is consisting of three key elements: substantive knowledge, skills, and values. Substantive knowledge is essential for the practice of the profession;

skills provide the ability to apply knowledge to practice; and values foster those career values necessary for success.

When designing a learning and teaching strategy the development of personal skills must be given priority. In doing so, the following points should be taken into consideration-

(a) Will the approach increase the student's understanding of the relevance of the subject area?

(b) Will it have a positive impact on the perception that economics is difficult?

(c) Does the approach fulfill the needs of students, institution and industry alike?

(d) Is the academic profile and rigor of the subject being maintained?

(e) are the criteria of any awarding bodies being met?

Essential development skills of trainees through job training programmes-

Communication Skills: The ability to communicate effectively verbally and through the written word

Basic Analysis Evaluation: Problem solving skills demonstrated through the use of appropriate examples and data like managing the operations, tour planning, tour costing& pricing, service, and negotiation with vendors, etc.

Information Technology Skills: Students are encouraged to use information technology by utilizing software packages for presentation and for statistical analysis of data

Management Skills: Introduction of modern management approaches and techniques; management skills of finance, marketing and human resource; portfolio of tourism management

Team Work: Within the industry, the ability to work as a part of a team is essential. Students are encouraged to identify appropriate areas for co-operation and development of team building skills; develop and create work culture; implement security and safety regulation; manage and control costs.

Objectives

1. To study the demographic profile of the students pursuing tourism education in India.
2. To study the effectiveness of job training programs on different aspects.
3. To suggest remedies for the best practices of industrial training for developing efficient human resource.

A random sample of 102 post graduate students is collected from different university departments and institutes located in different parts of the country which offer tourism education through direct mailing using structured questionnaire after studying relevant literature. The questionnaire contains 15 items covering demographic profile of students, motivation of students to join tourism education, their quality of job training and overall satisfaction on other parameters of training programs. Ranking and Likert scale (1-5) is used to get sample response. Further, percentage analysis is used to reach meaningful findings.

Table 1: Demographic profile of students (n=102)

	Responses	Percentage
Sex		
Male	71	69.60%
Female	31	30.39%
Income		
	0-50,000	2 5.88%
	Over 50,000 to 1 Lac	7 20.58%
	Over 1 Lac to 1.5 Lac	12 35.29%
	Over 1.5 Lac to 2 Lac	10 29.41%
	Above 2 Lac	3 8.82%
Area of bachelor level degree		
	Rural	2 5.88%
	Semi-Rural	3 8.82%
	Urban	29 85.29%
Stream at bachelor degree level		
	Science	5 14.70%
	Humanities	19 55.88%
	Commerce	10 29.41%
Source of information		
	Newspaper	11 32.35%
	Internet	2 5.88%
	Friends/Relatives	15 44.11%
	University/Institute Information Handbook	6 17.64%
Area of students joining tourism education		
	Rural	4 11.76%
	Semi-Urban	3 8.82%
	Urban	27 79.41%

A significant of 79.41% students join tourism course from urban areas. The stream of joining intake of students in tourism education at bachelor degree level stands as Humanities 55.88%, Commerce 29.41% and Science 14.70%. 44.11% students get information about tourism education from their friends/relatives followed by newspapers 32.35%. Electronic media is the least source of information 5.88% to the aspirants. 85.29% students obtained their bachelor degree from urban areas and rest from semi-urban and rural areas who join tourism education. The sample survey reveal that 64.70% students belong to the families with annual income between 1 lac to 2 lac and the least 5.88% below Rs. 50,000 annual. 69.60% male and 30.39% female students join tourism education.

The findings of table 1 suggest that tourism education should be made more popular in semi urban & rural areas. Proper planning & formal writing to the colleges may be sent so that more quality human resource could opt such courses. Again, all stream students should be encouraged to pursue tourism education considering multi disciplinary & inter disciplinary nature of tourism. Information about tourism education is required to be popularize through electronic media by University/ Institute website which has quick and wide coverage. This is high time to analyze the fee structure of prevailing tourism education in comparison to other professional courses in order to take strategic advantages. More than double of male students take admission than female in tourism education. There is need to further research on this aspect of inequality and stringent introduction of remedies.

Table 2: Why Students Join Tourism Education ? (n=102)
(Figures shown in parenthesis are in percentage)

Ranking	1	2	3	4	5	6	7
a) This course has good money (after passing)	3 (2.94)	27 (26.47)	18 (17.64)	16 (11.76)	28 20.58	6 5.66	15 14.70
b) It has good career growth	60 (58.82)	9 (8.82)	12 (11.76)	9 (8.82)	9 (8.82) (2.94)	3 (0)	0
c) It's a new field/course	21 (20.58)	24 (23.52)	24 (23.52)	6 (5.88)	9 (8.82)	9 (8.82)	9 (8.82)
d) In support of your personal	6 (5.88)	21 (20.58)	9 (8.82)	27 (26.47)	15 (14.70)	15 (14.70)	9 (8.82)
e) It has glamour	3 (2.94)	3 (2.94)	15 (14.70)	21 (20.58)	21 (20.58)	27 (26.47) (11.76)	12
f) It gives more chances to interact with external world	9 (8.82)	12 (11.58)	21 (20.58)	9 (8.82)	15 (14.70)	21 (20.58) (14.70)	15
g) For the sake of taking admission in premier institute /university	6 (5.88)	6 (5.88)	6 (5.88)	12 (11.76)	15 (14.70)	18 (7.64) (38.23)	39

Good career growth (58.82%), good money (26.47%) are the major factors of aspirants to join tourism course. The factor of only taking admission in premier university/institute (38.23%) and the statement- tourism industry is glamorous is the least attractive factors for the aspirants to join tourism course.

Only providing placement to the students should not be the sole aim of the department/ Institute rather they should look to the expectations of students in tourism industry as career. One should not forget the experience of students during job in industry and importance of their word of mouth. Department/Institute may position on the lines of expectations of aspirants before they announce tourism education program.

Table 3: Development of Skills of Trainees (n=102)
(Figures shown in parenthesis are in percentage)

Skills	Well Developed	Averagely Developed	Poorly Developed
Controlling	45(44.11)	48(47.05)	9(8.82)
Leadership Skills	39(28.23)	57(55.28)	6(5.88)
Planning Skills	45(44.11)	48(47.05)	9(8.82)
Communication Skills	48(47.05)	54(52.94)	0
Decision Making Skills	57(55.28)	39(28.3	6(5.88)
Presentation Skills	27(26.47)	60(58.82)	15(14.70)
Technological Skills	24(23.52)	48(47.05)	30(29.41)
Negotiation Skills	42(41.17)	51(50.00)	9(8.82)
Report writing	30(29.41)	45(44.11)	24(23.52)
Customer Care Skills	72(70.58)	24(23.52)	6(5.88)

The sample revealed that customer care skills (70.58%), decision making (55.28%) and communication skills (47.05%) are well developed by the trainees. The sample also indicated that technological skills (29.41%) is poorly developed by the trainees. Presentation skills (58.82%), leadership skills (55.28%) are averagely developed by the trainees.

Department/Institute should regularly receive feedback from the companies regarding the performance, improvement & involvement of trainees during on the job. Special guidelines can be imparted to the companies to improve the week areas of training, duration of training in different departments & trainee's involvement in managerial functions at different levels. Greater guidance should be given to the trainees on technological know-how, presentation skills and management competency.

Table 4: Trainee's Satisfaction with Job-Training (n=102)
(Figures shown in parenthesis are in percentage)

	Yes	No
Overall Training Program	60(58.82)	42(41.55)
Departmental Training Duration	60(58.82)	42(41.17)
System of Training	57(55.28)	45(44.11)

Only 58.82% students are satisfied with the overall training programs in tourism industry. 44.11% trainees are not satisfied with the system of training prevailing in tourism industry while 41.17% trainees are not satisfied with the duration of training in different departments.

A significant figure is unsatisfied with the system and duration of training in different departments. This is necessary that department/institute examine their job training policy/program of their students in consultation with industry players. There can be no compromise on the development of the skills and knowledge of the students and their stay during training program which has long-term significance.

Table 5: What motivate trainees to actively learn/work/participate during training period? (n=102)

Ranking	*1*	*2*	*3*	*4*	*5*	*6*	*7*	*8*	*9*	*10*	*11*	*12*	*13*
Management of the organization	33 (32.25)	9 (8.82)	6 (5.88)	12 (11.58)	12 (11.58)	6 (5.88)	3 (2.94)	3 (2.94)	6 (5.88)	3 (2.94)	3 (2.94)	6 (5.88)	0
Communication in the organization	3 (2.94)	9 (8.82)	9 (8.82)	6 (5.88)	6 (5.88)	6 (5.88)	6 (5.88)	3 (2.94)	3 (2.94)	12 (11.58)	9 (8.82)	24 (23.52)	6 (5.88)
Independent decision-making	0	6 (5.88)	9 (8.82)	21 (20.58)	6 (5.88)	12 (11.58)	15 (14.70)	6 (5.88)	6 (5.88)	3 (5.94)	0	12 (11.58)	6 (5.88)
Good leadership in the organization	3 (2.94)	15 (14.70)	24 (23.52)	15 (14.70)	6 (5.88)	0	6 (5.88)	12 (11.58)	12 (11.58)	3 (2.94)	6 (5.88)	0	0
Good supervision in the organization	3 (2.94)	15 (14.70)	12 (11.58)	18 (17.64)	12 (11.58)	15 (14.70)	0	15 (14.70)	6 (5.88)	6 (5.88)	0	0	0
Cooperation/co-ordination of co-workers	24 (23.52)	6 (5.88)	6 (5.88)	15 (14.70)	12 (11.58)	6 (5.88)	12 (11.58)	12 (11.58)	3 (2.94)	6 (5.88)	0	0	0
Fellowship offered by the organization	6 (5.88)	6 (5.88)	6 (5.88)	12 (11.58)	9 (8.82)	12 (11.58)	6 (5.88)	9 (8.82)	9 (8.82)	12 (11.58)	6 (5.88)	3 (2.94)	6 (5.88)
Trainees participation in management	3 (2.94)	30 (29.41)	9 (8.82)	15 (14.70)	9 (8.82)	12 (11.58)	9 (8.82)	3 (2.94)	3 (2.94)	0	9 (8.82)	0	0
Delegation of authority	3 (2.94)	3 (2.94)	6 (5.88)	6 (5.88)	3 (2.94)	21 (20.58)	3 (2.94)	12 (11.58)	3 (2.94)	15 (14.70)	15 (14.70)	12 (11.58)	0
Recognition and praise of your work	9 (8.82)	27 (26.47)	6 (5.88)	3 (2.94)	9 (8.82)	0	9 (8.82)	3 (2.94)	12 (11.58)	9 (8.82)	12 (11.58)	0	3 (2.94)
Setting job with the organization	3 (2.94)	6 (5.88)	12 (11.58)	9 (8.82)	6 (5.88)	3 (2.94)	9 (8.82)	6 (5.88)	9 (8.82)	9 (8.82)	12 (11.58)	9 (8.82)	9 (8.82)
Reputation of your company/organization in the market	12 (11.58)	15 (14.70)	3 (2.94)	9 (8.82)	0	3 (2.94)	3 (2.94)	12 (11.58)	18 (17.64)	0	15 (14.70)	6 (5.88)	6 (5.88)
Reputation of your academic institute/dept. in the industry	3 (2.94)	3 (2.94)	9 (8.82)	6 (5.88)	6 (5.88)	0	6 (5.88)	3 (2.94)	6 (5.88)	15 (14.70)	0	9 (8.82)	27 (26.47)

Management of the organization (32.35%), trainee's participation in management (29.41%) and recognition and praise of the trainees work are the main motivator factors for the trainees while reputation of the institute/department (26.47%) in the tourism industry, communication in the organization (23.52%) are the least motivator factors for the trainees to actively learn/work/participate during training period.

Company must recognize and ensure the contribution of trainees by involving them at different levels of management. This provides batter understanding of industry to trainees as well as maximum utilization of manpower in the form of trainee. Trainees feel motivated if company takes their presence seriously.

Significance of Findings

The findings of the study can be applied in the following areas:

1. The continuous transformation of accurate, timely and update information about the technological advancements and the latest trends in the industry so as to gain better understanding about the industrial requirements.
2. Active industrial involvements in developing and sharpening the students skills form time to time.
3. Industry orientation programmers for teachers.
4. Evaluation of training programmes and supply of feedback to the institutions.
5. Closer collaboration between industry and educational providers for benchmarking and setting standards for examination and certification.
6. Industrial participation at the time of entry level for the evaluation of basic and behavioral skills as required by the industry.

More scientific approach is required to be introduced in training program of the students. It is suggestible that all the department/institute in India may constitute a committee on the training programs of all the students. Firstly, institute will help to give uniformity to the tourism education and training program in country. Secondly, it may identify and balance the demand and supply of human resource in industry and also understanding the changing requirements. Relatively new departments, which are struggling with the problem of their student's training will also be benefited through the collective efforts of the committee.

REFERENCES

- Aiery, D., S. Johnson (1998). The Content of Degree Courses in the UK Tourism Management, 20 (pp. 229-235).
- Baum, T.(1995). Managing human resources in the European hospitality industry: A strategic approach. London: Chapman & Hall.
- Council for National Academic Awards (1993). Review of Tourism Studies Degree Courses. London.

- Gupta,I.C.(1995).Positioning of MTA programme paper presented in 'Tourism Education in India, seminar organized by IITTM G walior, India
- Johnson, S.(1997). Tourism Education in UK Universities: the issue of minimum core curriculum/body of knowledge for vocational tourism degrees, University of Surrey.
- Middleton, V.T.C. & Ladkin, A. (1996). The profile of tourism studies degree courses in the UK 1995/6. National Liaison Group for Higher Education in Tourism, The Tourism Society, London.
- Parsons, D.J., Cave, P.(1991). Developing managers for tourism. National Economic Development Office, London.
- Rise (1985). An assessment of costs and benefits of Sandwich Education Committee on Research in Sandwich Education, Department of Educational and Science ,London.

8

A Critical Comparative Analysis of Constraints of the Development of Tourism in India

Virendra thakore
* Assist Prof. in F & B Service **Lecturer in Tourism Management, Vivekanand Institute of Hotel and Tourism Management, N.H.-8/B, Kuvadava Road, Kuchiyadar, Rajkot-360003, Gujarat, virendrahariom@rediffmail.com
Achintya Mahapatra achintya4you@rediffmail.com

INTRODUCTION

Of late, tourism as an industry has made rapid advances in all over the world. The growth and potential of the tourism industry has now been recognized for special attention by both the Government as well as the private sectors. It is however, to be noted that in India educational system, tourism studies have remained as an under developed discipline. Simultaneously, not much effort has been made in creating awareness among the mass about tourism or in promoting research on the various effects of tourism. As a discipline, it has failed to harness human resources and has succeeded only partially in creating awareness and local participation. The National Action Plan for tourism recognizes the potential of tourism industry by admitting that it is capable of generating employment for about 13-14 million persons annually. Significantly this number has been predicted to touch double the present level before the turn of the century. The relevance of human resource and manpower training in the different areas of tourism industry is the most important factor of its development. At the same time it also has to be appreciated that such manpower is not required just at top or middle management levels. All the personnel involved in diverse activities at various levels need on equal professional approach with skills and knowledge to handle the operations at the positions they hold.

The increase of global tourism has marked to be quite dramatic, that is 13.2 million in 1951 tourism make it one of the biggest industries in the world by 1999, international tourism receipts exceeded US$, I earnings with US$ 74.9 billion. While Spain, France and Italy made around US $ 30 billion each, the United Kingdom earned US$ 20 billion and Germany, China, Austria and Canada registered US $ 10 billion each. The world travel receipts had an average growth rate scaling 20.38% in fifties, coming down to 10.07% in sixties and again going up-to 19.2% in seventies. The eighties and nineties of the twentieth century witnessed a downward trend due to world economic recession since 1986, Gulf war of 1990-91 and the on going disturbances in different parts of the

The patterns of international tourism at the global level testify to the fact that supplements the countries. Developed countries remain the major tourist generating and receiving countries of the world viewing tourism as an industry for the future, the developing countries view tourism as a panacea for the future, the developing countries view tourism as a panacea for solving their problems related to mounting foreign debt, poverty and unemployment.

The Minister of Tourism & Culture, Smt. Ambika Soni has said that the objective of the existing Tourism Policy of the Government is to position tourism as a major engine of economic growth and to harness its direct and multiplier effects for employment and poverty eradication in an environmentally sustainable manner. She was presiding over the meeting of the Parliamentary Consultative Committee of the Ministry of Tourism which was held at Bhubaneswar (Orissa) today.

The efforts made by the Ministry of Tourism & Culture in the last few years have had a salutary effect on the India Tourism. While the foreign tourist arrivals are expected to witness a growth of 78% in 2006 over 2001 (last 5 years), growth in the foreign exchange earnings is expected to be of the order of 122% during this period. India's share in world tourism, which was 0.37% during 2001 end, is likely to increase to 0.53% during 2006, Smt. Soni said. The Minister added further that as per the estimates, on an average, about 3.1 million additional jobs per year have been created directly and in-directly in the tourism sector in the last 4 years. Smt. Soni underlined that tourism is a priority sector because, among others, it is able to maximize the productivity of India's natural, human, cultural and technical resources; it is labour intensive and cottage or small industry based providing employment; it is capable of being primarily focused on rural areas with appropriate and relatively low cost programmes and it has extensive forward and backward economic linkages that build overall income and employment, especially for women and youth.

Giving details of her Ministry's initiatives in positioning & maintaining Tourism Development as a National Priority Activity, Smt. Soni said that a concerted effort has been made through the National Development Council (NDC) and other important forums by emphasizing that tourism is now considered the world over as a major engine of economic growth and several countries of the world have transformed their economies using the tourism potential to the fullest.

Other initiatives include the setting up of National Tourism Advisory Council as a 'think tank', the constitution of a Group of Ministers on tourism to improve policy integration and co-ordination. The development of a Tourism Satellite Account (TSA) to gauge precisely the contribution of tourism to the national economy using the methodology given by UN-World Tourism Organization and UN Statistical Division has provided an authentic tool to assess the success of the strategies. With a view to enhance India's competitiveness as a tourist destination, major policy initiatives such as liberalization in aviation sector; pricing policy for aviation turbine fuel which influences internal air fares; rationalization in tax rates in the hospitality sector; tourist friendly visa regime; immigration services, and; procedural changes in making available land for construction of hotels, allowing setting up of Guest Houses, etc. have been undertaken. These do not come directly under the purview of the Ministry of Tourism, but under the other Ministries and State Governments, have also been taken up vigorously, Smt. Soni said.

Smt. Soni said that the proposal to introduce Advance Passenger Information System (APIS) at airports to reduce delays in clearance of passengers at the immigration counters has already been accepted by the Ministry of Home affairs and notified. The system is being tested at Delhi Airport at present. This system, as ad when introduced, will not only reduce delays in clearance but would also facilitate introduction of the scheme of visa-on-arrival. With a view to promote India as a safe destination, all the States have been requested to deploy tourist Police at major tourist destinations in the States. The States of Andhra Pradesh, Karnataka, Goa, Kerala, Maharashtra, Himachal Pradesh, Rajasthan, J&K, Uttar Pradesh and Delhi have already deployed such police force. Matter has been taken up with Ministry of Home Affairs for issuing directions to other States, she added.

A number of steps have also nbeen taken to improve and expand the existing tourism products and their development. For expanding cultural and heritage tourism, integrated development of areas around these monuments is a prime activity. A few of the cultural and heritage sites/monuments taken up for development include – Red Fort, Humanyun's Tomb and Qutub Minar in Delhi; Somnath Temple in Gujarat; Heritage properties at Chail & Naggar in HP; Hampi in Karnataka; Gwalior fort in MP; Ajanta Caves & Sinhagad Fort in Maharashtra; Nahargarh Fort, Jaisalmer Fort, amber Fort & Hawa Mahal in Rajasthan; Somnath and Taj Mahal in UP etc. Illumination of monuments has also been taken up in a big way, and financial assistance is being provided for the purpose, Smt. Soni said.

A number of steps for the development of beach and coastal tourism have been taken. A number of sites on the west coast of India were identified for the development as beach resorts by the private sector. The sites on the beaches of Goa, Kerala and North Karnataka were taken up because of their easier access by air. Kochi in Kerala and the Andaman and Nicobar Islands were developed as international cruise destinations because of their proximity to international cruise routes and their exotic appeal. Smt. Soni informed that Rural tourism is being promoted as the primary tourism product of India to showcase rural like, art, culture and heritage at rural locates and in villages which have core competence in terms of crafts/handlooms/textiles/culture, etc. to tourists, thereby also spreading tourism and its socio-economic benefits to rural areas.

Smt. Soni said that steps have also been taken to promote wildlife tourism, adventure tourism, MICE (Meetings, conventions and Exhibition) tourism. In this context the Minister underlined the importance of developing world class international convention centers not just for the sake of tourism development but also for international domestic trade and commerce and added that presently, cities of Delhi, Mumbai, Agra, Bangalore, Cochin,

Goa, Hyderabad, Jaipur and Kolkata are being promoted as MICE destinations in India but facilities available today are not enough. Smt. Soni underlined that India's most unique tourism product in the last five years has been holistic healing and rejuvenation packages. She added that in focussing on this, the essence of Indian culture has been captured both for international and Indian visitors alike. States of Kerala, Karnataka and Uttranchal have taken up Ayurveda and traditional techniques of healing as also rejuvenation therapy in a big way.

Smt. Soni also underlined the need for physical infrastructure for tourism which ranges from ports of entry to modes of transport (airways, roadway, railways or waterways), to urban infrastructure such as access roads, power, water supply, sewerage and telecommunication. This underscores the need for inter-sectoral convergence of infrastructural schemes and programmes that could support tourist destinations, she underlined. For effective marketing of India tourism, a number of new initiates have been taken in the last few years. These include direct approach to the consumers through electronic and print media, joint sales efforts with the international airlines operating to India and direct cooperative marketing with the tour operators and wholesalers overseas. Ministry of Tourism is encouraging participation in travel marts like ITB, WTM, ATM, PATA etc. for promotion of India as a preferred tourist destination. These activities are in addition to the regular activities, undertaken by the overseas offices. A greater focus is being attached to the regions of China, North East Asia and South East Asia, Smt. Soni added and said that production of world class publicity material ranging from tourist information brochures, posters, scrolls, etc. with a common theme, that is, 'Incredible India' has been undertaken. The Members of the Consultative committee also visited Konark, which is a world heritage site and the Jagganath Temple at Puri. They also had visits to some other monuments in and around Bhubaneshwar like Lingaraj temple, Rajarani temple, Mukteshwar and Khandgiri-Udaigiri caves etc.

In ordinary parlance unemployment is a situation of individuals' joblessness at the prevailing wage rate. Lord Keynes expresses that unemployment is the result of deficiency in effective demand in advanced economics. Machine becomes ideal as a result of deficiency in effective demand. In consequence of machines idealness demand for labour falls. It implies that there exists a positive correlation between effective demand and employment. According to Lord Keynes, unemployment may be arrested by keeping the level of effective demand sufficiently. This type of unemployment shown in the advanced countries is termed as cyclical or frictional unemployment by Keynes. In developing or underdeveloped economy like India, cyclical or fractional unemployment is not more serious. Such type of countries are suffering from the problem of chronic under-employment or disguised unemployment in the rural sector and also suffering from the urban unemployment among the educated class. It should be noted that unemployment problem in under developed or developing countries is not the consequence of deficiency of effective demand but due to shortage of the economy should create higher rate of saving for capital formation by managing resources tactfully.

Scenario of South Asia and India

Most of the countries of South Asia like India, Pakistan, Bangladesh, Bhutan, Nepal, and Sri Lanka are passing through the second stage of demographic transition. In this stage countries must suffer from the problem of population explosion, unemployment and slow rate of economic growth. Out of 1.4 billion people of South Asia, 60% are in the working age group. Only 66% of the total age group participates as labour force. Employment growth rate are lower than GDP and labour force growth rates. Agriculture is the main occupation of the people, although it suffers from the lack of investment and low productivity. One third of the total population of South Asia is in poverty. Illiteracy in South Asia is also a mater of great concern. In South Asia major portion of the total unemployed is youth. In the year 1997, 70%of the total unemployment of Sri Lanka is youth 58% of the total unemployment of India is youth and 45% of total unemployment of Pakistan is youth. Declining trend of unemployment is public sector during the past decade dampens the prospects of employment of educated youth. Employment provided in the private sector is mostly in the semi-skilled or low-skilled section. In the year 1997, 41% of the total higher secondary passed youth of India was unemployed. In south Asia women have limited opportunity to get themselves employed. Two third of South Asia women are engaged in agriculture and agriculture related activities. Women from the majority in the informal sector, is very advance although they are failed to get reasonable opportunity and wages. In the year 1999 – 2000 male and female unemployment rate in South Asian countries shown in the table – I. the table shows the highest unemployment rate (16.2%) of women in Sri Lanka and lowest in Nepal (0.7%). In case of male unemployment, Sri Lankan rate (7.1%) is highest and Nepal is lowest (1.5%). Table – II shows over all unemployment rates of South Asian countries in the year 1999-2000. The highest rate of unemployment is 8.2% in Sri Lanka and lowest in Nepal, 1.1%. Unemployment rate in India is 7.3% in the year1999-2000.

Table 1: (Female and Male Unemployment Rates in South Asia, 1999-2000)

Countries	Female (%)	Male (%)
Bangladesh	2.3	2.7
India	10	7
Nepal	0.7	1.5
Pakisthan	14.9	4.2
Sri Lanka	16.2	7.1

South Asia's unemployment level is increased from 2.9% to 3.4% during the period 1995 to 2001. The unemployment rate of India has risen from 6% in 1994 to 7.32% in 2001(The Economic Survey of India). W.T.O has failed to generate more employment in South Asia because of the unilateral trade measures adopted by the developed countries.

India which is a thickly populated country in South Asia, has a very a very large labour force. The quality and productivity of the labour force is poor and low. Only 8% of the total work force is engaged in the organized sector and 92% is engaged in the unorganized sector.

Work force of the organized sector contributes near 40% of national output. The status of the labour in the organized sector is reasonably good but the working condition in the unorganized sector. The fastest growing industry in India is it. In the year 2002-03 it earns revenues of Rs. 11,700 crore. In the year 2004 the industry alone created 1.85 lakh jobs in Karnataka. Though the majority of the jobs are in Bangalore, the largest numbers of jobs were lost also Bangalore. During the post linearization and globalization period, the number of jobless workers in Karnataka is about 3 lakh. The number of closed state - enterprises in Karnataka is 27. 65% of workers become contract workers in Mumbai. Employees of Public sectors are forced to take VRS. The situation which implies the job security of workers is losing in India. Massive migration of laborers from rural areas to urban area is a serious problem of the Indian economy. 60% of the rural laborers of Orissa have migrated due to loss of jobs.

Table 2: Unemployment Rates in South Asia in South Asia, (1999-2000)

Countries	Rater (%)
Bhutan	1.4
Bangladesh	3.3
India	7.3
Nepal	1.1
Pakisthan	7.8
Sri Lanka	8.2

Extent of Unemployment in India

A projection of national sample survey (NSS) on unemployment reveals that 16 million persons were unemployed and 12 million persons were estimated to be severely under-employed during the year 1990. It implies that the total backlog of unemployed persons in the beginning of the Eighth plan period (1992-1997) is 28 million (Table - III). The net additions to the labour force during 1990-1995 had been expected to be 37 million. So the total number of jobless persons during the eighth plan period (1992-1997) would be around 65 million. It is further expected that in the next five years, that is during 1995-2000, labour force would increase by 41 million. Hence by the year 2000 AD, the total number of job seekers would be around 106 million. The Planning Commission, therefore, concludes, "Employment growth in the aggregate over the estimated employment of 300 million in 1990 would have to be about 4% compounded per annum if the goal of providing employment for all is to be achieved by the end of the Eighth Plan and over 3% per annum if it is to be attained by 2000 AD.

Table 3: (Projection of Unemployment for 1990-2000)

1	Backlog of employed in the beginning of 1990	28
2	New entrants to the labour force during 1990-1995	37
	Total unemployed for the 8th Plan (1+2)	65

3	New entrants to the labour force during 1995-2000	41
	Total Unemployed for the 9th Plan	106

Source: Compiled from the planning Commission, 8th Plan and 9th Plan

Table 4: Job-seekers of all categories registered with the employment exchanges in India (Figures in Thousands)

Years	Registration	Placement	Vacancies	Submission	Live Registration	% of P.I/ Vac.	% of Pl./ Sub	% Increase in L.R. over Previous Year
1994	5927.3	204.9	396.4	3723.4	36691.5	51.7	5.5	1.1
1995	5858.1	214.9	385.7	3569.9	36742.3	55.7	6	0.1
1996	5872.4	233.0	423.9	3605.9	37429.6	55	6.5	1.9
1997	6321.9	275.0	393.0	3767.8	39139.9	70	7.3	4.6
1998	5851.8	233.3	358.8	3036.6	40089.6	65	7.6	2.4
1999	5966.0	221.3	328.9	2653.2	40371.4	67.3	8.3	0.7
2000	6041.9	177.7	284.5	2322.8	41343.6	62.5	7.7	2.4
2001	5552.6	169.2	304.1	1908.8	41995.9	55.6	8.9	1.6

(*Source*: DGE & T, Ministry of Labour, Govt. of India, New Delhi)

Table - IV shows the year wise registration, placement, notified vacancies, submission made and lives registers during the period 1994 to 2001. The number of unemployed persons (Live Register) is increasing every year during the period 1994 to 2001. It was lowest in 1994 (3, 66, 91500) and highest in 2001 (4, 19, 95900). The nature of year wise registration during the studied period is volatile. But on an average 55 lakh to 60 lakh unemployed persons register their names in each year of study as job seekers. In the year 1997 maximum unemployed persons, about 63 lakh registered their names with various employment exchanges of India. The placement was maximum (2, 75, 000) in the year 1997. But after the year 1997 number of placement was decreased gradually in each year of study. In the year 1996, number of notified vacancies was maximum (94, 23, 900). But after the year 1996 it decreased every year except the year 2001. 'Submission made' in the year 1994 was 37, 23, 400. In the year 1997 submission was 37, 67, 800 and after the year 1997 submission decreased in each year of study gradually. The above discussion expresses the gravity and extent of unemployment in India.

Tourism Industry and Employment Generation

Tourism is one of the fastest growing industries in the world presently. It has become one of the most significant industries across the world. Now its position in respect of world is just below the oil and automobile industries. Tourism industry creates sufficient employment opportunity and brings foreign currency. To enhance national income, tourism plays a vital role. National integration and national understanding is maintained by the tourism industry. It plays a vital role in economic development of a nation, socio-culture and preservation of heritage. Tourism is an extremely labour-intensive industry with high linkage effect. As the world's largest export industry, tourism accounts for about 8% of the total world's largest export, more than 30% of the International trade in services, 10.7% of the global work force and about 12% of world GDP. According to the World Tourism Organization (W.T.O), in the year 2020 tourism will be an industry earning five billion dollars a day. The economic of the countries like Hong Kong, Singapore, Sri Lanka and small islands like Mauritius, Fiji, Malta largely depend directly or indirectly on this industry.

India is the sixth largest country in the world after China, Canada, Brazil, USA and Australia. The country is the mother of two primitive civilizations of the world. On is the Indus Valley Civilization and the other is the Aryan Civilization. India with her vast area, with her physical size and appearances, cultural heritage, splendid natural resources, coastlines, mineral, forest cover, old and antique buildings, Tajmahal, one of the seven wonders of world, monuments, beautiful temples and mosques, forts, hill stations, scenic beauty, springs, rivers, Canals, ponds, dams, flora and fauna, gardens, historical places, wild life sanctuaries can easily find a permanent place in the firmament of the tourism industry. The Government of India recognized tourism as an industry in the year 1967, establishing a department called 'Tourism and Civilization Aviation Department'. From this year the development of tourism in India is started. The Government of India Declared the year 1991 as a year of tourism, to give more impetus on tourism development. A report of the ministry of tourism and Civil Aviation reveals that India's gross foreign exchange earning from tourism was Rs. 283 crores in the year 1997. In this year India received 19.9% more tourists than the previous year. Share of business still confines to only about one per cent of the world's total tourist trade. In the year 1950 the total arrival of tourists in India was 15000. Up to the year 2004 the figure reached in 2.98 million. Now tourism industry is the third largest foreign exchange earner by producing gems and jewellery and ready made garments in India. Most of tourist coming to India belonging to the countries - UK, USA, Sri Lanka, Germany, France, Japan, Canada, Italy, Malaysia and Singapore.

The role of tourism industry in generation of employment is very significant. Tourism is a labour intensive industry. So a large number of job seekers can get employment in this industry. According to a report from the Ministry of Tourism, Govt. of India, number of people already employed in the industry is more than seven million. The number is about 2.4% of Indian total labour force. People directly or indirectly depends on tourism industry in India is around eleven million. Tourism Industry creates employment especially for hoteliers, restaurant owners, guides, local shopkeepers, merchants etc. The remarkable feature of the industry is that it employs a large number of both educated and uneducated women. Both skilled and unskilled women are employed in this industry. Women, in fact, out number men in hotels, airline services, travel agencies, handicraft and cultural activities are playing the major role in this industry. The estimated employment multiplier figure in the tourism industry is 2.36. It means the direct employment of 100 persons in tourism industry which create job for 136 persons in other sectors of our economy. From the view point of employment generation, this multiplier is very attractive than other industry-multiplier.

Problem Faced By International Tourism

Though India is having with all types of tourism potential, which has been already mentioned above, yet it is observed that no development is taking place in the field of tourism industry and the flowing of international tourist to India is gradually decreasing. For that aspect certain problems are responsible which will be discussed one after another.

1. Lack of Sufficient International Airport.
2. Lack of Transportation Facility.
3. Lack of Railway Connectivity to Tourist Destinations.
4. Lack of star Hotels.
5. Fear of Naxelite Problems Especially in Tribal Areas.
6. Lack of Preservation of Ancient Heritage Sites (Archaeological, Historical)
7. Lack of Road Communication.
8. Role of Media.

Due to the religious, cultural and natural point of view many international tourist are interested to come to this land. But it is the meter of regret that so far international Airport has been provided in India as per the requirements of tourist. This is the main hurdle for international tourist arrival. Hence an international Airport should be setup to give boost for tourism promotion.

As we know the transport and communication plays the vital role for the development of any industries. In the field of tourism industries this plays a major role. Some tourist places especially the states of North Eastern are situated at very interiors and no direct road and rail facilities are available. Some roads are totally damaged and no attention have been paid by the Government for the repair of that roads. Railway links has not been made to connect all the nock and corners of India. It touches only some fringes of main land. Hence the Railway network system should be extended to all the tourist places of India as much as possible. As a result the rapid progress of the tourism industry would take place, which will give a better tourism facility for its growth.

After transport and communication, accommodation facility plays the vital role for the enhancement of the tourist arrival to India. Though it is a vast sub-continent of Indian union having with many attractive tourist spots yet there are no sufficient star hotels for the international tourists. International tourists are facing lot of problem for their accommodation. Hence star hotels should be raised by the private sectors or public sectors. As a result they can stay comfortably and tourism industries will grow.

Fears of Naxalites are another cause of the decreasing potential of tribal tourism or eco tourism of India. When there is the danger to life and property and security has not been properly provided to the tourist, it is difficult to develop tourism in India particularly in this sector. So government should suppress the Naxalites violence and make safe the tribal areas for tourism development.

Now we are in 21st century, in the age of electronic media. Media plays a very important role in the promotion of tourism. Without bringing your products to the knowledge of the consumers nothing would sell. So to sell the tourism products marketing is essential. And for this task advertisement is necessary. So advertisement regarding the tourists destinations with the facilities, amenities, provided to the tourists to be highlighted in the newspapers, magazines and the most popular electronics media like television, radio etc.

Finally the exploitation and cheating of the local people at destination is one of the major problems of the International tourist as well as domestic tourist. Due to these factors the some times tourist are suffering a lot and it creates bad impression of the particular destination. As a result the influx of tourist to that place is decreasing day by day.

REFERENCES

- Krishna K. Kamra and Mohinder Chand, *Basics of Tourism*, New Delhi, 2004.
- Dr. D. Konar, *'The Scenario of Population Growth in India'*, Akansha Publishing House, New Delhi, 1st Edition, 2004.
- *Economic Survey*, Govt. of India, Various Issues.
- Amit Kr. Chakrabarty, *'JOHAR – Journal of Hospitality Application & Research'*, Vol. 1, No. 2, July 2006.
- Dr. S.N Tripathy, *Rural Development for Social Change*, Sonali Publication, New Delhi, in July, 2006.
- M.C Methani, Tourism, Yojana, Vol. 35, No 8, May 15, 1991.
- Website of the Ministry of Tourism, Govt of India, 2006.

9

New Trends in Tourism in India

Mrs. Vinay Goyal Khurania
Teacher Fellow,
Department of Tourism & Hotel Management,
Kurukshetra University, Kurukshetra

ABSTRACT

The globalization of economy has made tourism the prominent industry having customer base that is wealthier as well as technologically savvy. Information Technology, Low Cost Carriers, Budget Hotels, Revenue Management, Medical Tourism have created a paradigm shift in the tourism industry. Information Technology has been playing a major role in the tourism industry for a long time. Revenue Management is another technique that is being used in hotels, airlines, car rentals to maximize revenues. Low Cost Carriers and Budget Hotels have opened the door for middle tourist segments. Medical Tourism is boosting tourism industry and is viewed as a service sector. This paper analyses the latest trends to face the challenges of tourism and focuses on how tourism and new trends are closely associated and in what way their societal significance is treated as.

Key words: Information Technology, Low Cost Carriers, Revenue Management.

INTRODUCTION

The late twentieth century and the new millennium have witnessed the continued growth of interest in how people spend their leisure and non-work periods, particularly those times that are dedicated to travel and holidays. At a global scale this interest is becoming an international phenomenon known as tourism which is based on the use of leisure time to visit different places, destinations and localities. In 2002 the World Travel and Tourism Council (WTTC) estimated that travel and tourism as economic activities generated US $4421.1 billion, which is expected to grow to US$8613.8 billion by 2012 (Page,2006). There is a 4.5 percent increase in the demand for travel and tourism per annum, which is far in excess of the scale and pace of growth in the economies of most countries. At a global scale, the economic effects of travel and tourism are estimated by WTTC to be responsible for 198098000 jobs, which is equivalent to 7.8 percent of world employment in every 12.8 jobs. This number is expected to grow to 249486000 jobs by 2012. The screen of Indian economy is not untouched by the growing international significance of tourism. The vibrancy in the overall Indian economy and continuation of liberalization initiatives were the key boosters and have helped the growth ambitions of the tourism industry. In year 2005, the country got more prominence on the global tourism radar as India jumped from the ninth to sixth position in the UK's popular Conde Nast Traveler's list of favored destinations. India with its 8 percent GDP growth rate and stable economy has witnessed an all round development especially in the travel and tourism sector. Any increase or decline in this sector mirrors economic trends. The qualitative development trends in tourism are not only confined to sustainable development of tourism, increased market segmentation rather they have metamorphosed this industry as a quiet distinct market. Low Cost Carriers, Revenue Management, Budget Hotels, Space Tourism, Service Apartments, Loyalty Travel will shape the future of tourism.

Objectives of the Study

This study is undertaken for the following objectives:

(i) To explain the latest trends in the Indian tourism sector such as Information Technology, Low Cost Carriers, Budget Hotels, Revenue Management and Medical Tourism.

(ii) To observe how closely IT and Tourism sector are associated.

(iii) To analyze the present scenario of LCCs in Indian as well as global context.

(iv) To examine how budget hotels are entering into Indian hospitality market.

(v) To appraise the revenue management strategy in operational context of some selected 5 star hotels in India.

(vi) To highlight how medical tourism is attracting the foreign tourists towards India.

Research Methodology

The present study is composed of primary data as well as secondary data. The primary data is collected through self-administered questionnaires from randomly selected 5 star hotels working in India. While the secondary data is managed through various journals, magazines, newspapers, studies and websites. The collected data are analyzed to reach at conclusions regarding the various latest trends on the horizon of tourism.

1. Information Technology in Tourism Industry

A new flexible tourism is on the horizon -today's trends are redundant tomorrow. The tourist sector has experienced rapid technological development. In this new tourism environment, information and technology are important for establishing a competitive advantage. At an individual business level, information technology is the main driver of change, requiring better management for tourism operations to harness their potential. It provides up-to-date, managed client data, and scope to search for and select a wide range of products and experiences. IT enables forward looking businesses to respond to the demand for more up-to-date information and tailor made products. The World Wide Web also allows customers to undertake this process themselves, thus challenging the supply chain and its traditional role in selling tourism products. It is now widely adopted in the tourism sector, and innovation is likely to see further developments that will allow tourism products to reach a wider audience. Recent software launched by RWA –The 'sell it' software package –has made convenient for tour operators to compete for the online market by allowing clients to search by destination, departure point and holiday type. Canadian research on post 11 Sept, 2001 travel noted that these new trends have seen traveler behaviour changes, including demands for increased evidence of security, more road based trips, shorter trips and cruises, and a growth in the demand for safer destinations.

The partnership of information technology has grown even stronger since the deregulation of the US Airline Industry in 1978. Deregulation has made information technologies even more important to the tourism industry. It has further complicated the playing field with a large volume and wide array of rapidly changing information such include new airlines, new fares, new routes, forever changing prices, more alternatives, more confusion and a whole new vocabulary (yield management, no frills, frequent-flyer awards, halo effect,(Poon ,1993).

In the fast –growing tourism sector, new business processes called hypercompetition are emerging. D'Aveni (1998) identified four processes that are contributing to hypercompetition: -

1. The customer demand for better quality at lower prices.
2. Rapid technological change, enhanced through the use of information technology.
3. The expansion of very aggressive companies who are willing to enter markets for a number of years with a loss-leader product (e.g. low–cost airlines), with a view to destroying the competition so that they will harness the market in the long-term.
4. The progressive removal of government barriers towards competition throughout the world.

Infact, tourism is an extremely information-intensive industry. The rapid development of information technologies facilitates the speed and efficiency with which the industry's information is processed, stored, retrieved, distributed and otherwise manipulated.

Tourism Development and the Internet

The internet particularly is increasingly emerging as a platform to bring tourism products direct to the customer. Despite the challenging global economic environment, there is general shift of tourism arrivals towards developing countries. Growth rates of international tourism receipts were on average 50% higher in the major developing country destinations. The tourism sector is widely affected by internet which brings all the participants i.e. present & potential to the market. More than any other medium, the internet and its inherent interactivity empower people to find information quickly and precisely on any destination or recreation of their interest.

Table 1: Top 05 countries with highest number of internet users

# Country or Region	Internet Users, Latest Data and Date	Population (2006 Est.)	Internet Penetration Date	Source and Date of Latest	% Users of World
1 United States	205,326, 680	299,093, 237	68.6 %	Nielsen/ /NR Jan/06	20.1 %
2 China	111,000, 000	1,306,724, 067	8.5 %	CNNIC Dec/05	10.9 %
3 Japan	86,300, 000	128,389, 000	67.2 %	eTFore- casts Dec/05	8.4 %
4 India	50,600, 000	1,112,225, 812	4.5 %	C.I.Almanac Mar/05	5.0 %
5 Germany 997	48,721,	82,515,988	59.0 %	Nielsen/ /NR Jan/06	4.8 %
TOP 20 Countries	811,986, 333	4,064,319, 458	20.0 %	IWS - Mar.31/06	79.4 %
Rest of the World	210,876, 974	2,435,377, 602	8.7 %	IWS - Mar.31/06	20.6 %
Total World - Users	1,022, 863,307	6,499,697, 060	15.7 %	IWS - Dec.31/05	100.0 %

Source: http:/www.internetworldstats.com

As table-1.1 depicts and according to IWS (www.interworldstats.com) the number of internet users at the end of 2005 was around 1022 million. 15.7% penetration of internet has boosted not only tourism but all the business sectors all over the world. It was observed from the data that the global online usage growth rate accounts for approximately 183.4 percent all over the world by 2005. If we compare country wise, USA (20.1%) stands first as internet user, while china (10.9%) stands at second place and India (5.0%) is at fourth place. India was at eleventh place at the end of 2004. She jumped to fourth place as her share as user rose to 5%.

Internet in India: Despite India's technical outsourcing muscle, the country's internet penetration rate is low. JuxtConsult, a research based firm in New Delhi, surveyed Urban Internet users in April, 2005 talking to 30000 Indian web users about their liftstyle and their web use. Exhibit 1.1 shows that 15% web users are surfing the web less than once a day. About 40% use the net more than five times a day and 24% use it on daily basis.

Exhibit 1.1: Urban Internet users in India, by the frequency of usage, April 2005

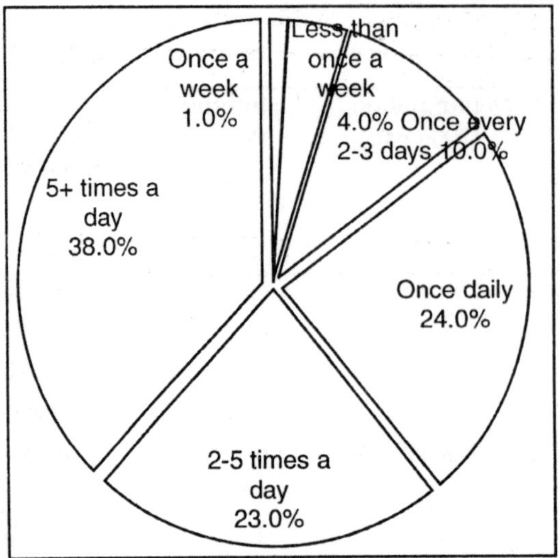

Source: JuxtConsult, August 2005

Tourism and IT- The challenges ahead: New Ideas are the seeds that ferment change. But whenever change is in motion, uncertainty arises. Radically innovative ideas are creating waves in the travel and tourism industry. Information Technology is only a part of the story for the tourism sector. As such, technologies are a vehicle- a means to an end, above all, technologies can become a powerful competitive weapon if creatively used.

2. *Low Cost Carriers*

A low-cost carrier or low-cost airline is an airline that offers generally low-fares. The concept originated in the United States before spreading to Europe in the early 1990s and subsequently to much of the rest of the world. The term originated within the airline industry referring to airlines with a low- or lower- operating cost structure then their competitors (Wikipedia, 2006). The global expansion of low cost carriers (LCCs) has defined recent adverse market trends, emphasizing the resilience of the airlines model and its ability to maintain the profitability and grow revenue in difficult operating conditions. As per FHRAI Magazine May-June 2005, the worldwide aircraft capacity fell by 8% between 2000 and 2003 while the capacity provided by LCCs grew by 69%.

Low-cost carriers pose a serious threat to traditional "full service" airline, since the high cost structure of full service carrier prevents them from competing effectively on price- the most important factor among most consumers when selecting a carrier. From 2001 to 2003, when the aviation industry was rocked by terrorism, war and SARS, the large majority of traditional airlines suffered heavy losses while low-cost carriers generally stayed profitable.

Basically 'Low Cost Carrier' business design is defined by three elements: -

Simple product

- No meals, drinks and snacks for free
- Narrow seating, no seat reservation, free seating, no frequent-flyer programs.

Positioning

- Non business passengers, leisure traffic, price-conscious business passengers,
- Secondary airports
- Competition with all transportation carriers (including rail and road).

Low Operating Costs

- Low wages, low cost of maintenance, cockpit training and standby crew due to homogeneous fleet.

As Bjorn Hanson, a hotel industry consultant from Price Water House Coopers says, "Travelers in general are more price sensitive to airfare than they are to hotel room rates. Often a low airfare will stimulate demand for travel even if the hotel prices are increasing."

Exhibit-1.2: Operating Costs (pence per seat-km)

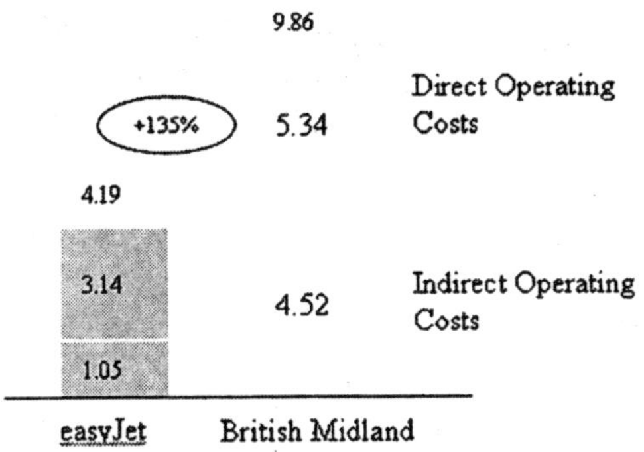

(*Source:* FHRAI Magazine May-June 2005)

The above diagram depicts that British Midland's unit costs are more than twice as high as easyJet's

Comparison unit costs: The cost advantage of low cost airlines are not primarily the result of radical cost management, but rather a natural offshoot of their business design. LCCs have the following advantages over the traditional airlines: -

- Narrower seating (higher capacity 148 vs.126).
- Higher plane utilization (10·7h vs. 8.4h) due to shorter turnaround times.
- Lower staff costs due to greater productivity. Generally lower wages and smaller staff (no service).
- Lower airport fees at secondary airports.

- No sales commission due to web sales.
- Low station costs due to simple handling and more efficient processes.

The concept of 'LCCs' or 'No Frill Airlines' though a global success is gradually catching on with the Indian traveler. LCCs is quiet affordable by the individual business traveler whether he is middle class or train traveler due to varied reasons. Firstly, main objective of LCCs is faster connectivity at a cheaper price which means no in flight services, no cabin crew to welcome abroad or serve hot towels, no piping hot meals etc. Secondly, the corporations are becoming cost conscious by cutting travel expenses and they are benefited by shifting from traditional airlines to 'discounters.'

The LCCs have brought tremendous benefits to the destinations and surrounding areas, which they serve in terms of higher tourism and business traffic. A very larger number of trips are being undertaken by people, which they would have otherwise not undertaken, just because of low cost. World- over, the low cost airlines phenomenon is beginning to transform the face of aviation and tourism industry. On the Indian front, the overall aviation is growing at 25%, the domestic market which is currently 19 million should increase to 45-50 million in the next five years. A well established example of this growing concept is Air Deccan, the airline that started off with one flight; while in 2005 it was offering 54 daily flights to 19 cities (fe Traveler, 2005).

However, the present scenario in Indian airline industry is different. The next couple of months could be very tough for the industry. There is bound to be high volume growth in the industry. But the challenge is to convert that into growth of profit (Business Today, 2006). One of the main issues for such alarming situation is the innovation by operators in route choices. Most low cost carriers like Jet Indian and Sahara and others are concentrating on Delhi and Mumbai routes. This has forced operator to lower the prices to attract customers leading to predatory pricing practices. Full cost-carriers are cutting the prices to low-cost levels, and some airlines are selling tickets far below the costs they occur.

Exhibit 1.3

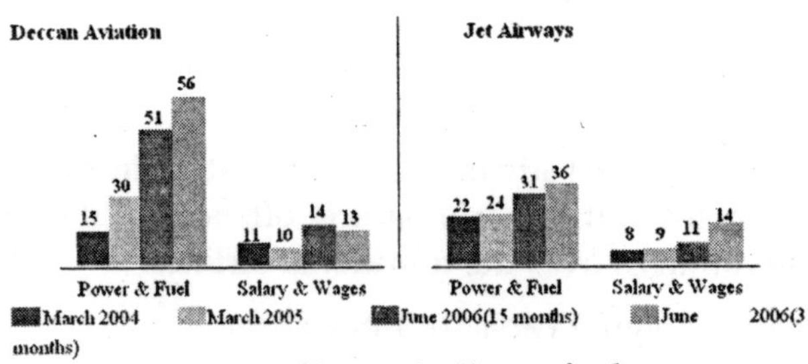

Figures in %age of sales

Source: CMIE

It is alleged that very high fuel and salary cost eat into airlines profit. This is exemplified by Deccan Aviations who brought the budget airline concept to the Indian skies, is now suffering a loss of Rs.341 crore on net sales of Rs.1,236.4 crore for the 15 months ended June

2006. Deccan added 20 new aircrafts on 56 new routes in the past 15 months but the escalating fuel costs accounting 51 percent of sales have eaten up its profits. For April-June quarter, wages and fuel swallowed away 69 percent of sales i.e. the net losses stands at Rs.110.26 crore on the sales of Rs.398 crore for the quarter.

Jet Airways too has been feeling the same pain on the wages and fuel fronts. For the year ended March, 2006, these costs jumped upto just under 40 percent from 33 percent in the previous year. The situation became worse in first quarter of 2006 when Jet suffered a Rs.45 crore loss with fuel and wages eating with almost half of sales (49%).

This story does not relate to only two airlines rather most of them are sailing in the same boat. A group of airlines head appealed to Air Aviation Minister, Praful Patel for the regulation of prices and restricting entry of new players. However, the government does not restrict the new entry, but promises to scrutinize their applications more closely.

3. *Budget Hotels*

The tourism sector has been overshadowed by one further trend -the rise of budget hotels or economy hotels. With inbound tourism growing at more than 25 percent and domestic travel fuelled largely by corporate and increasing popularity of low cost carriers, the hotel industry is fast realizing the potential of budget segment. After the elite class and the foreign tourists: the middle class is the third largest stratum constituting the visitors within India. Such visitors have a limited budget confining their stay in the budget hotels or economy hotels in India. Nearly a dozen chains including the global ones like the France based Accor group and two American groups, Choice hotels and Microtel -are planning to add capacity in the range of 3,000 rooms in the next five years, entailing a proposed investment of over Rs.1,000 crore(Outlook, July 2005). No-frill quality hotels can correct the skewed Indian market. In fact, budget hotels can do what low cost airlines have done- increase business volumes almost overnight.

Some of the new players include Hometel, Kamfotel, Courtyard by Marriott, Country Inns & Suites, Ibis and Fairfield Inn. IHCL last year launched the Indione brand that will build 500 hotels in the next ten years under the concept of Smart-Basics. Compared to its five starred cousins, Indione is a budget hotel and the differences are striking. There is no burly, thick mustachioed concierge to welcome the guests at Indione. Instead, there are airport like trolleys to carry their baggage to the rooms. No marble or granite floors or massive chandeliers in the lobby and certainly no Persian carpets. The factors like cleanliness, security and the core room product are key to mid segment hotel within which Smart-Basics fit in. IHCL has integrated Wi-fi and a cybercafe within the hotel premise to position the brand for the profile of corporate travelers who use the mid segment. Service need not be obtrusive and costs can be saved therein without actually depriving the guest of quality and at the same time giving the great privacy.

The budget hotels are characterized by cleanliness, simplicity, economy and provision of average amenities as desired by middle segment traveler. The scene of the budget hotel can be enjoyed by going through the following lines- a 17" plasma TV, a comfortable bed, a wardrobe, a direct dialing phone, a worktable, a big window and soothing contrast pastel colours or the wall. The rationale behind the move explains that the Budget Hotels will be premium in class and quality and economical in cost. It will be targeted at business travelers.

Table 3: What's on the menu

Hotel/Tariff	Future plans	USP
Indione, Bangalore Rs.900-950	10+ hotels by 2006 Investment: Rs.100 cr	The Tata brandname; cheapest among other comparable chains
Lemon Tree, Gurgaon Rs.1,900-2,500	5+ hotels by 2006 Investment: Rs.40-50 cr	Provides most services like a five-star including swimming pool and business centre
*Hometel, Gurgaon, Bangalore Rs.1,200-2,000	10+ hotels by 2007 Investment: Rs.100 cr	Room facilities comparable to five-star, will cut down on public space
*Ibis, Gurgaon, Bangalore, Pune Rs.2,000 and above	21 hotels by 2015 Investment: Rs.850 cr	Global brand; possible synergies in the future with Interglobe's own low-cost airline
*Choice Hotels' Sleep Inn, Delhi Rs. 2,500	10 hotels by 2008 Investment: Rs.100 cr	Internationally known; more upscale than traditional budget hotels
*Microtel Rs.1,800-2000	5 hotels by 2006 Investment: Rs.65-75 cr	Strong presence in the US market; Bigger rooms and larger public space

*Yet to commence operations

(*Source*: Outlook –the weekly news magazine, July 2005)

The global market reflects that the budget hotel market is most highly developed in France, where two companies -Accor and Group Evergure-run two thirds of Europe's branded budget hotel rooms. The UK is emerging as the second largest budget hotel market is Europe. In 2000 there were 47,000 beds in budget-hotel in the UK and it was expected that it would expand to 1,03,000 by 2005. The third largest budget hotel market in Europe is in Germany and is dominated by Accor's brands. The hotel chain domination of the European budget sector reflects its profitability; this sector has low staffing requirements (a full time staff of 20 can operate a 100 room hotel) and the costs of construction are modest (Cross, 1997). This expanding segment is taking business away from existing 5 star hotels because prices are comparatively cheaper.

While making an analytical study of this table, it is found that the Tatas have selected Whitefield the heart of Bangalore to start their latest venture, Indione. The Indione properties will be built on the basis of cookie cutter model, the science of which has been rigorously worked out so it's easy to replicate to a large extent. Sarovar Park Plaza is planning to offer in its proposed 50 budget hotels under a new brand Hometel. They would be knocking off a lot of public space like the lobby, banquets and lawns. No room service or multiple restaurants. But there will be no perceivable difference between budget hotel rooms and five star acommodation (Outlook, 2005). Accor India has tied up with Interglobe, a travel services firm to establish its Ibis brand of budget hotels. Accor India accepts even the figure of 3,000 rooms is nowhere near the optimum. In the next five years. India would need close to 25,000 rooms in this segment. With almost all the ambition expression plans still in the pipeline, it will take at least a few years before many cities have two or three quality budget hotels.

4. Revenue Management

An interesting new trend is the development of revenue management strategies. To develop profitability, larger hotels have adopted the revenue or yield management strategies that were pioneered in the airline industry. By identifying peaks and troughs in hotel bookings from previous years, hotels can then provide for a predicted pattern of demand based on experience. Using such models, hotels can then charge prices based on likely demand for future room capacity and seek to balance supply with demand to maximize occupancy. The hotel monitors the booking rate and can adjust prices according to future demand, thus flexibly responding to market conditions. This takes into account the expected business mix, and the profitability of each segment, since filling a hotel with low yielding sectors such as air crews is unviable and these need to be mixed with full price and discounted business. For smaller hotels, investment in yield management computer systems (as well as training and know -how) may previously not have been attractive, but these systems can now be accessed by non chain hotels via the internet for a monthly fee. Today revenue management has become one of the more potent tools used in pricing and revenue management. Now used by all airlines and by the great majority of hotel companies, RM is extending its scope to other service sector industries and some type of manufacturing. As a user of RM, the organization can expect to generate everywhere from 3% to 8% additional revenue resulting in potential increase of 50% to 100%. Here are the success stories of few names who gained the following without any increase in major capital investments(Cross, 1997).

- American Airlines -\$500 million increase in annual revenues.
- Marriott Hotels -\$100 million increase in annual revenues.
- National Car Rental turned the company from the brink of bankruptcy to compan growing at 20% annual rate.

RM is a set of forecasting techniques used to determine whether the price should b raised or lowered in order to maximize the revenue. Sheryl Kimes of Cornell Universit writes, "Yield (or revenue) Management is a method of managing capacity profitably. The term 'yield' in the airline industry refers to revenue per available seat mile. It can b applied to other industry by altering into revenue per available time based unit (such a room).

Measurement of Revenue Per Available Room Night (RevPAI)

In hotels –Average Room Rate = Total Revenue/Total Available Rooms

Suppose a 100 –room hotel sold

-30 rooms at \$40

-30 rooms at \$50

-30 rooms at \$60

resulting in total revenue = 30x40+30x50+30x60=\$4500

RevPAR =\$4500/100=\$45

Yield Management Strategies

1. Economics 101 –Adopt a differential pricing policy
   a) fixed pricing – charge one price to everybody
   b) variable – charge different prices to different customers for an essentially san product.
   - Assume that different customers are willing to pay different prices fo different perceived values.
   - Customers segmentation is a key.
   - Identify the price sensitivity of each segment.

Exhibit- 1.2

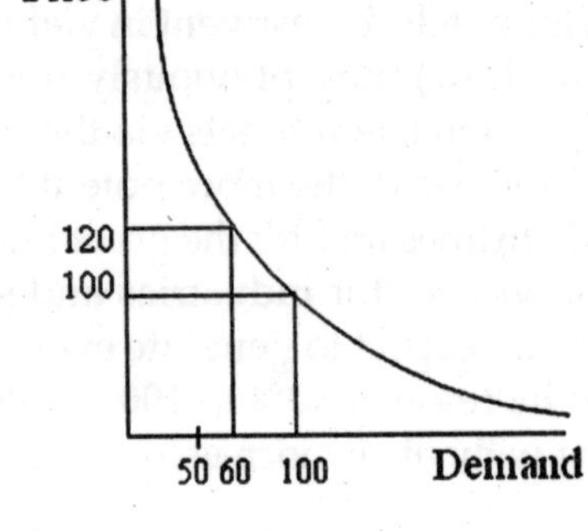

For a 100 room hotel Maximum possible revenue is a

$100 100 = $10,000

Maximum potential revenue = $120 x 60=$ 7,200

+

$100x 40= $ 4,000 $11,200

Increase in revenue amounting to $1,200. This increase in the revenue is due to lifferential pricing

2. Customer Segmentation –This concept has been around in the hospitality marketing since ages and is represented in two forms: -
   a) Product segmentation and differentiation
   b) Market segmentation

Product segmentation involves what is to be done with a product or service to lifferentiate it from other or competition.

Market segmentation is a marketing technique that targets a group of customers with pecific characteristics. In YM, the market is segmented to increase acceptability of the product and maximize revenue from every market segmentation. The generally used egmentation is based on

- Usage -leisure/business
- Period of stay – days of week – busy or low period
- Length of stay.
- Booking patterns.

3. Rate Fences:-

Rationally built in barriers to prevent customers willing to pay higher rates from taking advantages of lower rates.

Examples:-

Time of usage – Day of week

$60 rate on weekends v/s $100 rate on weekdays

Length of usage – short stay v/s long stay

$100 for one night v/s $90 for two nights

4. Forecasting: -

- Making prediction about future.

There are three rules of good forecasting.

a) It must be at right level of detail.
b) An appropriate amount of data must be analyzed.
c) Frequent reforecast must occur.

Table 4: Working of Selected Five Star Hotels in India

Hotel Name	Status	Year of Establishment	Year of YMS	% + Profits	Month of higher occupancy	Month of Slow occupancy.	RevPAR peak/slow
Le Meridien Restaurant & Convention Center Kochi	5 Star	2001	2002		Sept.-Dec	Apr.-Jun	
Radission Windsor Ltd, Jallandher	5 Star	2001	2001	30%	Oct.-Mar.	Apr.-Sept	2000/1500
Hotel Hindustan Int., Kolkatta	5 Star	1964	2005	7-10%	Oct.-Feb.	Mar.-Sept	4000/2200
The Park, Kolkatta	5 Star Deluxe	1967	Early future		Nov.-Jan.	May-Aug	2300/2000
Taj Bengal, Kolkatta	5 Star Deluxe	1989	1999		Nov.- Mar.	July-Sept.	5500/4000
Taj Residency, Calicutt	5 Star	1997	2003	10%	Sept.-Mar.	Apr.-Aug	1300/1200
Taj Malabar, Kochi	5 Star Deluxe	1986	2003	11%	Nov. -Feb.	May-July	8000/4000
Trident Hilton, Bhubneshwar	5 Star Deluxe	1985	2004	20%	Nov.-Jan.	May-July	2750/1600
The Oberoi Cecil, Shimla	5 Star Heritage	1997	NA		May.-Jun.	August	5200/3400
Trident Hilton, Chennai	5 Star	2001	1995	ARR+	Aug.-Mar	Apr.-May	4500/4000

Source: Primary Data

Working of Revenue Management in Indian 5 Star Hotels

In order to have an insight into operational framework of RM in 5 star hotels, the researcher mailed the questionnaires to these properties. Although the response was not very encouraging, only ten 5 star replied back. After analyzing the data, it was found that 80% of the respondents were implementing yield management systems in their properties

They opined RM as the most important management/financial strategy. Infact, YM is a 'management approach' in which computer based technology can help the hotel managers to realize the full potential of YM. In the survey only 50% of the hoteliers claim to have a computerized Decision Supports Systems (DSS) essential for the implementation of YMS. YM system demands that all staff should be familiar with the yield philosophy of the hotel and trained in specific yield techniques. While format YM techniques are enhanced by computer applications, managers used to structure their training programmes so that they include a primary focus on human resource input. Interestingly, only 60% of the hoteliers claim the presence of system of training and educating the employees. Five of the managers believed that staff is empowered by being involved in planning and decision making process and they also believed that this helped in reducing staff turnover. When asked about any incentive scheme in the properties, 50% of the hotels were rewarding the staff with incentive programmes under YMS. Since none of the hotels in sample was operating a formal YM system, incentives were volume oriented not profitability. Generally hotel management teams used strategies and tactics aimed to reduce uncertainty and increase profitability. Regarding the familiarity with yield management practices, 90% of the hotels know when to eliminate or restrict the discount allocations and only 80% know when to require a minimum length to stay. 9 out of 10 hoteliers claimed that they used discounting in the periods of low occupancy. During the course of study, it was found that eight hotels were using upsell as a strategy to increase profitability while 60% of the hotels used cross sell as a strategy. It was quiet heartening to note down that all hotels were hosting or organizing different events like marriages, meetings, festivals, seminars, conferences and others to increase the profitability. Whether the respondent hotels were aware of the latest market trends, 9 out of 10 hotels in the sample has the information about occupancy rate of the competitors. Although they did not mention clearly the reasons for collecting competitors' rates, it may reasonably be enough to suggest their main aim was to ensure the similar rate structure in their own establishments. Eight of the respondents were satisfied with their business being better than competitors, while one of them was not aware of this fact and the last one claimed that competitors were having better business.

Future of Revenue Management: The hospitality industry has been focused to explore methods of enhancing profitability. To eliminate or reduce in house services is a short term approach which conflicts with the aim of industry and overbooks sustainable growth. The entry of RM techniques can improve the hotels' competitive stance and enhance overall profitability. However, the benefits will accrue only when management has the capacity to fully understand the concept and the aptitude to learn essential YM techniques. RM is decidedly myopic. As technology develops and business environment continues to evolve, new opportunities to advance RM are continuously created. Our challenge as leaders in the field is to capture these opportunities. As Kimes point out 'If YM is to be likely successful, companies must seriously address both the technical and non technical implementation issues and must be prepared to embrace and anticipate future technological change.'

Medical Tourism: Things are hotting up in India like never before and the heat generated is not the outcome of seasonal or climatic changes. With Indian tourism industry growing by leaps and bounds, the visitors include not just those willing to see the Taj or the Konark temple, or experiencing the Goan beaches or enjoying the snow valleys in Kashmir. Tourists from abroad are flocking to India as India is set to become the health care destination of the world. More and more overseas patients are coming to premier hospitals in India. Our health care industry is growing at 30 percent annually. As per C I I-McKinsey report, medical tourism is stated to become a $2.3 billion industry by 2012, next to the IT sector.

Basically, the patients from the abroad can be categorized into three categories. In Punjab, more than five lakh NRIs make annual visits home. This single largest group of visitors is a big source of revenue, especially for the dental treatment and costmetic surgery market. The second large group covers Britons and US citizens who visit India while combining their vacations with low lost cosmetic surgery or dental treatment. The third one is from poor African Nations or SAARC countries where the medical facilities are not developed. The Escorts Heart Institute and Research Centre (EHIRC) in Delhi said that of over 1,500 foreign patients received last year, about 700 were from non SAARC countries including the US, UK, CIS and the Gulf, a significant change from previous years.

The combination of high quality, world class and affordable cost health care services is attracting a regular stream of foreign patients to India. Indian corporate hospitals are conforming to international standards, but the cost of treatment is about one eighth to one fifth of that in the US or the UK. From the table-1.5 it can be analyzed that replacement (single knee) in the US costs $ 22,000, best in India, a top of the line health care facility would charge about $ 6,500. Advanced rhinoplast surgery at a top teartiary care hospital in India costs $2,000 as against $ 10,000 in the US.

Table 5: Bargain Prices

Treatment	India	Us
Coronary Artery Bypass Grafting	$6,600	$60,000
Knee Replacement (Single Knee)	$6,500	$22,000
Rhinoplasty (nose job)	$2,000	$10,000
Bone Marrow Transplant	$26,000	$2,50,000
Root Canal Treatment	$100	$1,000

Source: - Outlook –the weekly magazine, 13th Feb, 2006.

The treatment cost includes the cost of medicines and healthcare delivery. Room charges for a day in a top Indian hospital are Rs.3,000 –Rs.5,000, whereas they come to $1,000-1,500 a day in the US. Most of the major hospitals and clinics list their prices on their websites. These are even 25 to 30 percent less than those in Thailand. The Indian government is planning to achieve uniform price band for top corporate hospitals in India, to ensure almost similar prices for overseas patients. The Confederation of Indian Industries has also suggested a price band for overseas patients that would leave little scope for price cutting. The commonest treatments for which medical tourists are flocking to India are cosmetic procedures like liposuction, tummy tuck, breast implants, and breast reduction, more reshaping, facelift, botox injection, filler injunctions and dental treatment. Increasing number of patients flocking to India is supported by a number of valid reasons. Most of them are escapees from western medical crises: whether it's long waiting lists or exorbitant costs. Today India is well equipped with the latest infrastructure and medical technology. Indraprastha Apollo Hospitals, New Delhi can boast of being India's first JCI accredited hospital. JCI (the international arm of the Joint Council of Accreditation of Healthcare Organizations) is considered the gold standard in healthcare and 46 hospitals worldwide have got this accreditation.

Fortunately for the tourism ministry not all medical tourists confine themselves to hospital rooms. Kerala known as God's own Ayurvedic Paradise is being promoted by as a 'global healthcare destination'. So after incredible temples, incredible tigers and incredible yoga, it's now going to be incredible doctors backed by incredible technology.

A new dimension to medical tourism is called 'reproductive tourism' in India. The couples find arranging for surrogate mother in India to be far cheaper than the thousands of pounds they spend or fertility treatment in Britain. Indian medical infrastructure is now being increasingly used by British nationals for reproductive purpose. The Guardian recently reported that such treatment has become big business in India and was now worth Rs.20 billion ($450 million).

As medical tourism grows, it is attracting critics also. They say that medical tourism should be held responsible for the gross distortion of priorities for a country failing miserably to meet the healthcare needs of its own people. Healthcare cannot be treated as a product. This type of medical tourism will distort prices in private sector. Eighty percent of Indian patients are dependent on private sectors and hospitals. Medical tourism will result in Indians competing for treatment with people whose incomes are 30 times higher. First of all, we must substantially and visibly improve access to state health services before we go in for medical tourism Thailand first created its medical infrastructure and then went for medical tourism. Medical tourism is a form of exports of services. Is it feasible to export wheat when there is a severe shortage of wheat in India?

Conclusion: Seeing tourism on the horizon of new trends, industry players virtually have to be masters of innovation in order to survive. In a sea of change, where innovative sharks are gobbling up small and big fishes alike, players have to use their ingenuity to survive. Change is the demand of time. Innovation is definitely the way to go. Infact, a number of travel and leisure companies have gained the competitive edge mainly because of their creativeness and willingness to dare. No doubt, many of these innovatives have been copied by others, it has given some inventors sufficient lead-time, experience and economic rent (monopoly profits) to stay ahead of competition. The future of travel and leisure industry will lie in more innovation.

REFERENCES

- Brotherton B&Mooney S. (1992). Yield Management Progress and Prospects. *Journal of Hospitality Managemen. 11(1).*
- Cornell HRA Quarterly Conference Report. (1990). Yield Management Magic. *The Cornell HRA Quarterly. 31(2), 14-15.*
- Cross Robert.(1999). Revenue Management -Hardcore Tactics for Profit Making and Market Domination. *University Press (India) Ltd.*
- Employment News. (2004 Sept. 25 to Oct. 01). Vol._,
- FHRAI Magazine. (2005, May-June). V, P.
- http:/www.internetworldstats.com accessed.
- Ingold Anthony, McMahan Beattie Una & Yeoman Ian in 2nd Edition of Yield Management.
- 'India wins over, 'out' patients' Singh Vijay Komal, (2006, April 08). *The Tribune, Chd.*
- 'Is medical tourism the next big thing after information technology and the BPO?' *Outlook* (2006, Feb.12). *62-69.*
- Poon Auliana in Tourism, Technology and Competitive Strategies, 1993.
- Stephen J. Page Tourism Management-Managing for change Accommodation. 165-178.
- The trends which are likely to shape the rapidly evolving Indian business travel segments 9-17 Charmaine Fornz and Bhishan Manusukhani in Business Traveler June 2005.
- Who need a concierge. Outlook (2005, July). 46-47.

Section II

Tourism Impacts

10

Beach Tourism Impacts-the Case of Beachfront Developments at Kovalam

M.R.Dileep
Faculty in Tourism
Kerala Institute of Tourism and Travel Studies (KITTS)
Residency, Thycaud, Thiruvananthapuram
Kerala, Inida

ABSTRACT

Beach and coastal tourism is a prominent kind of tourism in the world and in US, beaches are the leading destinations. Coastal tourism is key to US economy and thus has a deep impact on the economic health of the country (Chawla, 2004). Coastal areas are the transitional areas between the land and sea, marked by a very high unique biodiversity. The coastal areas are under high population pressure in different parts of the world and coastal tourism activities add to it since, in many coastal areas, tourism represents the most important economic activity. Thus, coastal areas face high environmental vulnerability in addition to socio-cultural. A variety of impacts on environment can be identified due to tourism activities in the coastal areas. Waste generation, physical change, resource overuse, etc. are the major reasons behind it and all lead to physical, ecological, hydrological, aesthetic, health related and socio-cultural impacts. Aesthetic/visual pollution due to construction on the beach frontage and the problem of beachfront developments are the impacts relatively less discussed in the international scenario. The after effects of beachfront environment deterioration are many. Ultimately, the loss of natural beauty of the destination will result in decline in tourist arrivals along with other environmental issues. Against this backdrop, an attempt has been made to examine the increasing level of beachfront developments and corresponding aesthetic consequences at Kovalam, one of the prime beach tourism destinations in India.

Keywords: Beach Tourism, Coastal Tourism, Environmental impacts, Beachfront developments, aesthetic pollution.

INTRODUCTION

Just thirty years of tourism generated a lot of impacts at Kovalam, one of the finest beaches in India. Loss of green cover in the beachfront, which led to decline of natural beauty, is one among them. Constructions of various kinds, ranging from high-rise buildings to tiny structures; government owned establishments to anonymous; large chain hotels to tiny petty shops, situated on the beach deteriorating the natural beauty significantly. A thick row of buildings has been vanishing the charm of the destination. A viewer from the sea can see a concrete fort instead of lush green coconut grove, which was the core of the attraction of Kovalam Beach years ago.

Beachfront developments constitute one of the important impacts of coastal tourism. World over, large number of beach destinations is facing the problem of beachfront developments. Aesthetic Pollution, Visual Pollution and Environmental Rape are some similar terms used interchangeably to denote the impact due to beachfront developments. Beaches in Spain are usually cited as example for denoting the environmental rape due to beach tourism development (Cooper, et.al, 2000). As far as Kovalam is concerned, the intriguing natural beauty is undoubtedly the most vital component of its attraction as a tourism product. But, as mentioned above, the charm of the destination is on the decline due to the declining in its green cover on the beach frontage because of the growing construction activities. Against this backdrop, an attempt has been made to address the problem of beachfront developments and the corresponding aesthetic consequences focusing on Kovalam.

Beach Tourism

In international tourism, Beach resorts have formed a 'niche' of their own and beach tourism is a major segment of leisure tourism sector. Beaches are leading destinations in many parts of the world and beach tourism has led to an overall development of tourism in those areas. (Mogan,1999). History reveals that, Beach/Coastal Tourism is one of the oldest forms of tourism. (Chawla, 2004). Simply, Beach is a shore of an Ocean, Sea or lake covered by sand or smooth stones. From the tourism perspective, Beach, according to Whyte (2004), is a 'liminal space', which has two dimensions. First, 'material space' when it is a *boundary zone where the hint of celestial forces is whispered by the ebb and flow of tides, a space neither land nor Sea, a zone of uncertainty that resonates with the sound of ever changing seas, a setting that is , by turns, calm, tranquil, and soothing or agitated, unruly, and frightening*. Second, it is a 'cultural space' where *border land that allows both difference and hybridity while facilitating the tactile tug of land or sea to reveal for many, but not all, spaces of heightened sensibilities that are temporary, personal and elusive.*

Beach Tourism utilizes the aesthetic and environmental values of the beach and it combines land water resources. Beaches attract tourists due to a variety of motivations in which relaxation, love for water and sand and even adventurous sports are the major among them. In Beaches, visitors may seek a space where the stress of normal working lives is temporarily suspended, cultures merge, egalitarianism flourishes and bonds of friendship are forged (Whyte, 2004). According to Smith (1991), Beach tourism development passes through a few distinct stages. In the very beginning it would be a no-tourism zone with only indigenous settlement around. In the next stage some tourists, particularly domestic, will discover the destination. Establishment of an accommodation unit is the third stage, which will be a landmark, and it will be followed by additional developments leading to an identifiable resort area and it constitutes the next stage. Sooner or later, tourist arrivals would see growth and gradually, a business area would be developed, thus evolves the next stage of its development. Spreading of accommodation units and others into inland areas would constitute the sixth stage. Slowly the area will be converted into urban area and a fully urbanized resort would be emerged sooner. It includes seventh and eight stage of development of beach tourism destinations respectively.

Marine Tourism is a related term and activities involved in it ranges from an individual wind surfing to people holidaying on a Cruise Ship. Marine Tourism is defined as the tourism which includes 'those recreational activities that involve travel away from one's place of residence and which have as their host or focus the marine environment (where the marine environment is defined as those waters which are saline and tide affected)' (Orams, 1999.). Coastal tourism is another term often used interchangeably with Beach tourism in tourism literature.

Beach Tourism Impacts

The benefits in the economy and society due to tourism in beaches hardly require any discussion. On the contrary, the negative impacts on various spheres like society, culture and environment need further discussion, though it had been there for some time. A wide range of issues can be identified due to the development of tourism in a Beach. It would not be surprising to reveal that sex tourism is increasingly seen associated with beach tourism world over (Herold, et. al. 2001). The development of second generation Sun and Sand tourist destinations was accompanied by considerable environment deterioration. It has been an established fact that beach developments are usually been associated with tourism. Due to the over use beaches, coastal areas and natural resources over there are facing deterioration (Aguilo et.al, 2005).

According to Gartner (1996), there are mainly two types of tourist activities that are the reasons behind the environmental impacts due to coastal tourism. Inherent attractiveness is the one, which results in a common form of beach activities and associated developments to accommodate tourists demands. Access points for tourists, land transformation and sewage discharge into the marine environment constitute the other one. Pollution by waste water, dumping of solid waste, oil seepages and spills, discharge of hotel waste, garbage, noise and traffic emissions, encroachment of buildings, facilities and roads, excessive use of natural resources, destruction of natural areas, beach erosion due to constructions, sand dune removal and dredging, erosion of reefs and coral, etc. are the major environmental issues commonly discussed due to tourism development in a Beach. Damage to sand dune due to recreational use of the beach has far reaching environmental impacts since dune vegetation acts as a barrier to erosion. (Equations, 2003; Newsome, et.al, 2006). Shoreline erosion is expected to increase due to the development in the beach frontage.

The development of tourism facilities can also lead to a decline in the aesthetic quality of the environment. 'Aesthetic Pollution' is common type of impact usually discussed in connection with beach tourism development. The effect of environment on the senses is known as environmental aesthetics and such qualities of tourism facilities, like beauty, very much on the eye of the beholder. An observer can easily distinguish between planning and offensive settings (John, 2000). Environment pollution is as much aesthetic as physical. Holloway (1994) remarks that an area of scenic beauty attracts more number of tourists, so more and more of the natural landscape is lost due to tourism development. The progression of this situation will result in loss of wooing natural/scenic beauty, which may eventually results in the movement of tourists to some other destinations that are tranquil and beautiful. Cooper et.al. (2000) states that the construction of tourism super structure utilizes real estate and may detract from aesthetics. They opine that the building of high-rise hotels on the beach frontage is an environmental impact that gathers headline status. They argue that it is a kind of environmental rape, though the rate is less as compared to that occurred during 1960s and 1970s.

The term 'aesthetic pollution' is more connected with the construction in a natural and/ or traditional set up and the design of construction in a manner that avoids natural/ traditional/indigenous style of buildings/constructions. Holden (2000) is of the view that the uniform style of development along many coastlines of the world ignores local architectural style, building traditions and materials. Architectural pollution, related but different term, refers to 'the inability to integrate resort design and infrastructure development into inherent characterization of the natural environment (Gartner,1996). Gartner is of the opinion that poorly and inappropriately designed facilities can clash with environmental surroundings, creating aesthetically unappealing facilities'. Visual Pollution can also be attributed to the insensitivity in the design of buildings for tourism (Holloway, 1994).

The coastline, a magnet for tourists since time immemorial, has raised concern about sustainable development. New approaches to shoreline management give more focus on those concerns. Coastal Tourism has grown dramatically, especially during the post 2nd World War era. The increasing damage to the environment due to developmental activities necessitated Shoreline Management Plans (SMPs) and they are being practiced in some countries. According to Jennings (2004), a few reasons are responsible for the changing relationship between coastal tourism and shoreline management- an increase in and the changing nature of tourist related pressure at the coast; advances in shoreline management approaches; the geo-morphologic behaviour of coastal system and projections of near future climate and associated sea level change.

Coastal Tourism and Beach Front Developments in India: the case of Kovalam

India has over 7500 kms of coastline interspersed with beautiful beaches. She has some fine beaches that have been luring tourists from world over for a very long time. Beahes in Goa (Colva, Calangute, Vasca, Dauna Paula, etc.); Mahabalipuram, Madras and Rameswaram in Tamil Nadu; Kovalam and Varkala in Kerala; Puri in Orissa; and beaches in Pondicherry, Andaman and Nicobar Islands and Lakshadweep are the examples for them. Natural beauty is the cardinal component of beaches in India, particularly the beaches in Goa and Kerala. They are the more exposed beaches to tourism developments and hence those face more environmental issues due to tourism than the rest. A range of environmental issues, majority of the earlier discussed issues can be identified in these beaches. But, they are not discussed here since it is beyond the scope of this paper. As far as Goan beaches are concerned, they have been experiencing proliferation of new buildings, particularly along the Aguada-Chapera strip. For example, the number of medium to large scale development under construction between Aguda Fort and Baga had increased from 12 to 45 (Wilson 1996). But Wilson argues that they have not been transformed into a concrete jungle with high-rise buildings on the Beach frontage, compared to beaches in Spain and many other European Countries. Beachfront developments are a common phenomenon connected with coastal tourism and serious concern has not been given so far on it, barring some destinations, which do consider the beauty of the beaches and take measures to preserve it in its natural form to the possible extent.

Kovalam: Nature's beauty at stake: A concrete jungle on the rise

Kovalam, a small fishing village on the coast of Arabian Sea, situated about 14 kilometers away from Thiruvananthapuran (Capital city of Kerala state), enjoys a distinguished position among the best beaches in India. This beach destination mainly involves four crescent shaped beaches. 'Chasing the Monsoon', written by Alexander Frater (1990) narrated with exceptional sensitivity and wit the towering influence of nature and especially monsoon over the lives and culture of India and her people. The enchanting beauty of Kovalam during monsoon season is also mentioned in it. Lonely planet (2000), a world popular travel guide described Kovalam as a hippie idyll; a picture perfect tropical beach; traditional Keralan fishing village thirty years ago, but it mentiones that the charm of the destination has declined to a large extent.

It was in 1930, Kovalam rose into public attention. Shree Chithira Thirunal Balarama Varma, the late Maharaja of Travancore (erstwhile small princely kingdom, now part of Kerala state) first brought Kovalam to the public eye as a summer retreat. Halcyon Castle at Kovalam was built during then. It is reported that in the early 1940s the Travencore Public Works Department (PWD) has undertaken some constructions near the beach. Tourists in small numbers started to arrive at Kovalam by then (Vijayakumar 1993)

Real development started when Government of India, realizing the potential, decided to develop tourism at Kovalam during mid 1960s. They had earmarked some area for the same. The developmental efforts necessitated rehabilitating some local fisher folk and that evoked unhappiness among them. The area had been used for developing 'enclave tourism'-tourism in a closed environment. A five-star hotel-Ashoka Beach Resort-was set up inside and thus the beach has passed a milestone in the history of its tourism development, which can be compared to the third stage as suggested by Smith. The arrival of Dr.Karan Singh, the then minister for civil aviation in 1972 brought Kovalam into the national attention. Kovalam thus gradually entered into further sages of its growth. Kerala Government has also entered into Kovalam beach area by constructing a Beach resort, Hotel Samudra built by KTDC. Private entrepreneurs rushed into Kovalam with small as well as large establishments. Local bodies and state authorities chalked out development plans during mid 1970s. Significant change happened afterwards and majority of the beach area has been occupied for constructing permanent or temporary business establishments in all scales. Department of Tourism has introduced many infrastructure facilities required meet the requirements of tourism activities at Kovalam (Zero waste, 2001).

One beach in the southern area was previously used as a holy place for the Hindus where they paid tributes to their ancestors by immersing ashes and bones in the sea after the cremation. Due to that, it was known as Avad Thurai'(Vavadu thurai). After the emergence of Kovalam as a beach destination, Europeans used the beach for sunbath, swimming and other tourism activities. Lured by the virgin and enchanting beauty of it- the tropical paradise-, tourists repeatedly visited it and called it Eve's (Hawwa) beach. The tourism at Kovalam has grown dramatically since then and 1980s and early 1990s have witnessed maximum growth in the case of tourist arrivals. Simultaneously, tourism business activities were also increased which led to the increase in construction activities. Arrival of charter flights by 1995 spurred the business initiatives at Kovalam. It has been reported that more than five hundred business establishments are there in the Kovalam Tourist Area (around 2.5 square kilometers) (Zerowaste,2001).

On the Beachfront itself, a wide variety of establishments are there. A survey was done along the Beach to find out the number and types of establishments and it reveals that 352 establishments are there found operational operational, situated from a distance 1 km form the beach. The result is given in table.01 and represented in figure.01. Around 60% of them are situated at a distance less than 500 mts from the beach. The establishments are of different types like hotels, resorts, lodges, home stays, ayurveda massage centers, bakeries, tour operators, travel agents, restaurants, coffee shops, tailors, textiles, handicraft shops, STD/ ISD/Internet centers, guest house, studio, general shops, etc. All such establishments are observed to be generating waste materials and thus contributing towards pollution, in addition to the other forms of impacts. Concentration of buildings is maximum in the beachfront.

Table 1: Establishments in the beachfront at Kovalam

Sl. No.	Type of establishment	Number of establishment
1.	Accommodation establishments	69
2.	Curio shops	57
3.	Tours and travels	19
4.	Refreshment centers (restaurants, coffee shops, etc.)	67
5.	Foreign exchange centres	10
6.	Hospitals	02

7.	Ayurveda/Panchakarma Centres	18
8.	Tailors	19
9.	Textiles	11
10.	Communication centres (STD/ISD/ PCO, Internet Centres)	15
11.	ATMs	04
12.	Shops/Stores	38
13.	Others	23
	Total	352

Source: Field Survey

Among the diverse range of establishments, accommodation and refreshment centers constitute the largest category (20 and 19 percentage respectively). Both those categories of establishments produce waste in a big manner. Ayurveda centers constitute the next highest category. Majority of them are situated very near to the beach and the type of construction vary from one to another. The style of architecture also varies, neither modern nor traditional. It seems that, barring some larger hotels near the beach, the rest lack a planned approach in terms of the style of construction, seems to be built hastily.

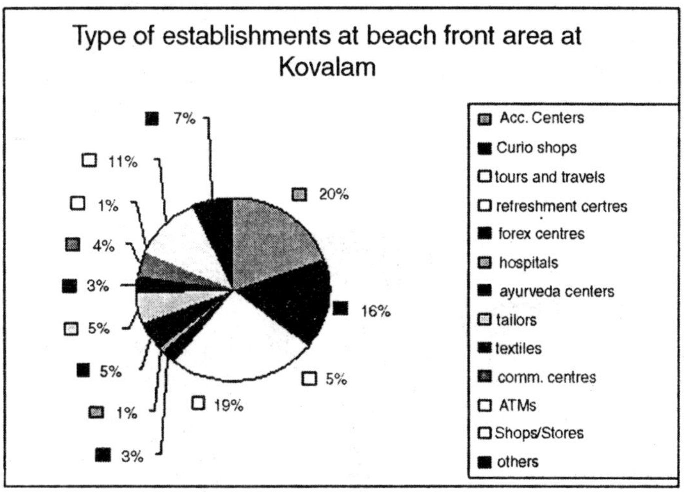

Figure: 1

It is a surprise that the owners and authorities of those establishments do not have any concern about the loss of natural beauty due to the constructions. While enquired about it, they are of the view that the establishments are inevitable there for delivering service to the tourists to cater their needs. Very small space in a building itself has been converted for doing business. An area of just 20 sq.ft would be sufficient enough for a retail outlet. An STD PCO needs lesser space. The height of the buildings is also devoid of aesthetic concern. Many constructions are incomplete structures and strong enough to have further constructions on them. It means that height of the buildings may go up again, which will supplement to the hideousness due to constructions. Overall, the style of construction is also do not follow aesthetic sense.

New constructions on the beach frontage

Beach encroachment is another threat due to the constructions on the beach frontage. It seems that new establishments are competing for occupying more beach space, which resulted in increasing rate of beach encroachment. If the situation persists, the beach will be narrowed, and lesser space will be there for the beach tourism activities. More importantly, fishing activities are still there on almost all the beaches in Koavalam and the beach encroach-ment will pose threat to it too. Currently, a harmonious relationship exists between tourism and fishing activities and the fishing process itself is an attraction for many who visit the beach. Also, walkers on the footpath along the beach coast sometimes face difficulty for smooth movement due to the encroachment into it by the business establishments situated beside it.

Businesses on the beach frontage: disturbance for walkers

To understand about the opinion of the host and visiting population, the tourists as well as members of local community were informally enquired about the loss of natural beauty of Kovalam due to constructions. Tourists (seventy five were surveyed) have wide complaints about beachfront developments and also of the opinion that establishments at the beachfront are one main reason behind the presence of huge amount of waste and litter on the beach. Among the surveyed tourists, 28% were repeat visitors. They are of the opinion that natural beauty is on the decline. They are worried that if the construction activities progress at this pace, the destination will be a common beach and it may not be able to lure many in the future. The rest of them also commented that Kovalam would be incredibly beautiful if the constructions were not there and still they are of the opinion that the natural beauty must be restored. The existing natural beauty of the Kovalam is one main reason why they have visited Kovalam. Around one hundred members of the local community were also discussed about the issue. They were unanimous in their opinion that the beach frontage has been destroyed for construction activities and it is menace in Kovalam. Local community is struggling to buy land due high price. Many of them recollected themselves the memories about Kovalam during 1960s and even before. They said that Kovalam beachfront had no buildings during then, barring one or two. The scenery from the beach was amazing and the beachfront was with rows and rows of green coconut trees interspersed with cliffs or sand forms. Altogether, the beaches were enchanting for any visitor.

The buildings lurking beneath the greenery

Natural beauty might not have been a serious issue when tourism was officially started at Kovalam. Rather, interest would have been to give more facilities to tourists to get maximum enjoyment. It is apparent that, tourism development in India generally does not follow proper research, where as in the international scenario, research is an important predecessor of any development. During 1960s, impact assessment in tourism was rarely done. Also, during then, Tourism was believed as 'non-polluting', 'smokeless' industry with little impacts on society and culture. At Kovalam, the government started the developments in the beach frontage by constructing a conclave tourism centre-ITDC beach resort on the seacoast. Government again continued occupying beach for construction and the second important construction was done by KTDC, a quasi-government establishment. A small portion of beach has been separated by fencing from common usage by the ITDC Ashoka Hotel authorities. That portion was used only for the tourists stayed in the hotel. After the sale of it to a private agency, that continued, though they faced some protests. Private entrepreneurs were latecomers to Kovalam and they only followed the government constructions. Majority of the constructions came up after 1985. The coconut tree laden beachfront has become a concrete jungle in just twenty years.

Superstructure development: a concrete jungle on the rise

New building-Provisions for taller constructions

CRZ (Costal Regulation Zone Government of India) regulations had little influence on the construction activities at Kovalam. Most of the establishments are concentrated in southern beaches (near to Lighthouse) where a large number of establishments are located on both sides of small crisscross pocket roads leading from the beach. Recent reports say that the construction activities continue without much difficulty. A study report says that in Kerala, tourism activities contributed more than 28% of the CRZ violations occurred in Kerala with 26% of violations falling in the No Development Zone (NDZ) (Nandakumar & Muralikrishnan, 1999). It is six years old figures and the situation will be lesser than that. Leela Kovalam Beach Resort (former ITDC-Ashoka Beach Resort), a famous national brand hotel is also continuing constructions on the beach frontage, neglecting all restrictions. As discussed earlier, the identified 352 establishments are situated in just a distance from 1 km from the beach and vast majority of them are seen in a distance of less than 500 mts from the beach. The developments on the beachfront is a clear case of violation of CRZ regulations, experts say.

Distant view of developments in a beach frontage at Kovalam

Constructions on beach frontage

Tourist arrival trend to Kovalam marred by unexplainable fluctuations after 1980. But the trend is not at all awful, not showing consistent growth, particularly after 1990. In the year 2000, Kovalam was visited by 44,440 foreign tourists while the next year only 29,700 tourists arrived. In 2003, more than 42,000 tourists visited Kovalam. (Dept. of Tourism). If we analyze the tourist arrival trends to Kovalam, it can be found that over 15 years, Kovalam has lost the importance as the most important destination in Kerala. In 1988, seventy three percentage of the tourists visited Kerala visited Kovalam, but in 2003, it has declined to 14 percentage. On the positive side, it is good sign that Kerala could diversify the product range. But on the other side, Kovalam has lost its prominence as the most important destination in Kerala (Dileep,2004). Loosing natural beauty might have contributed in the declining of glory of Kovalam. One factor should be kept in mind that there are thousands of beaches in the world, but many are coming to Kovalam from all over the world since Kovalam has some peculiarities, of which the natural beauty is undoubtedly a major factor.

One of the cliffs covered by constructions

Is there any way out?

In the international scenario, the problem of environmental issues due to beach tourism, like in the case of other forms of tourism, was a matter of hot discussion and debate. But still, the scenario continued and still continues in Kovalam. It reveals that physical planning was least bothered aspect during the process of development at Kovalam whereas how to increase the number of tourist arrivals was the sole aim. Recently, Government of Kerala has announced a Special Tourism Zone Act aiming at social, cultural and environmental conservation and preservation at destinations and Kovalam is one destination included in it.

Loss of natural beauty due to buildings

If the rate of construction continues, very soon, Kovalam would not be able to claim itself as a major destination in India, especially in Kerala. The problem of beachfront development at Kovalam should be an eye opener for tourism developments in other beaches in Kerala. Beach at Varkala, which has a different geographical feature, reported to be exceeded the limits. In this circumstance, naturally a question would arise-what could have been done? Things can not changed all of a sudden. But the existing greenery can be preserved to a great extent. There are arguments that if accommodation establishments and others are not there near the beach, it will reduce the level of enjoyment of tourists. But at the same time it has to be noted that the enjoyment opportunity is provided at the cost of its future. Also, the modern tourists won't demand the authorities and developers to cut down trees and build a concrete jungle.

A review of regulations followed in some parts of the world would reveal some factors to minimize beachfront development and aesthetic pollution almost to nil. Some destinations do not allow constructions near the beach, up to 500 metres or even more. In some destinations, regulations have been introduced to restrict the constructions to a height not greater than that of the palm trees. Mauritius is an example of it. (Cooper.et.al. 2000). In certain other areas, only small temporary structures are allowed near the beach. This may not require cutting down of trees and vegetation near the beach. All such efforts will prevent aesthetic loss due to constructions and aesthetic/visual pollution substantially.

A stream to beach carrying pollutants

But, it has to be noted that such issues are site specific and measures have to be chalked out at the destination/site level. Establishing of a large shopping area/complex could have made some difference since majority of the centers near are basically shopping related. The beach frontage has already occupied for business, but, better late than never, different departments under the government and local bodies have to act together for finding out solutions for the situation at Kovalam. Certain activities have to be urgently followed, like, prevention of further constructions, identification of an area for shopping malls, imposing need for registration (fact is that only less than 25% of the centres in the tourism area are registered with concerned authorities), chalking out laws and regulations to prevent constructions, undertaking researches and studies, developing strategies, plans and policies, involve representatives of all stakeholders in decision making, monitor progress periodically, etc. More importantly, let the local community and the entrepreneurs understand that the beachfront developments lead to loss of natural beauty that will eventually result in loss of charm of the destination to attract tourists. Already the issue has been highlighted by a few dailies and the government, with the help of local self-government agencies, have come up to prevent further constructions. But, difference can be made only if strong and integrated approach has been taken. If a destination dies in a short span of time, it will pose more issues for the society in and around it.

According to Oram (1999), an integrated coastal zone management and tourism development is more beneficial if it is done in the early stages of evolution of the beach as a tourism destination. He has described four types of management strategies to mitigate the coastal developmental issues. The are: Regulatory Management strategies-the most traditional and common strategies used to manage and mitigate beach front developments; Physical Management strategies- another kind by which, instead of heavy and high rise and permanent buildings, small and temporary structures can be developed; Economic Management Strategies- which can be imposed like heavy taxation, license fee, etc; and Educational Management Strategies, which can be practiced by which voluntary behaviour can be encouraged. Awareness programmes, literature, seminars, instructions can be organized for creating awareness about the issue related to beachfront development. In Kovalam, the destination is in the last stages of development life cycle, as discussed early, has been converted into an urban like area and hence, immediate measures are required to be implemented. Urgently, further construction activities have to stopped. Unregistered constructions can be demolished since it may not pose any legal problems. Apart from those, physical, economic, regulatory and educational management strategies have to formulated and followed for the future.

CONCLUSION

World over, good beaches are major tourism destinations and as a consequence, tourism and corresponding developmental activities along the coastal lines are creating different types of environmental impacts. Of which, beachfront developments and consequent loss of natural beauty is an important one, though not given due share. India has a number of fine beaches and among them, Kovalam occupies a prominent position. Intensive tourism activities were started only forty years back, but, within this period, it is fast becoming a concrete jungle. A study has undertaken to examine the situation at Kovalam. It reveals that more than three hundred establishments are found operational at the time of the survey, in a distance less than one kilometer from the beach. Of those, majority is situated close to the beach, in distcance less than 500 metres. CRZ regulations hardly influenced the construction activities at Kovalam. All establishments, particularly hotels and restaurants, produce waste in a big manner.

Beach encroachment is another problem identified, since many entrepreneurs are competing to occupy more space on the beach. The constructions on the beachfront do not follow any aesthetic pattern. Due to the constructions on the beach frontage, the natural beauty of the destination that was and is the most fundamental component of Kovalam's attraction is on the decline in a serious manner. The tourists as well as local community have complaints about the loss of natural beauty of the destination. The tourist arrival figures also do not show a consistent growth pattern; instead the statistics reveal that Kovalam is loosing its position as the most important destination in Kerala. The case of Kovalam should be an eye opener for beach tourism developments in other parts of the country and many measures can be taken, including imposing rules and regulations, undertaking awareness programmes, etc. to prevent beachfront developments and loss of natural beauty of the destination.

REFERENCES

- Aguilo E, Alegre J and Sard M, 2005, The persistence of the Sun and Sand Tourism model, Tourism Management, 26, pp219-31
- Chawla R, 2004, Coastal Tourism and Development, Sonali Publicatiions, New Delhi.
- Cooper C, Fletcher J, Gilbert D and Wanhill S, 2000, Tourism Principles and Practices, II edition, Longman, Esex, England.
- Department of Tourism, Government of Kerala, Various Publications including annual statistics, Thiruvananthapuram.
- Dileep M R, 2004, Kovalam Struggling, A study on current tourism scenario at Kovalam, SAJOPS, 5(1).
- Equations, 2003,Eeighing the GATS on a development scale: The case of Tourism in Goa, Equations, Bangalore.
- Frater Alexander, 1990, Chasing the Monsoon, Viking Books India, New Delhi.
- Gartner C N, 1996, Tourism Development: Principles, pProcesses, and Policies, Van Nonstrand Reinhold, New York.
- Herold E, Garcia R and Demoya T, 2001, Female Tourists and Beach boys: Romance or Sex Tourism, 28, 4, pp 978-97.
- Holloway JC, 1994, The Business of Tourism, III Edition, Longman, Essex, England.
- Jennings S, 2004, Coastal Tourism and Shoreline Management, Annals of Tourism research, 31, 4, pp 899-222
- John J P, 2000 Australia, Environmental aesthetics, in Jafari J, (C.Ed.), Encyclopedia of Tourism, Rutledge, London.
- Lonely planet, Kerala, 2000, Lonely planet publishers, Australia.
- Mogan R, 1999, A novel, user based rating system for tourist beaches, Tourism Management, 20, 1999, pp 393-410.
- Nandakumar D and Muralikrishnan M, 1999, Mapping to Extend of Coastal Regulation Zone Violations of the India Coast, National Fish Workers Forum, Thiruvananthapuram.
- Newsome D, Moore AS, and Dowling KR, 2006, Natural Area Tourism, Ecology, Impacts and Management, Viva Books, New Delhi.
- Orams M, 1999, Marine Tourism, development, impacts and management, Routledge, Newyork, pp9)
- Smith R, 1991, beach resorts: A model of development and evolution, land scape and urban planning, 21: 189-210)

- Vijayakumar, B, 1993, Impacts of Tourism at Kovalam, Mphil Thesis, Unpublished, Kerala University, Thiruvananthapuram.
- Whyte PR, 2004, The Beach is a Liminal space, in Hall CM, et.al, A Companion to Tourism, Blackwell Publishing, UK.
- Wilson D, 1996, Paradoxes of Tourism in Goa, Annals of Tourism Research, 24, (1), pp 52-75.).
- Zero Waste, 2001, Zerowaste at Kovalam-draft report, Thanal and Greenpeace, Thiruvananthapuram.

11

Impact of Tourism Industry on Environment

Dr. S.husain ashraf (Reader)
Department of Commerce
Aligarh Muslim University
Aligarh

Travel, from the very beginning of history has-had a fascination for man. The urge to know the unknown, to discover new strange places, to seek change of environment and to achieve new experiences, inspired mankind to move from one place to another place. Most of the travels in the past were almost unplanned, having not much significance, but as civilization developed and moved further, conscious trends began to invade the world. Infact, the history of civilization is a rather chronological account of tribes and class leaving the land of their forefathers and going in search of new horizon.

Though the concept of travel is very old, the term 'Tourism' as we know or mean it today is of relatively modern origin, just five or six decades old. Industria-lization have created great pressure in present human life; speed, stress and strain have made it more necessary for people to relax and refresh their body and mind. Speedy means of transport and communication have made travel an easy affair. Prosperity, leisure, improved education, technological and scientific advancement coupled with the quest for pleasure and recreation are major motivations for travel.

The whole concept of pleasure travel has changed quite drastically during the past thirty years. Tourism in pre war day was only for more affluent, leisured and well-educated people who were content to enjoy scenery, art, culture and flavour of different lands. This concept was however replaced by something totally different from earlier concept. Today, tourists have very different ideas about travel. He comes from a wider social set-up and his tastes, desires are much more varied.

Today tourism is a big business. It has become a major worldwide industry and is expected to show continued strong growth. In the past two decades international tourist arrivals grew nearly three fold, and international tourists receipts rose from approximately us $ 22 billion in 1970 to about US $ 600 billion in 2000. If domestic tourism and travel were included, these figures would be much higher. According to a study carried out for American express travel, travel and tourism accounted for a sell of about US $ 1916 billion in 1987, making it the largest source of employment in the world. Over the last two decades, the bulk of tourism went to Western Europe, North

America and East Asia. The Mediterranean region accounted for an average of 36 percent of international.*

Tourism expenditure as a contribution to gross domestic product (GDP) varies widely from one country to another depending on the size of the economy and land of expenditure, but it contributes over 13 percent to the global GDP. Tourism industry with US $ 3,300 billion is also the largest employer with direct employment to 262 million, constituting 10.5 percent of global work force. What is more, in coming future global travel and tourism revenue is expected to increase to $6.3 trillion in the next decade. Even in India, the tourism industry's foreign exchange earnings are worth around 3.2 billion*. This clearly reflects the level of prosperity the world has reached where leisure becomes the priority. All this seems difficult for any sector to occupy such a key slot in the world economy, which will remain same in the coming millennium.

ENVIRONMENT - THE MEDIUM OF SURVIVAL

Environment may be defined as the sum total of all conditions and influences that affect the development and life of all organs. The human environment consists of physical, biological and social influences. Environment may also be defined the sum of substances and forces external to the organism in such a manner that it affects the organism's survival. Since man's life is regulated by air, land, water, flora and fauna, they automatically becomes the constituents of man's environment. This environment is in a continuing state of change. Environment would include not only the immediate surrounding but also a variety of matters connected with the human activity and its impact on natural sources. Like other animals, men depend on environment and become an important environmental factor with respect to other members in an eco-system.*

People have always cared about the environment, though their perception of environment issues and their attitudes have involved over the centuries. In the earlier part of this century environmentalism was essentially synonymous with wildlife conservation and considered to be the domain of prescient and often privileged few. Since the 1960s, environmentalism has become a movement with widespread popular support and an extensive range of interests. The United Nations Conference on the Human Environment convened in Stockholm in 1972 was a turning point in history of environmental awareness. Growing public pressure, backed by scientific finding in the late 1960s and early 1970s on the pollutants and environmental degradation, stimulate the necessary political will. The debate that took place in the early 1970s, based essentially on air and water pollution, brought home the fact that environmental degradation is caused not only by industrialization but by the poverty and lack of development. The environment movement has since become concerned with all aspects of the natural environment: land, water, minerals, living organisms, life process, the atmosphere, climate, polar ice-caps, remote ocean deeps, and even outer space.

So, the environment is a complicated dynamic system, with many interacting components. Our knowledge of these components, of the interactions between them, and of the relationship between people, resources, environment and development has undergone profound evolution over the past two decades. We now realize that unless development is guided by environmental, social, cultural and ethical consideration, much of it will continue to have undesired effects, to provide reduced benefits or even fail together. Such 'unsuitable' development will only exacerbate the environmental problems that already exist.

Recent years have seen the development of another phase of the environment movement. This is characterized by the concern evinced by some important, complex, and widespread problems, and by the organization taking place on a national and international scale around these issues. Examples are acid rain, the disposal of hazardous wastes, global warming, loss of biodiversity, depletion of the ozone layer, marine pollution, deforestation and the interaction between peace, security and environment.

Our ever-increasing demands and unprecedented progress of science and technology has brought about great changes in the natural environment. A multinational survey of public and leadership perception of environmental issues covering 14 countries - Argentina, China, Hungary, India, Jamaica, Japan, Kenya, Mexico, Nigeria, Norway, Saudi Arabia, Senegal, West Germany and Zimbabwe - showed a remarkable agreement between the public and leadership about the state of the environment, which shows that it is getting worst 'day by day.* Effective action on these environmental issues requires a wide range of skills considerable academic knowledge on the part of those involved; an ability to organize activities in the often widely-separated areas in which issue surface; political skill to deal with the government, industries, special interest groups and individuals who play major role in such issues; and an ability. To communicate with and through the media about these issues.

At last we can say that environment is a medium of survival because all living organism are dependent for their survival on the environment. All our basic necessities like air, water food and shelters are received from environment. It is the duty of the present generation to maintain the whole soreness of environment for the prosperity, generation after generation. All human beings have an equal right to live in a clean and healthy environment. The environment health will reflect the quality of life on this planet.

RELATIONSHIP BETWEEN TOURISM AND ENVIRONMENT

The relationship between tourism and environment is one of a delicate balance between development and safeguarding the environment. One of the elements of tourism is scenic beauty, which is a part and parcel of natural environment. More and more tourist get attracted to the place where they can have some natural things to explore like mountains, forest, wild life, sea beaches, desert etc. Also, influx of tourist is more at those places where the environment is clean and preserved in its natural form.

Burdened by foreign debt and desperate for hard currency, many developing countries have, however, shrugged off their worries that tourism could degrade the natural environment the beautiful resource that makes them attractive. These shortsighted policies have, in fact, and led to a marked degradation of the environment in some countries, which now keeps many tourists away. It would take years and massive financial resource to redress this degradation and reaccelerate tourism again.

On the other hand, in today's world of environmental awareness, environment also gets benefited from tourism. Efforts have been made in many countries to establish and-or develop protected areas to save wild life and environment. Many wild life sanctuaries and national parks raise funds through tourism for their protection and development.

So, the tourism and environment are both interrelated and can contribute to each other. Environment got appreciation through tourism and tourism is enjoyed by masses because of environment. We can say that environment is one of the important raw materials of tourism industry, without which it cannot produce a good product.

FORMS OF TOURISM DIRECTLY RELATED TO PHYSICAL ENVIRONMENT

Although whole of the tourism phenomenon is based on the physical environment but there are some specific forms of tourism which are directly related to natural environment. Some of them are:

1. Adventure Tourism

Refers to tourist activity which involve a certain element of physical challenge and sometimes danger. It includes such activities as trekking and mountain climbing, white water rafting and camping safaris. Stringent environmental controls need to be applied for these activities in environmentally sensitive areas such as trekking and climbing on mountains and scuba diving on coral reefs.

2. Ecotourism

Refers to ecologically based tourism which is a form of specialized nature tourism that emphasizes small scale operations of tours to natural areas and many include visits to place like wild life sanctuaries, national parks, mountains, forest, etc. Emphasis is placed on environmentally sensitive development and visitors use.

3. Water Transport Tourism

Refers to boat travel on rivers, canals and lakes as well as larger sea-going cruise ship travel. Yachting is also a type of water transport tourism.

4. Camping and Caravan Tourism

Refers to provision of camping grounds and caravan parks for use by tourists traveling through or staying in the area. Caravans (also called Recreational Vehicles-RVs) are small mobile homes used for recreational travel. Camping grounds and caravan parks need to be carefully located; with suitable layout in attractive environmental settings, and provided with adequate infrastructure

5. Farm and Rural Tourism

Refers to functioning farms (or ranches or plantations) that supplement their income with some form of tourism business usually providing accommodation, meals and the opportunity for learning about farm activities.

PHYSICAL IMPACT OF TOURISM

The physical impact of tourism may be subsumed under the category of environmental impacts.

Studies on physical impacts of tourism have followed two main lines of enquiry; studies on physical impacts which are reviewed as they relate to different environment types, e.g. coastal areas, mountain regions, oceanic island, and studies which are based on identification of certain resource requirements and environmental impact common to all ecosystem, e.g. water and energy resources, atmosphere, etc.

In the wake of tourist activities distinctive ecosystems mountains, coastlines and oceanic island develop environmental problems specific to their characteristics. Mountains, for example, exhibit low resilience to mass tourism, problems of landslides, rock falls, destruction of vegetation and wildlife with alterations in the physical structure. Coast lines develop a peculiar morphology based on linear development parallel to the coast and problems of sewage, pollution of beaches, disfigurement of coastlines, erosion of dunes and unaesthetic construction of buildings on soft landscape. However, others argue that management can lead not only to conservation of Natural beauty and wildlife but also enhance environmental quality.

Strain on infrastructural facilities have been reported for urban centres. These centres suffer from loss of residential amenities to locals through conversion of residential apartments to hotels, traffic congestion, lack of parking space, and strain on urban infrastructure, e.g. sewage disposal and water supply.

Problems of noise, litter, and increased erosion from overuse of paths and trails also characterize rural centres which are open to tourism. There are additional conflicting situations arising from both tourism and agriculture being land and labour intensive. Increased competition for land and labour, damages of vegetation, harassment to livestock have been reported by a number of researchers.

Tourism's impacts often are categorized using groups like "direct" and "indirect" or "on-site" and "off-site". Using the latter groups, some on-site impacts include:

- Soil erosion and compaction;
- Disturbance of wildlife;
- Trampling of vegetation (or coral in the case of marine tourism);
- Removal of vegetation (e.g. collection of plants or firewood) ;
- Accidental introduction of exotic species;
- Increased frequency of fire; and

- Litter and vandalism.

Some off-site impacts include:

- Reclamation of land for infrastructure(e.g., coastal hotels for marine tourism);
- Water and air population; and
- Purchase of souvenirs utilizing threatened or endangered species (e.g. black coral).

ANALYSIS

While tourism is universally hailed as the most desirable activity, the world of scholars raised eyebrows. A few call it good, many denounce it bad, often ugly. Negative impact of tourism are invariably linked up with mass concentration of visitors at particular time and space. But all environment are not alike. Some have resilience to absorb activity, others are only too fragile to accommodate minor disturbances. Much can be said on the type of activity and the use-pattern and management of resources. All do agree that wholesome management of resources results in positive effects, though such a situation is hard to achieve. Economics of tourism, more often than not, overrides other considerations of pith and marrow, resulting in resource damage at the end, which may be irreparable lose in many cases of sensitive or unique ecosystems. By its very nature tourism is said to be self-destructive. This is more true for developing countries like India where economic wellbeing is preferred to action against pollution because it costs or may be lack of prophylactic attitude of the planners and the developers.

Mostly economists has seen the 'good' and 'worthwhile' in tourism, as it earn foreign exchange, creates employment opportunities, improves infrastructure, diversifies economy, improves standards of living of the hosting communities besides patching up regional disparity. Example of positive impacts on environment can be cited from backward areas and mountain regions abounding in scenic resources. Haryana in India is the living example where marshes and barren wasteland were converted into tourism scenes'. Apart from this tourism can be a means of supporting the conservation of natural areas and increasing environmental awareness among residents and tourists.

With this seemingly bright side of the coin, scholars argue that the other face is less then good. Some social scientists and geographers have tried to study the precise adverse impact on some destination and they have commented that over crowding, traffic snarl, congestion and space misuse or overuse have been due to unguarded and badly planned tourism. Environmentalists are more loud in their attack, a sort of 'Green Mafia'.

According to the above discussion we can say that, tourism industry has both type of impacts on physical environment i.e, positive as well as negative. Negative impacts are in the form of increased carrying capacity resulting in deterioration of the place, careless attitude of tourists about the site and its environment, threat to the destination's flora and fauna, waste disposal problem, disturbance in the natural habitat of animals because of craze among the tourists to buy things which are made from different endangered species of plants and animals etc.

On the other hand tourism also has some positive impacts an natural environment, they are in the form of conservation of national parks and - wildlife sanctuaries through the revenue generated by tourism, enhancement of scenic environment at different places of tourist interest by planting trees etc. making the environment of the tourist place-clean and green as the tourist will prefer to have these qualities at the site etc.

Although the tourism had both negative and positive impacts on environment, but due to lack of proper planning and management, the negative impact is more. But we can't say that tourism is bound to influence environment negatively. It can have more positive environmental impact, provided, there should be an efficient planning and management of tourism projects. Other reason of increased negative impacts is the lack of awareness among the tourists and local people about the environment. This problem c an also be solved by educating tourists and local people about environmentally sound tourism development in the region. This way positive impacts of tourism on environment negative impacts can be reduced to minimum.

In the end we can say that there is nothing good or bad, it is the planner and developers that make it so. There are many example of good tourism development in India and overseas- and bad tourism is in abundance. Tourism is going to stay with us, critics or no critics. More thing of nature would be in high demand. Protect and preserve them for tourism and from tourism. The planners have an obligation to the present generation and to posterity- perhaps they would need these assets more then we do as the supply would be scarce. The prime task is to organise our natural resources for our present need and for tomorrow. Once we have an inventory of these resources then alone we can think of creating 'tourism zone'. Admittedly we cannot give tourists all our environments which may be too precious or ecologically too sensitive. Some zones have to be protected and preserved, may be for future use or for 'no tourism', because we cannot sacrifice our environment on the altar of tourism. So, the need of the hour is "environment friendly tourism development".

REFERENCES

- Tolba, Mostafa K., "Saving our planet-challenges and hopes" (Chapman & Hall), P. 170.
- Magnet (Internet Magazine), January, 2001.
- Datt, Mridula Narayan, "Ecology and Tourism" , (Universal Publishers Distributors), P. 4.
- Tolba, Mostafa K., "saving our planet-challenges and hopes" (Chapman & Hall), P. 225.
- Lindberg, Kreg & McKercher, Bob, "Ecotourism: A Critical Overview," (Cognizant Comm. Corp.) P. 71.
- Singh, Tej Vir, "Tourism Recreation Research, "Vol. X, No . 1, P. 3.

12

Impact of High Occupancies on Waste Management - A Concern for Hotel Housekeepers

Dr. Mohinder Chand, Reader
Department of Tourism Management, Kurukshetra University, Kurukshetra - Haryana
E-mail: mohinderchand@rediffmail.com
Ashish Dahiya
Lecturer, Hotel Management - Birla Institute of Technology, Mesra Ranchi - India. Ph- 0651 2275648, Fax - 2275401, Cell- 09431175462
e-mail: adahiya@bitmesra.ac.in
Lata S Patil
Vice Principal, Bharati Vidya Peeth's College of Hotel & Tourism Management, Belapur, Navi Mumbai - Maharashtra
E-mail: lataspatil@yahoo.com

ABSTRACT

Today, hospitality industry has recognized as a socio-economic instrument for the development of a nation. Its contribution has been appreciated by the various countries irrespective of their size and structure at global level. The Government of India has accorded hospitality the status of "high priority industry" to enable sustainable development of the sector. Hospitality industry include hotels, motels, way side amenities, restaurants, beach, hill and desert resorts, heritage properties and other kind of tourist complexes which provide accommodation for or cater to the food requirements of both domestic and foreign tourists. It has been experienced that increase in tourism activity triggers hotel room sales. In fact, room sale is directly proportional to increase in hotel revenue that is why maximum hotels as part of their expansion & growth pay emphasis on maximising hotel room sales so as to earn more profits. Many times occupancy levels go as higher as 150% or even more. Thus, in the process of achieving higher occupancy staffs are being provided both training & extra incentives to achieve the targets. However, hotel management often forgets to pay attention on the carrying capacity. Therefore, one common problem which is being faced by the housekeepers' remains unattended is the concern of solid waste management. The waste in hotel is in terms of solid, liquid & gaseous. Recognising these vary facts an attempt has been made to examine the impact of high occupancies on materials & waste management in selected hotels in the context of hotel housekeepers.

Keywords: Housekeeper, Hotel, Solid Waste Management, Plastic Toiletries, Room Occupancy.

INTRODUCTION

In 2005, the Indian hospitality industry experienced tremendous growth over the preview years in terms of hotel occupancy, ARR's and hotel rooms. The industry is a significant growth area employing over 12 million people accounting for 8.5% of the total workforce. There are more than 3.50 lac catering outlets in the country serving over

Table 1: Projected accommodation requirement during the Xth plan (2002-2007)

Catogories	2002	2003	2003	2005	2006	2007
Five star	26,347	27,807	29,617	31,497	33,567	42,197
Four-star	8,551	8,841	9,171	9,541	9,951	11,611
Three-star	22,783	24,443	26,353	28,543	31,063	40,783
One-& Two star	22,342	23,092	23,992	25,072	26,312	30,902
Haritage class	2,124	3,624	5,694	7,754	10,014	19,454
Total	82,147	88,107	04,027	102,407	110,007	114,917
Rcoms						

15-20 million meals a year and earning more than 5 millions every year (2005).

Sources: Ministry of Tourism, Government of India, 2005.

Till the end of March 2002, there were over 1,570 hotels (1-star to 5-star category only) comprising 82,147 rooms spread across India. This is an abysmal figure for a country of India's size and population. About 70 per cent of these rooms are in the 3- to 5-star deluxe category hotels, out of which 32 per cent of the rooms comprise 5-star and 5-star deluxe hotels; 38 per cent for 3- and 4-star hotels; and the rest 30 per cent constitute the remaining 1 and 2-star and heritage hotels. Looking at the above statistics we can estimate the solid waste disposal from the hotel rooms itself. As the no of guest supplies are on a higher end in three stars & above hotels the total solid resulting from rooms thus would be more. Looking at the potential of tourism, there will be a manifold requirement of hotel rooms. Demand for rooms might grow at approximately 18 per cent across the country in 2003/04 (according to HVS estimates) and is growing at 15-20 per cent in the current fiscal. It is estimated that another 65,000-80,000 rooms will be added across the country, to be able to meet the increase in demand. Preliminary data indicates that, at best, there are currently only 35,000-40,000 rooms expected to enter the market in the next five years under different stages of planning and construction. (2004, HVS). Thus, the problem of solid waste disposal is going to be increased proportionally.

In fact, hotel industry consumes a vast range of goods in construction and operation. They generally use huge amounts of energy, consume large amounts of water and generate disproportionate amounts of waste. Hotels are fortunate in that there are many things they can do within existing hotel operations, often at little or no cost, that will save them money both in the short and long term. If a hotel that is minimising its energy and water consumption, if it is making efficient use of resources and reducing waste without compromising on quality or standard of service, it will increase the competitiveness of the hotel business. Moreover, so along with their own responsibility to the environment, they are well positioned to encourage others-including their suppliers and business partners - to do the same. Therefore, hotels can play a formidable role for change towards sustainable development. The range of goods used by the hotel industry is vast and covers most of the manufacturing base of an economy from building materials to furniture and fittings. Hotels also use full range of professional services from advertising agents to merchant banks and communicate via diverse media. This interdependence with so many other businesses gives hotels a unique opportunity to challenge business partners to help in environmental mission and to look at how they might change their own activities to be more environmentally conscious. It is vital that hotels make their customers aware of their schemes and educate them to (seek cooperation) co-operate with hotels in their initiatives (2003). By spreading the word they can influence their competitors. However, caution need to be exercised in reviewing the 'green initiatives' taken 'yesterday' are still remaining green even 'today'. For example: the harmful effects of propellants used in spray cans were not known till very recently (ozone depletion). Therefore one has to keep abreast of the new and emerging environmental challenges and maintains flexibility in mending the ways of environmental protection. A number of leading hotels in India has launched proactive programs to improve the environmental performance of their products, processes, services, and facilities. However, challenges faced by the hotels include (1) gauging their performance against others within their industry and (2) identifying solid waste management efficiency improvement opportunities. But such initiatives have not been much publicised, may be due to the high level of competition in this sector. According to the survey of HVS, some of the international chain of hotels operating in India does not even have an environmental policy in place while their counterparts in other countries are known for their green image. However, of late, the scenario in India is rapidly changing for better, as the local and global environmental pressures are becoming increasingly evident. Indian hotel industry is just beginning to realise that energy and environmental management is the cutting edge strategies for their business profitability. This can be illustrated with an example, the environmental initiatives of Maurya Sheraton (The Welcome Group of Hotels) have been paid off when the US President preferred the most environment friendly Hotel in the capital, i.e., Maurya Sheraton, during his recent visit (March, 2000) to India. Today, hospitality industry, with the establishment of International Standards for Environmental Management i.e., EMS, ISO 14001, is taking advantage of implementing these standards that are comparable across the world. Thus, hotels have recognized as a formidable force in influencing a substantial and diverse body of people by challenging the suppliers about the environmental impact of their goods and services and by asking if there might be alternatives. Moreover, the more hotels demand environmentally friendly goods, the greater the market will be and cheaper the goods will become to obtain which would be good news for everyone as well as for the environment (FHRAI, 2004).

Therefore, for the housekeeping department of hotels, waste can be divided into four major identifiable categories.

- Plastic toiletries-such as shampoo bottles, bath foam bottles, combs, shower caps, toothbrushes, and toothpaste tubes.
- Unused portions of soap.
- Slippers
- Newspapers.

Besides the above cited categories there are other types of solid waste which needs proper planning and strategy such as shown in the table 1 resulting from Hotels.

Table 1: Various Solid Wastes Resulting from Hotels

Various Solid Wastes Resulting from Hotels

Description	*Area Found*
Placemats	Coffee Shop/ Room Service Pantry
Used Stationery	Offices, Guest Rooms
Glass Covers	Guest Rooms, Offices
Coasters	Offices, Banquets/ Guest Rooms
Bubble Bath Bottle	Guest Rooms, Suites
Shampoo Bottle	Guest Rooms, Suites
Moisturizer Bottle	Guest Rooms, Suites
Loofah	Guest Rooms, Suites
Used Match Box	Guest Rooms, Suites,
Facial Tissues	Bar, Banquets
Ear Buds	Rooms, Public Cloakrooms
Cotton Buds	Cloak Rooms, Rooms
Used Comb	Guest Rooms, Suites
Comb Case	Cloak rooms, Guest Rooms, Suites
Tooth Brush	Guest Rooms, Suites
Used Paste	Changing Rooms, Guest Rooms,
Dental Kit Cover	Suites, Guest Rooms
Stitching Kit Cover	Guest Rooms, Suites
Hotel Info Cards	Guest Rooms, Suites
Shaving Razor	Lobby, Guest Rooms, Suites

Shaving cream	Guest Rooms, Suites
Shaving Kit cover	Guest Rooms, Suites
WC Band	Guest Rooms, Suites
News Papers	Guest Rooms, Suites,
Magazaines	Cloak Rooms
Packing Material	Offices, Guest Rooms, Suites
Glass Bottles	Offices, Guest Rooms, Suites
Laundry Bags	Restaurant, Banquet,
Plastic Bottles	Guest Rooms,Bar, Banquet, Rooms, Room Service
Shoe Bags	Guest Rooms, Suites
Shoe Shine	Bar,Coffee Shop,Guest Room, Suites
Broken Glasses	Guest Rooms, Suites
Food Packaging	Guest Rooms, Suites
Aluminum Foils	Bar, Banquet,Guest Rooms, Suites
Dried Flowers	Pantry, Room Service, rooms
Twigs n Leaves	Pantry, Room Service, Restaurant
Cola Cans	Rooms, Lobby, Cloak Rooms
Paper Cups	Flower Room, Garden
Pen/ Pencils	Rooms, Room Service
Printed Matter	Staff Cafeteria
Others	Rooms & Offices

Review of Literature

Today, hoteliers are more conscious about the environment not only to protect itself from the government laws but to attract the clients and compete in the international volatile hospitality marketplace. The concern about waste management in the hospitality industry goes back to the 1980,s however, after the Rio Earth Summit in 1992 hoteliers have become increasingly proactive in environmental protection. The trend has changed when the Prince of Wales participated in the International Hotels Environmental Initiative (IHEI) in 1993 all over the world. In 1993 Eleven international hotel chains consented to cooperate and initiated the development of a manual to embrace a comprehensive campaign to advance environmental performance in the hotel industry Regionally, the Asian Pacific Rim echoed this global initiative and organized the Asia Pacific Environmental Initiative, consisting of 16 hotel groups to further drive the environmental movement (Mackie, 1994). In the same year, the Hotel &Catering Institute Management Association participated in Green Globe (1994), which was established by the World Travel and Tourism Council. Subsequently, environmental protection has been continuously addressed and has increasingly attracted notable public attention.

In the advanced countries, concern about solid waste management grew significantly in the early 1990s. Particularly, the "garbage crisis" was raised as an issue by trade journals in 1990 and 1991 (Crosby, 1990; Foss, 1990; Hasek, 1991; King, 1991; Townsend, 1990). To cope with this, trade associations began to develop resource packages about solid waste management and published monthly articles on this topic (Crosby, 1990). Published articles in this period emphasized the environmental movement and approaches taken by the hotels and catering operations in order to address the solid waste problem (Shanklin, Petrillose, & Pettay, 1991). Scholars claimed that the government and the private sector should be more concerned about the shortage of landfills and thus should act more proactively to solve the problem (Cummings & Cummings, 1991; Environmental Protection Agency, 1989; Schwartz &Miller, 1991).

Cummings (1992) stated that despite a trend towards recycling in last few years our modern society still continues to generate huge quantities of waste. We have to recognise that waste management is not simply a matter of disposing unwanted & sometimes hazardous output and it is important that we differentiate between waste minimisation & waste management must be given the highest priority because not only does it conserve resources but also can save considerable amount of hotel's money.

Pettay, (1992) studied the type and volume of waste generated by hotels but the study evaluated only two selected hotel properties in the process The following year, future research directions for "green" hotels were proposed (Nicholls&Nystuen, 1993; Shanklin, 1993), and a case study on solid waste minimization practices was subsequently undertaken in amegaresort (Cummings, 1997). Many researchers have also conducted related studies to addressed the estimation and the environmental accounting of municipal solid waste (Chan & Lam, 2001) and assessed the waste generated in foodservice operations (Wie & Shanklin, 2001) and environmental tactics (Revilla, Dodd, & Hoover, 2001)'.(Wilco Chan & Kevin Wong 2003). These studied have pointed out that there is a dire need for waste management in the hotel industry so that they may meet the environmental norms. As for as India is concerned no such study has been conducted except the few steps have been taken by hoteliers in context to suitability & environmental concern such as Uppal's Orchid - Ecotel Hotels have been striving for excellence in this field. Indian Hotel Company - Taj Group of Hotels is paying considerable attention on recycling of Paper. The stationery including the visiting cards of Executives of Taj Group is of recycled eco-friendly paper.

Recognizing these very facts the present study has been conducted on the topic "impact of high occupancies on materials & waste management in selected hotels in the context of hotel housekeepers".

Research Objectives

The study is based on the following objectives:

- To provide a review of key concepts and issues related to solid waste management in Indian hotel industry,
- To study the impact of solid waste on room Occupancy in the selected hotels,

- To suggest remedies for improvement of solid waste management in the selected hotels in particular and other hotels in general.

Research Methodology

Paper focuses on studying the impact of higher room Occupancy on solid waste management in the selected hotels as a new approach for controlling the room occupancy. The data have been collected through an interview method comprising a questionnaire of 17 questions. 5 about demographic profile of respondents and 12 about the impact of high room occupancy on solid waste management practices. The variables have been selected on the basis of review of previous literature. The sampling method was convenient which was designed in such a way that it would give an appropriate representation to the study. Of 45 respondents approached and interviewed only 30 (66.67%) respondents provided complete information.

For the present study five star deluxe, five star and four star hotels were selected located in major cities. These hotels were selected as they account for 75% of the market share in India. Respondents in this study were asked to rate the importance of each of the 12 solid waste management variables on a 5-point Likert scale ranging from 'not at all, minimally, moderately, significantly and substantially. Mean and standard deviation statistical tools were used for analysis and interpretation of data.

Results and Discussion

Survey responses asserted that the solid waste management issues are pivotal significant for any managerial decision in the hotel industry therefore every employee should take their responsibilities seriously. Study indicated that while improvements were always being discussed with the hotels, there was a need for better supervision of the hotels and routine meetings. The importance of the Eco-Hotel Rating Program for the hotel's public relations and to help the hotels become more aware of the need to protect natural resources was emphasised. Table 2 shows the mean of Amounts of waste produced per room/guest is 4.22 with a confidence interval of 65%. The mean weight was based on information available from the experienced housekeeping staff. It is therefore suggested that more attention should be paid to the recycling of various types of plastic materials. For instance, the installation of lotion dispensers could be an alternative. Also, the selling of newspapers to waste collectors for recycling should be promoted, and the return of soap remains to special collectors should be considered. The Amounts of waste produced per room/guest, Solid waste production (segregation), Use of chemicals (housekeeping) were a common problem. There were differences between the actual operations, standard operating procedures, and the responsibilities outlined in the policy document. However, according to the standard operating procedures, there were clear-cut that the hotel should follow the guidelines. Moreover, the standard operating procedures highlighted the importance of separating waste produced per room/guest from other waste for safety reasons. In practice, hotels kept waste separated but did not use the categories of waste described in the standard operating procedures. Many managers stated that they used special bins with different colours for paper, metal, glass and plastic waste when waste was sold directly to waste dealers. However, that degree of waste recycled very from hotel to hotel depending on the policy of that hotel. Since ihe hotel staff did not have proper procedures and equipment for keeping the waste separated, it seemed pointless for the hotels to continue separating waste into different types of recyclables.

The table indicates that the mean value of Solid waste disposal comparatively very high followed by current performance of the hotel concerning with waste management practices. Regarding the question that occupancy rate has any impact on the solid waste management more than 70 per cent respondents agreed that huge solid wastage was due to higher occupancy. Even the quality of room was considered affected by this variable.

68 % respondents said that the proper place is needed to be redesigned with separate compartments for the different materials; however, 30 % respondents did not think that compartments on the waste would work well. It would be difficult for the hotels to consider alternative systems for waste separation and collection because the existing practices are different in all hotels. The dumping of waste on the floor and the tearing of plastic bags made picking up waste from the hotels more time consuming. Possible causes of the problems were identified to be a communication gap between hotel managers, engineering and stewards and the lack of staff appointed by the hotel to ensure that proper separation of wet and dry waste occurred. It was also stated that hotel managers knew about the problem but did not do anything about it. In the hotel's evaluation of the program, it said that the reason why hotel waste was getting mixed was because hotel employees did not care about or did not understand how to do reduce, reuse, recycling and source separation. It was common for hotels to run out of bins for wet waste because bins would get broken and then not get replaced. The hotels would then place the wet waste in plastic bags or use dry waste bins for wet waste. At least one of these plastic bags would break every day because the plastic bags were not strong enough for the weight of the wet waste. It would take a lot of time to clean up the garbage from the floor. The shortage of bins would also result in the mixing of wet and dry waste.

Thus, the results show that the higher room occupancy has a profound impact on the solid waste management practices in the selected hotels. The study also highlighted that the involvement of housekeeping staff is very pertinent to achieve the Organisational goals.

Table 2: Waste Management Practices in the Sample Hotels

Variables	Actual operations producers (mean)	Standard operations producers (mean)
Amounts of waste produced per room /guest	4.22	.876
Amounts of waste recycled	4.32	.853
Amounts of residual waste	4.21	.826
Amounts of liquid waste	4.09	.697

Solid waste disposal	4.43	.723
Solid waste production(segregation)	4.07	.944
Use of chemicals (housekeeping)	4.22	.876
Solid waste disposal	4.33	.807
Past performance of hotel	4.32	.853
Occupancy rate,	4.21	.826
Number of rooms available	4.09	.697
Number of guests and staff, types of guest rooms	4.17	.890

Table 3: Waste Management Practices - Hotels Monitoring Quantitative Performance

Variables	Actual operations producers (mean)	Standard operations producers (mean)
Amounts of waste produced per room/guest	3.21	3.76
Amounts of waste recycled	2.32	3.02
Amounts of residual waste	4.60	3.87
Amounts of liquid waste	3.76	2.98
Solid waste disposal	3.02	2.86
Solid waste production(segregation)	2.34	3.65
Use of chemicals (housekeeping)	4.33	4.67
Current performance of hotel	4.51	3.76
Past performance of hotel	3,59	3.50
Pccupancy rate,	2.43	3.54
Number of rooms available	3.18	3.76
Number of guests and staff, types of guest rooms		

The results demonstrate that the housekeeping department provides various types of facilities to the guests which have profound impact on environment. On the other hand laundry system can consume large quantities of energy and water, a regular guest-room can generate various kinds of solid waste, and the air ventilation system can affect the guest room's indoor air quality. Therefore, the housekeeping should run its operations in such a way as to reduce consumption of energy and water, recycle and reduce solid waste, reuse recycled materials, revise purchasing procedures and freshen guest-rooms' indoor air quality. Moreover, housekeeping can influence the success of a hotel's solid waste management programme because guest-rooms and guest corridors consume more than 23 per cent of the hotel. With an effective solid waste management programme, which includes employee education and training, housekeeping staff can reduce energy consumption as part of their daily routines. The study also demonstrates that housekeeping department should have proper segregation, recycling and waste disposal procedures to protect environment and reduce operating expenses

Finally, the discussion revealed the following initiative taken by the hotel housekeepers in the industry with relation to the solid waste management

Solid Waste Management Initiatives

- Bed linen/towels are reused for making dusters, face cloths, scarves, swab cloths, waiter clothes etc.
- Segregation system of wet and dry garbage is adopted for recycling, reuse & recover the waste Left out cooked oil is sold for manufacturing soap
- Old carpets are reused as far as possible otherwise sold to the scrap contractor. Wherever possible, reduce, reuse, and recycle waste is adopted for food, plastic, water or any waste material.
- Bed linen/towels are given to orphanage/ used as discard for cleaning
- Segregation is done by the type and sold for recycling
- Reverse side of the paper are used for photocopying and envelopes are reused in internal office communication
- Soap cakes once used by guests are used in Laundry / housekeeping
- Left out unused fruits are turned in to salads and purees

Other Initiatives

- More than 90% of bulbs used in the hotel are energy efficient such as CFL, Fluorescent.
- Timers switch on/off street/neon lights.
- VFD is installed for soft starter.
- Double speed motors installed for improved working and energy efficiency
- Capacitor Bank & BMS are installed to conserve energy.
- Economisers are used in the boiler to recover the heat from the hot exit gas, which is used for preheating the water fed to boiler.
- Solar energy is used for terrace lighting.
- Urinal sensors installed in public toilets to conserve water (30% reduction in total water usage).
- Taps with aerators are installed conserving 40% of total water usag.
- Drip irrigation method is adopted for gardening W/C Flush of 6.5 litres used against normal usage of 8 - 10 litres flushing

- Energy cards are placed in the guestrooms and energy conservation training's are conducted for the staff.
- Bulbs used in the hotel are energy efficient bulbs such as CFL, Fluorescent.
- Road lights, Public area and corridor lighting have centralised on/off control operated by photocell.
- Economisers are used in the boiler to recover the heat from the hot exit gas, which is used for preheating the water fed to boiler.
- Orifice is provided in each water outlet to monitor the water usage.
- Using both sides of paper for internal communication to save a few trees.
- Judicious use of light and other forms of electricity so as to reduce energy consumption thereby reducing dependence on fossil fuels and other energy sources.
- Helping our people understand dire need to use water in the right quantity and avoiding wastage.
- Wherever possible substituting cloth for paper and adhering to usage of handmade paper.

Conclusion and Suggestions

The finding of the study should be interpreted with caution, given the study's limitations. In particular, it is a single study, therefore the perception scale used in this study need further development and testing. The study also encountered the problems associated with responses provided bye respondents and small sample size. However, this study provides a framework for developing system pertaining to solid waste management in the selected sample hotels in India. In fact, in the hospitality industry, the complexity of issues associated with solid waste management makes solid waste planning and management a challenging task for the housekeeper. The findings of the study helps to clarify the problem situation by providing a description of the various solid waste management variables and issues involved with implementation of solid management practices and the housekeeper's role in the sample hotels. Further, the study demonstrated how a housekeeper acted as the facilitator between waste producers and waste haulers, helping to ensure that waste reduction, collection, recycling and disposal was conducted in an acceptable way through the development of contracts, standard operating procedures, record keeping and evaluation mechanisms. Thus, the impact of high occupancies on materials & waste management in selected hotels may sustainably minimise by enhancing the proactive role of hotel housekeepers.

Based on the results obtained in the present study, the following strategies have been recommended:

- The involvement of housekeeping staff is very pertinent to achieve the organisational goals of minimizing the waste management.

- Development of solid waste management awareness programmes for both staff and guests.
- More active role of top management is the essential ingredient for the effective and extensive solid waste management practices.
- Introduction of solid waste management award scheme \ accreditation scheme and solid waste audit.
- Hotels should focus on environment-friendly image and highly professional management.
- Government should formulate clear laws and incentives programmes to promote solid waste management practices.
- Training and partnership programs would help organisations share experiences and lessons learned as they develop and implement their solid waste management practices.

REFERENCES

- India, Travel and Tourism - Forging Ahead, 2004 Travel and Tourism Economic Research, World Travel and Tourism Council, 2004
- Industry Overview: Tourism- 2004 Integrated Databases India Limited, Ref: website:
- Manav Thadani, Managing Director and Deepika Malkani, (Editors) Hotels in India - Trends and Opportunity, - HVS International, New Delhi / November 2004.
- Incredible India, Department of Tourism E- News Letter, Tourism Statistics, 2003
- Indian Hotel Industry Survey 2003-2004, HVS International, Federation of Hotel and Restaurants Association of India and CNN.
- Hotel Industry Trends, 2005, Ministry of Tourism Govt. of India, New Delhi.
- D.M. Upasni and Ms Lynn Wilson, a Case study of The Orchid, Mumbai, India, Hospitality Rating: 5-STAR # Rooms: 245, Architect: (USA) - HVS ECO Services. , 2003.
- Inderjeet Singh and Axel Michaelowa, Indian Urban Building Sector: CDM Potential through Energy Efficiency in Electricity Consumption -; HWWA Discussion Paper 289, Hamburgisches Welt-Wirtschafts-Archiv (HWWA), Hamburg Institute of International Economics, 2004.
- Manav Thadani and Deepika Malkan (2004) Hotels in India - Trends and Opportunity; - HVS International, New Delhi.)
- A Business Guide for Reducing Waste, EPA/530—K-92-004, U.S. EPA, Office of Solid Waste, 401 M Street SW, Washington, DC 20460, 713-941-4452.
- Business Recycling Manual, Resource Systems, Inc. and INFORM, Inc., 381 Park Avenue S., New York, NY 10016-8806, 212-689-4040.

- Hammer, M. S. And Townsend, J. M., *Eco-Purchasing in Hotels and Motels.* Florida Energy Extension Service, Institute of Food and Agricultural Sciences, University of Florida, Gainesville, FL 32611.2002.
- Hotels - CO2 Emissions Trends - Internal Communications, IRADe, 2005.
- Climate Change and Hotel Industry - Opportunities for CDM Projects. Workshop Proceedings, Goa, 18 June 2005 (IRADe).
- Environmental systems Branch Development Alternatives B-32, Tara Crescent Qutab Institutional Area New Delhi - 110016 Website: www.devalt.org.
- Cleaner Practices for Environmental Management in Indian Hotel industry (2000) Development Alternatives, New Delhi.
- Environmental Management for Hotels, The Industry Guide to Best Practices (1996) International Hotel Environment Initiatives (UK).

Waste reduction in hotels and motels -A Guide For Hotel and Motel Managers,Georgia Hospitality Environmental Partnership ,The University of Georgia, March, 1996.

13

GATS and Trade in Tourism Services-Implications for India

Manjula Chaudhary
Professor
Department of Tourism and Hotel Management
Kurukshetra University

ABSTRACT

GATS (General Agreement on Trade in Services) is the first multilateral trade agreement covering the services including tourism. Its implications for tourism are being debated on different forums since the beginning of GATS. Like all other services covered under GATS, opening of trade in tourism too has its advocates and critics. While its proponents are counting its merits to forward the case of opening of international markets the opponents are criticizing it for ignoring human rights and environmental issues. Countries heavily dependent on tourism have been watching the developments very carefully and have been forwarding their concerns. India has not yet raised these issues effectively as it has done for agriculture subsidies and TRIPS. But the pace at which tourism has been growing in the country in the past few years, its implications shall be felt sooner. GATS impacts will be reflected in international tourism as well as in huge domestic tourism operations.This paper provides an outline of GATS, its legal principles and explains the concerns of parties involved in its implementation. Furthermore, it considers the case with special reference to India.

Key Words: GATS, Tourism, Opening of Markets, Indian Tourism

INTRODUCTION

Tourism is a an important economic activity that alongwith travel related services accounts for about 11 percent of World GDP, 7.9 percent of world export earnings and 7.8 percent of global employment. Traditionally it is dominated by the northern countries that are main tourism generators/receivers and earners/spenders. Lately Asia Pacific is emerging as an important tourism generating and receiving region. It is one of the oldest areas of economic activity covered under the WTO's (World Trade Organization) General Agreement on Trade in Services (GATS). In 1994, when services were negotiated for the first time in international trade agreements, 119 out of 127 countries agreed to liberalise tourism and tourism-related services. There was no other service sector in which countries made as many commitments as in tourism. Developing countries especially opened up Hotels und Restaurants to foreign investors. In view of its importance WTO held a symposium in Feb 2001 to discuss issues of tourism and GATS. And in the further rounds of negotiations more commitments are expected to be signed.

Objectives

The objective of this paper is to explain how are the existing commitments and future negotiations going to impact tourism? Why developing countries are getting increasingly skeptical as more understanding is being developed? Why are some countries insistent on pushing it fast?

Framework of GATS

An understanding of general framework of GATS and its applicability in tourism gives insight into the above issues. GATS provides a detailed framework for the international trade in services. This includes modes of services and the different types of commitments to be made for the regulation of these services. It also provides for preparedness of developing countries where certain exemptions may be given as well as countries can also choose the commitments to be signed.

GATS recognizes four modes for the supply of services in international trade.

Mode 1: Cross-border supply of services; Mode 2: Consumption abroad; Mode 3: Commercial presence; Mode 4. Temporary movement of natural persons.

A country's obligations under GATS can be divided under two headings: (1) General obligations and (2) Specific Commitments. General obligations apply directly and automatically to all members and services sectors. Under these members are required to accord (a) Most Favoured Nation Treatment (Art II) to all the WTO members (a country has to extend immediately and unconditionally to services or service suppliers of all members treatment no less favourable than that accorded to like services and suppliers of any other country) and maintain (b)Transparency which requires members to publish all measures of general application and respond to other members' queries. Specific commitments are commitments laid down in individual country schedules and concern specifically designated sectors.

The scope of these commitments may vary across countries and sectors. Specific commitments concern (a) Market Access (Art XVI) which states that 'members give no less favourable treatment to the services and service suppliers of other members than is provided in its schedule of commitments' and (b) National Treatment (Art XVII) which implies that members do not discriminate between foreign and domestic services or suppliers. Art XVI specifies the following six measures affecting free market access that may not be applied to foreign services or suppliers unless they are clearly specified in the schedule – limitations on (1) the number of service suppliers (2) the total value of services transactions or assets (3) the number of services operations or the total quantity of service output(4) the number of persons that may be employed in a particular sector or by a particular sector (5) measur that restrict or require supply of the service through specific types of legal entity or joi venture (6) percentage of participation of foreign capital or total value of foreign investme (www.wto.org).

Tourism Activities under four Modes of Supply

Tourism activities fall under all the four modes of supply but mode 2 and 3 accou for major share of tourism business.

Mode 1: Cross-border supply of services; It includes travel consultation throug traditional and electronic channels. India is developing as an important centre fc outsourcing that includes travel too.

Mode 2: Consumption abroad; all international tourism comes under this categor where tourists cross national boundaries to consume services. It is most important form c trade in tourism and accounted for 783 million tourists and USD 623 billion in 2004. I India it was worth USD 3 billion and 2.3 million people.

Mode 3: Commercial presence; international service providers sell tourism services b establishing presence in different countries. Hotels, Travel agencies all set up bases i different countries to sell their services.

Mode 4. Temporary movement of natural persons; People or service performers trav to different countries to seek employment.

Tourism Regulation under the GATS framework

WTO classification of tourism as a service sector under GATS is relatively narrow an implies that other service activities such as transport, business, distribution and recreationa services, which are directly or indirectly linked to tourism, are not considered to be touris services for the purposes of international trade. There is virtually no single services are that is not either directly or indirectly linked to trade in tourism services. The effect c GATS liberalisation in this area is thus likely to be broader than if one was only considerin the current commitments in "tourism and travel related services".

The World Trade Organization/General Agreement on Trade in Services (WTO/GATS lists the tourism industry under the category "Tourism and Travel Related Service"

(TTRS). GATS commitments in the tourism sector (sector 9 out of the 12 main GAT sectors) can be divided into four sub sectors (A–D) as indicated below (WTO, 1990):

Sector 9. Tourism and Travel Related Services.

A. Hotels and Restaurants (incl. Catering)

B. Travel Operators and Tour Operators

C. Tourist Guide Services

D. Other

In terms of existing GATS commitments, the first three sub sectors have associated listing under the United Nations' "Provisional Central Product Classification" (CPC) as detailed below.

A. Hotels and restaurants (including catering) (CPC 641-643)

CPC 6411 (Hotel lodging services)

CPC 6412 (Motel lodging services)

CPC 6419 (Other lodging services), the last of which is further separated to include holiday camp services, youth hostels, etc.

CPC 642 (Food serving services)

Restaurant services (CPC 6421),
Self-service facilities (CPC 6422),
Catering services (CPC 6423)
Other (CPC 6429).

The CPC 643 classification (Beverage serving services for consumption on the premises) is composed of

Services without entertainment (CPC 6431) and
Services with entertainment (CPC 6432).

B. Travel agencies and tour operators services (CPC 7471)

C. Tourist guides services (CPC 7472)

D. Other.

Commitments in Tourism under GATS

Countries have signed a large number of commitments regarding their trade regimes or aspects of tourism services within the WTO framework. Yet these commitments are considered limited in scope as is evident from following-

- Tourism services under GATS classifications are "distinctly limited in scope" when compared with the actual range of tourism-related services activities.
- Tourism evidently has a substantially higher level of liberalization than any other GATS sector, with about 120 Members (counting the EC as one), making commitments, full liberalization definitely has yet to be achieved within even this limited classification. At the very least, the WTO obviously has more than 120 Members. Members have made maximum commitments under the Hotels and restaurants sub-category, the number of commitments then begins to fall, with less than 100 commitments under Travel agencies and tour operators; less than 60 commitments under Tourist guides services; and less than 20 commitments under the "Other" sub-category.
- In respect of the four modes of supply under GATS, Tourism is no exception to the general pattern of the highest levels of full market access (i.e. "None", meaning no restrictions entered in the Schedule) being giving to consumption abroad,

followed by significantly lower levels for cross-border supply and commercial presence, with only minimal levels for Mode 4, the movement of natural persons. What is surprising, however, is that even for consumption abroad, that is the right for citizens of a country to travel abroad to consume tourism services, the level of full liberalization never rises above about 80 per cent for any of the four sub-categories (Dale B. Honeck, 2001)

The total number of commitments signed in tourism are 246, with 108,80,45,13 in A, B, C and D categories respectively. The details of these are summarized in the Tables 1,2 and 3 category wise.

Table 1: Category A-Hotels and Restaurants Commitments (108 commitments)

Type of Trade	Barriers to trade	Fully open market access	No restrictions to national treatment
Cross Border Trade	Lack of Technical feasibility	42 (39%)	50 (46%)
Consumption abroad	Hard currency regulations	98 (90%)	95 (88%)
Commercial presence	Licensing, non-automatic approval, registration, permit.Economic needs test - 9 countries. On the type of entry: joint ventures, incorporation, branches. Requirement for foreign capital equity ranging from 30% to 51%. Differential taxes, the requirement to employ a certain number of nationals or provide training for them, availability of work permit or prior residency.	75 (69%)	89 (82%)
Movement of natural persons	Nationality, citizenship or residency. More favourable treatment is accorded to topmanagement or specialists, if their entry is related to the commercial presence.	9 (8%)	29 (27%)

Source: UNCTAD. TD/B/COM.1/EM.6/2

Table 2: Category B-Travel Agencies and Tour Operators services (80 commitments)

Type of Trade	Barriers to trade	Fully open market access	No restrictions to national treatment
Cross Border Trade	Commercial presence necessary	44 (55%)	50 (63%)

Consumption abroad		66 (82%)	66 (82%)
Commercial presence	Economic needs test. Number of foreign travel agencies allowed fixed as a share of domesticagencies or below certain number. Operations allowed in the market of inbound passengers. Establishment in a form of joint venture, incorporation, private limited company; branches or subsidiaries not allowed. Limits on foreign equity. Mandated employment of local staff, including on the board of directors. Residency requirement.	44 (55%)	66 (82%)
Movement of natural persons	Nationality, citizenship or residency. More favourable treatment is accorded to topmanagement or specialists.	7 (9%)	16 (20%)

Source: UNCTAD. TD/B/COM.1/EM.6/2

Table 3- Category C & D Tourist Guide services (45 commitments) and other services(13 commitments)

Type of Trade	Barriers to trade	Fully open market access		No restrictions to national treatment	
		Tourist Guide Services	Others	Tourist Guide Services	Others
Cross Border Trade	Lack of Technical feasibility	24 (55%)	25 (56%)	6 (46%)	7 (53%)
Consumption abroad	None	41 (91%)	41 (91%)	12 (92%)	13(100%)
Commercial presence	Non-automatic approval, licence, permit. Establishment as a private limited company. Nationality, residency. Exams, entree fees. Supply of service only through travel agencies.	32 (71%)	36 (80%)	7 (54%)	7 (54%)
Movement of natural persons	Nationality, Preference to top management or specialists.	1 (2%)	8 (18%)	2 (15%)	6 (46%)

Source: UNCTAD. TD/B/COM.1/EM.6/2

GATS Negotiations and Commitments in Future

Future negotiations will move for more commitments from more members and trade under all the modes will see effects of globalization. To assess these implications many factors must be considered and the total impact will depend upon multitude of factors like country's tourism management system, regulatory environment, and government policies. A number of important issues considered restrictive now are expected to come up for discussion. Economic needs test provision and use of other discretionary measures like licensing and authorization for regulating market access will demand improved commitments for creating favourable climate for investment. Access to and provision of tourism-related information with the emphasis on GDSs is another important area as GDSs is dominated by few countries and few corporations. Any restrictive measure for the access of information will be against the spirit of open markets. Developing countries will emphasize the movement of service providers.

In a broader perspective each supply mode has associated benefits and problems. Countries have different strengths under the modes. Developed countries may have edge in the mode 3 whose big corporations will find it easy to open bases in developing world while developing nations have it under mode 4 whose people are ready to migrate to distant lands for better job avenues. All countries will focus on the modes where their strength lies and will ask for larger commitments but at the same time will also calculate the impacts of trade in other modes.

A very important development in this area is adoption of cluster approach. It involves listing all the activities together in a group or cluster that are related to tourism. For example air transportation is one such service that is listed separately under GATS and there are many more. This hinders an appropriate understanding of the impacts of tourism. A system of Tourism Satellite Accounting (TSA) is being developed with the support of UNWTO (World Tourism Organization) and WTTC (World Tourism and Travel Council) as a national accounting tool to better measure the impact of tourism on national economies. The TSA system is now being used as the basis for an Annex on Tourism Services that would group a broader "cluster" of tourism-related services. In addition to the traditional tourism services, this "cluster" approach expands the list to include air, sea, rail and road passenger services, certain financial services, navigational aids and tourism information services (Smithies Richard, 2001, ILO 2001).

When this cluster as an annex will be brought for liberalization, countries will loose the flexibility of existing system where only very narrow range of services are opened.

Criticism of GATS

GATS and its implications are being discussed since inception and some rounds of talks and negotiations in the past ended without any consensus for opposition from member nations. Particularly developing countries have felt that opening of markets will not be good for their economies as their corporations are not yet competitive enough. GATS is often being criticized for not giving full thought to all the implications of its provisions. Some concerns are-

Lack of full Commitment

The move for open trade has been initiated by Northern countries that are not reciprocating equally by opening up their markets to the service exports of Southern untries. Particularly under the mode of 'supply of natural persons' restrictive immigration les exist in developed nations. Southern countries too use barriers of licensing, technical andards setting and grant subsidies for the domestic sectors in tourism.

If governments attempt to control foreign investment in any way, once they had mmitted to GATS they could be legally challenged by investing companies under the ispute settlement procedure within the World Trade Organisation. Consequently vernments could face real difficulties in trying to limit negative environmental, social d cultural impacts in their country. Governments also face difficulties in making the nployment of local workers or the use of local products and materials a condition of foreign vestment. It could also render a government powerless to stop tourism development on digenous land and sacred sites, in response to community protests.

The adoption of broad market access commitments across the tourism sector could ohibit countries from protecting sensitive areas and regulating their use. Limitations on e number of excursions in a sensitive zone or restricting certification and licensing for o-tourism could be illegal under GATS. Adopting national treatment commitments could so make it difficult to pursue many eco-tourism policies, such as those that require local mmunity participation in projects (www.foe.co.uk).

GATS contains general exceptions to the agreement on the basis of the need 'to protect uman, animal or health' (Article XIV). The lack of specific environmental exception may eaken the possibility of a ruling supporting the necessity of regulations to protect the vironment (WWF, 2001, Outreach 1999). A research by Bendell and Font (2004) pointed ree areas where sustainable tourism standards and GATS principles conflict:

- Standards often restrict visitor numbers to environmentally sensitive areas - GATS calls for unrestricted market access and limiting numbers may prevent some companies from operating in an area
- Standards have criteria for using local labour, food and materials, especially in developing countries - GATS requires that local and foreign companies are treated equally.
- Standards require that tourism development is compatible with local culture - GATS states that development should not be discriminated against because of its 'foreign character'.

Mariama Williams (2002) mentions that the direct impacts of the GATS as it relates to urism would include-

- The GATS would allow foreign companies to merge or take over local companies. This is a threat to indigenous-owned and operated sustainable tourism initiatives.
- The GATS would allow upward pressure on the exchange rates with implications for real wages, price of land and other resources as well as for traditional exports such as agriculture, mining and fishing.
- Domestic regulation rules may impact governments' use of taxation policies to prevent de-industrialisation and de-agriculturalization.

- Governments will not be able to mitigate or limit the impact of the outflow of repatriated earnings from FDI, which will result in reduced welfare.
- GATS may also prove detrimental to eco and heritage tourism development.
- The GATS also has serious implication for pro-poor tourism that attempts to generate net benefits to the poor. The core of this strategy is to 'unlock opportunities for the poor with tourism rather than to expand the overall size of the sectors. But this requires domestic regulation to remove some barriers to entry and to enhance their ability to participate effectively in tourism.

Dominance of Developed Countries

Berne declaration quotes examples to raise its concerns about GATS and the different interests of countries. The developing countries are putting their case for the abolition of regulations and in 2000, the United States requested under the WTO the following deregulations:

- Abolition of limitations to the share of foreign firms in a joint venture.
- Abolition of restrictions with regard to the sale or renting of property
- Abolition of the requirements of Economic Needs Tests
- Abolition of the imperative to collaborate with a local partner.
- Abolition of local players' access to government programmes or tax incentives
- Abolition of the imperative to employ local personnel
- Abolition of limitations to the repatriation of profits

According to the EU, the following regulations currently in place should also be abolished:

- Jordan requires foreign travel agents to have their tours conducted by local companies.
- Egypt limits the number of hotels and restaurants and demands an economic needs test. Casino services are permitted only in 5-star hotels.
- Barbados charges a special tax on the sale or purchase of land, shares and stocks by foreigners, according to the value of the transaction.

Furthermore, the EU is also trying to abolish restrictions that require foreign companies to collaborate with local partners. However, it is this kind of collaboration in tourism that can significantly increase the local and regional value added. Such regulations are also important in order to make it easier to hold companies accountable in cases of non-compliance. The assets of locally registered companies can be confiscated through local courts, while foreign multinationals are able to easily transfer their assets.

GATS and Tourism in India

Tourism in India is late starter in modern sense and currently accounts for 5.3 % of GDP and 10.3% of its export earnings. It provides employment to 23.7 million people ie.

6% of work force. Currently its international tourism size is small with around 3.5 m people in the current year but its domestic base is huge estimated at 300 million. Outbound too is promising with 5.5 million currently. Sensing its growing weightage in the economy the government increased its Tourism Budget of 110 Cr in 9th plan to 2900 Cr in 10th plan.

Commitments Signed by India in Tourism

India has signed commitments only under A and B categories and none under C and D (WTO,1998). The commitments under A and B category are given in Table 4.

	Limitations on Market Access		Limitations on National Treatment	
Category of tourism Services → / Modes of Trade in Services ↓	A	B	A	B
Cross Border Supply	Unbound	Unbound	Unbound	Unbound
Consumption Abroad	Unbound	Unbound	Unbound	Unbound
Commercial Presence	Only through incorporation with a foreign equity ceiling of 51 per cent	Only through incorporation with a foreign equity ceiling of 51 per cent	None	None
Presence of Natural Persons	Unbound except as indicated in the horizontal section	Unbound except as indicated in the horizontal section	Unbound except as indicated in the horizontal section	Unbound except as indicated in the horizontal section

Source:http://gats-info.eu.int/gats-info/nwtosvc. pl?COUNTRY=India and http://www.wto.org.

Suresh K.T. (2003) says that the examination of Indian commitments in tourism shows that while six possible limitations are possible, India's entry under Mode 3 (commercial presence) shows that it has chosen to invoke only item 6, a limitation on the participation of foreign capital. This could imply that henceforth any regional or local government policy that could limit the number of service suppliers, total value of transaction or assets; the total number of service operations or quantity of service output; the total number of natural persons and require a certain type of legal entity or joint venture can possibly be challenged as violating India's market access commitments. Governments may successfully defend their policies as legitimate but it leaves them open to challenges under the WTO dispute settlement system, which may not be the appropriate body to deal with the pros and cons of democratically evolved domestic policies. It is also important to mention that in the present negotiations the only way forward for India is to either maintain the status quo or remove item 6.

Implications for the Industry

These limitations invoked to regulate the market access may not be very useful. The foreign investors will invest within the legal framework but may further aggravate the environmental damage in view of existing violation of Coastal Regulatory Zones, Environment Protection Act and Environment Impact Assessment by tourism industry (Christine Pluss and Mariane Hochuli, n.d.). And in future more commitments for greater liberalization will be on WTO agenda. GATS guidelines may not support the regulatory system in the country. India is going for empowerment of local bodies and any commitment in tourism may require large-scale consultation with local bodies that have encouraged community participation in tourism.

The fact that the GATS also applies at the local level causes serious setbacks to important processes of decentralisation under way in a number of countries. In India, for example, such a process that is to grant more competence to local self-governments found entrance into the constitution only in 1992:Now that we have for a short time been learning to establish democracy at community level, these processes are endangered by the multi-lateral GATS agreement, which will have impacts even at the local level (Suresh K T, 2003).

CONCLUSION

Following inferences can be made from the above arguments:

Tourism in India can no longer be sidelined and this is supported by its increased contribution to economy. It has large domestic base and its international tourism is growing fast. This makes for a fit case to consider GATS vertical commitments seriously so that domestic preparedness can be made well in advance.

Even with commitments signed only in A and B category the limitation is only one and it opens Indian market for commercial presence. The other regulatory measures used for curtailing this access in the name of environment, local or human considerations shall be subject to dispute settlement with WTO. And it might be very difficult to defend the country's logic. So limitations shall be used as allowable than not using these and later contending cases for other regulatory mechanisms.

Further negotiations will bring more commitments for signing and may be the annex through cluster approach. India shall study all the impacts in tourism very carefully as it has done for other areas in Doha round.

Sooner or later world will become an open market place and only through judicious and balanced approach by making its industry competitive on the one hand and on another adopting cautious approach during negotiations, can give India an advantage. As put by Soloman Ranjan (N.D.)- A number of factors have to be balanced in WTO's *"Liberalization with a human face"* and UNWTO's *"Travel and transport from the imaginary of Jules Verne to 21st century reality"*.

REFERENCES

- Angela Kalisch. Report Tourism as Fair Trade - NGO Perspectives. In bulletin of Tourism Concern's Fair Trade in Tourism Network, Issue 3, Winter 2001/Spring 2002. www.tourism concern.org Accessed 30.11.06
- Bendell J. and Font X. (2004). Which tourism rules? Green standards and GATS'. *Annals of Tourism Research.* 31/1. id21 Research Highlight, 6th February 2005.www.id21.org
- *Briefing GATS primar* (Nov 2002). www.foe.co.uk
- Christine Pluss and Mariane Hochuli. Perspectives on Tourism: Tourism and GATS- GATS Dilemma in the web of Tourism. Eqations. Banglore,India.
- Dale B. Honeck. *Overview of GATS Disciplines and Commitments. Symposium on Tourism Services.* 22-23 February, 2001. World Trade Organization, Geneva. www.wto.org
- IATA (1999). Liberalisation of Air Transport and the GATS. www.iata.org Accessed 2.12.06
- ILO(2001 April). Human resources development, employment and globalization in the hotel, catering and tourism sector. www.ilo.org Accessed 1.12.06
- Mariama Williams (2002, April). General Agreement on Trade in Services. Tourism Liberalization, Gender and the Gats. International Gender Trade Network. Economic Literacy Series.
- Outreach (1999, April 21). GATS undermines sustainable development in tourism.V4(9).
- Position paper by the Berne Declaration and the Working Group on Tourism and Development, Switzerland on the World Trade Organization's Policy of Liberalising the Tourism Sector. www.evb.ch Accessed 1.12.06
- Ranjan Soloman (n.d.). Tourism-A challenge for the 21st century. www.travelwirenews.com/articles. Accessed 12.1.06

- Smithies Richard (2001), *Airline views on the proposed tourism annex to the GATS*, WTO/OMC symposium on Tourism Services. Geneva, 22-23 February 2001.)
- Suresh K T (2003,Feb). Interrogating the GATS from an Environment Perspective: The case of tourism. GBER Vol. 3 No. 3 pp 6 - 14.
- UNCTAD secretariat (1998, April 8) International Trade in Tourism-Related Services: Issues and Options for Developing Countries. TD/B/COM.1/EM.6/2
- WTO (1990, October 23). second Secretariat paper, "Classification of Tourism-Related Services", MTN.GNS/TOUR/W/1/Rev. 1.
- WTO (1998,Sep 23). Tourism Services. S/C/W/51. Background note by Secretariat. www.wto.org Accessed 19.12.06 www.wto.org
- WWF International (2001). *GATS and Responsible Tourism-Policy statement.* Sep 2001.

14

Environmental Impacts of Tourism: Global Perspective

Dr. Vinay Chauhan (Sr. Lecturer) and Suvidha Khanna (JRF),
Centre for Hospitality and Tourism Management, Faculty of Management Studies, University Of Jammu, J&K.

ABSTRACT

The rapid development of tourism all over the world, has led lots of the people and environmentalist more and more concerned about impact of tourism on environment. Infact, the degree and intensity of the impact depends upon the level of the contact between tourist and host, the stage through which the destination is passing through, type of tourism, seasonality, degree of local control over the industry, type and scale of the development, specific activities undertaken at the destination, characteristics of the destination area etc.

Realizing the significance of the environment for tourism, an effort is made to conduct a research in terms of understanding relationship between tourism and environment. The study also examines the impacts of tourism on the environment in global perspectives. Finally study suggests some of the strategic options as to how tourism can be used as a tool for conservation.

The study points out that environment whether natural or man-made is an essential component of tourism. The study highlights various conservation and preservation strategies, these include - integration of tourism into overall policy for sustainable development, focusing on Environmental Impact Assessment (EIA), strategic management of tourism development having partnership and pro-active initiatives by Industry, regular monitoring, technological adoptions and practicing appropriate compliance mechanisms. The study also highlights conditions for success such as involvement of stakeholders, information exchange and Capacity Building

Key words: Tourism, Environment, Impacts and conservation strategies.

I. INTRODUCTION

Tourism industry has attained prestigious position owing to its rapid and spectacular growth over the last few decades, and today it has been recognized as a significant factor in the economy of many nations especially in the developing countries like India. However, ironically the rapid growth and development of tourism in the 20th century has produced both problems and opportunities and its impact has been seen both positive as well as negative. The pressures placed upon the destination areas have raised and the consequent effects are apparent. (France,L.,(1997). This problem is much serious as on today, because this problem started as early as 1960s Christaller(1964) has mentioned about expending peripheries as holidaymakers began to travel further afield.

Although it is not possible to develop tourism without incurring environmental impacts, but it is possible with efficacious planning to manage tourism development in order to minimize the negative impacts and encouraging positive impacts. The expansion of tourism mostly leaves behind a trail of litter and destroys the fragile forest habitat and wildlife. Seasonal influx increases the population and densities resulted in physical congestion in areas like- beaches, ski lopes and historic centers (J.K, Sharma, 2000). Farrell (1999) highlights on sustainable tourism that is conveniently defined as all types of tourism that are compatible with or contribute to sustainable development. Sustainable tourism depends on encouraging the desirable and discouraging the undesirable (Reynolds & Braithwaite, 2001). In fact, impacts of the tourism can be explained as the changes in the destination areas, which occur as a result of industry. These changes can be of various types but generally speaking these impacts can broadly be grouped in to three categories i.e. economical, social and environmental. In reality these can overlap as all these three can occur simultaneously. It is commonly observed that economic impacts are generally positive whereas environmental and social are less desirable. The degree and intensity of the impact depends upon the level of the contact between tourist and host, the stage through which the destination is passing through, type of tourism, seasonality, degree of local control over the industry, local participation, type and scale of the development, specific activities undertaken at the destination, characteristics of the destination area, stage of the development, and the policy context in which tourism occurs. Establishing a nation wide planning process that prevents the destruction of tourism by tourism and protects the environment is still not too late for some Mediterranean countries although the environments of many are already severely damaged. (Karan, French, 2005).

Objectives of the Study

Realizing the significance of the environment on tourism , as it is well said that the means of achieving and maintaining sustainable tourism growth will be challenging of the coming years (Choi & Sirakaya, 2005), an effort is made to conduct a research in terms of understanding relationship between tourism and environment. The study also examines the impacts of tourism on the environment in global perspectives. The research also suggests some of the strategic options as to how tourism can be used as a tool for conservation.

SECTION II
TOURISM AND ENVIRONMENT - RELATIONSHIP

With the rapid development of tourism all over the world, lots of the people and environmentalist are becoming more and more concerned about its impact on environment. International tourism has been going through a phase, in which the opportunities for making quick profits from exploiting what were regarded as freely available natural resources, dazzled the eyes of government and businessmen, as well as many local residents.(Middleton&Hawkins,1998).

The Johannesburg Submit, devoted a separate session to sustainable tourism and consequently, (Buckley, 2003). It should be remarked that this declaration came at a time when the year(2002) had already been declared The International Year of Ecotourism by the United Nations and tourism was getting maximum publicity. PATA and WTO have devoted a full time conference at Bali in 1993, to discuss the relationship between tourism and environment and have laid down some guidelines. Environment today, has acquired a broad definition. It includes not only land, air, water, flora and fauna but also encompasses people their creation, social, economic and cultural conditions that may affect their lives (Learner, S.C., 1997). The environment is an integral part of tourism development, in their improvised state and the community depend on environment for their livelihood and substance, as a result there is a more of extraction than about conserving them for tomorrow, and the result is opposite to the sustainability.(Bansal,S.P, and Gautam, P.,(2005). Tourism receiving environment is the totality of the destinations and includes not only natural or physical components, but also the socio-cultural practices of the indigenous population. Within the total resource are discrete, smaller scale environmental resources, e.g lakes & mountains, which may be affected independently by the tourists- environment interaction (Tiwari,S.P.,1993,pp250-51).

Tourism resources available in the various countries consist of the same time of space, facilities and values. These are resources whose use cannot be left controlled without the risk of their deterioration, or even their destruction. The satisfaction of tourism requirements must not be prejudicial to the social or economic interest of the population in the tourist area, to the environment, or above all to natural resources which are fundamental attraction of tourism, and historical and cultural sites. All tourism resources are part of heritage of mankind.

Environment whether natural or man-made is an essential component of tourism. Modifications are unavoidable if we have to promote and develop tourism, but these modifications should be done aesthetically and without greed applying the principle of conservation. Conservation really means effective use of resources. It implies safeguarding the visual beauty of the countryside. Conservation of wildlife means survival of all living things - flora and fauna, providing them ample space to live, grow and breathe natural air. Environment whether natural or manmade, is the most fundamental ingredient of the tourism product. However, with the tourism activity, the environment is inevitably affected or modified either to facilitate tourism or during the tourism process.

SECTION III
IMPACT OF TOURISM ON ENVIRONMENT- GLOBAL PROSPECTS

Negative impacts from tourism occur when the level of visitor use is greater than the environment's ability to cope with this use within the acceptable limits of change. Uncontrolled conventional tourism poses potential threats to many natural areas around the world such as soil erosion, increased pollution, discharges into the sea, etc. It often puts a strain on water resources, and it can force local populations to compete for the use of critical resources.

Infact, there are three main impact areas: natural resources, pollution, physical impacts.

Some Astonishing Facts about Tourism Impacts :

- In Italy, 80% of the sewage waters from the 120 largest coastal cities gets dumped into the Mediterranean without even being treated
- The Mediterranean waters are recycled only through the Straits of Gibraltar….. Approximately once every 80 years.
- Tourism contributes to 7% of all pollution in the Mediterranean Sea
- Cruise ships in Caribbean produce more than 70,000 tons of waste every year!
- By 2030, Florida will also face other climate change challenges with the potential to affect tourism, including increasing wildfires and the loss of coral reefs due to higher sea temperatures.

In less than 25 years climate change will have a radical impact on the global travel industry, according to the Holiday 2030 report launched by Halifax Travel Insurance.

3.1. Depletion of Natural Resources

Tourism development can put pressure on natural resources when it increases consumption in areas where resources are already scarce.

3.1.1. Water resources

The tourism industry generally overuses water resources for hotels, swimming pools, golf courses and personal use of water by tourists which can result in water shortages and degradation of water supplies, as well as generating a greater volume of waste water.Golf course maintenance can also deplete fresh water resources. An interesting study reveals that An average golf course in a tropical country such as Thailand needs 1500kg of chemical fertilizers, pesticides and herbicides per year and uses as much water as 60,000 rural villagers.(Source: Tourism Concern, www.tourismconcern.org)

3.1.2. Local resources

Tourism can create great pressure on local resources like energy, food, and other raw materials that may already be in short supply. Because of the seasonal character of the industry, many destinations have ten times more inhabitants in the high season as in the low season. A high demand is placed upon these resources to meet the high expectations tourists often have (proper heating, hot water, etc.).

3.1.3. *Land Degradation*

Increased construction of tourism and recreational facilities has increased the pressure on these resources and on scenic landscapes. Forests often suffer negative impacts of tourism in the form of deforestation caused by fuel wood collection and land clearing. For example, one trekking tourist in Nepal - and area already suffering the effects of deforestation - can use four to five kilograms of wood a day.

3.2. Pollution

Tourism can cause the same forms of pollution as any other industry: air emissions, noise, solid waste and littering, releases of sewage, oil and chemicals, even architectural/ visual pollution.

3.2.1. *Air Pollution and Noise*

Transport by air, road, and rail is continuously increasing in response to the rising number of tourists and their greater mobility. One study estimated that a single transatlantic return flight emits almost half the CO2 emissions produced by all other sources (lighting, heating, car use, etc.) consumed by an average person yearly. (Mayer Hillman, Town & Country Planning magazine, September 1996. (Source: MFOE, www.mfoe.u..net.com).

Noise pollution from airplanes, cars, and buses, as well as recreational vehicles such as snowmobiles and jet skis, is an ever-growing problem of modern life. In addition to causing annoyance, stress, and even hearing loss for it humans, it causes distress to wildlife, especially in sensitive areas. For instance, noise generated by snowmobiles can cause animals to alter their natural activity patterns. As per Idaho news, in winter 2000, 76,271 people entered Yellowstone National Park on snowmobiles, outnumbering the 40,727 visitors who came in cars, 10,779 in snow coaches and 512 on skis. A survey of snowmobile impacts on natural sounds at Yellowstone found that snowmobile noise could be heard 70% of the time at 11 of 13 sample sites, and 90% of the time at 8 sites. At the Old Faithful geyser, snowmobiles could be heard 100% of the time during the daytime period studied. Snowmobile noise drowned out even the sound of the geyser erupting. (Source: www.Idahonews.com)

3.2.2. *Solid waste, Littering and Sewage*

In areas with high concentrations of tourist activities and appealing natural attractions, waste disposal is a serious problem and improper disposal can be a major despoiler of the natural environment - rivers, scenic areas, and roadsides. For example, cruise ships in the Caribbean are estimated to produce more than 70,000 tons of waste each year. UNEP magazine for environmentally sustainable development points out that The Wider Caribbean Region, stretching from Florida to French Guiana, receives 63,000 port calls from ships each year, and they generate 82,000 tons of garbage. About 77% of all ship waste comes from cruise vessels. The average cruise ship carries 600 crew members and 1,400 passengers. On average, passengers on a cruise ship each account for 3.5 kilograms of garbage daily - compared with the 0.8 kilograms each generated by the less well-endowed folk on shore. (Source: Our Planet,www.ourplanet.com/imgversn/planethme.html)

Construction of hotels, recreation and other facilities often leads to increased sewage pollution. Sewage runoff causes serious damage to coral reefs because it stimulates the growth of algae, which cover the filter-feeding corals, hindering their ability to survive. Changes in salinity and siltation can have wide-ranging impacts on coastal environments.

3.2.3. Aesthetic Pollution

Often tourism fails to integrate its structures with the natural features and indigenous architectural of the destination. Large, dominating resorts of disparate design can look out of place in any natural environment and may clash with the indigenous structural design. A lack of land-use planning and building regulations in many destinations has facilitated sprawling developments along coastlines, valleys and scenic routes. The sprawl includes tourism facilities themselves and supporting infrastructure such as roads, employee housing, parking, service areas, and waste disposal.

3.3. Physical Impacts

People and planet highlights that In industrial countries, mass tourism and recreation are now fast overtaking the extractive industries as the largest threat to mountain communities and environments. Since 1945, visits to the 10 most popular mountainous national parks in the United States have increased twelve-fold. In the European Alps, tourism now exceeds 100 million visitor-days. Every year in the Indian Himalaya, more than 250,000 Hindu pilgrims, 25,000 trekkers, and 75 mountaineering expeditions climb to the sacred source of the Ganges River, the Gangotri Glacier. They deplete local forests for firewood, trample riparian vegetation, and strew litter. Even worse, this tourism frequently induces poorly planned, land-intensive development.

(Source: People & the Planet, www.peopleandplanet.net)

3.3.1. Physical Impacts of Tourism Development

The development of tourism facilities such as accommodation, water supplies, restaurants and recreation facilities can involve sand mining, beach and sand dune erosion, soil erosion and extensive paving. In addition, road and airport construction can lead to land degradation and loss of wildlife habitats and deterioration of scenery.

In Yosemite National Park (US), for instance, the number of roads and facilities have been increased to keep pace with the growing visitor numbers and to supply amenities, infrastructure and parking lots for all these tourists. These actions have caused habitat loss in the park and are accompanied by various forms of pollution including air pollution from automobile emissions; the Sierra Club has reported "smog so thick that Yosemite Valley could not be seen from airplanes". This occasional smog is harmful to all species and vegetation inside the Park. (Source: Trade and Environment Database, www.american.edu/ projects/mandala TED/yosemite/html)

3.3.2. Depletion of the Ozone Layer

Ozone depleting substances (ODSs) such as CFCs (chlorofluorocarbon) and halons have contributed to the destruction of this layer. The tourism industry may be part of the problem; direct impacts start with the construction of new developments and continue during daily management and operations. Refrigerators, air conditioners and propellants in aerosol spray cans, amongst others, contain ODSs and are widely used in the hotel and tourism industry. Emissions from jet aircraft are also a significant source of ODSs. According to Tourism Concern, scientists predict that by 2015 half of the annual destruction of the ozone layer will be caused by air travel. UNEP's OzonAction Programme works with governments and industries, including the tourism industry, to phase out ODSs and find safer alternatives. UNEP has developed extensive information and guidance on how many types of businesses can eliminate ODSs and contribute to preservation of the ozone layer.

3.3.3. Climate Change

Global tourism is closely linked to climate change. Tourism involves the movement of people from their homes to other destinations and accounts for about 50% of traffic movements; rapidly expanding air traffic contributes about 2.5% of the production of CO_2. Tourism is thus a significant contributor to the increasing concentrations of greenhouse gases in the atmosphere. Air travel itself is a major contributor to the greenhouse effect. Passenger jets are the fastest growing source of greenhouse gas emissions. The number of international travelers is expected to increase from 594 million in 1996 to 1.6 billion by 2020, adding greatly to the problem unless steps are taken to reduce emissions. (Source: WWF)

Tourism not only contributes to climate change, but is affected by it as well. Climate change is likely to increase the severity and frequency of storms and severe weather events, which can have disastrous effects on tourism in the affected regions. Some of the other impacts that the world risks as a result of global warming are drought, diseases and heat waves. Malaria, the world's largest killer, has resurfaced in Spain, and it is estimated that changes in climate will result in parts of the country becoming a suitable habitat for malaria-carrying species of mosquito by the 2020s.

3.3.4. Natural Disasters

Catastrophes like floods, earthquakes, wildfires, volcanoes, avalanches, drought and diseases can have a serious effect on inbound and domestic tourism and thus on local tourism industries. The outbreak of the foot and mouth disease epidemic in England earlier this year (2001), for instance, has severely affected Great Britain's inbound tourism market. A BHA/Barclays Hospitality Business Trends Survey found that 75% of hotels in England, 81% in Scotland and 85% in Wales continued to be affected by the foot and mouth outbreak, and over 60% forecast a decline in business in the June-September 2001 period.

3.3.5. Physical Impacts from Tourist Activities

Trampling Tourists using the same trail over and over again trample the vegetation and soil, eventually causing damage that can lead to loss of biodiversity and other impacts.

Such damage can be even more extensive when visitors frequently stray off established trails. Following table depicts some of the major impacts as caused by tourist activities

Trampling impacts on vegetation	Trampling impacts on soil
Breakage and bruising of stems	Loss of organic matter
Reduced plant vigor	Reduction in soil macro porosity
Reduced regeneration	Decrease in air and water permeability
Loss of ground cover	Increase in run off
Change in species composition	Accelerated erosion

Source: University of Idaho , www.its.uidaho.edu/rrt484/484INTR97/

The example of this is Safaris and wildlife watching activities have a degrading effect on habitat as they often are accompanied by the noise and commotion created by tourists as they chase wild animals in their trucks and aircraft. This puts high pressure on animal habits and behaviors and tends to bring about behavioral changes.

3.3.6. Tourism and Ecological Sensitive Areas

Sensitive areas hold the main assets on which the tourism industry depends, so conservation is a must. UNEP strongly believes that tourism can make a contribution to the protection of sensitive areas through financial contributions, provision of environmental infrastructure, improved management, awareness raising and education, and by the creation of protected areas, national parks, cultural and natural sites. Ecotourism is of special interest to UNEP for its relationship with conservation, sustainability, and biological diversity. As a development tool, ecotourism can advance the three basic goals of the Convention on Biological Diversity *(Source : Convention on Biological Diversity, http://www.biodiv.org/default.shtml)* :

1. Conserve biological (and cultural) diversity, by strengthening protected area management systems (public or private) and increasing the value of sound ecosystems;
2. Promote the sustainable use of biodiversity, by generating income, jobs and business opportunities in ecotourism and related business networks, and
3. Share the benefits of ecotourism developments equitably with local communities and indigenous people, by obtaining their informed consent and full participation in planning and management of ecotourism businesses.

In the field, well-planned and managed ecotourism has proven to be one of the most effective tools for long-term conservation of biodiversity when the right circumstances (such as market feasibility, management capacity at local level, and clear and monitored links between ecotourism development and conservation) are present. On the other hand, tourism has the potential to create beneficial effects on the environment by contributing to environmental protection and conservation. It is a way to raise awareness of environmental values and it can serve as a tool to finance protection of natural areas and increase their economic importance.

3.3.7. Tourism impact on beaches, islands and coastal areas-

Marine ecosystems suffer from the waste disposal by otels, littering by tourists, fuel seepage from ships and other boat traffic. The European marine ecosystem has probably been the worst affected because it is an inland sea, thus it has a longer self-cleaning process due to the limited tide. Out of all the components affected in this ecosystem, coral reefs are the most vulnerable. Reefs can be harmed by trampling from scuba divers and snorkelers, untreated sewage dumped from hotels or the resort cities themselves, and many developing countries use coral for construction of hotels and roads. The biggest driver of development in the European coastal zone in recent years has been tourism. Europe is the world's largest holiday destination, with 60% of international tourists, and business continues to grow, by 3.8 % a year. The greatest activity is along the Mediterranean coastal zone, with France, Spain and Italy receiving respectively 75 million, 59 million and 40 million visitors a year. These represent increases of between 40 and 60% since 1990. France and Spain are the world's top two tourist destinations.As the big resorts of the western Mediterranean fill up, areas to the east are becoming increasingly popular, including the Greek islands, Cyprus and Malta. Malta receives more than a million tourists a year, three times its permanent population.

Tourism is the largest sector of the economy in many coastal zones, and construction of hotels, apartments and other tourist infrastructure is the dominant form of development.

In French coastal regions, tourism provides an estimated 43 % of jobs, generating more revenue than fishing or shipping. This dominance of tourism is reflected in the seasonal changes in population density, with an influx of both tourists & people to work in the tourist industry each summer.

Peak population densities on the Mediterranean coasts of France and Spain reach 2300 people per square kilometre, more than double the winter populations. A further 40 %increase in peak populations is expected in the coming 20 years. (*Source http://reports.eea.europa.eu/state_of_environment_report_2005_1/en)*)

3.3.8. Tourism Impacts on Coral Reefs

Coral reefs are under threat, suffering from decline and degradation due to a combination of natural and anthropogenic factors. The scientific community is in agreement about it and the press talks about it. Fifty-eight percent of the world's reefs are potentially threatened by human activity. Overexploitation and coastal development pose the greatest potential threat *(Source :WRI, Bryant et al. 1998, www.wri.org/indictrs/reepisk.htm)*

Assessments made in late 2000 show that 27% of the world's reefs have been effectively lost, with the largest single cause being the massive climate-related coral bleaching event of 1998. This destroyed about 16% of the coral reefs of the world in 9 months during the largest El Niño and La Niña climate events ever recorded.

(Source: Global Coral Reef Monitoring Network www.gcrmn.org/)

SECTION -IV
CASE STUDIES

4.1. Case study on negative impact of tourism on the ecology of JAMAICA

Jamaica is an island paradise located in the northern Caribbean. It is one of the islands that is visited by hundreds of thousands tourist annually. The main attraction is its natural beauty: sandy beaches, clear water, distinguished wildlife, and, of course, warm climate. Jamaica has been once known as the land of wood and water, and the rich diversity of flora and fauna is still amazing to this day. There are reported to be about 3,000 species of flowering plants alone, 827 of which are not found anywhere else. There are also 25 species and 21 subspecies of birds which are found nowhere else.

Jamaica relies heavily on its tourism industry; however, in the process, ecology of the island is suffering. Every little thing that is done to accommodate tourists sets Jamaica one step back on the environmental scale. This is also due to the fact that there is little done to improve present conditions of the island. The government, in an attempt to encourage tourism investment, has let the hoteliers to keep their money where they want. All of the profit is usually kept in private offshore accounts or invested in other projects overseas. Thus, it is not even certain what percent of the money generated from the industry is put back into the national economy and improvement of the ecology. As a result:-

- The island's visiting population has more than tripled in twenty years – now equal to almost half the size of its native, resident population. An increase in the tourist population of this magnitude poses very similar challenges and problems as any other kind of population increase.
- In addition ,unfavorable conditions, and more pressure caused by constant overuse of these territories by people makes it more damaging to the island and its inhabitants.
- The heavy flow of tourists is also related to the pollution of the environment. The use of airplanes to transport people to and from the island, growing number of vehicles contribute to pollution. Pollution ranges from unclean air to contaminated waters, and, in the case of Jamaica it's both.
- Jamaica's inadequate sewage disposal system has been the cause for worries for some time now, throughout the island.
- The deposits also stimulate the overgrowth of algae that smothers coral reefs. Also, due to the deposits of disposals, there is an increase in nutrients in the water which cause fluctuations in the oxygen supply and distribution. This affects all aquatic life and is a source of various diseases through seafood.
- This pollution has caused Water Shortage.
- The consequences of the sewage disposal system include degradation of coral reefs. Without coral reefs the beaches will disappear as well as supporting fishing, diving, and snorkeling operations, all of which are important assets of tourism industry.

- According to researchers the fish population in the area around the damaged coral reef thinned during the period of two years (the length of observation period).
- Decline in Biodiversity, deforestation and destruction of Ecology.

4.2. Indian Scenario

The main impact of climate change on Goa will result from rising sea levels, with this very flat, low-lying area extremely susceptible to even the smallest rise. By 2030, beach erosion and inundation of shoreline properties is likely to be a real problem. Kerala is also low-lying and susceptible to rising sea levels, and is likely to encounter similar problems, although due to its size less people will be affected. Nevertheless, the coastal zones that support much of the tourist trade will suffer increasingly from beach erosion and inundation in the run-up to 2030 and beyond. Both Goa and Kerala are within the Indian Ocean's cyclone belt, and will be affected by the increase in the number of more powerful cyclones predicted to occur due to climate change; a trend that may already be apparent. This will raise the probability of wind damage and coastal flooding due to storm surges, exacerbating further the problems caused by rising sea levels. Climate change may also result in a more unpredictable Monsoon, leading, on the one hand to severe flooding, and on the other to periods of extended drought, causing water shortages.

4.3. Maldives and Seychelles

The big problem for the Maldives is undoubtedly rising sea levels, with most of the 200 or so inhabited islands rarely rising more than 1 - 2 m above sea level. By 2030 sea-level rise will certainly have caused major beach erosion, and at worst may have started to submerge substantial areas of the islands. Salt-water intrusion of aquifers is likely to make individual islands uninhabitable, while the loss of coral reefs due to rising sea temperatures will mean the death of dive tourism. By the end of the century, the Maldives could be largely submerged and uninhabited, and their tourist industry destroyed. Loss of its beaches and coral reefs will also take a serious toll on tourism in the Seychelles, but the higher topography - up to 900 m in places - will at least ensure that the country does not vanish beneath the waves.

The changing impact of the tourist trade could have a marked impact on local and global economies. The industry represents 3.6 per cent of the planet's total GDP, in 2005 was estimated to employ 243.4 million people, providing 8.7% of the world's employment.

SECTION V
CONSERVATION AND PRESERVATION STRATEGIES

As environmental degradation has been increasing due to human use and misuse, it is imperative for the present generation to identify those activities, which are environment friendly besides being economically and cultural viable.(Bansal,S., 2003)Sustainable development and eco tourism has been proved a great success in this direction, to an extent that Rose and wall has mentioned ecotourism as a potential strategy to support conservation of natural ecosystems, while at same time promoting sustainable development(Rose and Wall,1999). Some of the strategic interventions that can be applied in tourism are discussed as under.

Integration of Tourism into Overall Policy for Sustainable Development

A. National Strategies: Ensure that tourism is balanced with broader economic, social and environmental objectives at national and local level by setting out a national tourism strategy that is based on knowledge of environmental and biodiversity resources, and is integrated with national and regional sustainable development plans.
   - Establish a national tourism strategy that is updated periodically and a master plan for tourism development and management.
   - Integrate conservation of environmental and biodiversity resources into strategies and plans.
   - Enhance prospects for economic development and employment while maintaining protection of the environment.

B. Interagency Coordination and Cooperation: Improve the management and development of tourism by ensuring coordination and cooperation between the different agencies, authorities and organisations concerned at all levels, and that their jurisdictions and responsibilities are clearly defined and complement each other.
   - Strengthen the coordination of tourism policy, planning development and management at both national and local levels.
   - Ensure that all stakeholders, including government agencies and local planning authorities, are involved in the development and implementation of tourism.

Development of Sustainable Tourism:

A. Environmental Impact Assessment (EIA): Anticipate environmental impacts by undertaking comprehensive EIAs for all tourism development programmes taking into account cumulative effects from multiple development activities of all types.
   - Examine impacts at the regional national and local levels.
   - Adopt or amend legislation to ensure that EIAs and the planning process take account of regional factors, if necessary.
   - Ensure that project proposals respond to regional development plans and guidelines for sustainable development.

B. Legislation & Standards: Sustainable tourism should be supported with following standards
   (i) Legislative Framework: Support implementation of sustainable tourism through an effective legislative framework that establishes standards for land use in tourism development, tourism facilities, management and investment in tourism.

- Strengthen institutional frameworks for enforcement of legislation to improve their effectiveness where necessary.
- Standardise legislation and simplify regulations and regulatory structures to improve clarity and remove inconsistencies.
- Strengthen regulations for coastal zone management and the creation of protected areas, both marine and land-based, and their enforcement, as appropriate.
- Provide a flexible legal framework for tourism destinations to develop their own set of rules and regulations applicable within their boundaries to suit the specific circumstances of their local economic, social and environmental situations, while maintaining consistency with overall national and regional objectives and minimum standards.

(ii) Environmental And Regional Standards : Protect the environment by setting clear ambient environmental quality standards, along with targets for reducing pollution from all sectors, including tourism, to achieve these standards, and by preventing development in areas where it would be inappropriate. Ensure that tourism and the environment are mutually supportive at a regional level through cooperation and coordination between States, to establish common approaches to incentives, environmental policies, and integrated tourism development planning.

- Minimise pollution at source, for example, by waste minimisation, recycling, and appropriate effluent treatment.
- Take into account the need to reduce emissions of CO2 and other greenhouse gases resulting from travel and the tourism industry.
- Adopt overall regional frameworks within which States may wish to jointly set their own targets, incentive and environmental policies, standards and regulations, to maximise benefits from tourism and avoid environmental deterioration from tourism activities.

Management of Tourism : Tourism management should consider following parameters

A. Initiatives by Industry : Ensure long-term commitments and improvements to develop and promote sustainable tourism, through partnerships and voluntary initiatives by all sectors and stakeholders, including initiatives to give local communities a share in the ownership and benefits of tourism.

- Structure initiatives to give all stakeholders a share in the ownership, to maximise their effectiveness.
- As well as global initiatives, encourage small and medium-sized enterprises to also develop and promote their own initiatives for sustainable tourism at a more local level
- Consider integrating initiatives for small and medium-sized enterprises within overall business support packages, including access to financing, training and marketing, alongside measures to improve sustainability as well as the quality and diversity of their tourism products.

B. Monitoring : Ensure consistent monitoring and review of tourism activities to detect problems at an early stage and to enable action to prevent the possibility of more serious damage.

- Establish indicators for measuring the overall progress of tourist areas towards sustainable development.
- Establish institutional and staff capacity for monitoring.
- Monitor the implementation of environmental protection and related measures set out in EIAs, and their effectiveness, taking into account the effectiveness of any ongoing management requirements for the effective operation and maintenance of those measures for protection of areas where tourism activities take place.

C. Technology : Minimise resource use and the generation of pollution and wastes by using and promoting environmentally-sound technologies (ESTs) for tourism and associated infrastructure.

- Develop and implement international agreements which include provisions to assist in the transfer of Environmentally Sound Technologies (ESTs) for the tourism sector, such as the Clean Development Mechanism of the Kyoto Protocol for energy-related issues.
- Promote introduction and more widespread use of ESTs by tourism enterprises and public authorities dealing with tourism or related infrastructures, as appropriate, including the use of renewable energy and ESTs for sanitation, water supply, and minimisation of the production of wastes generated by tourism facilities and those brought to port by cruise ships.

D. Compliance Mechanisms : Ensure compliance with development plans, planning conditions, standards and targets for sustainable tourism by providing incentives, monitoring compliance, and enforcement activities where necessary.

- Provide sufficient resources for maintaining compliance, including increasing the number of trained staff able to undertake enforcement activities as part of their duties.
- Monitor environmental conditions and compliance with legislation, regulations, and consent conditions
- Take into account compliance and reporting requirements set out in relevant international agreements.
- Use incentives to encourage good practice, where appropriate.

Conditions for Success : There are condition for success and these include :

A. Involvement of Stakeholders : Increase the long-term success of tourism projects by involving all primary stakeholders, including the local community, the tourism industry, and the government, in the development and implementation of tourism plans.

B. Information Exchange : Raise awareness of sustainable tourism and its implementation by promoting exchange of information between governments and all stakeholders, on best practice for sustainable tourism, and establishment of networks for dialogue on implementation of these Principles ; and promote broad understanding are awareness to strengthen attitudes, values and actions that are compatible with sustainable development.

- Exchange information between governments and all stakeholders, on best practice for sustainable tourism development and management, including information on planning, standards, legislation and enforcement, and of experience gained in implementation of these Principles.
- Use International and regional organisations, including UNEP, can assist with information exchange.

C. *Capacity Building* : Ensure effective implementation of sustainable tourism, and these Principles, through capacity building programmes to develop and strengthen human resources and institutional capacities in government at national and local levels, and amongst local communities; and to integrate environmental and human ecological considerations at all levels.

- Develop and strengthen their human resources and institutional capacities to facilitate the effective implementation of these Principles.
- Transfer know-how and provide training in areas related to sustainability in tourism, such as planning, legal framework, standards setting, administration and regulatory control, and the application of impact assessment and management techniques and procedures to tourism.
- Encourage contributions to capacity-building from the local, national, regional and international levels by countries, international organisations, the private sector and tourism industry, and NGOs.
- Encourage assistance from those involved in tourism in countries which have not yet been able to implement sustainability mechanisms in training at the local and national level in the sustainable development of tourism in co-operation with the Governments concerned.

REFERENCES

- Christaller(1964), in France,L.,(1997),The Earthscan Reader in Sustainable Tourism, Earthscan publishing, London.
- Learner,S.C.,Tourism in Bali-Social Impact,1977.
- Tiwari, S.P., (1993), Tourism Dimentions, Atma Ram and Sons, New Delhi, pp250-51).
- France,L.,(1997),The Earthscan Reader in Sustainable Tourism, Earthscan publishing, London.
- Seth, Pran,(1997), Successful Tourism Management, Vol I, Sterling Publishing Pvt Ltd., New Delhi.
- Middelton,Victor T.C., and Rebacca Hawkins,(1998),Sustainable Tourism: A Marketinf Perspective, Oxford:Butterworth and Heinemann,p-232.

- Rose,Sheryl, and Wall Geoffrey,(1999),Ecotourism Towards congruence between theory and practice Tourism management, 20.pp.123-133.
- Our Planet (1999), UNEP magazine for environmentally sustainable development, volume 10, no. 3, 1999, www.ourplanet.com/ imgversn/ planethme.html)
- Sharma, J.K. (2000), Tourism and Development: Design for ecological Sustainability, Kanishka Publishers & Distributors, New Delhi.
- Reynolds P C and Braithwaithe D (2001): towards a Conceptual framework for wildlife Tourism, Tourism Management, Elsevier Science Ltd., Vol. 22(1), pp. 31-42.
- Bansal,S.,Ecotourism (2003), An Answer to Ecosystem Conservation, Tourism development Journal, Vol.1,No.1,2003,IVS,HPU Shimla.
- Bansal,S.,Ecotourism (2003), An Answer to Ecosystem Conservation, Tourism development Journal, Vol.1,No.1,2003,IVS,HPU Shimla.
- Buckley,R.(2003), Case Studies in Ecotourism, Oxon: CABI Publishing.
- Karan.Baha.Mehmet and Fench, Ron (2005), The Structure and Financing of a New NTO for Northern Cyprus, Tourism Development Journal, Vol. No. 2 & 3, No. 1
- Bansal,S.P, and Gautam, P.,(2005), camping - An Emerging Trend of Eco Tourism(A study of selected camping sites of Himachal Pradesh), Tourism development Journal, Vol.1,No.2&3,IVS,HPU Shimla.
- The European environment - State and outlook 2005, http:// reports.eea.europa.eu/ state_of_environment_report_2005_1/ en
- Choi, H.S.C., and Sirakaya. E (2005): Measuring Resident's Attitude toward Sustainable Tourism: Development of Sustainable Tourism Attitude Scale, Journal of Travel research, vol.43, Pp. 380-394.

  http:/ / www.unep.fr/ pc/ tourism/ policy/ principles.htm
- www.saxakali.com/ caribbean/ ekozyr.htm
- Convention on Biological Diversity, http:/ / www.biodiv.org/ default.shtml
- OceanPlanet,http:/ / seawifs.gsfc.nasa.gov / OCEAN_PLANET / HTML/ education_threats.htm)
- University of Idaho , www.its.uidaho.edu/ rrt484/ 484INTR97/
- Trade and Environment Database, www.american.edu/ projects/ mandala.TED/ yosemite/ html)
- People & the Planet, www.peopleandplanet.net
- Tourism Concern, www.tourismconcern.org)
- Global Coral Reef Monitoring Network (GCRMN) www.gcrmn.org/
- UNEP's Energy Programme, www.uneptie.org/ energy/
- World Wide Fund For Nature, www.wwf.org

Section III

Strategies and Sustainability

15

Towards Sustainable Approach to Culture-Tourism Relationship: the Issues in Question

S.S.Boora (Reader)

Department of Tourism & Hotel Management, Kurukshetra University, Kurukshetra-136119, Haryana (India)

ABSTRACT

Tourism development and its impacts are the two major areas of concern in tourism. The development of tourism through out the globe has brought, on the one hand, immense economic opportunities and benefits. On the other hand, it has put immense pressures on the natural environment, societies and cultures. While sharing the benefits of tourism development, the communities at the destination had been on the receiving end – all leaving behind a trail of deprivation and gaps. The culture – tourism relationship under mass tourism has resulted in the change in the value system, behaviour and the identity factor. The community structure, family relationships, collective traditional life styles, ceremonies and morality of the host community too are greatly influenced by tourism.

The absence of sustainable approach in the process of tourism development is more discernible in case of developing countries where inadequate legal and social controls have given ways to the defaulters. These defaulters have come out with their narrow agenda of reaping commercial profits over the existing socio-cultural environment. The development of sex tourism, in number of developing countries is a manifestation, besides others, of this development. The major area of neglect is the careful concern for the culture-tourism relationship and incorporation of that concern in the policy framework needed for development The whole debate focuses on inculcation of a sustainable approach towards culture-tourism relationship.

The present paper develops a holistic view of the culture-tourism relationship that gives a theoretical construct for the future discussion particularly in view of the nature of development and its consequences for the host cultures. The paper will also examine the concept of sustainability and its application for the cultures.

INTRODUCTION

In the second half of the twentieth century, tourism has developed into a major economic, cultural and social phenomenon that has made it a much sought - after economic activity in the modern world. The economic potency of tourism can be realized from the amount of wealth and employment it generates that, in turn, leads to the socio-cultural changes. In 2004, 766 million tourists visited various destinations across the globe generating the wealth to the tune of US $622 billion. The average annual growth of tourists' arrivals of 6.4 per cent for the period 1950 - 2003 signifies tremendous potential and splendid performance of international tourism (WTO, 2005) securing for it the status of an important agency for economic development. The proven capacity of tourism to generate revenues and employment brought tourism on the development agenda of number of countries. But the focus of concern was primarily the economic one and that was achieved at the cost of environmental and socio-cultural concerns in number of cases. These trends, noticed at number of places, created an imbalance in the culture-tourism relationship. The nature of development under mass tourism - the most popular pattern of tourism development, widened this imbalance and created a situation where further development of tourism was significantly resisted and opposed even violently at certain destinations.

The impact of tourism on the culture at the destination had been a subject of central concern atleast among the academicians and the environmentalists. (See below). The UNEP identifies the following impacts of tourism on culture, which requires a sustainable handling of tourism development.

NEGATIVE SOCIO-CULTURAL IMPACTS

I - Change or Loss of Indigenous Identity and Values

- Commodification
- Standardization
- Loss of authenticity and Staged authenticity
- Adaptation to tourists' demands

II - Cultural Clashes

- Over - exploitation of socio-cultural carrying Capacity
- Economic Inequalities
- Irritation due to Tourist Behaviour
- Job Level Friction

III - Physical Influences Causing Social Stresses

- Resource Use Conflicts
- Cultural Deterioration
- Conflict with Traditional Land - uses

IV - Ethical Issues

- Crime Generation
- Child Labour
- Prostitution and Sex Tourism

Despite being the fact that tourism has contributed significantly to the socio-cultural growth at the destination (Richards, 1996) but in view of the magnitude of negative impacts, the positive contribution or the 'development' (as is described popularly) stands hollow. The term 'development' is defined and interpreted in terms of tourism only and thus forms the primary concern. The social and cultural growth receives the secondary consideration. Tourism development is the outcome of the conscious efforts but socio-cultural development is more a matter of chance that may or may not provide opportunities for growth. The basic flaw lies in the approach towards culture-tourism relationship where the complimentary role between the two is negated and the singular objective of tourism development is given preference. Unfortunately, this very singularized and popularized economic dimension of tourism and its pronounced supply and demand axioms have conditioned the whole notion about tourism in itself and in respect to other conceptual and operational realms. For example, when culture is viewed from the demand/supply angles, it is suddenly reduced to a tourism commodity - an attraction which influences the choice of a destination, where tourists consume their packaged experiences, where cultural production is shaped by the wishes of the market, where the visited population is cast and animated in that image, and where the supply-side host and demand-side guest interact. But even this very supply/demand construct suggests that tourism is more than an economic activity. Tourism, as recent studies reveal about its complex inward/outward functions and structures, is most and foremost a socio-culturally embedded phenomenon with diverse dimension and untold influences, of which economics is but one (Jafar Jafri, 1997).

CULTURE-TOURISM RELATIONSHIP: A THEORETICAL CONSTRUCT OF INTERACTION

Cultural tourism designates a system of relationships involving people through interaction that is based on the symbiotic relation of 'give and take'. The concept of interaction is crucial to understand the symbiotic character of relationship between the host and the tourist. Surrounding and influencing the actual tourist-host contact is a range of inputs, influences and infrastructure extending beyond the immediate bounds of tourism. Fundamentally, this wide participation and involvement is present because tourism is regarded as likely to deliver economic benefits. Therefore, the stage and players to be viewed are necessarily extensive in considering how cultural conflicts in tourism might be resolved (Boniface, 2002). Since the guest and the host does not represent one homogeneous group and possesses innumerable diversities - geographical, social, cultural, economic etc., the impact is to be understood in view of these diversities. In other words, the nature of impact depends upon the nature of culture, which the tourists represent. Thus, the interaction between the host and the guest involves the intricacies and complexities - all making i difficult to diagnose the role and limits of host and guest and that, ultimately restricts a mutually acceptable and beneficial relationship. Many a times such interaction leads tc development of conflict that contributes for growth of inequality but considered as inevitabl (Robinson, 2002).

Culture – Tourism Relationships
Types and Interactions

Types of Society/ Culture	Nature Society/ Culture	Characteristics Society/Culture	Degree of Impacts
Industrial	Comparatively open	Less prohibitive to change, rather more responsive to change; Convenience rather than honouring traditions, more social freedom	Industrial to Industrial interaction - Less impact Industrial to agrarian interaction - More Impact Industrial to Tribal interaction- High Impact
Agrarian	Comparatively Moderate	Initially resistive to change, traditional,	Domestic interaction- Less impact Between local & foreigner interaction-more impact
Tribal	Comparatively closed	Avoids interaction, lives in isolation,	If interaction takes place - risk of high prefers to avoid any kind of interaction, thus attracts no impact.

The destinations world over fall into either of the three types of societies viz. industria agrarian and the tribal ones. Each type of society and culture possesses specific set of value traditions, norms and usages that shapes the attitudes, beliefs and perception of its member These contents of the social order prepare the responses of the members that develop a outlook about the world around them. When an interaction under tourism takes plac between any two cultural groups, there comes into action a set of responses that determine the basis of relationship between the host and the guest.

The main question arises - when this interaction leads to imbalance in the cultur tourism relationship? A close look into the character and persona of the interacting partie would reveal the presence of a situation where the tourists exercise a commanding an dominating position and the community or the hosts are put at the receiving end. Th positions thus acquired are based on the premise that tourism and tourists brings economi benefits to the local people. The culture of the host faces subordination to the culture of th tourists.

Since the industrial society forms the major part of the tourism market and th destinations, the degree of cultural impact will be less in comparisons to the agrarian societie as the tourists and host share so much in common in the industrial social set up. The agraria society, primarily in the developing countries, receives greater degree of impact when th tourists belong to industrial society and the host represents the agrarian society. The mo the cultural gap between the tourists and the hosts, the more is the degree of impact. Th host, in such situation, becomes subservient to the wants and demands of the tourists. The impact percolates from the 'above' to the 'below' i.e. from the dominating party to the receiving party. Similar situations can be noticed in case of other societies.

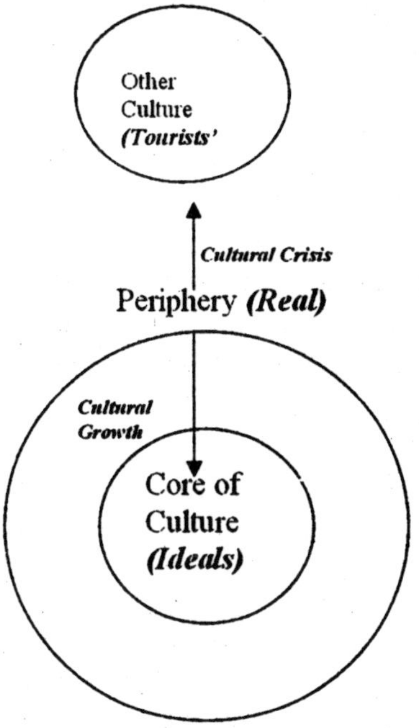

Fig. 1

The beginning of impact takes place at the periphery and then gradually percolates to the 'core' of the cultural system. The damage to a culture is more when the system at the 'core' is influenced. The core of the culture comprises of the ideals and principles over which the entire edifice of culture is created. The 'core' provides the distinct identity to the culture and a system of values, norms and beliefs is designed to preserve the 'core'. The other dimension relates culture to the periphery that provides occasions, channels and platforms for interaction with the outer world. The impact of tourism first, as stated earlier, begins at the periphery, which, gradually, over the years percolates towards the core. The culture faces the identity crisis when tourism as a force akin to the host culture disturbs the harmony of the 'core'.

DOES TOURISM LEAD TO CULTURAL GROWTH?

Tourism is described as an engine of growth not only economic but socio-cultural as well. The benefits of tourism are summarized as follows by UNEP:

POSTIVE SOCIO- CULTURAL IMPACTS OF TOURISM

- Tourism as a force for Peace
- Strengthening Communities
- Facilities developed for tourism can benefit residents

- Revaluation of culture and traditions
- Tourism encourages civic involvement and pride

The socio-cultural impacts of tourism described here are the effects on host communities of direct and indirect relations with tourists, and of interaction with the tourism industry. For a variety of reasons, host communities often are the weaker party in interactions with their guests and service providers, leveraging any influence they might have. These influences are not always apparent, as they are difficult to measure, depend on value judgments and are often indirect or hard to identify (UNEP, 1996). Here two main issues come into picture.

1. Does tourism lead to material changes that improve the quality and socio-economic standards of the host community?
2. Does tourism leads to cultural growth?

The question of sustainability is to be addressed in these two contexts. Tourism is known to have contributed to the economy of the destination. But the distribution of benefits of economic development had not been found to be uniform in number of cases. The economic development has taken place but the majority of the benefits have been shared by the entrepreneurs and the government. Even the employment opportunities give a little relief to the employment problem of the community. Majority of the employment is of menial nature that too at the level of grocery suppliers, security men, gardener, plumbers, electricians, waiters, peons, rickshaw pullers, auto drivers, workers in amusement and entertainment sectors, in restaurants and hotels etc. Employment at the subsistence level may not be described as a great economic contribution of tourism for the community at the destination. Moreover, the resources used to attract the tourists – cultural and natural, and the entrepreneurs to reap greater benefits use over which the community has greater right and custodianship. The sustainability, thus, requires settling the issue of custodianship of the resources and their management with community at the core of the affairs.

The second issue "does tourism leads to cultural growth?" needs to be handled in the context of proper explanation of the concept of 'cultural growth'. The cultural growth revolves around the movement between the two cardinal points in culture - one, that forms the 'periphery' and, second, that consists of the 'core' (Figure 1). The core possesses the core values or the ideals of the culture, which remains, more or less, same through out the period of its existence. The traditions of the culture nurture these ideals. These traditions bestow a distinct identity to the culture. The periphery reflects the 'real' face of the culture that interacts with the external agencies. Here, the people are indulged in their day-to-day activities and interact frequently with the outsiders to derive the means and modes of livelihood. The periphery establishes contact with the 'core' of the culture and the outsider agency at the 'periphery'.

The cultural growth here signifies the movement of the 'real' towards the 'ideal' and more the narrower gap between the 'real' and the 'ideal' the more it moves towards growth. Likewise, the wider the gap between the 'real' and the 'ideal', the more crisis the culture experiences. The sustainability in the culture-tourism relationship lies in the restoration of the interaction between the 'core' and the 'periphery' and any departure or distance from the core and that too towards other culture (which is here represented by the culture of tourists) causes a negative impact on the host culture. The thesis here is not to snap every interaction between the host and the tourists but to draw a line of sustainability. There is no harm in using culture for tourism so long as the host culture remains unspoiled or unexploited at the hands of tourism. But, since tourists are the dominating group, the hosts are put at the receiving end.

Sustainability: Issues in Question

The discussion above amply makes it apparent that negative social impact of tourism on the culture arises because of the community's inability to protect itself from the dominating part of the tourists' culture. The host fell subservient to the demands and expectations of the tourists and, as a result, the culture starts moulding itself to the tastes and likings of the tourists. There is no end to these changes and ultimately a situation of imbalance in the culture - tourism relationship emerges to the extent of culture being relegated to the status of a commodity. The main issues that qualify for discussion can be identified as such:

1. The culture or the community at the destination should have greater participation and involvement in the decision-making process
2. The exploitation of resources should not be allowed to the extent of depletion of those resources for future.
3. The culture at the destination should have adequate means and mechanisms to identify its cultural priorities and that too in the context of the tourists.
4. The distribution of economic benefits from tourism should be seriously looked into and the community should get her due share. The share of the community should be determined in relation to the loss and exhaustion of natural and other resources used for tourism development.
5. Address the problems of inequality and indifference at the level of the local culture and community

The sustainability, in this context, should be interpreted to conserve the 'core' without compromising on the ability of the culture and her people to derive economic benefits from tourism.

REFERENCES

- Boniface, Priscilla, 2002. Tourism and Cultures: Consensus in the Making. In Robinson, Mike & Boniface, Priscilla (eds.) *Tourism and Cultural Conflicts,* CAB International, Wallingford
- Jafar Jafri, 1997, Tourism and Culture: An Inquiry into Paradoxes. In: UNESCO/ AIEST Proceedings of Round Table, *Culture, Tourism, Development: Critical Issues for the XXIst Century,* UNESCO, Paris.

- Richards, G. 1996, The Scope and Significance of Cultural Tourism. In Richards, G. (ed.) *Cultural Tourism in Europe,* Cab International, Wallingford.
- Robinson, Mike. 2002, Cultural Conflicts in Tourism: Inevitability and Inequality. In Robinson, Mike & Boniface, Priscilla (eds.) *Tourism and Cultural Conflicts,* CAB International, Wallingford.
- United Nations Environment Programme: Social Impacts of Tourism; www// http.unep/tourism.org
- *World Tourism Organization Report, 2005, Madrid*

16

Rural Tourism: Best Solution for Environment Preservation & Rural Development

Dr. Ravi Bhushan Kumar[*]

INTRODUCTION : THE PROBLEM AREA

For last five decades of independence from British rule, all governments have tried their best theoretically and practically to eradicate poverty from rural areas where 72% population of India lives in about 5.76 lakh villages (Census of India, 2001), but the success is very far from realisation. There are several constitutional safeguards to protect the rights of Indian citizens e.g. Equality of opportunity in matters of public employment (art. 16)

- Prohibition of traffic in human beings & forced labour (art. 23)
- Promotion of educational and economic interests of SC, ST & other weaker sections (art. 46)
- Duty of state to raise the level of nutrition and the standard of living and to improve public health (art. 47)
- Organization of agriculture and animal husbandry (art. 48)
- Protection and improvement of environment and safeguarding of forests and wild life (art 48-A)
- Protection of monuments, places and objects of national importance (art. 49)

Above-mentioned articles are few examples of the sacred feeling enshrined in our constitution for betterment of rural folks. To achieve the mentioned goals central government with cooperation of state government launched several welfare schemes such as IRDP, NREP, TRYSEM & JRY, but the condition of villages has not changed to desired extent. On Aug. 23, 2005, Rural Development minister Mr. Raghuvansh Prasad Singh passed a revolutionary bill, named as 'Rural Employment Guarantee Bill, 2005; which ensures at least 100 days employment per year in every household. For strict monitoring and vigilance a village committee or panchayat will play a principal role in selection, implementation & monitoring of schemes, initially the progamme will be implemented in 150 districts, later on 50 more districts would be added in the list. (Times of India, Aug. 24, 2004)

However the fruits of this revolutionary bill, as claimed by UPA Govt., will ripen in long period. The critics are very skeptical, whether this bill also may not get same fate as others got.

The rural economy is dominated with primary occupation e.g. agriculture, fishing, wild product collection etc. Its share to GDP is very poor. About 72% working people contribute to 24% of GDP (Economic Survey 2004). About 70% of cultivated land is depended on monsoon rain due to lack of irrigational facilities but their share in crop production is about 30% of food production. The land holdings are small & fragmented. Besides these factors the agriculture is suffering from several environmental problems such as alkalinity, salinity, soil erosion, sheet erosion, lowering of water table, floods, drought and several natural calamities, that's why agriculture has been always 'gamble of monsoon'.

This gamble has created deep rooted poverty. Dependence on monsoon rain water has resulted into unemployment, underemployment and disguised employment. Rural peasants have very small period of gainful employment. After sowing and harvesting they remain idle. The welfare programmes have failed to provide jobs for 183 days in a year. The landless marginal farmers & educated youth are compelled to migrate to urban areas. The rampant poverty, low literacy level, high mortality rate at child birth, high morbidity rate of toddlers, low availability of health and other civic facilities are general features of rural area. These factors have accentuated in several socio-economic & administrative problems. The widespread naxalitie problem is an outcome of poverty.

Here tourism can be one of the rescuers. Indian villages have large variety of attractions which can attract both domestic as well as foreign tourists. Rural Tourism is an alternate form of tourism in which the professional and commercial practitioner such as travel agents, hoteliers, escorts etc. are not involved, rather the local village folk are the entrepreneurs, who provide food and accommodation with guide & other services. These enterprises are small scale, traditionally operated in traditional surroundings and relatively in geographically isolated region.

OBJECTIVES

- To understand the problems of rural economy.
- To evaluate the variety of tourist resources of Indian villages.
- To know status of rural tourism in India.
- To understand the role of rural tourism as environment saviour.
- To analyse relationship between rural development and rural tourism.

METHODOLOGY

About 5.76 lakh villages are spread throughout India with a great variety of physiological, anthropological, social, economic and cultural features. Their features are very complex. It is very difficult and impossible to study all. Even sample survey is very difficult.

The researcher is fortunate to travel whole India several times from interior of Ladakh to Kanyakumari and from Gujarat to West Bengal-Sikkim. This article is based on the observations of researcher. The statistical information are taken from different sources published by government publications, books, journals and newspapers.

RURALITY IN INDIA

The definition of village, country side, rural area varies from country to country. In several countries the population size has been taken as important parameters while physical and socio-economic parameters have been adopted by several countries. 'The countryside can be defined as those areas which lie beyond major town and cities and which are therefore 'rural' opposed to 'urban', it includes a number of features such as forests, reservoirs, canals, beaches & agricultural land (Sharplay 1996, p. 13). The OECD (Organization for Economic Cooperation & Development Report, 1993) has also adopted similar definition whereby rurality includes all social and economic activities outside immediate economic influence of urban centers. In brief the non-urban natural environment with physical features are major determinant of rurality. In India like varied country, only physical features can not be very important, because the villages of Punjab & Haryana are better than several urban areas of other states.

The definition of 'Census of India' is more scientific, it defines a rural area (as opposite to urban area) as an area that has :—

1. A population less than 5,000 persons.
2. The population density less than 400 persons/Sq. Km.
3. That seventy five percent of working male population may be engaged in agriculture and allied economic pursuits.

This is very scientific and objective definition, it may have several exceptions, but by and large most acceptable. There are several villages which are very large with very dense population, but their occupational structure is based on primary sector.

If we see the figure of census, then we find that there has been a gradual decline in rural population at very steady rate.

Census year	Rural Population (as % of total population)
1901	89.2
1911	89.7
1921	88.8
1931	88.0
1941	86.1
1951	82.7
1961	82.0
1971	80.1
1981	76.7
1991	74.3
2001	72.22

The figures show a gradual decline, i.e. increase in urban population. But urbanization does not mean the actual development of area. Urbanization may be a result of large size migration from rural to urban area due to marriages, better job opportunities and developed civic amenities. Whenever a road is constructed in any region, a ribbon type settlement appears with large number of non-agriculture service. In such cases urban like feature does not really brings development. There may be some superficial changes, but the beliefs, rites and rituals, dialects and social behaviours seldom changes. So these can be termed as extended villages, because their basic characteristics are similar to rural areas.

TOURIST RESOURCES OF RURAL INDIA

There are two main types of tourist resources:—

a) Natural, e.g.— Mountains, hills, forests, lakes, sea, rivers, flora and fauna etc.

b) Cultural or man made, e.g. — forts, palaces, temples, sculptures, fairs and festivals, handicrafts, music and dance etc.

Indian villages are very rich in a combination of both types of tourists resources. Some of them are worth to be mentioned separately.

1. Natural Beauty- the main means of economy of rural area is based on primary sector, i.e., agriculture, mining, fishing, hunting, wild product collection etc. so, most of the Indian villages located in the lap of nature in different types of physiographic environment i.e. mountains, hills, plateaus, plains, coastal beaches, deserts, forests etc. Many of them can be developed as tourists destinations by virtue of their beautiful locations, e.g. the settlements located in the Himalayas, along coastal areas, in wild areas, in deserts of Rajasthan, in the valleys of Ladakh etc.

2. Activity Based Tourist Resources—A large number of villages are rich in activity based tourists resources. They are spread throughout the India. Such resources are mountains, hills, valleys, forests, water bodies (e.g. rivers, lakes, lagoons etc.) and forests. There is an increasing trends of activity based tourism in whole world and India is not an exception. If the visitors like to indulge in such activities, the local youth can get jobs as guide, escorts, trainers etc. e.g. for guiding in wild life areas, for water tour in lagoons, for trekking and mountaineering and skiing in the Himalayas, most of the working youth are local people. So such tourism provides opportunity in accommodation, guide and several other activities in several ways.

3. Historical Monuments—A large number of historical monuments/ archaeological sites are located in rural areas. They are spread throughout India. Many of them are very popular among the both; domestic as well as foreign tourists e.g. Khajuraho, Nalanda, Rajgrih, Bodh Gaya, Sanchi etc. When they are accessible with good surface transport, then the number of tourists also increases. Tourism in such areas does not provides job opportunities only in small hotels, restaurant and *dhabas*, but the rural artisans also get jobs, their inherited skilled art survives

and with the income from tourism maintenance and renovation of ruins and beautification of the area can be done. In India, there is lack of funds for general developmental works. In this regard tourism may be a boon for the tourist areas.

4. Fairs and Festivals– India is a land of joy and festivity through out the year. Most of them are celebrated in rural set up. The venue of most of fairs is located in rural areas. Many of such fairs and festivals are now widely popular, such as Holi of Barsane, Teej of Rajasthan, Dussehara of Kullu, Elephant Procession of Kerala, Buddhist festivals of Ladakh and Sikkim etc. The tourists are attracted to enjoy their traditional rites and rituals. Many tour operators include such fairs and festivals into their packages at respective destination. Though there are several changes in recent years, they still exhibit the kaleidoscope of Indian society.

5. Music and Dance– The physiography, climate, history, culture, rite & rituals are reflected in the music and dance tradition of India. The rural India is very rich in folk dance and music. Though films and T.V. have diluted and corrupted their impacts, yet they have popularized several of folk dances and music. They are among the strongest image-maker of any destination. The Yaksha Gana of Karnataka, Lama dance of Ladakh, Kalbelia dance of Rajasthan etc. are widely known. Perhaps they might not be primary attraction of a destination, but they are important secondary attractions, e.g. In Camel Safari of Rajasthan, the folk dances and musicians are essentially accompanied items during stay time in night.

6. Handicrafts- Handicrafts are creations of rich traditions of a place, which are outcome of local raw materials, traditions and long experience of locals. There are several unique products made up of stones, terracotta, bamboos, textiles, metals etc. Several parts of India are world famous for their specific artistic handicrafts. These handicrafts give an image to the area. When a customer or tourists purchases a product of visited area, that souvenir imprints a permanent image of that area for long period. Tourism helps in the maintenance and revival of dying tradition of artistic handicrafts. If tourism develops, then the artists are saved to be exploited and converted as labourer.

7. Other Attractions- The costumes, dresses, rites, rituals and several other forms of culture are also attracting the visitors. These elements are making images of that places. The tourists are attracted by unique cultural features of the destinations. The colourful turban of Rajasthan, Phiron on Kashmiri, Lungi of South Indians, Lehnga- Choli of Rajasthani women are attraction for other culture people. The marriage ceremony, methods of worship etc. are one of the attractions for tourists. They can enjoy such things in original form in original place.

It is not possible to mention the types of tourist resources in short time and place. However, it is clear that India has a lot of tourist resources to offer to all age, sex and income groups of tourists in all seasons in all parts of India. However, the resources of rural areas for tourism purposes are yet to be tapped. We have to concentrate to exploits its full potentia1.

THE STAKE HOLDERS OF RURAL TOURISM

Rural tourism requires cooperation and coordination between stakeholders for successful operation. The main stake holders of rural tourism are: –

Local communities – they will be the hosts. They provide accommodation, food and guide services. They will be main trainer in adventure sports e.g. water sports, ice based activity etc. Such enterprise needs very small investment, but they will get jobs with supplementary income.

Tourism departments (of state and center) play key role as they introduce, promote and patronize destinations. They develop needed infrastructure. They enforce and monitor policies and strategies. They ensure standards of services and save against exploitation.

Private Sector – they provide several supplementary services e.g. – access (transportation), training to trainers (in case of adventure tourism) etc.

Government – It develops policies, strategies, land use plans and regulations. It ensures basic infrastructural and financial supports. It ensures environment's protection, visitor safety, protection against exploitation of hosts and guests, law and administration control. In short, without government will and support it is very difficult to think about tourism in such areas where people have never heard about it.

RURAL TOURISM AS A SAVIOUR OF ENVIRONMENT

The conflict between man & environment exists since the appearance of man as homo sapiens. Whenever the word 'development' is used, it always denotes industrial and economic development that exploits natural resources ruthlessly. The rural areas are normally depending on agriculture and allied economic activities such as cattle rearing, fishing, wild product collection etc. Such places are facing several types of environmental problems, such as clearance of natural vegetation, large-scale deforestation, killing of wild animals etc. construction of roads in such areas disturbs natural drainage system. Deforestation & road construction leads to soil erosion, soil creeping and land sliding (especially in hilly terrain).

Pumping out water for irrigating crops results into lowering of water table & drying up of water channels. In several parts of Punjab, Haryana, Rajasthan and West U.P., where State & Central Governments have provided canal irrigation facility, the main problems are water logging, increasing salinity and alkalinity of soil, so a large area is becoming infertile.

In brief, most of economic activities lead to environmental problems.

Tourism is such special activity which is mostly done in marginal utility area, e.g. the coastal beaches are full of sands & bushes with cliffs and wilder vegetation. These are not suitable for any economic activity or human settlement, but they are most suitable places for tourism. Similarly, hilly and mountainous terrains, forests, deserts, islands, coral reefs etc. are attracting large number of tourists.

When tourism starts in rural area, it does not need change in land use, rather the rural landscape — thatched houses, crops, trees, dresses, costumes, rites and rituals etc. become attraction. Tourists come to see these things e.g. large number of tourists visit to Ladakh, Rajasthan, Himachal etc. to see the rural folk, their life style in rural environment. Thus tourism does not need change in land use as any factory can do.

When tourism begins at any place, the local people are very cautious. Gradually, they understand the benefits of tourism, then they themselves involve in tourism. They realize that it is for their benefit to keep their places attractive, so they start conservation. We can see several examples in different parts of India e.g. Goa, Kerala, Uttranchal, Jammu & Kashmir and other Himalayan states, where the people started to maintain & beautify their destination to keep them attractive. In these places forestation, soil conservation, water management, animal protection programmes are done by themselves to improve the environment.

RURAL TOURISM FOR RURAL DEVELOPMENT

Rural areas have their own limitation. Most of them are located in relatively isolated, inaccessible areas. They devoid of proper civic amenities. They are lacking opportunities for economic activities. They have very poor infrastructural facilities such as all weather roads, sewage, electricity, supply of potable water etc.

The tourism action plan of 1992 and 2002 planned by Department of Tourism, Government of India, emphasize on the diversity of Tourism. It focuses on the 'spread out effect' of tourism to dilute the ill effects of mass tourism. Rural tourism is one of the best solutions to it. Considering this fact several state governments have taken several steps to promote and develop rural tourism in their states. Among such states, the main are—Rajasthan, J&K, Haryana, Himachal Pradesh, Uttranchal, Chhattisgarh, Madhya Pradesh, Kerala, Goa, Karnataka, West Bengal, Sikkim, Jharkhand and North-eastern states. The central government during the period of Dr. Jagmohan (Former Minister for Tourism & Culture) planned to introduce rural tourism in 39 selected villages. It is very popular in several parts of India. Among them the newly created states i.e. Uttranchal, Jharkhand and Chhattisgarh are bestowed with natural pristine beauty and unspoiled tribal culture. So, their emphasis is more on nature based eco-tourism, in which main stake holders would be the local tribal folks.

Among the Himalayan states it is very popular in trans Himalayan region, H.P., Sikkim, Darjeeling and Arunachal Pradesh. In fact, the trekkers and mountaineers visit to the inner and isolated region of the Himalayas where there are very few commercial accommodation facilities, so the visitors have to take the services of local folks. Sikkim is now taking several steps to develop rural tourism. Rajasthan is top receiver of foreign and Indian tourists. This state is specially known for its cultural attraction. Among those attractions traditional Rajasthani life style unaffected by western influence is very popular. The Hindi films have also made it very popular. The camel safari to rural areas is very popular from very long period. In Goa, the Konkani dance and music with Portuguese architecture attracts large number of tourists. In brief, the beauty of rural areas can be seen anywhere in India.

The state government in above mentioned states have taken several steps to encourage local people to involve them as main host. The local people accommodate them with paying guest facilities, i.e. accommodation, food and guide facilities. In several sports e.g. water sports (in lakes, sea, and rivers), skiing, trekking, wild-life tourism the locals are best escorts, guides & trainers.

Tourism is a harbinger of development process. Being a labour intensive service industry it can accommodate all, from illiterate persons as sweeper and guard to literate as guide and manager. Tourists need personalized services. Many studies done in different parts of the world have shown that rural tourism makes an important contribution to the local economy both at the level of the individual farmer and region as a whole. The vacationers not only sleep and eat in rural areas, but they also engage in recreational activities and purchase of local products, particularly souvenirs. Rural tourism provides job opportunity, brings money, raises their living standards, upgrades literacy level and general awareness about the world. The local governments also provide better infrastructural and political support. In this way rural tourism can bring holistic development to an area. If the multiplier effect is taken into consideration, then the local economy extends far beyond the households of a village, this alternate source of income will provide stability of income in case of failure of monsoon. In the report of FICCI (2001) it was observed that "the tourist expenditure circulates locally and the leakages are low, a significant improvement can be made in the income and living standards of the people of the region or locality.

CONCLUSION

The real success of any country does not lie in the growth of GDP, but in its equal distribution. The mechanism of 'spread out effect' or 'trickle down effect' is very poor in India. It is a common case of developing nation in which there are vertical growth of region rather than horizontal.

The rural tourism gives opportunity for extra income, particularly in lean season of agriculture. The rural youth can be best trainers for activity based tourism e.g. trekking skiing, water sports in white water or sea water, wild-life tourism etc. The exposure with outer world may broaden the mental horizon of rural folk. The interaction creates emotional bond with others that leads to universal brotherhood. This is the demand of time.

The rural India has a very large potentiality to offer natural and cultural tourist products

REFERENCES

- Butler (1998). Conclusion: The sustainability of tourism and recreation in rural areas, in tourism and recreation in rural areas (eds.) Butler, Hall and Jenkin, Toronto wily.
- Cavaco, C. (1995). Rural Tourism: the creation of new tourism space, in tourism region, space and restructuring, (eds.), Montanari and Williams, Chichester, wiley
- Chand, Mohinder & Ravi Bhushan Kumar (2005). Rural Tourism: A New Approach to Sustainability, SAJOSPS, Kerala.

- Dernol (1991). About Rural Tourism and farm tourism, Tourism Recreation research, 16, 3-6.
- FICCI. International conference and exhibition on rural tourism in India, Sept. 8-12, 2001.
- Greff (1994). Is rural tourism a lever for economic and social development? Journal of sustainable tourism, 2, 22-40.
- Hoggart, K., Butler, & Black (1995). Rural Europe: Identity and change, London, Arnold.
- Hummelbrunne, K. & Miglbauer, E. (1994). Tourism promotion and potential in peripheral areas: The Austrian Case, Journal of Sustainable Tourism. 2, 41-50.
- Jafari J. (1988), Retrospective and prospective views on tourism as a field of Study. Paper presented in the
- Richard and Lesley, (2004). Rural Tourism-10 years on, International Journal of Tourism Research, 6, 119-124.
- Richard, G. (1996). ed. Cultural Tourism in Europe, Wallingford, Oxford
- Robert, L. and Hall, D. (2001). Rural Tourism and recreation : Principles to Practice, CAB Publication, Walling ford.
- Sharma, B.A. Rural Tourism: It's a niche that India can offer, Financial Express, 25th August 2004, New Delhi.
- Sharpley, R. (1997), Rural Tourism: An Introduction, International Thomson Business Press, London.
- Singh, T.V. (2002). Altruistic Tourism: Another shape of sustainable tourism. The case of Kanda community, Tourism Management, Vol. 50, no. 4.
- Tourism Policy 2002, Ministry of Tourism, Govt. of India, Delhi.
- Travel Trend Today, Jan. 2004.
- Constitution of India, Publication Division, Govt. of India, Delhi.
- Times of India, August 24, 2005

Census of India 2001, Govt. of India.

(Footnotes)

* *Reader, Dept. of Tourism & Hotel Management, Kurukshetra University, Kurukshetra-136119 (Har.)*

17

Tourism Policy in a Unique Supranational Context: Strategies and Organizational Structure of Tourism Development of the European Union

Emese Panyik, Carlos Costa
Department of Economics, Management and Industrial Engineering
University of Aveiro, Portugal

ABSTRACT

In theoretical and empirical terms, the various forms and different levels of community participation in tourism development have provided new sights in recent planning and development paradigms of tourism research. Local, regional and national levels have broadly been analysed and conceptualized, whereas the distinctive characteristics of supranational community participation have not been much considered in the literature. The European Union (EU), as a unique intergovernmental and supranational formation, currently encompassing 25 countries of Europe, presents suitable conditions to examine the organizational system and strategies of tourism development at the supranational level through its initiatives and provisions in tourism. In fact, however, tourism was not implemented to, and consequently adopted as one of the policy areas of, the Amsterdam Treaty - the latest amendment Treaty of policy issues of the European Union. At present, competences and responsibilities in tourism area are scattered over three coordinative bodies: the Tourism Unit and the Tourism Advisory Committee of Enterprise and Industry Directorate-General of the European Commission and the Committee on Transport and Tourism of the European Parliament. The aim of this paper is to briefly review the evolution of EU Tourism Policy and thus to critically analyse its position in the system of EU policies by various factors such as actors, competences and decision-making. Within this context, distinctive characteristics as potential competitive advantages of supranational tourism development in the tourism market are recognized.

Keywords: *Supranational tourism development, Tourism policy, EU*

INTRODUCTION

During the last decades, particularly after the ratification of the Maastricht Treaty of the EU in 1993, tourism policy in Europe went through structural changes and innovation in many countries showing the existence of a continuous concern to improve administration management by ways of adapting structures, investing in new product development and reinforcing public-private partnership (WTO, 2003). Particular attention was given to the role that the European Union could play in tourism development and the advantages it could provide to the Member States and the Community as a whole. At the early stages of the formation of the Union, tourism was seen as an area with the responsibility primarily attached to the Member States and of little direct concern to the Community (Pompl and Lavery, 1993). The aim of this paper is to briefly review the uneven and not yet completed evolution of EU Tourism Policy and thus to critically analyse its position in the system of EU policies.

From a theoretical perspective, *supranational* tourism development is a *vertical* approach as opposed to *international* tourism policy which is a *horizontal* approach of tourism development strategies beyond the national level, both operating with different techniques, methodologies and organizational structures. This study attempts to recognize the distinctive characteristics of supranational tourism development as potential competitive advantages in the tourism market.

Community Participation in Tourism Development at the Supranational Level - Issues *above* National Borders

In theoretical and empirical terms, the various forms and different levels of *community participation in tourism development* have provided new sights in recent planning and development paradigms of tourism research. It is believed that participatory development approach could facilitate implementation of principles of sustainable and therefore more effective long-term tourism development (Tosun, 2004). Moreover, it has also been seen as an instrument to improve the professional basis of tourism development planning (Pearce, Moscardo, & Ross, 1996). The existing typologies of participation developed by Arnstein (1969), Pretty (1995) and Tosun (1999) recognize various forms based on the degree of power distribution, i.e., the degree of external involvement and local control, and the power relationships between them. Besides these forms, as a categorical term, community participation allows the involvement of people, citizens or a host community in their affairs at different levels - local, regional, national - under site specific conditions (Tosun, 2004).

In general, literature on community participation deals with the *local* and the *regional* level of communities, whereas the distinctive characteristics of community participation beyond the *national* level have not been much considered in the analyses. The rationale for considering *supranational* level within this context is twofold: First, political community definition, that sets up a criteria system of territorial (borders), social (citizenship) and psychological (common identity as membership) elements, explicitly includes supranational formations. Community levels have a *relative nature*, that is to say, one is indefinable without the other in the social, political and economic space. Second, the European Union (EU), as a unique intergovernmental and supranational formation, currently encompassing 25 countries of Europe, presents suitable conditions to examine the organizational system and strategies of tourism development at the supranational level through its initiatives and provisions in tourism.

More precisely, the Union can be placed on a theoretical continuum that stretches between two ideal-typical modes of governance: the *intergovernmental pole*, where the central players are the national executives of the member states and the *supranational pole*, where centralized governmental structures possess jurisdiction at the supranational level (Gerven, 2005). The pace and the nature of European integration, which shows a great unevenness (Sweet and Sandholtz, 1998) have depended crucially on the allocation of competences and the decision-making procedures, as well as on the attitude of the various Member States to the process (Corbett, 2002).

Out of the three pillars of the EU structure, the principles of supranationalism dominate obviously in the first, the so-called *European Communities* pillar, whereas in the case of the second *Common Foreign and Security Policy* pillar, and the third, *Police and Judicial Co-operation in Criminal Matters* pillar, powers of the different EU institutions are significantly limited. Indeed, the main institutions of the Union are, according to their function and type, characterized by either intergovernmentalism or supranationalism. The European Commission is, no doubt, the most "integration-driven" European institution (Gerven, 2005), the hallmark of supranationalism, together with the European Parliament.

Intergovernmentalism is represented by the Member State governments and parliaments and, at the European level, by the Council of Ministers.

Taking all this into account, the draft Constitution of the EU, if adopted, would have the effect, as regards legal procedures and voting requirements, to move the Union on the continuum between intergovernmentalism and supranationalism further into the direction of the latter (Gerven, 2005).

Specific Attributes and Continental Differences of European Tourism

Before presenting the tourism supply-side structure of the EU, it may be useful to outline the main features of the demand-side of the European tourism market.

Europe, with the greatest diversity and density of tourist attractions among the continents, is the most visited tourist destination in the world, accounting for 49 per cent of the international tourist arrivals and 52 per cent of the international tourism revenue (World Tourism Organization – WTO, 2004). Europe is also the main generating market in the world. Although the current level of overall international tourist arrivals is amounted to 763 million, it is forecasted that *only Europe itself will register 717 million incoming international tourists in 2020*, as opposed to the current 422 million, showing an average annual growth rate of 3 per cent (WTO, 2001).

Tourism in Europe is largely domestic. More than 80 per cent of the tourism activity recorded is attributed to its own citizens (EUROSTAT, 2004).

In structural terms, small and medium-sized tourism enterprises (SMEs) play a vital role. European tourism is rather an SME-dominated sector, with over 99 per cent of firms employing fewer than 250 individuals.

Tourism is an essential economic activity in the EU in terms of GDP, employment, and external trade in services. Tourism currently holds 5.5 per cent of the EU GDP, 6 per cent of employment, and 30 per cent of total external trades in services. The EU will keep obtaining annual growth rates in tourism above the average rates of the economy. Furthermore, it is admitted that tourism in the next decade may generate up to 3.3 million jobs in the European Union (Rita, 2000).

Development and Structural Changes of Tourism Policy in the European Union – a Chronological Approach

Prior to the early 1980s, and most notably before the coming into force of the Merger Treaty in 1967, which gave a framing to the modern Union and constructed the current institutional system, including the single European Commission, the cardinal actor of EU Tourism Policy, the European Union as a *polity* had not been diversified enough to handle such specific policy areas as tourism. Nevertheless, the Commission already faced with the general problems the emerging tourism raised on a Community scale, and compiled a draft inventory with proposed further action in 1971. (SEC(71), 1971) This inventory comprised of discussions on four main categories: general problems of tourism (such as tourism promotion, the length of tourism season), the problems of tourism enterprises, the problems of tourists and statistical problems in tourism.

In view of the rapid expansion of tourist activity in the European Community and the inter-relationship between tourism and a large number of Community activities, the European Commission in 1982 formulated initial guidelines for a Community policy on tourism (EEC-NTOs, 1983). In regard to the fact that the not any Treaty throughout the history of the EU even mentioned 'tourism' before the Maastricht Treaty in 1992, this document already denoted the potential of tourism as a key factor for the tasks of Article 2 of the Treaty of Rome (1957), as part of promoting closer relations between the Member States and stimulating economic development. This very first selection of the areas affected by tourism, focused particularly on transportation, working conditions, regional development, environmental protection and European heritage. (COM(82),1982)

Furthermore, another legal basis for EU tourism policy, as Davidson (1998) recognizes, is the chapter 'the free movement of persons, services and capital' in Articles 48-73, since the European Court confirmed by a judgement that EU nationals travelling abroad within the EU are 'recipients of services'.

In parallel, cooperation among the National Tourist Offices of the member states already started by launching a series of discussions entitled 'The Economic Significance of Tourism within the European Community' commissioned by the British Tourist Authority, with the participation of all the then 10 members of the EU. The major drawback to the formulation of a Community tourism policy on tourism was found to be the lack of an adequate statistical base (EEC-NTOs, 1983).

The first Council resolution on the subject, of 10 April 1984, acknowledged the importance of tourism for European integration and invited the Commission to make proposals. (EP, 2006)

Although an important step forward was taken with the establishment of the Tourism Advisory Committee in 1986, its role remained rather consultative, based on mainly facilitating exchange of information, consultation and co-operation in tourism among member states. (Council Decision 86/664/EEC). Each member state is required to send the Commission an annual report on the most significant measures taken, and those it intends to take. (Johnson and Thomas, 1992) However, this was the most important and tangible of those measurements that had been adopted by the Council of Ministers for the first time, as conclusions of the paper 'Community action in the field of tourism'. (COM(86) 32, 1986) In sum, these resolutions aimed at *standardization* of information on hotels, *harmonization* of legislation on package travel, *promotion* of a better seasonal and geographical distribution of tourism and *easing* of controls and formalities applicable to national of the Member States when crossing intra-Community borders. In the same year a budget line was instituted to fund a Community contribution to joint promotion efforts by Member States in markets outside the EC. On the basis of these endeavours towards cooperation, the EU's ministers responsible for tourism have met the Commission on a regular basis from 1988 on, to discuss Community policy and to exchange information on their respective national tourism policies (Davidson, 1998). On their first formal meeting in 1988 the participants designated 1990 as the 'European Year of Tourism' and adopted a preliminary programme.

Also, as an upshot of the directive on harmonization of legislation on package travel, the directive on package travel had been issued in 1990 (Council Directive 90/314/EEC), designed to protect consumers who contract package travel in the EU.

Initially, tourism policy had been included in Directorate-General (DG) VII for Transport, but in 1989 it was transferred to DG XXIII for Enterprise Policy, Tourism and Social Economy. DG XXIII was then renamed to Directorate-General Tourism and Commerce of the European Commission, still, with a modest budget and a relatively small stuff.

Additionally, the legal base for tourism in the EU also lies in the consequences of the establishment of the Single European Market. The aim of the Single European Act, which came into effect on 1st July 1, 1987, is to encourage economic integration not least in the tourist industry of the EU. This already raised the question for the European Commission, what form a European tourism policy should take if this was to accompany steps towards the common internal market. As in other sectors, the objective of such a policy was to simplify adjustment for the tourism industry to the internal market and the planned economic and monetary union. (EC – DG XXIII., 1996)

Following upon resolutions of the meeting of Ministers responsible for tourism of the Member States in 1988, the decision of the Council of Ministers to declare the year 1990 'The European Year of Tourism' was designed to emphasize the role of tourism and to develop a coherent and integrative policy approach (Council Decision 89/46/EEC). On one hand, the modest budget and the short, only twelve-months-long period limited the efficiency of the operations within this initiative, but on the other hand, it has been considered as the main inspiration for the increased levels of Community measures undertaken in support of tourism ever since. (COM(96) 29, 1996) Most notably of all, in the end of the Year, the ministers of tourism approved a new *'Community action plan to assist tourism'* for a three-year period between 1992 and 1995, in full consultation with the tourism trade sectors (Lickorish, 1991). The *horizontal approach* of tourism was indicated to be strengthened in many different ways, from tourism product development and tourist market segmentation to cross-border co-operation and international promotion.

The Treaty of Maastricht in 1992 included, for the first time, 'measures in the sphere of tourism' in the list of Community activities foreseen in support of the Community's overall objectives (Article 3t). However, the Treaty gives no particular guidenance for a community tourism policy and even up till now, there is still no *direct* legal base for Community measures on tourism. (COM, Enterprise and Industry DG, 2005)All the same, the full endorsement of the Maastricht Treaty was the overture of the unified Europe and impacted overall decision-making processes and policy formulation at national, regional and local levels as tourism policy has been given a 'European' dimension (Pompl, W., Lavery, P., 1993).

The Declaration No. 1 of the Maastricht Treaty made further provision derived from the implementation of tourism in the Treaty in Article 3t, that the question of introducing a Title relating to it into the Treaty be examined by the intergovernmental conference of the Member States in 1996 on the basis of a report which the Commission would submit to the Council. The purpose of *'Green Paper on Tourism'* (1995) was to fulfil these requirements of the Declaration as well as to facilitate and stimulate thought on the Union's role in assisting tourism (COM(95) 97). In this path, it is considered to be the pioneer of analyses carried out on the role of the Union in the field of tourism ever since, implying a review on previous community actions, community added values in general and suggestions on possible developments in the role of the union as regards tourism.

The progress of the formulation of tourism policy came to a standstill following upon the Green Paper in 1996 when the European Commission adopted a proposal for a Council Decision on a First Multiannual Programme to assist European Tourism (*'Philoxenia'* 1997-2000), designed to stimulate the quality and competitiveness of European tourism. The Council of Ministers could not be able to reach a unanimous agreement on the proposed programme and, although it received the favourable opinion of the European Parliament and other European institutions, the Commission formally withdrew its proposal in April 2000.

Major attention, from this time on, has been given to the subject of Tourism and Employment process, based on several conference and council conclusions (European

Conference on Tourism and Employment, 1997, Council of Tourism Ministers, 1997, Luxemburg European Council on Employment, 1997). The latter entrusted the *High Level Group on Tourism and Employment*, composed of qualified tourism experts from all Member States, to give a practical orientation to these results and examine the conditions under which the potential of tourism for employment can be enhanced.

As a sequence, four working groups were set up within the frameworks of the recommendations of the Group in 2000, dealing with the following topics:

- Facilitating the exchange and dissemination of information, particularly through new technologies (*Working Group A*);
- Improving training in order to upgrade skills in the tourism industry (*Working Group B*);
- Improving the quality of tourist products (*Working Group C*);
- Promoting environmental protection and sustainable development in tourism (*Working Group D*).

In addition, a special working group, entitled 'managing the impact of new technologies in the tourism sector' (*Working Group E*) started working in early 2001 (COM. DG ENTR, 1997). *Working Group C* took a particular consideration on the possibilities of more intensive use of Structural Funds for quality improvements of tourism products. According to its conclusions, the three principal financing categories foreseen by the regulations are productive investments, infrastructure investments and the development of indigenous potential. (Final Report of *Working Group C*, 2001) The five key issues, represented by the working groups, (information, training, quality, sustainability and technology) were presented in (COM (2001) 665 final) in 2001.

The Commission series, *'Community measures affecting tourism'* (1997-1999, 2000) attempted to illuminate the cross-sectoral and fragmented nature of tourism from the view of the European Union policy structure. Many Community policy areas, thus several Directorate -General are, while not designed specifically in terms of tourism objectives, interact with tourism, that is, affected by or have a direct effect on it. Similarly, a range of support programmes, either directly for tourism investments or complementary support of other policy areas such as the Structural Funds for regional development are available for tourism (Tab.1). This calls for a broad framework of co-ordination between these policies and measures and strengthens the argument for an overarching tourism policy with a long-term outlook. The latter concept has widely been supported in the literature (Lickorish, 1991; Johnson and Thomas, 1992; Rita, 2000; Pils, 2001; Akerhielm, Dev, and Noden, 2003; etc.) and ultimately has also been included in the first Council Resolution adopted specifically on tourism, in 2002 (C/8447/02, 2002). Also, to promote the dialogue between public sector, tourism industry and private stakeholders, the Resolution prompted the organization of an annual European Tourism Forum, and launched the implementation of Tourism Satellite Accounts to facilitate the process of measuring the economic impact of tourism in the Member States and to gain relevant statistical information.

The first European Tourism Forum, held in Brussels in 2002, in concordance with the main European Institutions, as regards with the conclusions of *Working Group D* on sustainable development of tourism activities which became a key category in the Commission Communication *'Working together for the future of European tourism'* endorsed the proposal on developing an *Agenda 21* guideline for sustainable actions in all levels for the increasing European Tourism sector (COM, Enterprise and Industry DG, 2002) and set up a Tourism Sustainability Group (TSG) in 2004.

In recognition of the importance of key-issues in tourism to crop-up and emerge throughout the history of the European Union such as employment, regional development, sustainability and European integration, the new EU Constitutional Treaty (signed by the 25 Member States and the 3 candidate countries on 29 October 2004 in Rome and unanimously adopted on 18 June of the same year) includes a proposal to add tourism to those areas where the European Community can take 'supporting, co-ordinating or complementary' action and thus made provision for a new legal basis to this effect. Article III-281 lays down the objectives of this policy and establishes the means of action. This new EU 'competence' would give the EU moderate powers to legislate in support of existing, national initiatives on tourism, but would not allow it to harmonise national legislation. Any new laws would be subject to qualified majority voting and the co-decision process (joint approval by the Council of Ministers and the European Parliament). However, the new competence will only come into effect if all 25 Member States ratify the Treaty and this is by no means certain. Referendums in France and the Netherlands rejected the text of the Constitution on 29 May and 1 June 2005 respectively. In the light of these results, the initiative deadline for ratification assigned in the Treaty, 1 November 2006, has been postponed till an undefined date of *mid 2007*. Subsequently, a period of reflection, explanation and discussion is currently under way in all countries. Until then, the EU will be limited to taking forward non-legislative initiatives.

Table 1. Index of EU support Programmes and Instruments Available also for Tourism per Directorate-General, 2006

Directorates-General affected by tourism in the EU	EU support programmes and instruments available also for tourism per Directorate-General
Agriculture DG	EAGGF, LEADER+, SAPARD
Economic and Financial Affairs DG	EIB, EIF, JEV, EBRD.
Education and Culture DG	Leonardo da Vinci, Socrates, Youth Programme, Tempus, Culture 2000, European City of Culture, European Cultural Month, Media Plus
Employment and Social Affairs DG	ESF, EQUAL, EURES
Energy DG	Intelligent Energy Europe, Save, Altener, FP6, Coopener, STEER
Enterprise and Industry DG	Multiannual Programme for Enterprise and Entrepreneurship, JEV, EICs, IRC, European Venture Capital, Small Business Envoy, MGCs, eBusiness Campaign, Business Partner Search Database, SMIE, Gate2Growth
Environment DG	Life
Fisheries DG	EIFG

Information Society DG	FP6, *e*-Content, *e*-TEN, Asia IT&C
Internal Market DG	SOLVIT
Regional Policy DG	ERDF, INTERREG, URBN, Innovative Measures, EBN/BIC Network
Research DG	FP6, CORDIS
Development DG	EDF
Enlargement DG	PHARE
External Relations DG	TACIS, MEDA, Asia Programmes, ALFA, URB - AL, Asia - Urbs, Asia - Link, EU Gateway to Japan Export Promotion Campaign, ETP
Trade DG	Market Access Database

Source: EU support for tourism enterprises and tourist destinations, European Commission, 2004

The current structure of EU Tourism Policy

At present, EU activities, competences and responsibilities in tourism area are scattered over three coordinative bodies: the Tourism Unit and the Tourism Advisory Committee of Enterprise and Industry Directorate-General of the European Commission and the Committee on Transport and Tourism of the European Parliament. In addition to these divisions, the European Travel Commission joins The National Tourist Organisations (NTOs) of 37 European countries, with the majority of EU-members, acceding and accession candidate countries, in order to promote Europe as a tourist destination in third countries.

The organizational structure of the main coordinative body, the Tourism Unit is shown in Fig.1. This division is responsible for planning and implementing Community-wide initiatives on tourism as well for coordinating activity in tourism between Member States at the national level and between other DGs of the Commission at the European level as it is related to tourism.

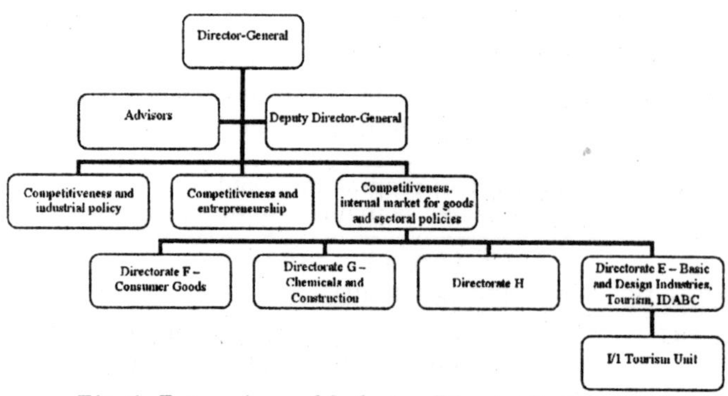

Fig. 1. *Enterprise and Industry Directorate-General, I/1 Tourism Unit, 2006*

The system of Directorate-Generals of the Commission is comparable to the national governments' ministries given the fact that each of them is responsible for specific tasks or policy areas. From this comparative view Enterprise and Industry Directorate-General corresponds to a mixed portfolio ministry which combines tourism with other related functions. The National Tourism Administration (NTA) model (Inskeep, 1994), describes the general structure of a single or divided Ministry or Department of Tourism as a diversified system organized into various sections and sub-sections whereas the Tourism Unit is an indivisible, single unit under Directorate E of 'Competitiveness, internal market for goods and sectoral policies' section of the DG. The functions of the model NTA structure are typically divided into four main sections: Marketing services, statistics and research, planning and development and education and training which are shaped to and inserted in the overall government structure. In the European Union, these functions are, however, not aggregated and coordinated exclusively by any of the divisions involved in tourism, but rather handed selectively to each with different legal base originated from different institutions. The fact that tourism is represented in low-level subdivisions alludes to a disproportionately law recognition and priority of the subject whilst the wide legal source (presence both in the legislative and executive bodies, implications in the Treaties and in the future Constitution), and the recently launched draft of a renewed tourism policy (COM(2006) 134 final) gives solid base for steps taken forward towards a more embedded Tourism Policy in long terms at the European level.

CONCLUSIONS

At the European level there has so far been no success in exploiting the potential of a coherent EU tourism policy and there is still no direct legal base for Community measures on tourism. Decision-making in tourism is hampered by restrictive conditions, which means that any act of the Council of Ministers in the field of tourism needs unanimity among all member states. Furthermore, tourism development in the EU has always been linked to key development categories such as employment, sustainability and regional development, not least because of the intersectoral nature of tourism, and scarcely has been treated as a policy for its own. Nonetheless, with regard to the thematic orientation of European tourism policy, it can be said that areas of mutual intrest for politics and business are attracting growing attention. As Johnson and Thomas (1992) notes, the EU has developed a rudimentary but nevertheless evolutionary tourism policy that is capable of expansion into an effective and timely action programme.

Given both the role of tourism in the European Economy but also the constraints to growth in this sector, the competitiveness of the European tourism industry is an issue of key concern. Consequently, the future development of a sustainable tourism policy for or in Europe must be seen critically in this context.

REFERENCES:

- Akerhielm, P., Dev, C.S., and Noden, M.A. (2003). Neglecting the tourism opportunity Cornell Hotel and Restaurant Quarterly. Ithaca - Vol. 44. No. 5-6.
- C/8447/02, (2002). Draft Council decision on the future of European tourism. Council of the European Union. Brussels.
- COM(82), (1982). Commission of the European Communities. Initial guidelines for a community policy on tourism. Brussels.
- COM(86) 32, (1986). Commission of the European Communities. Community action in the field of tourism. Brussels.

- COM(95) 97, (1995). Commission of the European Communities. The role of the Union in the field of tourism. Brussels.
- COM(96) 29, (1996). Commission of the European Communities. Report from the Commission on Community measures affecting tourism. Brussels.
- COM Enterprise and Industry DG, (2005). Facts and Figures about European Tourism.
- COM, Enterprise and Industry DG, (2002). Agenda 21 - Sustainability in the European Tourism sector. Brussels.
- COM. DG ENTR, (1997). European Comission Final Report Brussels: Enterprise and Industry DG, 4 and 5. Conference on 'Employment and Tourism: Guidelines for Actions' Final Report of Working Group C 'Improving the quality of tourist products', June 2001.
- Council Decision 86/664/EEC, 22 December 1986, OJ No L 384, 31.12.1986, pp. 52.
- Council Decision 89/46/EEC, 21 December 1988, OJ No L 17, 21.1.1989, pp. 53.
- Council Decision 92/421/EEC, 31 July 1992.
- Corbett, R. (2002). European Parliament's role in closer EU integration. Palgrave Macmillan,Gordonsville, VA, USA.
- Davidson, R. (1998). Travel and tourism in Europe. Addison Wesley Longman Ltd., NY, USA.
- EC - DG XXIII., (1996). Transnational Partnerships in European Tourism. EC, Luxemburg.
- EEC-NTOs (1983). The economic significance of tourism within the European Community. A Fifth report by the working group of the national tourist organizations of the EEC. London, UK.
- EP, (2006). European Parliament Fact Sheets. 4.15.0. Tourism. http://www.europarl.europa.eu/facts/default_en.htm
- Gerven, Van, W., (2005). European Union - A polity of states and peoples. Stanford University Press, Palo Alto, CA, USA.
- Inskeep, E.,1994. National and regional tourism planning. Methodologies and case studies. WTO/Routledge series, London.
- Johnson P. and Thomas B. (eds.), 1992. Perspectives on tourism policy. Biddles Ltd., Guildford&King's Lynn, London, UK.
- Lickorish L.J., (1991). Developing a single European tourism policy. Tourism Management Vol. 12.,No.3., pp. 178-184.
- Pearce, P.L., Moscardo, G., & Ross, G.F. (1996). Tourism community relationships. Oxford, Elsevier Ltd.

- Pils, M. (2001). Europe needs a co-ordinated tourism strategy. Bulletin, Newsletter from the IFN-Network, No. 16., Wien, Austria.
- Pompl W. and Lavery, P.,(eds.)(1993). Tourism in Europe: Structures and developments. CAB International, Wallingford, Oxford, UK
- Rita, P. (2000). Tourism in the European Union. International Journal of Contemporary Hospitality Management 12/7. 434-436.
- (SEC(71), 1971). Commission des Communautes Europeennes. Projet d'inventaire des problemes du tourisme a l'echelle communautaire. Bruxelles.
- Tosun, C., (2004). Expected nature of community participation in tourism development. Tourism Management, in press. 1-12 Available online from 25 February 2005, Elsevier Ltd.
- WTO, (2003). Tourism market trends: Europe. 2003 Edition. WTO, Madrid, Spain.
- WTO, (2001). Tourism 2020 vision, www.world-tourism.org

18

Anticipation of Heritage via Local Community Participation: Case Study of Orchha (India)

Dr. Devesh Nigam, *Assistant Professor*
Institute of Tourism & Hotel Management
Bundelkhand University, Jhansi-284128(U.P.)
&
Vinay Kumar Narula, *Research Scholar*
Alaggapa University, Tamilnadu

ABSTRACT

For many local communities in developing countries and elsewhere, the existence of large attractions nearby generates both benefits and costs. This paper examines some of the dynamics of the complex, nested relationships among host communities, their local heritage sites, and heritage tourism structures. Orchha in Madhya Pradesh, India, is used to illustrate the discussion of power, displacement and control, local participation, and the role of "heritage tourism management" in developing countries. It further offers some reflections on how tourism Planning and management might encourage small-scale local tourism enterprises for the benefit of both the host and guest populations.

Keywords: *Government planning, community participation, hosts, economic Relationship*

INTRODUCTION

Tourism's rapid international growth since the 60s has been well documented. Despite the recent sequence of external shocks since the September 11 terrorist attacks on the United States, including further bombings in Bali, Kenya, and Madrid, as well as the SARS epidemic and Iraq war in 2003, tourism is now the world's largest industry (WTO 2002, 2004a). Since the 60s, international tourism has been promoted as a major component of economic development and "modernization" strategies for many countries (OECD 1967; WTO 2004b) and seen as a "passport to development" (De Kadt 1979). In light of this expansion, many less developed countries (LDCs) were encouraged by multilateral institutions, including the World Bank and OECD, to host international tourism (OECD 1967). Given tourism's economic significance in most less develop countries, planning assumes a central role within the local political economy and highly detailed tourism development plans are created, with national, regional, and local master plans drawn up (Hall 2000b; Inskeep 1991).

The heritage tourism sector has received relatively little attention from scholars interested in the concept of sustainable tourism. With a few notable exceptions (Anfeld 1994; Cope 1995; Croft 1994; Johnson and Thomas 1995; van der Borg, Costa and Gotti 1996), the academic literature has preferred to concentrate on the cultural, educational, and practical conservation aspects of heritage tourism. Yet the heritage sector represents a highly significant component of tourism in many developed economies. For example in the United Kingdom, the heritage sector has been described as "a major strength of the British market for overseas visitors" (Markwell, Bennett and Ravenscroft 1997:95) and is estimated to generate around 28% of all UK tourism expenditure annually (Carr 1994). The heritage sector has also been vaunted as a major potential growth area for tourism in the UK (Prentice 1993a). In view of the economic significance of heritage as a tourism "product", it is curious indeed that so little interest has been shown in assessing the conditions that must be met in order to secure its sustainability. It is surprising that so little academic attention has been paid to exploring the relationship between heritage tourism and sustainability because the two concepts evidently share a common theme. Sustainable development has been defending as a process which ensures that "we pass onto the next generation a stock of (natural and built) capital assets no less than the stock we have now" (Pearce 1992:4). However, for many local or ''host'' communities located close to large heritage attractions, such development raises many issues. This paper considers tourism planning and its relationships to local communities and their economic development. In essence, it argues that there are two main aspects affecting present approaches to planning and local communities: the issue of power relations and the economic case for local community involvement.

Heritage Tourism and Local Community

International tourism, in addition to its economic contributions to wealth-creation, investment, and employment, also plays a significant role in the construction of many countries' national identities and, particularly, how a country wishes to be perceived by others. However, the ''real'' images portrayed in marketing material—whether of colorful local costume, ancient monuments, or ''tropical paradise'' beaches— are, highly contested realities that have been carefully constructed. In India , the focus of this paper that for Orchha , the Religious paradise image was deliberately engineered by the Ministry of Tourism, India , to facilitate economic development and to replace the late 50s popular imagery of India as a dangerous, chaotic place. This is particularly necessary following the terrorist bombing in 1993 & 2006 in Mumbai, India's premier destination,. Further, the serial bombing in the different cities in India in 200 5has made the management of India's image as a destination even more problematic than it was before. As a country covering a large geographical area, India has many tourism sites, including natural attractions such as Himalayas & Like so, charismatic large fauna, ancient human constructions such as the world heritage sites of Humpi & Taj Mahal and cultural attractions. Given the existence of heritage sites including temples, monuments, fortifications, and palaces, Ashworth (1997) raised the fundamental question alluded to earlier: whose heritage is this? In India constitutionally multicultural concept found since 5000 years earlier. It is an image that could appear to be dissonant with the present local community. Therefore, the historical specificity of any given attraction may be helpfully considered as a being a social construction. In other words, its particular meaning and significance are in fact created and then shared by a particular human society at a given time and place in world history. Any analysis of the site should be viewed within this context. This paper considers in more detail the nature of the complex relationships between the tourism attraction and the local host community.

Local Communities as Central Point

Of the variety of models addressing tourism impacts, (Britton's, 1989) approach, based on the "Dependency Theory", maintains that in order to understand the tourism industry one must consider the organisation of international tourism and examine the structure of the peripheral (host) economy. On the other hand, (Preister, 1989) considers Britton's "Dependency Theory" to be to global for use at local level. He claims that locally affected people are not shaped passively by outside forces but react as well, at times even changing the conditions of the larger system, and that the outcome of Heritage tourism development is a negotiated process.

Communities are a basic element in modern Development. They are the focal point for the supply of accommodation, catering, information, transport facilities and services. Their local natural environment, buildings and institutions, their people, culture and history, all form core elements of what the tourists come to see. Whether as towns, villages or cities, every community has tourism at one level or another, and is affected by the growth and development of the industry (Godfrey & Clarke 2000: 3).Government plan based on Community Participation are the most suitable for a development where the community is participating actively in the decision-making process. Clearly, governments should be involved in establishing guidelines and formulating laws to guide the planning and implementation of Heritage Conservation. However, this is not enough. Local community involvement is necessary to enhance or to further develop sustainable communities. An important precondition is that Heritage tourism development will be community based yet it needs the support of locals, regional and national governments. (Inskeep) points out that host communities must have a right of voice in shaping their future community and has called for the maximum involvement of the local community to maximise socio-economic benefits of tourism for the community (In Tosun 2000: 616). In doing so, the first thing to achieve is the local communities' understanding on the importance and the repercussions of tourism development in their region in order to encourage an authentic participation and involvement. Local communities and the various stakeholders must be familiar with the process to appreciate it and thereby support it (Cottrell, 2001: 7).

Role of Local Community

- Local Community Participation

- Implication of a Plan
- Government plan For Heritage Tourism

Literature Review:

Heritage, "the 'buzz' word of the 1990s" (Palmer 1999:315), is regarded as one of the most significant and fastest growing components of tourism (Alzua, O'Leary and Morrison 1998; Herbert 1995). It is referred to as something which needs to be managed (Cheung 1999) and marketed (Bennett 1995) differently. The subject is of increasing interest from a range of disciplines and its study is perceived as useful for understanding social behavior of individuals and society as a whole (Hewison 1987; Nuryanti 1996). Research has focused on the growing "heritage industry" (Conlin 2001; Hewison 1987) where researchers often differentiate between cultural (Richards 1996), natural (Hall 2000), and built (Laws 1998) elements. This paper focuses upon what is generally called cultural heritage, but for convenience the term heritage is used throughout. The literature commonly investigates and clarifies elements associated with prevention of heritage and role of the local community(Crang 1999; Halewood and Hannam 2001; Garrod and Fyall 2000).Earlier work in this field in Ghana (Bruner 1995), and at the Irish National Heritage Park (Johnson 1999) refers to perception as a factor relevant in understanding behavior of local Community. Cheung (1999) indicates that a heritage destination can have different meanings for different people. (Herbert and Piccini (1999) believe that what is presented stimulates thought and notions based on the individual's background. Michael (2002) asserts that heritage tourism should not be viewed in terms of arbitrary issues, but should take into consideration sociopsychological needs. Another study of relevance here concerns residents' attitudes. Uriely, Israeli and Reichel (2002), taking into account local people's religious affiliations, argue that the relationship between the local residents and the heritage presented can influence the locals' attitudes towards development. (In Nazareth, in the case of 240 HERITAGE TOURISM their study). Geographic and psychological literature suggests that in order to understand individual behavior in a specific space, it is necessary to reveal certain aspects of the links between the individual and that space (Zube 1987; Zube, Sell and Taylor 1982). Although all these studies used perception, this concept was not explored in relation to the specific issue under scrutiny here. Nevertheless, the literature suggests that some links are relevant to the understanding and this relationship is examined in this paper. In fact the literature contains two main approaches to the precise phenomenon under study. The first and most common is to regard it as tourism in places categorized as heritage or historic places. An example of this approach is illustrated in Seale's description "the visitors to heritage areas/sites" (1996:486) or Laws' arbitrary classification of those visiting castles as heritage tourists (1998). The second approach emphasizes that the contents of a place are linked to the local people, as illustrated by Strauss and Lord. In their opening sentence, they indicate "history is a popular theme for recreational travel"

Research Aim

The primary aim of this paper is to explore the Heritage tourism potential in the study area using previous multivariate statistical measures of community segments and their five attitudes toward future tourism development. The secondary aim is to spatially represent these Segments and attitude factors on to the modified boundaries of tourism Development to determine what Social implications they might have for the agencies that promote Heritage tourism in this area.

Study Method

This research is an outcome of three consecutive fields Survey undertaken from August 2005 to May 2006. Although data was collected from Orchha, it was decided for the final analysis to join Local Community participation with Anticipation of Heritage. However, care was taken to include all the communities in the survey so as to get a glimpse of the overall resident attitudes and perceptions. The fine tuning of the two page research instrument was undertaken by the two researchers in the year 2005 (Nigam &Narula, 2005).

Local People as Participants

For this study a stratified purposive sampling framework was undertaken in order to get the balanced view. Residents were selected from all walks of life, age, gender, educational background, and involvement with tourism industry. A sample of 105 residents was collected within the tourism product region .Although the over all sample for this study consisted of 300 people, only 267 were used for the final results. The salient features of the sample are: male: female ratio was around 79:21; the mean age of the sample was 35.6 years (range 18-57 years); 12% were Graduate, 33 % not married ; 46% had dependent children living at home ; and mean length of residence was 10 years with 70% of residents living in the Study Area for more than 20 years.

Materials (Questionnaire)

The administered questionnaire consisted of three well separated sections (only two of which are relevant to this research. The first section consisted of five heritage *tourism and five attitude statements* based on a five point (Likert) scale for the sample to choose.

Factor generation

Factor 1-Tourism: Negative impact (Heritage Tourism development has negatively impacted on the quality of life of the local community)

Examples of items on the final scale are:

1. General quality of life has deteriorated thanks to tourism in my region
2. Heritage Tourism development has change the face of our cultural and heritage properties

Factor 2-Tourism: Positive impacts (Tourism development has benefited the community)

1. Through tourism development our local culture gets better national respect.
2. International tourism in my place has helped to local Community serve the better picture of country to the world

Factor 3-Tourism: Positive change (Tourism has promoted local infrastructure)

1. Thanks to tourism the recreational facilities have got a facelift.
2. My region would be a dull place if heritage tourism did not develop to this extent

Factor 4-Tourism: Negative change (Tourism industry is perceived as insular and self-serving)

1. Tourism benefits those who are promoting it for profits
2. Tourism has increased the cost of living in my region

Results and discussion:

The primary aim of this paper is to explore the Heritage tourism potential in the study area using previous multivariate statistical measures of community segments and their five attitudes toward future tourism development. The Segment distribution of community groups in terms of location within Orchha. The Factor is regional distribution of attitudes toward future Heritage tourism development. The conceptualization of results formed around the notion that while tourism planners had failed to widely consult with local community members living in Study area, the communities in this Study area will vary in their composition and their attitudes toward future heritage tourism development. A survey of this result allows tourism planners to effortlessly determine the residential location of types of community members and their positive and negative attitudes toward heritage tourism development. By overlaying proposed future tourism development planners (tourism industry and local / state governments) can readily identify the acceptance (residents with positive attitudes) or social impacts (residents with negative attitudes) on the related community. Using the factor segment as a tool, distributional characteristics of attitudes can be discerned. This segment clearly shows that respondents within Orchha have varied views about the impact of tourism on economy and lifestyle. These respondents acknowledged the significance to tourism, though they are also cautious and skeptic about its impact on culture and economy.

Factor 1, labeled "high Connection and negative attitude" indicated that the host communities, which are more connected with tourism, have more appreciation of heritage tourism as an economic development instrument. It can be seen in the results that the resident clusters with *low industry connection but with a strong negative attitude and high industry connection but with a negative attitude score over other clusters.* Similarly, the factor distribution inside this Area reveals the governance of the factors *strong negative impact strong positive change* and the *strong positive impact.* This particular study area enjoys being proximity to the biggest heritage tourism generating region –. The tourism development strategies envisaged for this region are increasing the yield by converting the predominant day trips into overnight stays. Perhaps, some of the urgent infrastructure issues such as sewerage treatment and clean water supply through the Orchha could be more important to the residents than the ever increasing visitor demand on these necessities. The public agencies and the concerned local councils need to show more pragmatic approach with regard to the implementation of the envisaged developments since the overall resident attitude does not seem to be heartening. Local government initiated tourism plans and endeavours need to be friendly towards the cluster which has strong negative attitudes with very low industry connection, this cluster has large number of well educated males, married with pre-adolescent children, live close to the major tourist attractions for five to twenty years. By involving and listening to this cluster local tourism associations could increase the Awareness for tourism in the Area in the future. In the attitudinal cluster dispersal shows a dominance of *low connection negative attitude* followed by *high connection positive attitudes* over other two clusters. The factor scattering shows a combination of the dominance of *strong positive change and strong positive impac*t factors over other factors. Perhaps, at the completion of the designed three phase heritage tourism plan, with the expected economic upturn, the resident attitude might change for the better. The strategies proposed towards developing the area's infrastructure, Heritage classification, accommodation and touring should open the avenues for those who hold a *Strong Positive Impact* and *Strong Positive Change* attitudes.

CONCLUSION

In regular tourism, tourists believe they provide some benefits to the Local community in different ways. They buy handicrafts, seeing the cultural programmes, give some money to the artists or donate some used clothing to the villagers. The tourists truly believe they are benefiting the Local area or local Communities, but in many cases it may not at all. This will give many of the negative impacts on regular tourism. Local communities can manage their own tourism program and get benefits from Heritage tourism. But of course, in most cases, it does not happen by itself. It does need the right guidance and facilitation, at least in the beginning stages, in order to be feasible and successful tourism policies.

This paper suggests the need for a radical rethinking of the relationships between such sites and the local host communities. In particular, a new approach to tourism planning is urgently needed. This is seen in issues of power and control, and also in the economic case for local community participation. The following suggestions are offered, while recognizing that the historical specificity of each LDC, different regions within each country, types of attraction, local contexts, political economy of power relations, and particular characteristics of any given tourism authority, should not lead to the "one size fits all" approach (Simpson and Wall 1999). In light of all this, how then might a start be made? First, tourism departments and local authorities could engage with and listen to the local communities who live within and near attractions. The main concerns of the local people about the site, their level of involvement, "ownership" of the site, the mix of local and outside control of businesses, and ideas and concerns about managing the site all constitute appropriate agenda items. Listening to local communities is only the beginning of the process of increasing local participation. One possible way forward is through creating effective partnerships between host communities and the authorities, so that local people feel that the attraction is their heritage site as well as the tourists' (Black and Wall 2001). While structural, financial, and cultural issues could impede implementation (Tosun 2000), it is a valuable objective to work towards. As well as listening to the views expressed by the host community, planners and decision makers need to recognize the legitimate existence of small-scale businesses and the informal sector in plans for the development of regions, new resorts, or in the upgrading of existing attractions, including their roles in an integrated tourism system.

Ratter (1998) proposed the idea of "planagement", where small areas are seen as being like complicated ecosystems, thus requiring the careful fusion of planning and management, hence the term. The implementation of such ideas perhaps awaits a new generation of planners to be in place in many LDCs to begin explicitly to include the people "outside the plans". Again, more than just lip-service being paid to local participation is required. As Tosun (2000) noted, there is also commonly a need for education of both planners and local people. He argued that some developmental nongovernmental organizations might have a useful role to play given their experiences with participatory development at the community level. The UK Department for International Development's interest in pro-poor tourism might facilitate further initiatives (DFID 1999; PPT 2004; Roe et al 2004) Increasing local participation will require facilitating access to capital, in particular micro loans for small businesses. Research in Yogyakarta demonstrates that the capital needs of small tourism businesses are minimal, but to obtain loans for startup capital or improvements they are hampered by lack of collateral which reduces access to banks and other lenders (Hampton 2003). LDC governments might learn from the success of the (nongovernmental) Grameen Bank in Bangladesh (The Guardian 2004) by encouraging the formation of specialized tourism micro credit agencies. Investment incentives could be created for small and medium-sized businesses, while placing strict limitations on new large hotel developments. This, of course, assumes that the encouragement of local small-scale businesses appears desirable, rather than a continuing "bigger is better" mindset. This may be the main obstacle to any movement towards increasing local participation. In addition, given the major role of external funding in much LDC tourism, a continuing focus on large-scale projects to capture economies of scale may be difficult to change. Free or highly subsidized basic training (perhaps funded by the national tourism departments) would assist many small-scale businesses.

The aim would not be to replicate Fordist business methods, but rather to encourage post-Fordist, niche production and facilitate a better understanding of both international and domestic markets. Training could include craftwork production, marketing, distribution, appropriate sales techniques, and (for those working with international tourists) English language tuition (Roland 1999). Research by Cukier (2002) in Bali found that training also enhanced employability and facilitated employment for local people. In the final analysis, the empowerment of local communities to benefit from tourism in LDCs requires a radical rethinking of present planning priorities, although it is recognized that the political economy of local structures and the elites' vested interests are also highly signifi-cant. Further, the role of transnational corporations as key actors is also crucial, as external capital can facilitate real change in the host society, or it may merely prolong the existence of a rentier class (Gunder Frank 1967) expropriating some of the surplus enroute to the industrialized countries. This also raises the fundamental issue of whether—under conventional international tourism—low income countries have merely exchanged one form of dependency for another (Britton 1982; Brohman 1996; Mowforth and Munt 2003; Tosun 2000). If "empowerment" of local people is to become more than just a buzzword or hopeful sentiment, it clearly requires the participation of local communities in partnership with the state, its agencies, and the large operators rather than being a passive "host" community that happens to have a major attraction on its doorstep. As Tosun comments: "community participation in the development process cannot become much of a reality unless specific and deliberate strategies at local, national, and international levels are developed" (2000:626). Concerning the latter, the gradual international acceptance of the principles of the 1992 Rio Earth Summit, especially those of Local Agenda 21, gives some hope that local communities may benefit from a new approach to planning and managing local assets. In the same way, the increasing acceptance of the need for meaningful participation of local people also provides hope that heritage sites may be able to generate real economic and social benefits for their local host communities.

REFERENCES

- Aditjondro, G. 1995 Bali, Jakarta's Colony: Social and Ecological Impacts of Jakarta-based Conglomerates in Bali's Tourism Industry. Asia Research Center Working Paper No. 58. Perth: Murdoch University.
- Ashley, C. 2000 The Impacts of Tourism on Rural Livelihoods: Namibia's Experience. ODI Working Paper 128. London: Overseas Development Institute.
- Ashley, C., C. Boyd, and H. Goodwin 2000 Pro-Poor Tourism: Putting Poverty at the Heart of the Tourism Agenda. ODI Natural Resource Perspectives (51). London: Overseas Development Institute.
- Ashworth, G. 1997 Elements of Planning and Managing Heritage Sites. In Tourism and Heritage Management, W. Nuryanti, ed., pp. 165–191. Yogyakarta: Gadjah Mada University Press.
- Ashworth, G., and B. Van der Aa 2002 Bamyan: Whose Heritage was it and What Should We Do about It? Current Issues in Tourism 5:447–457.
- Berry, S., Conservation, Capacity and Cash Flows: Tourism and Historic Building Management. In Tourism: The State of the Art, A. V. Seaton, ed., pp. 712± 718, 1994, Chichester: Wiley.
- Bramwell, B., and B. Lane,, Interpretation and Sustainable Tourism: The Potential and the Pitfalls. Journal of Sustainable Tourism, 1993, 1:71±80.
- Bramwell, B., and B. Lane, eds. Rural Tourism and Sustainable Rural Development., 1994, Cleve don: Channel View.
- Chambers, R. 1983 Rural Development. Putting the Last First. London: Longman. 1997 Whose Reality Counts? Putting the First Last. London: Intermediate Technology Publications.
- De Kadt, E., ed. 1979 Tourism, Passport to Development? Oxford: Oxford University Press.
- Debbage, K. and D. Ioannides, eds., 1998, the Economic Geography of the Tourist Industry. London: Routledge.

- DFID (Department for International Development) 1999 Tourism and Poverty Elimination: Untapped Potential. London: DFID.
- Din, K. 1993 Dialogue with the Hosts: An Educational strategy towards sustainable tourism. In Tourism in South-East Asia, M. Hitchcock, V. King and M. Parnwell, eds., pp. 327–336. London: Routledge.
- Dumarcay, J. 1978 Borobudur. Oxford: Oxford University Press.
- Ecoforum 1993 Fish, Curry and Rice: A Citizens' Report on the Goan Environment. Goa: The Other India Press.

19

Pilgrimage Tourism: A Resource for Sustainable Tourism Development

Bharti Gupta, _Scholar (UGC-JRF),_
Centre of Hospitality and
Tourism Management, University of Jammu,
Jammu.

The concept of sustainable tourism represents a set of principles, policy prescriptions and management methods that chart a path for tourism development in such a way that the destination area's environmental resource base- natural, built and cultural features- is protected for future development. Tourism activity if not managed properly leads inevitably towards environment resource's depletion. Different forms of tourism namely cultural, adventurous, recreation, conference etc. all have inherent features of causing negative impacts upon the environment. These negative impacts over the period of time become reasons for the decline of tourist inflow and thus depriving the coming generation of the benefits of tourism. This study highlights that from among various tourism forms pilgrimage tourism can achieve the goal of sustainability effectively as it is inherently having features most suitable for the sustainable tourism development. In addition to this a survey has been done which results that pilgrimage destination choice selection is very less affected by external factors which normally remain deterrents to tourism in case of other forms of tourism enabling the future generation to keep enjoying the benefits and thus supporting the sustainable tourism development.

Key words: - _Sustainable tourism, pilgrimage, deterrents, external factors, etc._

INTRODUCTION

As part of the process of rapid growth, the tourism industry has become more diversified, selling better targeted and more sophisticated products. The bulk if mass tourism is gradually being segmented into such varied sub markets as urban tourism, natural tourism, ecotourism, adventure tourism, sports tourism, religious tourism and recently even dark tourism (Gibson and Yiannakis, 2002; Mishara, 2000;Poria et al., 2001). All these tourism activities deal with provisioning of various services and it is based on the availability of the environmental resources, which are free to all. The intangibility aspect of services, the unique nature of the tourism product and the free ride of the environmental resources have made the management of this economic phenomenon very difficult. Tourism needs extra ability from the professionals of tourism to manage the subtle aspects of the industry. This demand from the professional if not met will lead to environmental resource base depletion and decline of tourism and thus killing of tourism by tourism. The growing awareness about the importance of environment as a result of environmentalism has directed the attention of tourism developer to develop tourism on the basis of sustainability.

Sustainable tourism development is a concept that represents a set of principles, policy prescriptions and management methods that chart a path for tourism development in such a way that the destination area's environmental resource base -natural, built and cultural features is protected for future development. (Batt.R.N.,2000). The sustainability therefore implies the amount of consumption that can be continued indefinitely without degrading stocks of natural and man made capital. Brundtland Commission gives the most referred definition for the sustainable developmnt in the report. It defines sustainable development as development that meets the needs of the present generation without compromising the ability of future generation to meet their own needs. (WCED, 1987)

The application of sustainability is the strategical need of the hour. The neglect of this issue will be harmful not only to environment but will ultimately put detrimental affect on human welfare. This study explicitly depicts the different inherent features related to pilgrimage tourism which can naturally contributes toward the objective of sustainable tourism development. It also highlights that decline of tourist inflow which is resultant in case of other forms of tourist activities not managed properly does not come up as a consequence in the presence of various deterrents in case of pilgrimage tourism.

Pilgrimage Tourism and Sustainability

Spiritual and religious tourisms, types of pilgrimage tourism have been into practice for many hundred of years. This form of tourism is represented by a strong desire to visit a place of personal religious of spiritual inclinations. From among the countries of the world India comes first in the range of religious diversity. India is also a hub for spiritual tourism granted by the need of master (guru) for spiritual enlightenment.

There are certain factors, which are common to almost all of the religions and spiritual practices. These common factors qualitatively support the norms of sustainability.

The factors are:

1. No excessive burden on the environment.
2. Killing of animals is mostly prohibited.
3. Maximum involvement of the local community.

4. Very less cultural difference between the hosts and the tourists.
5. Occur at certain times of the year only.

1. No excessive burden on the environment: Pilgrims needs are very limited. These are directed towards performing the religious/spiritual practices. Unlike other tourism forms it does not expect super infrastructure. Even the limited basic infrastructure may suffice the need. Pilgrims' demands do not include luxury hotels, recreational facilities, etc. which can be brought about by utilizing and disturbing the environmental resource base.
2. Killing of animals is mostly prohibited: Most of the religions except a few do not recommend for killing and eating animals. This prohibition thus protects the animals. In other forms of tourism hunting may be one of the recreational pursuit endangering animal's life.
3. Maximum involvement of the local community: Local community serves the needs of the pilgrims by organizing small businesses. Local community gains all the economic benefits by the spending of the pilgrims. Besides the ubiquitous needs of tourists like food, accommodation, transportation, pilgrims needs also include the particular needs related to the offerings that are to be made to the deity. Their particular needs at the destination may also correspond to the climatic conditions of the destination. Such needs are better understood and served by the locals. Pilgrim's spending on their requirement generates employment as well as income to the locals.
4. Very less cultural difference between the hosts and pilgrims: The nature of host-guest relationship determines the success or failure of tourism at destination. Smooth relations are developed when hosts feels that they are benefited from the activity. Smooth relations also develop in the absence of any disturbing difference in lifestyle and culture of the guest and the host. In pilgrimage tourism, participation of local community in serving the needs make them feel benefited. In addition to this there is very less cultural difference between these two groups. Thus leaving a least chance of hostility.
5. Occur at certain times of the year: There is a high level of seasonal factor present in case of pilgrimage tourism. Most of the pilgrims' activities are conducted in certain part of the year. E.g. Badrinath, Kedarnath have peak seasons in summers, as the two shrines remain closed in winters. Similarly for Amarnath yatra to Kashmir, the pilgrimage is only for two months .The shrine shri Mata Vaishno Devi in Jammu has tourist inflow throughout the year but still it has peaks and lows depending on the periodic summer vacations and Navratras.

This seasonal factor gives time to the destination to revitalize itself thus getting back its status quo in case of any disturbance caused in the nature's equilibrium there by achieving the aim of sustainability.

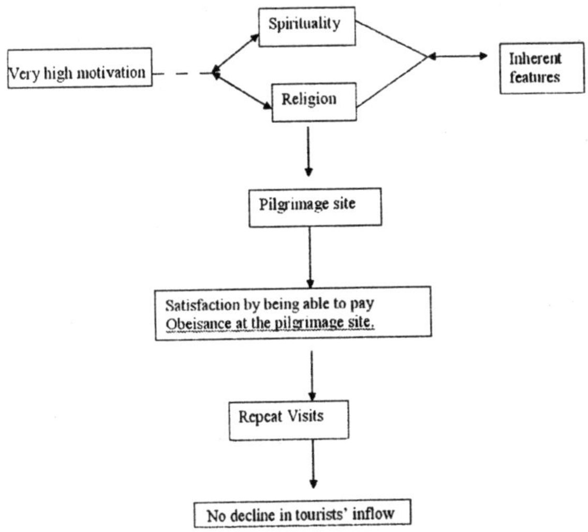

Fig. 1

- No excessive burden on the environment.
- Killing if animals is prohibited
- Maximum involvement of the local people.
- Very less cultural difference between the hosts and pilgrims
- Occur at the certain time of the year only.

The figure 1 shows that spirituality or religion is having inherent features, which achieves sustainable tourism. When the sustainability goal is achieved then it means that there is no depletion of resources. This ensures continuous flow of tourists to the destination, as there is adequate supply of resources. Exception to this flow could be the factors like change in the tastes of customers or trend.

The figure 1. also shows that the motivation level is very high in case of sustainable/ religious tourism . This motivation takes one to the pilgrimage site. Pilgrims' attainment of satisfaction comes after paying obeisance at the pilgrimage site. The proper facility / opportunity for paying obeisance is good enough to satisfy a pilgrim. His satisfaction induces him to come again for the same journey and the process. There is no decline in tourists'inflow as tourists continue to repeat their visit due to their high motivation level.

The high motivation level of pilgrims has been determined by a sample survey of around two hundred pilgrims to Mata Vaishno Devi and Shri Amarnath. In this survey

Yes and No questions are asked in for factors which mainly act as deterrents to tourism activity in case of other tourism forms.

Table 1. Assessment by pilgrims about the role of the following factors in influencing their pilgrimage destination choice selection.

Factors	Percentage (Yes)	Percentage (No)
1) Distance	82	18
2) Transportation cost	76	24
3) High accommodation cost	90	10
4) High price of the essential commodities	95	5
5) Non- availability of the facilities	75	15
6) Discomfort during the pilgrimage	96	4
7) Problems related to safety and security	97	3
8) Terrorism	86	14

The table 1 clearly shows that the factors, which are characteristically the deterrants for tourism donot, play any vital role in influencing the pilgrimage destination choice selection, as the response of majority of the respondents is negative.

This result indicates that the pilgrimage tourism is the type where the normal deterrents do not act as limiting factors for pilgrims to visit the particular place. This shows that the pilgrims are highly motivated to visit a particular place.

a. New Product Development

b. Application of management tools

- Carrying capacity analysis
- Environment Impact Analysis
- Valuation of environmental resources

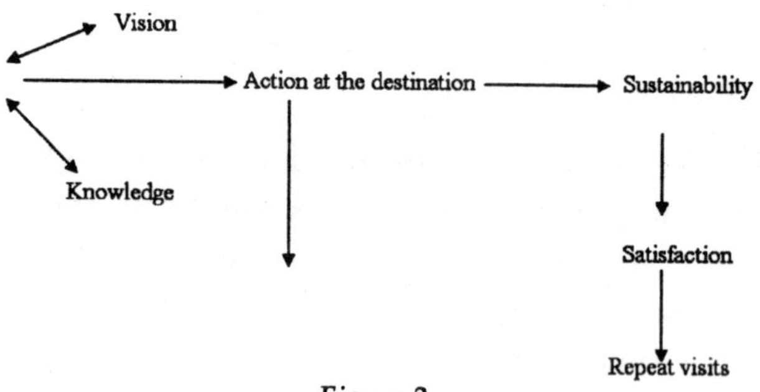

Figure 2.

The figure 2 shows that the knowledge and vision act as the source of creativity which enable the policy makers to take actions which involve New Product Development which is a strategy for growth and responsible for the continuous charm of the destination. In addition to these, management tools are applied which include carrying capacity analysis, environment impact assessment and valuation of environment resources. These management tools ensure that there is no depletion of resources. This adds to the charm of the destination and achieves sustainability. Visitors feel highly satisfied in the destination, which retain their beauty and resources. The satisfaction attained ensures further visits of the tourists to the destination and thus the subsequent benefits.

CONCLUSION

Sustainable tourism, which is the current rage for the tourism development policy makers, is not the trend but the need of the hour. The different forms of tourism do not ensure sustainable development unless certain actions are undertaken which involve application of management tools namely carrying capacity analysis, environment impact assessment and valuation of environmental resources; as well as new product development. From among the various forms of tourism, it is the pilgrimage tourism, which may not involve application of these management tools to achieve sustainability, as there are certain features inherent to this form of tourism, which leads to sustainability on its own. These features are no excessive burden on the environment; killing of animals is mostly prohibited, maximum involvement of the local community, very less cultural difference between the hosts and the tourists and occurrence at certain times of the year only.

In pilgrimage tourism the high motivation level influences the repeat visits. A sample survey of two hundred pilgrims to Shri Mata VaishnoDevi and Shri Amarnath yatra has revealed that the maximum percentage of pilgrims did not change their choice of selection to pilgrimage destination even in the presence of those factors which normally act as deterrents to tourism and this tendency of the pilgrims is a further support to sustainable tourism development as it helps the locals to accrue constant benefits of the consistent flow of tourists to the destination. The other forms of tourism attain repeat visits when there is achievement of sustainability that is there is no depletion of resources. The study shows that the pilgrimage tourism is the most suitable form from among various forms of tourism to the sustainable tourism development.

REFERENCES

1. Bhardwaj,S.M.(2000)"Hindu Places of Pilgrimage in India", University of California Press ,Berkeley.
2. Collins-Kreiner,N. and Kliot,N.(2000) 'Pilgrimage Tourism in the Holy Land: the behavioural characteristics of Christian Pilgrims, Geojournal,50,5-67.
3. Digance,J. (2003)" Pilgrimage at Contested Sites", Annals of Tourism research,30,1,143-149.
4. Dhar,T.N.and Gupta,S.P.(1999)"Tourism in Indian Himalaya", Indian Institute of Public Administration, U.P,Branch, Lucknow.
5. Fleisher, A., (2000)" The tourist behind the Pilgrim in the Holy Land", Hospitality Mangement,19,311-326.

6. Gibbons,P.P.R (1999) "Tourist or a Pilgrim",Association for Heritage Interpretation. Journal Article,St,Mary's University College StrawberryHill.http//www.heritageinrepretation.org.uk/j4A_tourist.htm
7. le Beau,B.F. and Mor,M.(eds)(1996)"Pilgrims and Travellers to the Holy Land", Crighton University Press, Omaha, NE.
8. Mishara,L. (1999)"Religious tourism in India", Mohit Publications,New Delhi.
9. Sizer,S.R.(1997)"The Hidden Face of Holy Land Pilgrimge Tourism" International Journal of Contemporary Hospitality Management,9,1,34-35.
10. Sizer,S.R.(1999)"The Ethical Challenges of Managing Pilgrimage to the Holy Land, International Journal of Contemporary Hospitality Managementy,4,2,85-90.

20

Tourism and Environmental Quality Management: Comparative Perspectives

Babu P George
Lecturer in Tourism Studies
School of Management
Pondicherry University, India
(Please address all correspondences to Babu P George at myselfgeorge@gmail.com)

Gopal Sami Poyyamoli
Reader
Department of Ecology and Environmental Sciences,
Pondicherry University, India

ABSTRACT

Tourism and the environment are intricately and inseparably interlinked, with many positive relationships as well as several irreversible negative impacts. Destinations of higher environmental quality attract tourists and in that process are also transmuted, either positively or negatively. Drawing evidences largely from the Indian context, the present paper analyzes the root causes of tourism related degradation in environmental quality and suggests alternatives that synergizes tourism and environment. Two case studies are presented: one to show how tourism produces inferior environmental quality and the other to suggest a practical means to overcome the apparent contradiction between conservation and development. It is concluded that the paradigm of eco-cultural tourism and the praxis of community based ecotourism could provide useful global frameworks with reference to which locally informed quality-tourism initiatives could be formulated and customized.

Keywords. *Environmental quality, tourism impacts, eco-labelling, eco-cultural tourism, case studies on Goa Tourism and RTS in Spain.*

INTRODUCTION

The quality of environment, physical and socio-cultural, provides a sustainable basis of competitive advantage for tourism destinations and firms. Environmental resources provide one of the most basic ingredients, a critical production factor, for the production of touristic experiences. They include natural scenery, islands, beaches, back waters, coral reefs, mangroves, mountains, valleys, waterfalls, ancient monuments, traditional and picturesque towns and villages and many more. They offer settings for the tourists to enjoy, live in, and relax. Tourism's relationship with the environment involves many activities that can have both adverse and beneficial environmental impacts. Many of these impacts are linked with the construction of general infrastructure such as roads and airports and tourism facilities including resorts, hotels, restaurants, shops, golf courses, and marinas. The negative impacts of tourism development can gradually destroy the environmental resources based on which it depends. Conversely, properly managed, tourism has the potential to create favorable effects on the environment by contributing to environmental protection and conservation. The natural resource base which supports tourism is heavily stressed in and around the major tourist destination areas.

The problem is that these areas now support large transient populations with high-income lifestyles and these impacts harm both the environmental quality of the destination areas and the people; i.e., the tourists as well as the local communities. Changes in the physical, spatial, and socio-economic structure of a tourist area as well as the existence of several, sometimes burdensome, environmental problems testify to the presence of these conflicts and the crying need for evolving appropriate strategies to manage the environmental quality, especially in the third world countries like India (Singh, *et al.* 1989). Yet, policy makers in such countries prejudice that the demand for environmental quality is low due to issues like poverty and the governmental policies largely ignore any voice calling for a better environment. Not only that, even in Kerala, the most advanced of all Indian states, any opposition to large-scale, polluting tourism projects by environmental and labor activists is often dealt with by the governmental machinery through totally undemocratic means (Sreekumar& Parayil, 2002). At present, the Indian Tourism Development Corporation (ITDC) and the State Tourism Development Corporations invariably restrict themselves to the tasks of setting up infrastructure, promoting holidays, etc. These organs of the state make only ad-hoc efforts to improve the environmental quality. This is self-evident from the "tell-tale symptoms" or "indicators" of degradation in environmental quality such as garbage dumps, foul smell, and exorbitantly high rates of all sorts of pollution in popular destination areas. One important reason why environmental conservation is perceived by the tourism industry stakeholders as antithetical to tourism development is the sheer lack of awareness about the unique and sustainable competitive advantage that a quality environment present at a destination region could provide to the tourism industry there (Hassan, 2000).

The present paper is conceptually weaved together with inputs mainly from the eco-tourism literature to throw light upon the interface between tourism and environmental quality. The paper argues that under certain conditions tourism and environmental quality are natural partners: properly managed, tourism can enhance rather than lower the environmental quality of a destination area. Two case studies are presented: one to show how tourism produces inferior environmental quality and the other to suggest a practical means to overcome the apparent contradiction between conservation and development.

TOURISM AND ENVIRONMENTAL QUALITY LINKAGE

Environmental quality related issues have already become a major area of investigation for environmental psychologists, tourism ecologists, and geographers (Altman & Wohlwill,

1983; Blangy *et.al.*, 1993; Bourassa, 1990; Daniel, 1990; Demick & Wapner, 1990; Höge, 1990;). Of late, interest in the topic has grown quite markedly which brought out in-depth analyses like the one provided by Davies & Cahill (2000). In their report, employing a framework developed from industrial ecology, these authors analyze the environmental impacts of tourism industry in the United States, where it is the third largest, behind only automotive dealers and food stores. According to most of the available studies, environmental quality refers to the quality of air, water, and landscapes that are aesthetically important attributes for attracting tourists.

Tourism's demand for environmental resources is not so simple to identify and analyze as it might appear at the first thought. This is because tourism is not a single economic activity with a rather standard pattern of input requirements and a standardized output. Tourism is a complex of interdependent and inseparable activities (that include travel, lodging, shopping, recreation, and services), each one with its own demand for inputs and characteristic outputs. The demand for the products of tourism is ultimately a holistic synthesis (not a mere addition) of these individual demands. Hence, the analysis of tourism demand for environmental inputs involves analysis of the demands made by its constituent activities as well as the interrelationships among these individual demands.

This demand analysis is important for two reasons:

1. Tourism development of an area must take into account the availability of local resources (ecological, cultural, heritage, and human) that are necessary for its growth and maintenance; and,
2. Tourism-related activities are to compete for the environmental resources of an area among themselves and with other economic activities (agriculture, industry, trade, transportation, etc) and conflicts among different uses/users are natural to arise. Depending on the developmental context, these conflicts result either in the deterioration of the quality of the tourist product and consequently bring losses to the tourism industry or culminate in a struggle for the domination of the most economically profitable activity.

The use of an area's environmental resources for tourism has two important consequences. Firstly, the quantity of available resources diminishes and sets limits to further tourism development in the area. Physically or economically non-augmentable resources like beaches and sites of natural or archaeological interest become limiting factors in this respect. For other types of resources, planning and managerial interventions must be made to maintain their quantity at levels necessary for continued tourism activity. Secondly, the quality of resources deteriorates with possible negative effects on tourism itself. This is because with increasing exploitation, the tourist product offered will become of inferior quality and the quantity of superior quality products available (which was the original reason for tourism development in that region) gets shrunk.

Tourism produces a variety of unwanted by-products that are disposed, intentionally and unintentionally, to the environment and adulterate it in that process; they are collectively called as the externalities by traditional economists. Moreover, as noted above, in the name of providing quality holiday experiences, tourism uses up and modifies natural resources affecting their quantity and quality available for tourism purposes themselves. It is an irony that developmental initiatives aimed at tourism ultimately detracts the tourists and destroys the tourism industry itself. Thus, sustainable tourism development depends in many important ways on the proper handling of the relationships between tourism and the environment. In 1996, in an effort to integrate tourism into the broader sustainability discussions, World Tourism Organization, World Travel & Tourism Council, and the Earth Council released their own action-plan, *Agenda 21 for the Travel and Tourism Industry*, outlining key priorities for governments, the industry, and others. (Inskeep, 1991; WTTC, WTO, and the Earth council, 1996).

In spite of the revolutionary strides in the technological realm and our lofty claims about progress, we have trapped ourselves in a vicious circle of self-deception by adopting the typical "boom and bust" tourism paths. The question is whether we, in the blind pursuit of rapid economic growth and more foreign exchange earnings can afford to sacrifice the higher environmental quality upon which tourism so strongly depends. Though we have already learnt many bitter lessons, we tend to overlook them due to the higher short-term gains from neglecting them and the longer gestation time for the negative impacts to manifest themselves.

THE AESTHETICS OF ENVIRONMENTAL QUALITY

Tourists are attracted to destinations of higher Environmental quality (Hull & Revell, 1989; Viljoen, *et al.*, 1988). Many top ranking destinations in the world are blessed with a variety of natural attractions such as tropical climate, unspoiled beaches, forests, country side, chilly hill tops with rolling grass lands, clear coastal waters, bewitching back waters, fresh flowing rivers, lush vegetation, and other scenic landscapes besides another set of destinations that are known for their ethnic diversity, arts and crafts, and architectural splendor. It has been noted that even in the case of those attractions where poor environmental quality is an integral part of the authentic tourism product, tourists preferred a staged version of the same product with better environmental quality features even though doing so would introduce some degree of inauthenticity (Inskeep, 1991).

The presence of natural outdoor environments in their authentic state is of utmost importance to psychological well-being (Godlee & Walker, 1991). Destinations that maintain low environmental quality are offensive, both visually and conceptually. According to Moore & Scott (2003), destinations of high environmental quality provides a set of positive meanings, beliefs, symbols, values, and feelings in the visitor and generates in them what these authors call as destination attachment, which is a sense of oneness or belongingness with the environment. In any outdoor tourism activity, human experience, knowledge, expectation, and socio-cultural context interact with environmental elements as entities to produce an outcome that affects both the humans and the environment (Pitt & Zube, 1987).The visual characteristics of landscapes that enhance the attraction of the destination areas such as moderate complexity and depth; moderately even ground surface; deflected vistas here and there; mystery elements though without an appraised threat; etc., are hence important for any tourism activity.

Since scientific landscaping is almost unheard in developing countries, their destinations suffer from great degrees of aesthetic pollution. Live Indian examples can be cited from Kashmir in the North to Kannyakumari in the South and Kovalam in the West to Calcutta in the East; even remote mountains like Himalayas and islands such as Andaman and Nicobars are not spared from degradation in environmental quality, thanks to poor tourism developmental practices. In coastal regions, the main causes of aesthetic pollution are large concrete constructions, unclean public toilets, haphazard arrays of street vendors, noise, plastic and sewage derived litter, dead animal bodies, scum, oil, etc. The recreational waters in many of the beaches have an exceptionally inferior turbidity, odor, and color over their natural backgrounds. In India, compared with many other destination countries, since a majority of visitor hours are spent in outdoor activities, the impacts associated with aesthetic pollution are far more pronounced.

Researchers from a variety of disciplines, using different perspectives on landscape aesthetics and psychological benefits, and focusing on different levels of human functioning, have provided consistent findings that natural landscapes in their unspoiled form, and especially in the case of a visible or known water presence, elicit higher aesthetic ratings than any other kind of landscape that has so far been investigated, together with consistent reports of highly restorative psychological benefits (Altman & Wohlwill, 1983; Balling & Falk, 1982; Brown & Daniel, 1987; Daniel, 1990; Fiedeldey, 1995; Herzog, 1985; Knopf, 1987; Purcell *et.al.*,1994; Ulrich, 1981). Among the diverse landscapes available, natural landscapes, especially the wilderness with visible or known water presence, attract the largest number of tourists, both national and international, noted Viljoen, *et al.* (1988). These authors describe wilderness areas as invariably rugged and undeveloped: there must be mountains and trees as well as an absence of people and manmade objects; and the area must be remote and access to it difficult. Rossman & Ulehla (1977) also investigated the psychological reward values associated with the use of natural areas and found that most of the rewards were rated in terms of the fulfillment of the desire for tranquility, emotional and spiritual experience, adventure, natural beauty, and escape from the hectic urban pace.

One of the paradoxes in aesthetic design is that the technical and touristic experiential definitions of environmental quality need not always be one and the same. Also, not all tourists hold similar aesthetic views on what make up a high or low quality environment. A survey conducted recently by one of the coauthors of this manuscript revealed that the exhibition of nudity of any sort by the tourists at the beachside is perceived by the local residents as disgusting; the domestic tourists were ambivalent to this, while the foreign tourists in general felt it as an integral part of the beach tourism experience. The public at times perceives the quality of recreational waters to be somewhat different from its actual microbial and chemical quality (Philipp, 1994). However, even though good aesthetics does not mean a high-quality environment, bad aesthetics always mean a low-quality environment (Dinius, 1981), meaning that the tricky task could greatly be simplified into choosing one of the many appealing alternative aesthetic formulations that is technically superior as well.

The above discussion on the aesthetics of environmental quality makes one to think that the beauty and grandeur of the destination environment could be one of the fundamental push factors for tourists. Putting differently, it is in nobody's interest to deplete the environmental resources for immediate and short-lived gains. On the other hand, sustainable advantages for the destination enterprises become possible only by making use of the rents obtainable from fostering environmental quality.

DEGRADATION OF ENVIRONMENTAL QUALITY: TOURISM RELATED CAUSES

It is not that tourism is the sole culprit in the degradation of environmental quality. In fact, impacts from other industries often have a more dramatic effect on the environment and can seriously affect tourism, which often depends upon unspoilt environment for its survival as a viable business. Some examples of this sort of effects are: pollution and the destruction of local marine and land species caused by oil spillages in seas; water pollution and algae booms due to agricultural run off or industrial discharges; and, destruction of corals due to destructive practices such as fishing with blasts and poisonous chemicals. But, these in no way mitigate the harm to environmental quality caused by tourism. The following are the principal causes of environmental degradation, which arise due to uncontrolled mass tourism activities:

- Inadequate sewage, solid waste treatment, and disposal facilities; deteriorating soil and water quality, causing visual pollution and bad odour.
- Storm water discharge due to inadequate drainage facilities, transporting silt and pollutant into water bodies.
- Shore line construction and dredging causing beach erosion and reef damage.
- Deforestation, aggravating flood damage, and siltation.
- Unplanned development and illegal encroachment - contributing to the destruction of wetlands, important as fish nurseries and wildlife habitats and as buffers against water pollution and coastal erosion; degradation of agriculturally fertile areas and wildlife habitats; ill-planned road network and its impacts on natural resources and the traffic itself.
- The big advertisement boards on highways to attract tourists cause visual blight in scenic landscapes; they destroy the natural scenic beauty, wilderness experience, outdoor recreation opportunity, and visibility values.
- Intentional and unintentional introduction of exotics and monocultures, thus decreasing the diversity of local germs.

These processes eventually affect the tourism industry by degrading environmental quality. Most of these negative impacts are constantly affecting the common property resources (CPRs), such as air, groundwater, and community lands. The CPRs are subject to individual use but not to individual possession. Yet, in the era of ultra-commercialization in everything, the necessity for the community cooperation to manage these vital resources on a sustainable basis is dismally ignored. Since the commons, especially the open access commons, are being overexploited by a majority of the stakeholders themselves due to the "free riders" syndrome, no significant voice exists there to bother about the commons that are essential for maintaining the ecological and socio-economic sustainability of the destination areas. Tragedy of the commons has become inevitable due to the unsustainable modes of tourism development like the uncontrolled and unplanned construction of buildings and allied infrastructures; especially the roads, bridges, and multi-storied buildings in highly sensitive areas, as well as illegal encroachments. Hence, we urgently need sustainable, alternative strategies for tourism, necessarily rooted in community-based approaches or community-controlled strategies.

TOURISM AND ENVIRONMENTAL QUALITY: TWO CASE STUDIES

Given below are two contrasting case studies that demonstrate how radically different outcomes could be produced by tourism-environment interactions depending upon the sort of developmental intervention strategies adopted. In the first study, tourism is sited as the prime culprit in destroying the environmental quality of a region namely, Goa in India. In the ultimate analysis, tourism in Goa in on a suicidal path; the saddest part is that while killing itself, it kills the nature and culture as well. The second study provides an example of how to creatively overcome the seemingly inherent contradiction between tourism development and the preservation of environmental quality. The Responsible Tourism System is a mechanism wherein those tourism and hospitality enterprises that responsibly manage environmental resources and preserve environmental quality are rewarded with appropriate eco-labels. This certification is an independent and trusted third-party assurance about the quality standards and the environmental ethics being practiced by an establishment to the customers that deal with it, and hence a vital competitive marketing plank.

Case study 1. Beach Tourism and Environmental Impacts in Goa

Since costal regions are already fragile ecosystems, the additional impacts generated by the human action associated with tourism, which often represents an exploitative relationship between man and environment, may cause to ring the death knell for these regions. This case study presents how tourism has negatively affected the environmental quality in Goa over the last quarter-century and discusses what measures can be adopted to bring the situation back under normalcy. It summarizes the environmental impacts of tourism development in Goa in the overall perspective of the provision of superior quality experiences to the visitors, which is the only certain way to retain them and regenerate more demand (Fleischer & Felsenstein, 2000). The matter presented here is culled out partly from the case-studies conducted by the postgraduate students of Goa University and partly from a review of literature. This study will be a valuable addition to the extant case-based literature on environmental quality related issues in tourism emerging from different national contexts (Price, 1981; Akama, 1996; Gartner, 1987; Spenceley, 2005).

A vast majority of incoming tourists to India invariably visits coastal regions and Goa is the Indian state with the most concentrated coastal tourism activities. Goa is a small coastal region on the west coast of India located between the Western Ghats and the Arabian Sea, where tourism began as an economic activity in the late 1960s, when western hippy travelers discovered its pristine beaches, idyllic villages, welcoming people, and of course the easy availability of drugs (Newman, 2001). Goa was under the Portuguese rule for four centuries until 1961 when it was finally handed over to India, which was a decisive influence upon the territory's identity and its unique selling proposition in the post-colonial era.

However, with the packaging of Goa as a major international tourist destination that began in the mid-1980s, the floating population of visitors exceeded the number of residents and the ill-effects of tourism became all the more visible. The state started to gain an unwanted reputation as a den of drugs, all-night partying, and nudism. In addition to the international tourists, domestic tourists too increasingly began to flock to Goa to have a gaze at the debauched foreigners.Under the economically powered hi-discourses, Goa has lost almost all traces of its rich past except in the inauthentic artifacts staged for conspicuous consumption, laments McCabe & Stocks (1998). These authors note that the region's non-tourist related economic activities like agriculture, salt-pan industry, aquaculture, and shellfishery have totally been lost to tourism.

Sawkar & Noronha (1998) lists out the multitudes of environmental woes associated with tourism development in Goa: beach degradation due to improper waste management by tourists; groundwater depletion and water scarcity due to over-exploitation for tourism industry; groundwater pollution due to improper waste management; beach and coastal erosion due to unsuitable infrastructure development; and so on. A study commissioned by TERI has investigated the changing land cover patterns of vegetation in the North Goa (Feoli & Giacomich, 2003) and concluded that the sandy areas, the coconuts and cashew plantations, and the dense woodlands have appreciably been reduced in area and the species diversity has decreased with the loss of vegetation. The satellite images also showed an exceptionally high spatial fragmentation in those villages that were the victims of tourism related urbanization. The natural flows of tidal waters and esturies have been badly affected and the shore-width has been diminished with sand dunes razed to make space for tourism activities.

A few decades back, Goa's beaches were beautifully lined by dunes of sand covered with vegetation. The dunes were formed above the high water mark by the sea-storms, each storm adding a little more sand, and the vegetation grew upwards through each successive deposit with a strong root system. Such a dune barrier protected the land behind it from flooding and erosion. However, the steady increase in the hotel construction, the hotel activities, the construction of other buildings and the heavy use of public beaches have led to the eradication of the dune barrier from along the beaches, resulting in the removal and deposition elsewhere of sand that was formerly held in place by the vegetation. The overall outcome of removal of the dune from the beaches is that Goa has seen an accelerated erosion of many of its lovely beaches. Besides this, cruises travelling in close proximity to the coastlines caused oil to wash onto the beaches, destroying not only the crabs and other marine life, but also causing discomfort for people using the beaches. With an anticipated overall increase in the tourism influx, it is high time to evolve an integrated approach to protect the environmental quality of the region and improve the socioeconomic conditions of the coastal communities.

The bitter realization that society, culture, and environment can no longer continue to be maidservants of conceited economic objectives is rampant all across the state now (Harding & Thomas, 2003). Goans have no blanket opposition to tourism, since their livelihoods are dependent upon it and since it has somewhat become ingrained into their social identity (Wilson, 1997). Rather, it is the nature of tourism development wherein they have little voice with regard to even those matters that directly affect their future that causes rebellion. The want preserve the pristine quality of their environmental resources that are the raison d'etre for quality tourism to Goa. Their nominal involvement in the environmental planning and policy decision-making generates in them a strong sense of alienation. Nevertheless, interestingly, instead of nurturing sustainable forms of development in order to minimise the negative impacts caused by tourism and to bring in the local population into confidence, the government of Goa continues to concentrate its full attention upon merely curbing the negative publicity so that even more multinational investments and tourist flows shall take place (Breda, 2005). It has a history of using even agencies like the World Tourism Organization (WTO, 1994) to further this end at all costs (Burns, 1994). The recent initiative of the present government to concentrate more upon promoting up-market tourism is touted as having the effect of minimizing the negative impacts of mass tourism; yet, the same could significantly jeopardise the structure of the Goan tourism industry which as of now is catered by small and medium scale enterprises where, at least in principle, local entrepreneurship is possible.

Tourists are attracted to Goa mainly for its unique natural and cultural resources. If care is not taken to preserve the natural habitat, that part of the industry which believes in quality tourism may ultimately be forced to withdraw from the state. Small patches of vegetation that now exist in isolated regions should be developed into dense natural parks, which is a sure means to earning some extra revenue too. Similarly, activities like fostering estuarine mangrove vegetation greatly add to the beauty of the coastline and can attract genuinely responsible tourists. Nobody can refute that the existence of healthy coastal habitats like wetlands, beaches and dunes, sea grass beds, mangroves, coral reefs, and estuaries is important to coastal recreation and tourism. Plantation of local species by hotel owners should be made compulsory. Constructions in the coastal belt should not be permanent, as these can disturb the water table and the ecosystem. For beach restoration, softer solutions like natural beach nourishment with flora could often be better than harder solutions like building sea-walls. Foreign tourists and the recreating domestic public stop going to areas where the waters are polluted or fishes are tainted and significant improvements in water quality is to be achieved by controlling both point and non-point sources of pollution.

Case studies conducted by Noronha *et al.* (2002) in Goa demolish the assumption that preventing tourist movements and controlling the intensity of impacts associated with these movements are one and the same. This means that while the recognition that tourism in Goa sustains upon a set of delicate resources is definitely to be reflected in the existing rules, the solution is obviously not in curbing all sorts of tourism activities. What is to be checked are the concentration of population and the associated increase in the density of infrastructure and facilities in certain ecologically sensitive areas. Also, policy measures should encourage the harmonization of tourism with more sustainable ways of livelihood like the traditional agriculture, which itself can be promoted as a unique tourism product. Future research in this region should target the development of contextually rich environmental quality markers that would enable the identification and quantification of environmental problems and act as monitors of ecological changes associated with tourism.

Case study 2. The Responsible Tourism System in Spain

Spain has been consistently maintaining a leadership position in terms of visitor numbers and revenue and tourism contributes to one-tenth of its GDP. Millions of tourists travel to Spain every year to enjoy the sunshine, heat, and other attractions that make it a favorite destination. While Spain is highly appreciated for hospitality, visitors complain that it scores poorly on environmental aspects with noise, dirty towns and cities, degradation of beaches and of sea animals and plants, among others. Some of the problems which Spain suffer due to tourism, either directly or indirectly, are: land speculation and mass urban development in rural areas; invasion of pristine natural zones and interiors; poor sanitary infrastructure; depletion of non-renewable resources; traffic congestion; alternations to traditional lifestyles; and so on. These problems are compounded due to the seasonality aspect of tourism to areas already under pressure from other activities such as farming, fisheries, and industrial development (Barke, 2004). In sum, the diversification which has resulted in the environment becoming a resource and the competition posed by rival destinations with better-preserved environments represent a threat to Spain's continued success in the tourism industry.

In this context, the Responsible Tourism System (RTS) was conceived after the World Conference on Sustainable Tourism (Lanzarote, Spain, 1995) as an independent system to provide hospitality and tourism enterprises with incentives to improve the quality of their installations voluntarily by adopting strategies for responsible management for quality tourism experiences and the conservation of natural and cultural assets. Responsible tourism management includes the conservation of environment and cultural assets; satisfying tourist expectations about the destination; and enhancing the quality of life of the host population, among others. The Institute for Responsible Tourism (IRT), Spain, is the body that manages the RTS measures, resources, and procedures.

There has always been a need for external and visible recognition to distinguish the efforts made by tourism establishments in the direction of advancing ecological ethics. The fact that tourism lacks universally accepted and objectively measurable parameters of quality of business practice has led to the booming up of many tourism enterprises advertising green holidaying opportunities. Alongside, quality control agencies established by the industry associations began to sell the rights to use quality assurance labels with the same business zeal, even without requiring or verifying that the recipient is truly committed to improving the environment Such labels, thus became a mere marketing strategy for the "greenwashing" firms. In the midst of these fraudulences, the Institute of Responsible Tourism stands apart and promotes tourism models that actively contribute to maintaining and protecting the cultural and natural assets of tourist destinations. Its ultimate objective is to promote sustainable development in the tourist industry and encourage the use of the endogenous skills of each destination and host community.

The IRT is most credited for its environmental quality certification initiative. The Biosphere Hotels seal of environmental quality provided by RTS is a form of accreditation for those hotels that take the environment into account in terms of energy and water savings, the use of cleaner forms of energy, waste management, minimal air pollution, promotion of ecological principles, and conservation of natural surroundings. The establishments that receive the seal must also meet an array of other requirements. As an incentive, a hospitality property following the guidelines and getting the RTS certification will be permitted to operate even in sensitive areas like the "Biosphere Reserves" (Biosphere Reserves generally include any area, region or territory that implicitly or explicitly complies with the requirements established at the Rio Earth Summit, 1992).

The IRT holds that responsible tourism establishments—that saves non-renewable sources of energy by minimizing their consumption, that have policies to minimize negative environmental impacts, that strengthen local economies and societies, that pledge to preserve cultural assets, and that live up to the expectations of responsible customers—need to be given proper incentives for them to reinforce the same behaviour. According to the RTS, environmental quality standards in the context of tourism could be operationalized in terms of the following:

- Environmental Quality: This set of criteria includes several physical factors within the environment, both inside and outside the establishment and in its activities, as well as the products and services it offers. The IRT studies how the hotel affects the health, safety and comfort of its customers and employees and how well their expectations are met in terms of quality and natural surroundings.
- Quality Tourism: These standards are related to the truthfulness of the establishment's advertising, its efforts towards customer satisfaction and other criteria involving customer service.
- Resource Conservation: The goal is to minimize the consumption of resources, especially those that are finite, through the use of conservation systems and other efficient ways of using resources. This category involves the actual physical components and systems used and the activities performed during basic hotel management processes, for both direct services provided to guests and for indirect services, such as internal affairs and management.
- Environmental Efficiency: Conscientious, responsible ways of managing the establishment should be used so that its activities play a proper role within its environmental protection policy. This category basically includes a set of criteria that ensure a minimal impact to the environment.
- Sustainable Development: These criteria will be applied to ensure compliance with the principles and objectives established at the many forums on sustainable tourism.

The RTS standards are customized depending on where they are applied; the different standards place special emphasis on specific issues like conservation of bio-diversity, the behavior of tourists in sensitive areas, architectural heritage related criteria, or criteria concerning ethnographic resources. For each of these standards, different quality assurance labels are given and currently, there are four such labels: "Responsible Tourism"; "Quality for Life"; "Heritage for Life"; "Animal Embassy".

The IRT certification is absolutely voluntary and the process of application is simple and straightforward. Once a firm decides to join RTS, it will be offered an initial round of counselling plus the set of guidelines and other documents. The firm is encouraged to introspect and then to perform an internal audit to see how much it complies with the RTS requirements. If this process generates optimistic results, the firm can offer itself for a third party audit by IRT. If the audit proves successful, the firm is awarded the appropriate Biosphere Hotels label, with the condition that the firm is willing to undergo re-examinations any time. Otherwise, IRT will offer the firm proper counseling to improve those aspects that did not come up to the required standard. The IRT has invested heavily in the continual development and dissemination of practical instruments for implementing a responsible tourism policy, especially in the accommodation establishments. This means that the industry receives accurate guidelines and points of reference in raising awareness of sustainable development projects and eco-friendly solutions in the tourist industry.

Thus, the first case study from India portrays the most common instances of the negative impacts of uncontrolled mass tourism upon environmental quality and the impacts of a deteriorating environment upon the tourism industry. Goa is not the only destination in India where environmental quality has been badly affected as an impact of tourism. Other beach destinations like Kovalam and Varkkala in Kerala and a number of hill stations especially in the Himalayan ranges have also been the victims of unchecked tourism development. The second case study from Spain, on the other hand, points out that improved environmental quality by the introduction of quality control systems has to potential to promote long term sustainable tourism in the region. While India can provide many such negative case studies, the more positive ones are emerging from other countries, especially those in the Western Europe (*See*, Ashley, *et.al.*, 2001; Goodwin *et.al.*, 1998).

In the recent years, the labeling of eco-friendly products has been introduced in a number of developed countries to assist in the protection of the environment. Tourism in the developing countries is a highly fragmented and heterogeneous industry and hence for the successful implementation of an eco-labeling scheme, the effective coordination of a number of agencies is sine qua non. Consumers, as well as manufacturers, have to be educated about the long term benefits of the scheme, and trustworthy non-governmental organizations have to take the mantle of certification. A study conducted in India by Santhakumar (2003) reveals that institutional deficiencies in the country become the major-most bottleneck in raising its environmental standards. Existing property right structures are the next culprit in producing a suboptimal environmental quality control regime (Cooter & Ulen, 2000). In such contexts, citizens' actions like civil disobedience movement may have to be advanced to meet the unmet demand for environmental quality.

TOWARDS A QUALITY ENVIRONMENT: ALTERNATIVE OPTIONS

Synchronized efforts to reach a sustainable balance between tourism activities and environmental quality are necessary for the quality of our environment and the quality of our lives. Based on the issues discussed here and elsewhere, we outline the following policy alternatives for the tourism industry (Inskeep, 1991; Mastny, 2001):

- Catalyze participatory research, planning, implementation, and monitoring strategies for community based tourism.

- Restructure tourism operations and management along environmental lines: this means reducing consumption of water, energy, and other resources; introducing environmentally sound methods of transportation; improving management, handling, and disposal of waste; and so on.
- Accelerate the transfer of environmentally sound technologies, practices, facilities, and management tools to the destination regions.
- Encourage the organizations in tourism to subscribe to environmental guidelines by a system of incentives (like subsidies, tax holidays, soft loans and awards) and disincentives (like fines, pollution taxes and in extreme cases ban/closure).
- Match tourism strategies with environmental quality, social equity, community empowerment, cultural integrity and economic efficiency to promote responsible forms of tourism activities.
- Enhance historical towns and revive the arts and crafts through tourism.
- Evolve pluralistic but integrated regional tourism policies with special emphasis on community based or community /govt. or community /private or community /private /govt. partnerships for long-term sustainable development.

Further guidelines aimed at the enhancement of environmental quality may be borrowed from the available knowledge databases. For instance, UNEP (1995) has prescribed a sophisticated set of environmental codes of conduct for tourism. Gonsalves (1991) has brought out a set of important guidelines for alternative tourism with reference to the third world. Mastny (2001) from the World Watch Institute has provided a few vital policy guidelines with lessons for quality tourism. The Green Globe program (WWF, 2000), the ECOTEL Certification awarded by HVS Eco Services, Certification Programs for Sustainable Tourism and Eco-tourism (Honey & Rome, 2001), Exemplary Practices by Canadian Tourism Commission (1999), and the National Eco-tourism Accreditation Program of the Eco-tourism Association of Australia and the Australian Tourism Operators Association are some of the noteworthy initiatives that aspire to practice these guidelines.

In fact, many of these policy alternatives have already been subsumed in the newly emerging paradigm of eco-cultural tourism (ECT) and it is a valuable framework to organize the environmental quality discourse. Because of the many forms in which ECT activities are offered by a wide variety of operators and because it is practiced by an even larger array of tourists from multiple backgrounds, there is no great deal of consensus about what it is. While there is no single universal definition for ECT, the present authors attempt to summarize its general characteristics in a way that would still enlighten its potential connections with the guiding principles of sustainable tourism (Wight, 1993; Ceballos-Lascurain, 1996; Goodwin *et al.*, 1998):

- It includes all nature-based forms of tourism in which the main motivation for the tourists is the observation and appreciation for admiring, enjoying or studying nature as well as the traditional cultures and heritage (both past and present) prevailing in relatively undisturbed or uncontaminated natural areas

- It contains participatory, interactive, educational and interpretation features
- It is generally, but not exclusively organized for environmentally /socially conscious small groups by specialized and small, locally owned businesses. Foreign operators of varying sizes also organize, operate and/or market ECT tours, generally for small groups
- It minimizes negative impacts upon the natural and socio-cultural environment
- It supports the protection of natural areas and the revival of culture by: generating equitable economic benefits for host communities (by providing alternative employment and income opportunities), organizations and authorities managing natural areas with conservation purposes, and adding value to local heritage, cultural and natural resources through sustainable tourist access to those resources and thus provides incentives for protecting them increasing awareness towards the conservation of heritage, natural and cultural assets, both among locals and tourists by participatory, interactive, interpretative, enlightening experiences.

Eco-cultural tourism as a praxis is superior to the conventional definitions of eco-tourism: it imbues 'eco' with 'cultural' and has in its ambit something beyond the natural environment, which is a pragmatic addition too. Extending responsible business practices beyond the environmental agenda to address the local economic and social aspects builds reputation, particularly for those tourism enterprises that want to establish a leadership role. The market is gradually shaping itself to reflect socially, environmentally, and culturally aware holidaymakers. These market trends require sumptuousness that goes beyond the confines of a truncated experience. There is market advantage and repeat business to be secured by enabling clients to enrich their experience and this will increase the local economic benefit, too (Neto, 2003). It is extremely plausible that, properly conceived and implemented, eco-cultural tourism could offer a panacea for many an ailment associated with the current tourism practice.

CONCLUSION

What sorts of tourism products are promoted and how, what is bought and consumed, how the wastes are handled, how the travel is made, and how the locals are involved – all these issues have their associated environmental impacts on the destination areas. As noted by Ashworth (1995), because tourism represents a series of heterogeneous products and services consumed in stages often from fragmented suppliers, quality of tourism experiences can not be measured by any single index modeled after the traditional economic analysis. Due to the complexity of the factors involved it may not be fully realizable to trace the root causes of environmental problems arising out of tourism activities in isolation and there exists a dearth of solid scientific evidence, which is used as an excuse in downplaying the impacts (precautionary principle). Yet, it is imperative and consensually agreed that tourism-environmental quality linkages occupy a central position in determining the limits to growth of tourism activities.

In the face of current human population increases and serious ecological degradation, intact and healthy ecosystems are becoming rare. Vested opinion sources make people believe that while attracting tourists seems difficult enough in the first place, talking of ecological and cultural sustainability and the economics of it would only drive the prospective tourists away and discourage the tourism promoters. The "its-not-in-my-face-yet and any how, we-need-the-foreign exchange" attitude is widely held. Not only that an informed understanding of the urgent necessity in integrating environmental conservation into our tourism promotion strategies is mired in propagandas, but also in casualty are a number of related concerns like recognizing the inseparable links between poverty, environmental quality, and sustainable tourism (Ashley *et.al.*, 2001). It is high time to realize that as the impacts of tourism continue to spread, it is increasingly important to steer it onto a more sustainable path—economically, culturally, and environmentally.

A broad range of stakeholders—including the tourism industry, governments, international organizations, nongovernmental groups, host communities, and tourists themselves—will need to be involved in engineering deep structural changes for a comprehensive quality revolution at all levels. Fortunately, representatives from many of these groups are already moving forward on some of the key issues. For instance, while concerns about tourism merely hovered at the fringes of discussions at the 1992 U.N. Conference on Environment and Development in Rio de Janeiro, these have been moved to the center of preparations for the follow-up World Summit on Sustainable Development in September 2002. Though still very few in numbers, hotels, tour operators, and other tourism businesses have already taken the preliminary steps to incorporate environmental and social sustainability measures into their daily operations, including reducing resource use and improving the treatment and handling of waste. They are embracing a wide range of voluntary initiatives, from developing environmental and social codes of conduct for their staff and clients to working to meet benchmarks for a diversity of tourism certification efforts. Yet industry action alone is not enough to ensure sustainable tourism development.

Governments at the national, regional, and local levels can supplement industry initiatives by implementing a wide range of policies and regulatory measures, from restricting environmentally damaging constructions to limiting the number of visitors allowed at sensitive sites. And they can work with citizens' groups and other NGOs to help local communities take charge of their own futures, providing them with the training and resources they need to oversee and manage local tourism developments. Despite certain intrinsic disadvantages as noted by Ashworth (1995), local governments can act as the most effective agents of quality assurance in tourism since they are closer to the problem areas and are likely to have the support of the local communities than anyone else. Meanwhile, tourists themselves can play a valuable role in steering tourism onto newer and qualitatively better paths. Visitor education programs can spur important changes in travel choice and behavior by helping tourists to become more aware of the impacts of their own activities on local environmental quality, economy, and culture (Mastny, 2001).

Synergizing tourism and environmental protection is impossible unless each understand the other's objectives and demarcate areas of intersection between them. Engineering an environmental quality revolution is a deeply challenging task that requires changing attitudes and priorities both at the higher levels in the policy making circles, as well as at the local levels. In the same vein of Marx, the present authors bring this paper to a close by noting that while we have had enough of studies and interpretations on environmental quality, what has gone unattended is the pressing need to really advance it.

REFERENCES

- Akama J.S. (1996). Western environmental values and nature-based tourism in Kenya.
- *Tourism Management, 17*(8), 567-574
- Altman, I. & Wohlwill, J.F. (1983). Human behavior and the environment. *Behavior and the Natural Environment, 6,* 17-34.
- Ashley, C, Roe, D. & Goodwin, H. (2001) *Pro-poor Tourism strategies: Making tourism work for the poor – a review of experiences.* PPT Report No1, ODI/IIED/ CRT, England, 53-55.
- Ashworth, G.J. (1995). Environmental quality, tourism and the environment In Coccossis H. & Nijkamp, P. (Eds) Sustainable Tourism Development, Avebury, Aldershot, 49-63.
- Balling, J.D. & Falk, J.H. (1982). Development of visual preference for natural environments. *Environment and Behavior, 14*(1), 5 - 28.
- Barke, M. (2004). Rural tourism in Spain. *International Journal of Tourism Research, 6*(3), 137-149.
- Blangy, S. & Nielsen, T. (1993). Ecotourism and Minimum
- Impact Policy. *Annals of Tourism Research,* 20(2), 357-360.
- Bourassa, S.C. (1990). A paradigm for landscape aesthetics. *Environment and Behavior,* 22(6), 787 - 812.
- Breda, Z. (2005). Tourism and the changing face of Goa. In George, B. & Swain, S.K. (Eds.). *Advancements in Tourism Theory and Practice.* Abhijeet Publications, 26-37.
- Brown, T.C. & Daniel, T.C. (1987). Context effects in perceived environmental quality assessment: Scene selection and landscape quality ratings. *Journal of Environmental Psychology,* 7, 233 - 250.
- Burns, P. (1994). Review of World Tourism Organization-National and regional tourism planning: Methodologies and case studies. *Tourism in Focus, 14,* 16-25.
- Canadian Tourism Commission (1999). *Catalogue of Exemplary Practices in Adventure Travel and Ecotourism.* Prepared by Pam Wight & Associates on behalf of the Canadian Tourism Commission, March, 1999, Ottawa, Canada.

- Ceballos-Lascurain, (1996).*Tourism, Eco-tourism and protected areas.* IUCN, Gland.
- Cooter, R. & Ulen, T. (2000). *Law and Economics.* Reading, MA: Addison-Wesley
- Daniel, T.C. (1990). Measuring the quality of the natural environment. A psychophysical approach. *Journal of American Psychological Association, 45*(5), 633 - 637.
- Davies, T. & Cahill, S. (2000). *Tourism and the environment: Environmental implications of the tourism industry.* Washington: Resources for the Future.
- Demick, J. & Wapner, S. (1990). Role of psychological science in promoting environmental quality. *Journal of American Psychological Association, 45*(5), 631 - 632.
- Dinius S.H. (1981). Public perceptions in water quality evaluation. *Water Resources Bulletin,* 17(1), 116–121.
- Feoli, E. & Giacomich, P. (2003). Land cover patterns. In *Coastal Tourism, Environment and Sustainable Development.* TERI, Goa, 121-130.
- Fiedeldey, A.C. (1995). *Implications for park management of tourist preferences for water landscapes.* Paper presented at the 103rd Annual Convention of the American Psychological Association, 11-15 August, New York, USA.
- Fleischer, A. & Felsenstein, D. (2000). Support for rural tourism - Does it make a difference? *Annals of Tourism Research 27*(4), 1007-24.
- Gartner, W.C. (1987). Environmental impacts of recreational home developments. *Annals of Tourism Research* 14(1), 38-57.
- Godlee F. & Walker, A. (1991). Importance of a healthy environment. *British Medical Journal,* 303, 1124-1126.
- Gonsalves, P. (1991). Alternative tourism: A third world perspective. *Lokayan Bulliten 9*(2), 23-28.
- Goodwin, H, Kent, I. Parker, K. & Walpole, M. (1998). Tourism, conservation and sustainable development: case studies from Asia and Africa. *Wildlife and Development Series, 11,* IIED, London, 88-93.
- Harding, P. & Thomas, B. (2003). *Goa.* Victoria: Lonely Planet Publications.
- Hassan, S.S. (2000). Determinants of market competence in an environmentally sustainable tourism industry. *Journal of Travel Research, 38(3),* 239-245.
- Hawkes, S. & P.Williams (1993). Conclusions. In *The greening of Tourism: From Principles to Practices in Tourism.* Hawkes, S & Williams, P. (Eds.) VAN, Simon Fraser University, Center for Tourism Policy and research, British Columbia.
- Herzog, T.R. (1985). A cognitive analysis of preference for waterscapes. *Journal of Environmental Psychology, 5,* 225 - 241.
- Herzog, T.R. & Bosley, P.J. (1992). Tranquility and preference as affective qualities of natural environments. *Journal of Environmental Psychology, 12,* 115 - 127.

- Hoge, H. (1990). Ecological perception and aesthetics: Pictures are affordance-free. In Landwehr, K. (Ed), *Ecological Perception Research: Visual Communication, and Aesthetics*, Berlin: Springer-Verlag, 105-121.
- Honey, M & Rome, A. (2001). *Protecting Paradise: Certification Programs for Sustainable Tourism and Eco-tourism, Inst. For Policy analysis. Accessed at* http://www.ips.dc.org/ecotourism/protectingparadise/*standardsforparadise.pdf on 24th march, 2004.*
- Hull, R.B. & Revell, G.R.B. (1989). Cross-cultural comparison of landscape scenic beauty evaluations: A case study in Bali. *Journal of Environmental Psychology, 9*, 177 - 191.
- Inskeep, E. (1991).*Tourism Planning: An Integrated and Sustainable Development Approach.* London: John Wiley & Sons.
- Knopf, R.C. (1987). Human behavior, cognition and affect in the natural environment. In Stokols, D. & Altman, I. (Eds.), *Handbook of environmental psychology.* New York: John Wiley & Sons, 783-825.
- Mastny, L. (2001). From Rio to Johannesburg: New Paths for International Tourism. Washington: World Watch Institute
- McCabe, S. & Stocks, J. (1998). Issues in social impacts of tourism research with reference to the Indian State of Goa. In Roy K.C. & Tisdell, C. Roy K.C. & Tisdell, C. (Eds.) *Tourism in India and India's Economic Development.* New York: Nova Science Publishers, 187-200.
- Meier, C.A. (1985). *A Testament to the Wilderness.* Zurich: The Lapis Press.
- Meyer,JL. and WT.Swank (1996). Ecosystem management challenges Ecologists, *Ecological applications,* 6(3), 738-740.
- Moore, D. & Scott, D. (2003). Place attachment and setting context: Attachments to a suburban park versus a trail within that park. *Forest Sciences, 49*(6), 877-884.
- Neto, F. (2003). A new approach to sustainable tourism development: Moving beyond environmental protection. Natural Resources Forum, 27(3), 212-222.
- Noronha, L., Siqueira, A., Sreekesh, S., Qureshy, L., & Kazi, S. (2002). Goa: tourism, migrations, and ecosystem transformations. *AMBIO: A Journal of the Human Environment, 31*(4), 295-302.
- Philipp. R. (1994). Memorandum. In *Bathing water.* Select Committee on the European Communities, House of Lords, Paper 6-I, London: HMSO, 131–137.
- Pitt, D.G. & Zube, E.H. (1987). Management of natural environments. In Stokols, D. & Altman, I. (Eds.) *Handbook of environmental psychology.* New York: John Wiley & Sons, 1009 - 1042.
- Price, C. (1981). The impact of tourism on the environment. *Journal of Environmental Management 12(3),* 279-80.

- Purcell, A.T., Lamb, R.J., Peron, E.M., & Falchero, S. (1994). Preference or preferences for landscape? *Journal of Environmental Psychology, 14,* 195 - 209.
- Rossman, B.B. & Ulehla, Z.J. (1977). Psychological reward values associated with wilderness use. *Environment and Behavior,* 9 (1), 41 - 66.
- Santhakumar, V. (2003). Citizens' actions for protecting the environment in developing countries: An economic analysis of the outcome with empirical cases from India. *Environment and Development Economics,* 8, 505-528.
- Sawkar, K. & Noronha, L. (1998). *Tourism and the Environment: Case Studies on Goa, India, and the Maldives.* Washington: The World Bank.
- Schroeder, H.W. (1991). Preference and meaning of arboretum landscapes: Combining quantitative and qualitative data. *Journal of Environmental Psychology, 11,* 231 - 248.
- Schroeder, H.W. & Daniel, T.C. (1980). Predicting the scenic quality of forest road corridors. *Environment and Behavior, 12 (3),* 349 - 366.
- Singh, T.V, Theuns, L. & Go, F.M. (1989).Towards Appropriate Tourism: The Case of Developing Countries. FrankFurt: Peter Lang.
- Spenceley, A. (2005). Nature-based Tourism and Environmental Sustainability in South Africa. *Journal of Sustainable Tourism, 13* (2), 136–170
- Sreekumar, T.T. and Parayil, G. (2002). Contentions and contradictions of tourism as development option: the case of Kerala, India. *Third World Quarterly,* 23(3), 529-548.
- Ulrich, R.S. (1981). Natural versus urban scenes: Some psycho-physiological effects. *Environment and Behavior, 13*(5), 523 - 556.
- UNEP (1995). *Environmental Codes of Conduct for Tourism.*
- Technical Report No. 29, United Nations Publication 95-111-D.2, Paris, 1-69.
- Viljoen, H., Van Staden, F., Grieve, K. & Van Deventer, V. (1988). *Environmental Psychology: An Introduction.* Johannesburg: Lexicon Publishers.
- Wapner, S. (1987). A holistic, developmental, systems-orientated environmental psychology: Some beginnings. In Stokols, D. & Altman, I. (Eds.) *Handbook of Environmental Psychology,* 1433 -1460.
- Wight, P. (1993). Sustainable ecotourism: Balancing economic, environmental and social goals within an ethical framework.
- *Journal of Tourism Studies 4(2),* 54-66.
- Wilson, D. (1997). Paradoxes of tourism in Goa. *Annals of Tourism Research,* 24(1), 52-75.

- WTTC, WTO & Earth Council (1996). *Agenda 21 for the Travel and the Tourism Industry: Towards Environmentally Sustainable Tourism.* Accessed from http://www.wttc.org/promote/agenda21.htm on 1 September, 2005.
- WTO (1994) *National and Regional Tourism Planning: Methodologies and Case Studies.*
- London: Routledge.
- WWF (2000). *Tourism Certification: An Analysis of Green Globe 21 and Other Tourism Certification Programs*-A report for WWF-UK: Synergy, 37-56.
- Zube, E.H., Brush, R.O. & Fabos, J.G. (1975). *Landscape Assessment: Values, Perceptions and Resources.* Stroudsburg: Dowden, Hutchinson & Ross.

21

Tourism Policy Framework for Further Growth and Development in Garhwal Himalaya with Special Reference to Tourism Attractions in Uttarkashi District

I. Kathirvel,
Research Scholar,
CMTHS, HNB Garhwal University

Sanjay Mahar
Research Scholar,
CMTHS, HNB Garhwal University

S.C. Bagri
Dean & Director
Centre for Mountain Tourism and Hospitality Studies
HNB Garhwal University, Srinagar Garhwal Uttaranchal

ABSTRACT

Since the last couple of years the world has witnessed the rapid tourism development which paves the way to the quest for the survival and dependence of the local community for their well being on tourism related activities. Despite of several policies formulated by the State Governments for the local people nothing seems to have come into the ground as far as the policy implementation is concerned. Because of the growing popularity of the study area in Uttarkashi districts, the interest of inhabitants to use the tourist potential of this region for the tourists is a glaring example of the proper in-house utilization of manpower for their self-reliance and livelihood. Infact, this area will face a considerable boom in the tourism in the next few years that may become a challenge for tourism development in sustainable manner. However the unlimited tourism potential of Uttarkashi has not been fully realized in the absence of a planned and coordinated strategy of tourism development. Inadequate capital investment in tourism infrastructure and limited private sector participation have been substantially responsible forth in the much rapid tourism development. Insights from these theme infact lead to a coherent and rigorous research. This research paper examines how the policy works systematically so that tourism can be tapped to its fullest extent. By using questionnaires, various depths and dimensions on different parameters have been sought. Perception of the local people, viability of the various tourism project have been examined which are quiet imperative for the development of tourism. It attempts to highlight the present infrastructure scenario of prevailing human resurce practices for the proper utilization of resources.

Key Words: *Infrastructure, sustainability, policy, local people*

INTRODUCTION

Pilgrimage has traditionally been a major segment of tourism in Garhwal Himalaya. Incidentally important places of pilgrimage of Hindu religions are located in Uttarkashi. Among these Yamunotri, Gangotri and Gangnani etc. are some of the best known places which always fascinates tourists. This is primarily because it contains the origins of the most sacred of India's rivers, the Ganga, and its illustrious sister, the Yamuna. There are innumerable local fairs and festivals of prime importance like Magh Mela and several other local fairs which always has a lot to offer to the tourists in the form of villagers ethnicity, culture, tradition, customs etc. Har-ki-Doon, Dodital, Dayara Bugyal, Kedar tal are also the fertile bounty of tourists thrills. The adventure enthusiasts and many more attractive tourist destinations are part of Uttarkashi. The sheer variety ranging from mountaineering, Trekking, skiing, skating, water sports to aero sports like hang gliding, para gliding make Uttarkashi one of the most attractive destinations for adventure sports not only in India but the world over. Along with the world-famous Govind Pashu Vihar wildlife sanctuary, Gangotri National Park, Uttarkashi has several other breath-taking destinations for Wildlife Tourism. Uttarkashi has a rare diversity of flora and fauna. This makes it an ideal area for developing ecotourism projects and activities like jungle safaris, trekking on mountain and forest trails, nature walks, catch and release angling for Mahaseer and other fish species. All these activities have to be conducted in a manner that promotes awareness of environment and helps maintain the fragile ecological balance. For the naturalist, there is a wealth of blooming flowers, rare species of which may be studies undisturbed, beautiful forested trails and Himalayan treks. The untouched, pristine beauty of its snow-clad peaks, rivers and forests provides all that a tourist could avail. The clean, fresh and invigorating environment makes Uttarkashi a preferred destination to relax and unwind.

Policy Aims and Objectives

The policy drawn by Uttaranchal Government for Uttarkashi district has some set of goals and objectives to be fulfilled. It's aim are to correct regional imbalances, provide for all its people equal employment opportunities, and control out-migration. The policy further would be helpful to eradicate poverty, enable all people to lead a productive life, and provide to its people minimum acceptable quality standards in life. The policy envisages education and health, and augment capital, infrastructure and resources to support growth and increased economic activity. It advocates to promote technology and innovation for agricultural and industrial up-gradation. It acts as a facilitator and encourages entrepreneurship to empower women and provide equal opportunities. It further ensures active participation of local communities in the development process and protects the natural resources, environment, forests and greenery of the district that constitutes its greatest wealth. It makes the Government effective, transparent, responsive and accountable and encourages public private partnership in infrastructure development and delivery.

In order to meet goals and objectives certain steps have been taken and Government is all set to achieve the vision. Some radical steps have been enlisted as follows:

Infrastructure Development Board was set up under the Chairmanship of the Hon'ble Chief Minister and a blue print has been prepared for the infrastructural development to make Uttarkashi as a model town of Uttaranchal. Furthermore, expeditious disposal of proposals involving interdepartmental policy issues and decisions on special dispensations have been started. It further started to undertake project development activities

Existing Policy Framework

To provide self-employment opportunities for local residents and encourage maximum participation of the host community in the tourism sector is a policy of Uttaranchal Tourism Development Board. Under this Scheme, assistance for the project to the extent fixed by govt. can be provided. Projects under this Scheme shall include fast food centres, setting up retail outlets for local handicrafts, plying of buses and taxis, provision of equipment of adventure sports, establishing small motel-like residential accommodation, setting up tourism information centres with PCOs/restaurants, tented residential facilities and garages. With the objective of boosting tourist traffic to Uttarkashi and enriching the quality and content of tourism products, attractive package tours will be developed and promoted, with the help of private sector tour operators and travel agencies, these will include air/road/rail travel, boarding and lodging, excursions, site visits etc. These package tours will be specially promoted for the various popular destination of the area. A list of the accredited travel agencies will be prepared. Rules for accreditation will be simplified. Assistance of such accredited agencies will be sought to enlarge tourism business. The salient features of Tourism Policy are as follows.

Augmenting Capital Investment in Tourism

- To develop infrastructure facilities in the tourism sector, it is proposed to invite domestic private sector investment, foreign investment as well as investment from non-resident Indians. Such capital investment is specially proposed for construction of star-category hotels, tourist -resorts, golf courses, large eco-parks, amusement parks, ropeways, children's parks and winter sports projects.
- In addition, efforts will be made to seek financial assistance from World Bank, Asian Development Bank and other international agencies.
- To ensure private capital investment and participation for the development of tourism, separate funds for tourism development will be established. Arrangements will also be made to mobilize finances for these funds through voluntary contributions from travel trade representatives, industrialists and other establishments connected with tourism. For this a separate set of rules will also be framed.

Human Resource Development

- Diploma and degree training programmes will be conducted in the Hotel Managements and Catering Institutes. Training institutes will be developed for specialized activities like adventure sports, aero-sports, water sports, etc in this region.
- Arrangements will be made for tourism awareness programmes, and short-term training in specialized tourism related activities and services such as catering, fruit conservation, cookery, running paying guest facilities, managing S.T.D. equipped tourism information centres, handicrafts/souvenir related activities for unemployed Graduates.
- Special training programmes developed for local women and for the youth in areas like adventure sports, trekking etc. will be established with participation of the private sector as well as experts.
- Private sector involvement in training programmes and establishing training facilities will be encouraged.

Publicity and Promotion

- Posters, pamphlets, guide maps and other tourism literature depicting the important tourism attractions in Uttarkashi shall be produced and widely circulated.
- An Uttaranchal Tourism website will be launched which will incorporate every information pertaining to each and every destination. Moreover, Website will contain vital information for making the tour more enjoyable and memorable. Apart from providing tourism related information, reservation facilities shall also be made available through the proposed website.
- Familiarization tours to tourist places in Uttarkashi shall be organized from time to time for members of various sections of the tourism trade and industry, media persons, departmental officers/employees.
- Organization of, and participation in Tourism Conferences/Seminars, Travel and Trade Fairs on a regular basis will be encouraged.
- In order to give wide publicity to places of tourist interest in Uttarkashi, efforts will be made to promote film shooting in the region. Action will be taken to establish a Film City in this region and the necessary infrastructure for film shooting will be provided.
- Information Centres and other tourist facilities will be provided and developed at railheads and convenient points on highways in Uttaranchal.
- Tourism related signages will be developed at all important highways, airports and bus stands for the information and convenience of tourists.

Pilgrimage Tourism

- Amendments in relevant statutory framework will be considered with the aim of streamlining the institutional arrangements pertaining to the Yamunotri and Gangotri (Two sacred temples of Char Dham Yatra) and creating a hub to facilitate pilgrimage tourists to visit "Char Dham" pilgrimage, and improving the facilities for pilgrims.
- Accommodation and facilities along the pilgrimage routes will be augmented and upgraded in a phased and coordinated manner and a Master Plan will be drawn up for this purpose.
- Action will be taken for the integrated development of the less developed and lesser known destination in Uttarkashi.
- Efforts will be made to develop integrated packages and facilities whereby pilgrims are also attracted to other tourism desitnations in the area.

Ecotourism

- Botanical Gardens-cum Heritage Centres and Theme Parks will be established in order to highlight the biodiversity of Uttarkashi.
- Integrated Eco-Tourism projects will be developed and established and steps will be taken to promote eco-friendly tourism activities like Jungle Safaris, Nature Walks, Mountain treks, Camping, etc. in a manner that also promotes awareness and sensitivity towards environment conservation.
- Tree plantation as a tourism linked activity will be given special attention. Action shall be taken in a planned manner to deal with the problem of non-bio-degradable wastes. Intensive campaigns to regulate plastic waste shall be launched with the assistance of the private sector and nongovernmental organizations.
- The use of earthquake resistant technology and techniques in construction of buildings, and use of local materials will be promoted and encouraged.
- Special attention shall be given to the aspect of carrying capacity while preparing tourism development plans.
- Action will be taken to develop projects for ropeways, amusement parks, golf courses, children's parks, lakes and ponds and generally augment entertainment facilities in places of tourism interest.

Leisure Tourism

Uttarkashi has innumerable locations which can serve as quiet retreats amidst exquisite natural beauty, for those seeking leisure away from the stresses of modern urban life. Special efforts will be made to develop leisure-oriented tourism spots including Health resorts spa centres, yoga and meditation centres etc. herbal treatment and naturopathy centres to attract such tourists. Action will be taken for development and promotion of village tourism and tourist villages at different places in the district. This would include development of basic facilities of clean and healthy food and comfortable accommodation to tourists in these villages. Together with mountain tourism activities in the surrounding areas, the historical traditions of the villagers, folk arts/culture and cuisine will be promoted as special attractions. Steps will be taken to develop the enormous potential in Uttarkashi for Corporate tourism by creating world class facilities and the constructions star category hotels. The private sector will be encouraged to participate in the establishment of high class Convention Centres and facilities for conferences, seminars, workshops, business meets, etc.

Adventure Tourism

A major thrust will be given to the promotion and development of the following adventure tourism activities in the region.

- There exists a great potential for trekking in Uttarkashi. A Master Plan for development of trek routes will be prepared and implemented.
- The facilities on various trek routes will be improved i.e. for camping, provision for safe drinking water and hygienic food.
- Arrangements will be made for pre-paid facilities for trained guides, porters, tents and apparatus on hire at the starting points of these treks.
- Special efforts will be made to ensure that the environment is not polluted during trekking and necessary guidelines will be prepared.
- Activities like river rafting, canoeing, kayaking etc. are becoming increasingly popular. At present, these are being conducted with private sector participation, along the Ganges. River rafting will be further promoted/extended to other areas of Uttarkashi. For this purpose, guides will be trained and employed from among the locals, who will also be assigned the task of protecting both the tourists and the environment. Steps will be taken to set standards and regulations for this purpose.
- Other water sports will also be developed and extended to various water bodies in Uttarkashi like Dodital, near by area of Tehri Dam and Maneri bhali, etc. Fishing/angling, including "Catch and Release" angling will be promoted in planned and regulated way.
- A Master Plan will be drawn and further develop action will be taken in a time bound manner to develop Dayara Bugyal in Uttarakashi district as an international winter sports centre.
- With the help of the Government of India and the private sector wherever feasible modern telecommunication facilities will be made available in the farflung areas of Uttarkashi.

- Adequate facilities will be developed to provide a high level rescue system for adventure sports and other tourism related activities. This will include provision of various rescue equipments like recovery vans, Repling, Piten, Jumar and walkied-talkie sets etc. A Rescue Co-ordination Committee will also be set up.
- Registered organizations/clubs connected with adventure tourism will be encouraged through grants. A separate set of rules will be framed for this purpose.

Modus Operandi of Plan Execution

- High level empowered Uttaranchal Tourism Development Board was set up with representation from leading tourism experts from private sector for Uttarkashi district. Master Plans prepared by leading consultants for new destinations and tourist Circuits with Vir Chands Sing Garhwari Tourism Self Employment Scheme launched for Involving local host communities in Uttarkashi. Efforts are made to give thrust on development of Ecotourism and Policy Framework for Ecotourism Development and Management have been released. A Centre for Ecotourism and Sustainable Livelihood has been established at Har-ki-Doon and pilot project based on public Private Partnership have been initiated position of air transport at Chiniyali Saur air strip is set up with its establish scheduled air service and connectivity with an national gateway.

Policy Proposal for Gangotri Pilgrimage Complex

Gangotri is one of the rarest of the rare pilgrimage hub of Hindu mythology. Different segments of tourists and pilgrimage visit Gangotri for spiritual solace and salvation since time immemorial travel through this sub region.

Table 1 Towns Enroute Gangotri – Yamunotri

Categories			
Dham I	Junction Town II	Major Towns III	Settlements.
Gangotri	Chamba	Narendranagar	Dobata
	Uttarkashi	Agrakhal	Cham
		Baldiana	Matli
		Chinyalisor	Gangnani
		Maneri	Harsil
		Bhatwari	Bharonghati
Yamunotri	Dharasu	Bramhakhal	Kharati
			Syanachatti
			Hanumanchatti
			Krishnachatti
			Jankichatti

Source: Tata Consultancy Service and Infrastructure (Pvt.) Company

The Gangotri town is located at an altitude of 3042 m from mean sea level. This township is situated on the banks of river Bhagirathi. This small township of approximately 750 habiotants is full of activity during the yatra season i.e. of approximately 750 habitants is full of activity during the yartra season i.e. May- October every year. During the time over 3000 yatris visit this place on an average day. The place of origin of the river Ganga is 14Km beyond the Gangotri town and is known as Gaumukh. The activities of the town are centered around the Gangotri Temple. The temple surroundings offer picturesque view consisting river Bahgirathi. The other important area is the ghat where the pilgrims take bath prior to the Darshan. The twon has got the requisite facilities for accommodation for different segments of yatris ranging from 75 bed capacity extended by GMVN and other small hotels, dharmashalas contributing another 200 beds of different hierarchy. For most of the yatris Gangotri is a day destination. The accommodation facilities are availed by the Yatris who go for trekking. The activities are governed by the Gangotri Mandir samiti having its base office at Uttarkashi.

The main settlement of Gangotri along with the accommodation facilities is located across the river Bhagirathi. The Gangotri temple along with the structures housing the small shops is along the main approach to the temple. These facilities constitute accommodation, restaurants, shopping and public conveniences. The broad features of the Destination Development Plan are

- Visitor management system to enhance the overall circulation of the visitors.
- Development of area surrounding the temple. The riverfront available at this complex is proposed to be used for enhancement of the present queuing area.
- Rearrangement of the existing shops.
- Site specific development within Gangotri town
- The existing plans for the augmentation of the facilities at the complex have been considered in the development envisaged. Exhibit 7.2 shows Gangotri Township and surrounding areas, which constitute the Plan.

The facilities plan envisaged for Gangotri town are as follows.

A Visitor Circulation

The town receives a peak visitor inflow of 1500-2000 per day on an average. All these yatris visit the temple. The temple is situated at the foot of the hills. The present approach to the temple is through series of shops, which block the view of river. The existing path and approach to the temple. Arrangements for first aid near the temple Complexes or near are almost absent. There is a need to improve this situation and create appropriate means of Visitor Management, so that the visitors would take with them a rich and memorable experience of their visit. To achieve this objective, it is necessary to provide facilities to the visitors in an organized manner through well-planned approach to the shrine. It is also essential to ensure appropriate Visitor Circulation with facilities to meet minimum and essential needs of the visitors near the temple complex. As a part of visitor management system it is proposed to have entrance to the temple from the ghat. The existing shops along the present approach are proposed to be realigned as per the new circulation plan. The shops on the existing path thus will be over looking the river. The pilgrims shall visit these relocated shops on their way back to Temple. The primary circulation pattern of the visitors is at present linear i.e. from the parking lot to the temple and back. However the settlement of Gangotri town exists on the other bank of the river Bhagirathi. There are steep water drops within the river width, which a normal visitor does not witness during the course of his visit. It is proposed to clear off access to the present bridge which offers the view of water fall. Further it is proposed to formalise the area in the backyard of the settlement so that the river view is visible along the walkway. Further the trek route that leads to Gaumukh needs to have base camo facilities.

Existing Proposals

The Govt. of Uttranchal has outlined certain developmental measures for Gangotri town. The estimates for the proposed works have been included in the Master Plan. These measures are pertaining to provision of street lighting, sewerage system, and water supply in the town and the betterment of roads.

Table II. Capital Outlay for proposed Development at Gangotri

Development Measures	Capital Outlay (Rs in Lakhs)	
New Bridge Link	30.00	
Betterment of Queuing area		
Relocation of shops blocking river view	7.20	
Relocation of Structures along new approach	39.00	
Construction of Token counters, lobby & Electronics display system		
Development of access along river & Entry from ghats	30.00	
Separate access to Taptakund & Redesign of Bathing area		
New entry point facilities	9.30	
Provision of Cloak rooms		
Development of Ghats	25.00	39.00
Augmentation of Accommodation	200.00	
Toilet block	10.00	
Betterment of Road Junctions		
Viewing Gallery	18.00	
Formalization of Street sections		
Face lifting of Existing shops	27.00	
Development of Shopping plaza		
Lake front development		

Provision of Railings	6.00	
Beautification of Temple	20.00	
Medical facilities	40.00	
Signage plan		2.70
Solid waster disposal in Town	6.60	
Enhancement of Communication facilities		6.00
Developmental measures in town		
Water supply scheme for the town	5.00	
Development of Parking lots	90.00	
Development of inner roads	10.00	
Drinking water portable units		30.00
Base camp for trekking route		15.00
Total	**573.10**	**92.70**

Source: Tata Consultancy Service and Infrastructure (Pvt.) Company

Yamunotri Town

The Yamunotri temple is located at an altitude of 3235m from mean sea level. The settlement of Yamunotri Township is situated on the banks of river *Yamuna.* This small township is full of activity during the yartra season i.e. May - October every year. During the time over 500-1000 yatris visit this place on an average day .The original place of origin of the river is 1 km beyond the Temple town. The activities of the town are centered around the Temple. The temple surroundings offer picturesque surroundings consisting river Yamuna. The other important place is the hot springs where the pilgrims take bath prior to the *Darshan.* The town has got the requisite facilities for accommodation for different segments of yatris ranging from dormitory of 40 bed capacity extended by GMVN and other small hotels, dharmashalas contributing another 600 beds of different hierarchy. For most of the yatris Yamunotri is a day destination. The settlement immediately before Yamunotri is Hanuman chatti. There is a trekking route from Hanuman chatti to Yamunotri, which is 11 kms in length. There does exist 3 kms of motorable road upto a settlement called Phool chatti. This reduces the trek route to 8 kms. At present the ponies/dolis take the pilgrims up to the shrine. The settlements enroute the trek are Jankichatti and Krishnachatti. The accommodation facilities are availed by the yatris who go for trekking. The activities are governed by The Yamunotri Panda samiti having its base office at village Kharsali near Jankichatti.

The town receives a peak visitor inflow of 1500 per day on an average. All these yatris visit the temple. The temple is situated at the foot of the hills. The present approach to the temple is through series of shops, which block the view of river. Arrangements for first aid near the temple Complexes or near are almost absent. There is a need to improve this situation and create appropriate means of Visitor Management, so that the visitors would take with them a rich and memorable experience of their visit. To achieve this objective. it is necessary to provide facilities to the visitors in an organized manner through well-planned approach to the shrine. It is also essential to ensure appropriate Visitor Circulation with facilities to meet minimum and essential needs of the visitors near the temple complex. As a part of visitor management system it is proposed to have entrance to the temple from the ghat. The existing shops along the present approach are proposed to be realigned as per the new circulation plan. The shops on the existing path on the riverside shall be remodeled. The existing shops have got extensions protruding the pathway resulting in an effective width of approximately 8 feet. It is proposed to redesign the entire stretch of area where the present shops are located. As per the plan the shops shall have a modular design so as to facilitate smooth flow of pilgrims, increase in the width of the approach along with sit outs overlooking the river. The existing structures near the temple need to be suitably altered to facilitate the circulation. As per the revised circulation plan the pilgrims reach the redesigned kund for taking bath prior to the Darshan. The access to the temple is proposed to be from the riverside through the proposed circulation. The exit from the complex is proposed to be from the other side of the kund.

Visitor Circulation within Town

In travel to Yamunotri the route involves 8 kms of trek. The route passes through two settlements of Jankichatti and Krishnachatti. These settlements are used as stopovers during the trek. Further Jankichatti settlement has got accommodation facility. The present trek route cuts across these settlements. It is proposed to provide an alternative route to avoid movement of ponies from within the settlement. It is proposed that construction of road from Phoolcahtti to Jankchatti is taken up in the first phase of the project. The improvement of road from Hanuman chatti to Jankichatti also needs to be prioritized. This shall reduce the trek route by 3 kms. The construction of road from Hanuman ct1atti to Janki chatti shall necessitate provision of parking facility at Jankichatti. Further the movement of ponies will be beyond the Jankichatti settlement. Thus as part of plan it is proposed to provide

a) Parking at Janki Chatti

b) Pony stand at Jankichatti at Yamunotri end with proper hiring facilities.

c) Development of Stopovers at Krishnachatti for ponies.

The present trek to Yamunotri is 8 kms long with a break at Jankichatti (5kms from Yamunotri) and Krishnachatti (2.5 kms from Yamunotri). The proposed road to Jankichatti shall reduce the route of trek to 5 kms. Further along the trek it is proposed to provide

- Railings along cliff edges.
- Widening of trekking path with a separate path for ponies. (iii) Pathway lighting
- Drinking water and Toilet blocks.
- Provision of pony stand.
- Rest Places.

The forest department has identified another route of reaching Yamunotri. It is proposed to develop the trek route as a separate access for returning from Yamunotri. The present trek route needs widening, however with separate paths for up and down travel the travel shall ease in future. However an alternative of delineating track for pedestrians and ponies need to be explored.

Table III. The cost figures for the proposed development

Development Measures	Capital Outlay (Rs in Lakhs)	
	Public	**Private**
Beautification of Temple complex	10.00	
Betterment of entry & Exit areas		0.90
Relocation of shops blocking river view	39.00	
Relocation of Structures along new approach		
Construction of shoe stands etc		4.80
Development of access road from Northern side	22.50	
Separate access to Taptakund & Redesing of Bathing area	5.00	15.00
Provision of Cloakrooms		
Development of Chats	50.00	
Segregation of ponystand & pedestrian pathway	180.00	
Provision of railings	0.90	
Face lifting of Existing Shops	13.50	
Development of temple surroundings	12.00	
Medical aid centre	40.00	
Provision of Street Furniture		150.00
Signage plan		15.30
Solid waste disposal in Town	7.50	
Enhancement of Communication facilities	6.00	
Public Conveniences	20.00	
Water supply scheme for the town	10.00	
Development of Parking lots		
Development of inner roads		
Drinking water portable units		11.70
Trek Route		
Betterment of Road - Hanumanchatti - Pholchatti	100.00	
Road from Phool - Jankichatti	300.00	
Lighting of trek rout	345.00	
Widening of Trek route	210.00	
Water standpoints along trek	15.00	
Repairs to steps	15.00	
Pony stand at Jankichatti	27.00	

Resting places	2.52	
Widening of trekking path	54.00	
Railings along cliff edges	4.50	
Water filtration units		3.90
Signage plan		1.50
Krishnachatti		
Realignment of pathway	10.8.00	
Betterment of facilities in settlement	57.00	
Ponystand	21.00	
Signage plan		9.00
Street furniture & paving	8.70	
Jankichatti		
Development of Parking lots	54.00	
Realignment of trekking route & paving	6.09	
Medical relief centre	80.00	
Augmentation of accommodation	9.15	
Ponystand	14.40	
Street furniture & Paving	7.74	
Signage plan		0.90
Total	1855.50	213.00

Source: *Tata Consultancy Service and Infrastructure (Pvt.) Company*

Conclusion

Tourism has the potential to become a mainstay of Uttarkashi economy, and needs to be developed in a planned and in a specific time frame so that plenty could be offered to tourists in Uttarkashi. In this backdrop, policy makers can recruit the top personnel from tourism background who are well acquainted with the tourism terminology and can execute the policies with ease and in a planned manner. The responsibilities of the policy personnel can formulate of a strategy for mobilizing private sector participation and investment in the tourism sector and can prepare of plans and guidelines for developing and strengthening tourism related infrastructure in the State. Preparation of plans for various tourism segments and activities, identification and development of projects and ensuring their timely implementation is on immense significance with establishment of standards/norms and framing of policy guidelines for various tourism activities and simultaneously allocating the resources for the development of the destination and ensuring that the work in completed within the stipulated time frame. The body of the these tourism personnel will advise the Government on all matters relating to tourism in Uttarkashi in consensus of the State Tourism Minister. The body constituting the top notch tourism personnel shall have the sole authority to appoint persons from the private sector and experts in tourism related matters. A Single Window Information/ Assistance Centre has to be created and it will, inter-alia provide the facilities including all tourism related assistance and information, sanctions for projects, escort services for obtaining clearances and approvals from other departments and services of specialists and consultancy agencies for planning, implementation and evaluation of tourism projects.

Establishment of world class infrastructure facilities should be the highest priority of the Government for the development of tourism in the region. In order to do this, special efforts can be made to mobilize institutional resources and private sector investment and participation. In this context the development of Chiniyali Saur Air Strip to attract large influx of foreign tourists is a notable example. Efforts have to be made to develop and upgrade existing air strips in the district. Integrated development plans will be prepared for areas around the airports and air strips. Participation of the private sector in this area will be sought wherever feasible. Special efforts will be made to develop and upgrade tourism accommodation at important tourist centres in Uttarkashi keeping in view the requirements and income levels of different categories of tourists. Apart from the State government agencies maximum involvement of organized private sector and local residents (having guest accommodation) will be encouraged in this sphere. In view of the provision shall be made for wide road netwrok to ensure hassle free journey. With the help of the Government of India and the private sector wherever feasible modern telecommunication facilities shall be made available in the far flung areas of Uttarkashi. Availability of Land and buildings for development of infrastructure facilities is of prime importance. Simultaneously to keep check on carrying capacity and the residential concern of the area. land will have to be identified and land Bank established for purposes of developing accommodation and other infrastructure facilities at important destinations and tourist spots alongwith the pilgrimage routes. Land can be made available, on reasonable terms/price or as equity, by the State Government to private entrepreneurs for tourism schemes. Regulations will separately framed for this purpose. In addition to the properties of the Tourism Department and Garhwal Mandal Vikas Nigam or Zonal Development Corporations, rest houses of the various departments such as the Forest Department, Irrigation Department and Public Works Department can be utilized properly for tourism activities. Private sector participation in the development and management of such facilities will be promoted and encouraged so that cost benefit analysis of the tourism can be done for necessary control on the tourism related activities.

On of the key aspects of tourism development is private sector participation in the tourism industry is of vital importance. Despite of several tourism policies it has been observed no tourism policy can flourish without an active participation of private sector. Development of accommodation facilities for the different categories of tourists, tourist resorts, specialized food restaurants, facilities for adventure sports, amusement parks and facilities, etc. are some areas which provide attractive investment opportunities and where private sector could play a vital role. For this, the facilities could be provided to the private entrepreneurs. A Compounding Scheme to be made applicable for fixing the rate of entertainment tax on hotels showing programmes on the various channels through cable operators or dish antenna. New tourism units in the district be allowed rebate/deferment facility in the payment of luxury tax for a period of five years from the date of commencement. The norms and procedures for determining luxury tax on hotels can be modified and simplified to arouse interest of private entrepreneurs. New ropeways installed in the district, be exempt from the payment of entertainment tax for a period of five years from commencement. New Amusement parks set up can be exempted from entertainment tax for a period of five years from the date of becoming fully operational. For this, standards will be specified to determine eligibility. Steps shall have to be taken to provide beer-bar licenses to hotel units with attached restaurant facilities. To ensure increased participation of the private sector in the area of tourism a consultative mechanism shall have to be established. In order to attract domestic as well as foreign tourists round the year, there is an urgent need to create efficient, modern and state-of-the-art infrastructure to cater to the specific needs of tourists of all categories. Augmentation of infrastructure facilities must be accorded the highest priority by the Government to ensure the hassle free amenities and facilities provided to the tourists. Apart from its pollution free environs, Uttarkashi also provides clear skies and bright sunshine during the winter months. Yet tourism in Uttarkashi has been mainly confined to the summer months. Winter sports activities like skiing, ice-skating and ice-hockey, water sports, winter trekking etc. need to be promoted, publicized and advertised to attract tourists throughout the year.

Round the year winter tourism can turn into a hot destinations when newer unexploited destinations are to be created, developed, promoted and opened for the tourists as well as maintaining, preserving the vast reservoir of the assets prevailing in those areas. In order to ensure the clean, healthy environment and maintaining the eco-fragility of the destination at all tourist destinations, it would be essential to identify specific target groups and tourism activities and provide facilities according to their special requirements. For instance, the pilgrim devotees have different needs and beliefs from those of a nature lover who needs different kind of facilities. The challenge is to identify the needs of different categories of tourists and provide for them in a comprehensive and integrated manner. New tourist destinations should have to be developed according to the tastes, preferences, creativity and charm of the tourists. Apart from pilgrimage, hill stations, cultural tourism Uttarkashi should open new avenues such as Ecotourism, Ethnic tourism, Rural tourism and many others in the interiors, which can be and need to be developed into attractive tourist destinations. The far flung areas of Uttarkashi are known for the Handicrafts, Cuisine, Customs, Souvenirs etc. are integral to tourism anywhere in the world. So also, in Uttarkashi, it will be essential to promote large scale production of souvenirs and artifacts based on the traditional arts and crafts of the region, and encourage a rich fare of high quality international, national and local delicacies and cuisines. To encourage traditional handicrafts, rural craftsmen will be provided the necessary training and craft bazaars and craft villages will be set up and developed. Stalls will also be made available for marketing the crafted goods, especially during the various fairs and festivals. Besides, space will be provided for development in the Tourism Department Hotels/Guest Houses for setting up Souvenir shops in order to showcase and market locally produced handicrafts. Publicity, promotional events and marketing of the tourism attractions of Uttarkashi at the national and international level has been inadequate, which is quiet evident from the much untapped potentiality of the region from tourism perspective. Planned and coordinated efforts are required in this direction, with the fullest utilization of modern information technology. Above all, Tourism in Uttarkashi needs to develop its own brand name, image and relationship marketing. The people employed in tourism are the backbone of this industry. No industry can flourish and bear fruitful result if it is run with the help of untrained personnel. So there is an acute shortage and emphasis must be given to special arrangements and up-gradation of existing institutions and facilities will be necessary for developing tourism entrepreneurship and management capabilities and training in specialized services such as guides, porters, chefs, housekeeping, etc. ensure the proper human resources development for the betterment of the tourism industry. The existing institutional arrangements need modernization and qualitative improvement. In doing so, it will be essential to provide for the maximum involvement and participation of the private sector, specialists and experts, and those concerned with the tourism trade and industry. It would also be essential to ensure coordination between different agencies involved in administration and management of tourism development. There has been a dearth of participation and involvement of the private sector, particularly in the organized sector, in the development of tourism in Uttarkashi. There is need to promote and encourage private sector participation in the development of modern tourist facilities and infrastructure and management practices in the State. Private sector participation is bound to bear fruitful result provided that Government provides them full financial support and other kind of laxity in rules and regulations.

REFERENCES

1) Ateljevic, Irena. and Doorne, Stephen. (2002) Representing new Zealand Tourism imagery and ideology. Annals of Tourism Research, 29(3): 648-667.

2) Bagri, S.C., (2000) Tourism in Uttarakhand Prospects for Sustainable Development. In Sati, M.C. and Sati, S.C., book Uttarakhand Statehood: Dimensions and Development, Indus, New Delhi.

3) Bagri, S.C. and Gupta, S.K., (2001) Tourism and Pilgrimage: Planning and Development Issues. In Kandari, O.P. and Gusain, O.P., Transmedia, Srinagar Garhwal.

4) Beerli, Asuncion. and Martýn. d. Josefa. (2004) Factors influencing Destination image. Annals of tourism research, 31(3): 657–681.

5) Belin, C. (2002) A new tool for destinations: Tourism-Site, information network for the sustainable development of tourism destinations in Europe. Journal of Cleaner Production, 10: 605–607.

6) Bentleya, Tim., Page, Stephen., Meyer, Denny., Chalmers, David., and Laird, Ian. (2001) How safe is adventure tourism in New Zealand? An exploratory analysis. Applied Ergonomics, 32: 327–338.

7) Budic, N.Zorica., Mary-Ellen, F. Feeney, Rajabifard, Abbas. and Williamson, Ian. (2004) Are SDIs serving the needs of local planning? Case study of Victoria, Australia and Illinois, USA.Computers, Environment and Urban Systems, 28: 329–351.

8) Collins, Alan. (1999) Tourism development and Natural capital. Annals of Tourism Research, 26(1): 98-109.

9) Daby, D. (2003) Effects of seagrass bed removal for tourism purposes in a Mauritian bay. Environmental Pollution. 125: 313–324.

10) Department of Tourism, Govt. of India, (1992) National Action Plan, New Delhi.

11) Department of Tourism, Govt. of India, (1998) Draft National Tourism Policy, New Delhi.

12) Ecotourism and Bulgaria - An Overview, (2003) Part of the Draft National Ecotourism Strategy, supported by United States Agency for International Development, Bulgaria Mission. Sofia, Bulgeria.

13) Enright, Michael. J. and Newton, James. (2004) Tourism destination competitiveness: a quantitative approach. Tourism Management, 25: 777–788.

14) Fallon, Liza D. and Kriwoken, Lorne. K. (2003) Community involvement in tourism infrastructure—the case of the Strahan Visitor Centre, Tasmania. Tourism Management, 24: 289–308.

15) Gale, Stuart & associates. and Pierce, lefebvre consulting. (2003) Land based ecotourismMulti-day hiking (backpacking and trekking). Economic development branch BC Ministry of sustainable resource management, British Columbia.

16) Gibbs, David. (2000) Ecological modernization, regional economic development and regional development agencies. Geoforum, 31: 9-19.

17) Gibson, Heather J., Willming, Cynthia,and Holdnak, Andrew. (2003) Small-scale event sport tourism: fans as tourists. Tourism Management, 24: 181–190.

18) Gossling, Stefan., Hansson, Carina. Borgstrom., Horstmeier, Oliver.and Saggel, Stefan. (2002) Ecological footprint analysis as a tool to assess tourism sustainability. Ecological Economics, 43: 199-211.

19) Handberg, R. (2002) Creating transportation infrastructure through state spaceport initiatives: Florida and other examples. Technology in Society, 24: 225–241.

20) Hope, C.A. and Klemm, M.S. (2001) Tourism in difficult areas revisited: the case of Bradford. Tourism Management, 22: 629–635.

21) Hsu Cathy, H.C., Kara,Wolfe. And Soo, K. Kang (2004) Image assessment for a destination with limited comparative advantages. Tourism Management 25: 121–126.

22) Jurowski, Claudia. and Gursoy, Dogan.(2004) Distance effects on residents'Attitudes toward tourism. Annals of tourism research, 31(2): 296–312,

23) Link, Heike. (2004) Rail infrastructure charging and on-track competition in Germany. International Journal of Transport Management, 2 :17–27.

24) Lusseaua, D. and Higham, J.E.S. (2004) Managing the impacts of dolphin-based tourism through the definition of critical habitats: the case of bottlenose dolphins (Tursiops spp.) in Doubtful Sound, New Zealand. Tourism Management, 25: 657–667.

25) Newsome, David. Moore, Susan. and Dowling Ross, (2002) Natural Area Tourism: Ecology, Impacts and Management, Channel View Publications.

26) Polat, Eylem H. and Olgun, Metin. (2004) Analysis of the rural dwellings at new residential areas in the Southeastern Anatolia, Turkey. Building and Environment, 39: 1505 - 1515.

27) Reyers, Belinda. (2004) Incorporating anthropogenic threats into evaluations of regional biodiversity and prioritisation of conservation areas in the Limpopo Province, South Africa. Biological Conservation , 118: 521–531.

28) Ritchiea, Brent. W. (2004) Chaos, crises and disasters: a strategic approach to crisis management

29) Russell, Roslyn. and Faulkner, Bill (2004) Entrepreneurship, chaos and he tourism area lifecycle. Annals of Tourism Research, 31(3): 556–579.

30) Selvam, M. (1989) Tourism industry in India. Himalaya Publishing House, India.

31) Sharple, Richard. (2000) The influence of the accommodation sector on tourism development: lessons from Cyprus. Hospitality Management, 19: 275-293.

32) Simpson, Lyn., Daws, Leonie. and Pini, Barbara (2004) Public internet access revisited. Telecommunications Policy, 28: 323–337.

33) Tata Consultancy Service and Infrastructure Private Company (2006), Tourism Planning in Garhwal Himalaya

34) Thomas, D. Winfred., Oliver king, D. I. Soundrapandi, J. and Narasimhan, D. Evolution of livelihood strategies among Geographically isolated hill tribes of South India. Department of Botany, The American College, Tamil Nadu.

35) Tosun, Cevat. (1998) Roots of unsustainable tourism development at the local level: the case of Urgup in Turkey,.Tourism Management, 19(6): 595-610.

36) Turkstra, Jan., Amemiya, Nelly. and b, Murgia, Jose. (2003) Local spatial data infrastructure, Trujillo-Peru. Habitat International, 27: 669–682.

37) UNEP Publication, (2002) Sustainable Tourism in Protected Areas: Guidelines for Planning and Management

38) Uttaranchal Tourism Development Board, Tourism Policy and Planning (2006)

39) Weiers, Stefan., Bock, Michael., Wissen, Michael.and Rossner, Godela. (2004)

Mapping and indicator approaches for the assessment of habitats at different scales using remote sensing and GIS methods. Landscape and Urban Planning, 67: 43-65.

40) World Tourism Organisation and United Nations Environement Programme (1992), Guidelines: Development of National Parks and Protected Areas of Tourism, Madrid.

ACKNOWLEDGEMENT

The author is sincerely thankful to the Uttaranchal Tourism Development Board (UTDB) and Tata Consultancy Service and Infrastructure (Pvt.) Company for readily providing and supplying the requisite and valuable data, facts and inputs which are vital and relevant for further growth, development and coherent research in Uttarkashi District of Garhwal Himalaya.

22

Micro Level Approaches Towards Sustainable Tourism

Dr. Sanjeev Bansal
Department of Economics,
Kurukshetra University,
Kurukshetra

Dr. Madan Singla
Lecturer in Commerce,
M. Agrasen College,
Jagadhri

ABSTRACT

Sustainable tourism in its purest sense, is an industry which attempts to make a low impact on the environment and local culture, while helping to generate income, employment, and the conservation of local ecosystems. It is responsible tourism which is both ecologically and culturally sensitive. Thus, sustainable tourism should make optimal use of environmental resources that constitute a key element in tourism development, maintaining essential ecological processes and helping to conserve natural heritage and biodiversity. It should also ensure viable, long-term economic operations, providing socio-economic benefits to all stakeholders that are fairly distributed, including stable employment and income-earning opportunities and social services to host communities, and contributing to poverty alleviation. Sustainable tourism development requires the informed participation of all relevant stakeholders, as well as strong political leadership to ensure wide participation and consensus building. Achieving sustainable tourism is a continuous process and it requires constant monitoring of impacts, introducing the necessary preventive and/or corrective measures whenever necessary. The present paper is an attempt to discuss some sustainability issues in tourism and suggest some concrete micro level approaches to attain it.

During recent years human beings have become more concerned about their survival on the earth. People throughout the world have been realizing that the biological richness of their environment is their most valuable resource and that its preservation is vital for sustainable development. Whether it is Stockholm Conference, Brutland Commission, Earth Summit or Rio Plus 5, sustainable development has been the hottest agenda. Sustainable development, as defined by the Brutland Commission, is 'development that meets the needs of the present generation without compromising the ability of the future generations to meet their own'. The definition makes it clear that sustainable development is about responsible entrepreneurship, product stewardship, long term planning and doing more with less. It calls for business and industrial activity that makes more efficient use of resources and reduces the output of pollution - solid waste, liquid effluents, noise and emissions.

Case of Tourism and Hospitality Industry in Sustainable Development

In the modern society, tourism has emerged as an economic activity of immense global importance. It has found a niche for itself as an effective instrument for generating employment, earning revenue and foreign exchange, enhancing environment preservation, rejuvenation of the culture and tradition and thereby facilitating overall development. Normally considered as a clean industry, the negative impacts of tourism start to occur when the level of visitor use is greater than the environment's ability to cope with this use. Today's problem of travel is that too many travelers are going too far too often within a limited area i.e., our planet. The World Tourism Organization estimated that there were 25 million tourists' arrivals in 1950. UNWTO's *Tourism 2020 Vision* forecasts that international arrivals are expected to reach nearly 1.6 billion by the year 2020. Of these worldwide arrivals in 2020, 1.2 billion will be intraregional and 378 million will be long-haul travelers. This increasing number can put enormous pressure on an area and lead to impacts such as soil erosion, increased pollution, discharges into the sea, natural habitat loss, increased pressure on endangered species and heightened vulnerability to forest fires (Buckley and Pannell, 1992). The present paper aims to discuss the negative environmental impacts of tourism and suggest some micro level approaches to attain sustainability in tourism.

Tourism and Air Pollution

Transport by air , road and rail is continuously increasing in response to the rising number of tourists and their greater mobility. To give an indication, the ICAO reported that the number of international air passengers worldwide rose from 88 million in 1992 to 859 million in 2004. one consequence of this increase in air transport is that tourism now accounts for more that 60 p.c. of air travel and is therefore responsible for an important share of air emissions (ICAO,2004). Road traffic also causes noise, dust, congestion and particulate emissions that are worsened in many cities by badly maintained exhaust systems. It is worth noting that many of the world's major tourism city destinations- Bangkok, Paris, Rome, Los Angeles, Mexico City, New York, Athens and Manila are also on the global list of urban areas with very poor ambient air quality. So, a strong case is there why tourism industry should concern for the rising air pollution.

Tourism and Water Pollution

Water is perhaps the tourism industry's most important resource. It is estimated that in most developing countries, a tourist uses 10 times more water every day than a local inhabitant. The tourism industry generally overuses water resources for hotels, swimming pools, golf courses and personal use of tourists. This can result in water shortages and degradation of water supplies as well as generating a greater volume of waste water. The wastewater has polluted seas and lakes surrounding tourist attractions, damaging the flora and fauna. Sewage runoff causes serious damage to coral reefs because it stimulates the growth of algae, which cover the filter-feeding corals, hindering their ability to survive.

Tourism and Depletion of Ozone Layer

Ozone depleting substances (ODSs) such as CFCs (Chlorofluorocarbons), HFCs (Hydro chlorofluorocarbons) and halons have contributed to the destruction of ozone layer. The tourism industry directly contributes towards ozone layer depletion because it is an important user of ODSs for refrigeration, air-conditioning and fire-extinguishing, as well as of foam insulation, upholstery and aerosol spray cans. Emissions from jet aircraft are also a significant source of ODSs. Tourists, especially those looking for sunshine and the 'open air' are among the first to feel the impact of high levels of UV B radiation, which is increasing skin cancers, cataracts and immunity system diseases. Damage to crops and marine life also means that key tourist resources are being negatively affected.

Tourism and Land Degradation

The hospitality industry is often held responsible for the expansion of urban sprawl and the use of hitherto untouched natural areas, especially mangroves, mountains and forests, for further development. Poor land use planning coupled with unsustainable siting, engineering and construction of tourism facilities can cause erosion, landslides and flooding. For example, in many low lying and coastal areas, tourist facilities constructed on the waterfront may increase these risks if natural protective features such as dunes and vegetation cover have been destroyed. Forests often suffer negative impacts of tourism in the form of deforestation caused by fuel wood collection and land clearing. For example, one trekking tourist in Nepal uses four to five kilograms of wood a day (Butler,1991). Building and construction often involves soil removal, land reclamation, filling, dredging and leveling, which can involve the removal and sometimes total destruction of the site's vegetation. This causes serious interruptions in the natural cycles of the surrounding ecosystem.

Tourism and Wildlife

Viewing, photographing and in some cases hunting wildlife are all important tourist activities. But over the last 30 years, the evidence suggest that tourism is again becoming a victim of its own success (Cater, et al,1993). Firstly, tourism interrupts the feeding and breeding animals and predator-prey relationships of animals. Especially at fault are tourist vehicles that chase and track down animals in order to get a good photograph. Secondly, the creation of game reserves has led to habitat destruction. For example, in recent years the elephant population in the game reserves of Central and Southern Africa has increased dramatically. These large number of reserves have uprooted trees and stripped away vegetation cover, reducing the food available for many browsing species such as the giraffe.

Thirdly, littering and waste dumps by tourists and hospitality lodges attract rodents, birds and species such as bears. It certainly affects the traditional feeding patterns of these animals and raise safety issues for tourists and local inhabitants. The use of animals for souvenir manufacturing is internationally banned but poaching still thrives everywhere. This will continue as long as skins, furs, horns, shells, tails,hoogs, tusks, claws and stuffed animals fetch high prices and as long as adequate revenues from tourism do not gitter down to the local population.

Tourism and Acid Deposition

Acid deposition and rain occur when emissions of sulphur dioxide (So2) and nitrogen oxides (No2) react in the atmosphere with oxygen, water and other oxidants to form acidic compounds. These acidic components fall on the earth as 'wet deposition' (rain, snow, fog) and as 'dry deposition' (particulate matter and gas). Acid rain leads to increased acidity of water, impaired tree growth and therefore causes forest degradation. Forest damage and the loss of species due to acidification mean the degradation of some of the tourism industry's primary sources. Dry deposition on historic buildings and other monuments increases the frequency and cost of maintenance and repair. High sulphar emissions can impair the health of tourists and local people by increasing respiratory and lung disorders such as asthma.

Micro Level Approaches to Ensure Sustainable Tourism

The above discussion clearly reveals that tourism industry effects as well as affected by environmental degradation in one form or the other. Together these may be termed as negative externalities or social costs of tourism industry. In the presence of these externalities the optimal allocation and utilization of a particular resource is not possible due to the unreal costs and prices facing the producers and consumers. To convert unreal costs and benefits into real, the internalization of these externalities is required. Internalization of an externality occurs when individual benefits or costs in using resources are adjusted so that the users involved consider the value of their effects on others when choosing to use resource (Hyman, 1983). The prerequisite for internalization is that the parties involved must be clearly identifiable and the monetary value of the interdependence among them must be measurable. At a very micro level, such as a particular hotel/ tourist, the parties involved may be identified, however the monetary measurement of the damage is somewhat difficult. To keep the model simple, here it has been assumed that it is possible to measure the positive as well as negative effect of one party on the other. It means that how much worth of rupees impact (+ve or –ve) a hotel/tourist have on the environment can be measured quantitatively. Given this, now the problem has been reduced to how these impacts can be internalized. Some micro level approaches towards internalization are discussed here.

Through Economic Tools

Economic tools such as corrective taxes and corrective subsidies can be used to internalize the externalities. Corrective taxes or Pigovian taxes are designed to adjust costs or benefits artificially and in such a way as to force buyers and sellers to consider externalities in their choices.

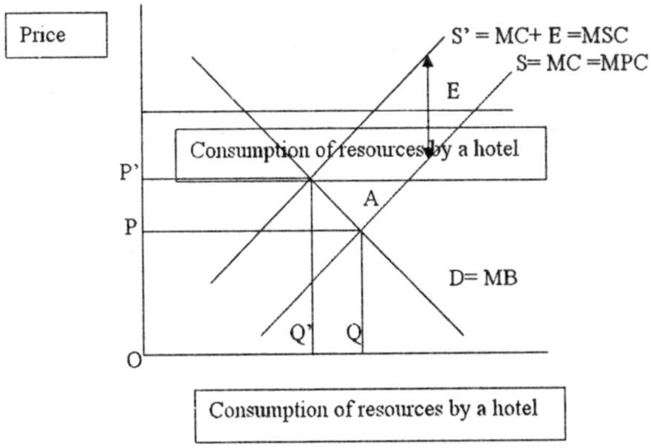

The operation of corrective taxes has been shown in Figure-I. The figure shows the relationship between the consumption of resources by a hotel and its price. It has been assumed here that the hotel have negative impact on the environment which is equal to 'E' per unit consumption of resources. To take an example, suppose a hotel threw waste equal to 'E' in a nearby flowing water stream against the consumption of resources by one guest. As the hotel has not been paying for such negative impacts so too much resources (OQ) have been consumed at too low prices (OP). A corrective tax can be imposed here to raise the costs of resource consumption, thereby, artificially raising the price to a level which will accurately reflect the scarcity of resources available for consumption. Since each unit of resource consumption causes 'E' Rs. of external damage to alternative users of the stream, it is an easy matter- in this case- to levy a consumption/ entertainment/ luxury tax on each unit of resource consumption equal to 'E'. The corrective tax, T, is therefore

$$T = E$$

This tax will raise the cost of consumption of hotels. Consequently, the marginal cost curve will shift up from S to S', where S' reflects MC+ E, which is a true marginal social cost of consumption. The increase in cost caused by the tax changes the market equilibrium from A to B, where the new price is P' and the quantity consumption is OQ'. This quantity is an efficient level of consumption as it is based upon the true costs and prices. In addition to raising the price and reducing the quantity demanded to the efficient level, the corrective tax will also results into following corrections:

1. A reduction in the value of losses to alternative users of the environment from EQ rupees to EQ' rupees.
2. The collection of TQ' =EQ' rupees of revenue from the hoteliers/ tour operators.

It is noteworthy here that the corrective tax does not reduce the environmental pollutants to zero. It merely raises the cost of consuming resources. Hoteliers/tour operators, as polluters, will compare this extra cost with other alternatives of waste disposal and decide how much of the environmental resources to consume given its increased price. Given the cost of alternatives- including the recycling of waste, purifying the waste before disposal, reducing consumption or going out of business – there will most certainly be a reduction in the waste emitted. The actual amount of reduction will depend on the availability and cost of alternative disposal methods relative to the corrective tax and the impact of tax on the profitability of the hoteliers.

One relevant issue can be raised regarding the ability of taxes to correct this market failure in case hoteliers are successful in shifting this tax burden to the tourists. The effectiveness of corrective taxes becomes doubtful as hoteliers are in a position to shift the whole burden to the buyer. In such a situation, the solution lies in simultaneous introduction of subsidies. The polluting hoteliers will be taxed as opposed to the non polluting hoteliers, which will receive subsidies. It will make the polluting hotels relatively costlier and the guests intake will certainly be negatively affected thereby reducing their revenues. So, for the polluters, corrective tax will work as a double edged sword.

Using Corrective Subsidies

A corrective subsidy is similar in conception to a corrective tax, however the later corrects the negative externalities while the former corrects the positive externalities. As discussed earlier, the operation of taxes will not bring the desired effects without the introduction of subsidies. In the tourism industry, there is no dearth of the firms which have taken initiatives to conserve energy, recycle water, build sustainable buildings and promote sustainable travel. These are positive externalities for the society in general, because they never enter the demand and cost function of the firms.

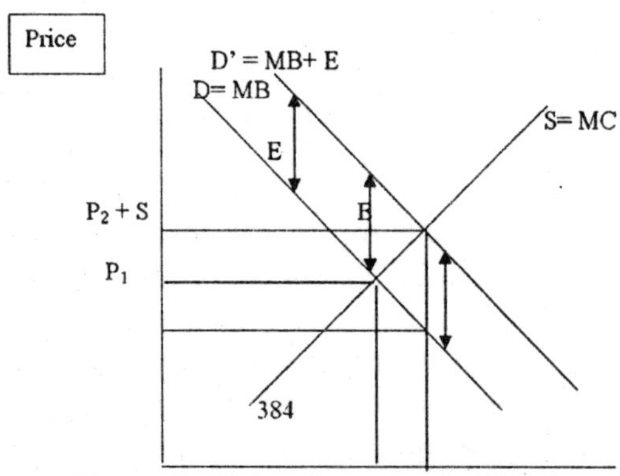

Figure-II Using Corrective Subsidies

P_2

Q_1 Q_2

Figure-II shows the operation of corrective subsidies. D and S are the demand and supply curves of environment friendly products/ conservation efforts. Assume that all these products/efforts result into external benefit equal to 'E' rupees. Before taking these positive effects into account, Q_1 level of environment friendly products/ conservation efforts will be chosen at a price of P_1. Q_1 is not an efficient level of products/efforts a sit is based on individual and not the social benefits. The optimality is attained at Q_2 level where marginal cost of the products/efforts becomes equal to their social marginal benefits. To reach this level, a corrective subsidy of S=E must be given. It will shift the MB curve to D′ and the optimal level will be at Q_2. Here, the producers of environment friendly products will receive a price of P_2+S but the hoteliers will pay only P_2 which is lower than the previously paid price i.e P_1.In case of conservation efforts, their total cost, which is equal to S will be given by way of this subsidy.

Through Voluntary Initiatives

Environmentally sound tourism development is not possible without wider range of voluntary initiatives. These initiatives are voluntary agreements and voluntary standards which promote product stewardship and environmentally responsible entrepreneurship.

- Voluntary agreements include environment related principles, Charters and code of conduct, which set out guidelines to environmentally sound operations and procedures;
- Voluntary standards not only provide guidelines but also indicate specific levels of environment related performance that need to be achieved.

Some of the developments in this area are worth noting:

- One of the popular international voluntary environment management standard in operation today is ISO 14000. it is a series of environment management standards and guidelines developed and promoted by the International Organization for Standardization. The series of most interest to tourism and hospitality is ISO 14001, which provides standards and certification of corporate environment management systems. Many tourism and hospitality business all over the world have already applied and received certification under ISO14001.
- An international food safety and hygiene programme that facilitates the Hazard Analysis and Critical Control Points (HACCP) is a systematic method using seven principles for analyzing a food process and determining the possible chemical, physical and biological hazards within it. The HACCP 9000 programme integrates HACCP, ISO9000 and food hygiene practices into one management system to ensure food safety and quality for a food/beverage plant or a food service establishment anywhere in the world.
- In 1992, the International Hotel Environment Initiative (IHEI), a non-profit charity programme has been developed by the International Hotel Industry for the benefit of hotels and the environment. The IHEI aims to promote the advantages of environment management as a fundamental part of running a successful and efficient hotel.
- In a joint initiative, the IH& RA, UNEP and IHEI published an Environment Action Pack for hotels in 1995. This user friendly guide is intended for use by all hotel employees and helps them in developing a practicable and effective environment management programme.

- The IH& RA's annual Green Hotelier and Restaurateur Environmental Award serves a triple purpose: to promote what the industry is doing to save environment; to raise industry's standards through identification of best practice; and to promote awareness of what still is to be done?
- The Green Globe American Programme is a joint venture between Green Globe and the Caribbean Alliance for sustainable tourism(CAST). This environmental and management programme promotes the membership and certification of travel and tourism companies and destinations.
- Eco-labels are of particular interest to small and medium sized tourism and hospitality businesses as they:
    1. Provide businesses with environment management information and expertise, which may not be available in-house;
    2. Allow tourists to identify directly and select environmentally responsible operators;
    3. Enable each business to develop an environment management system to suit its individual needs.

CONCLUSION

As tourism and hotel industry produce any negative as well as positive environmental impacts, so it is imperative that these impacts must be taken into account if the dream of sustainable development is to be fulfilled. The economic and public participatory approaches mentioned in this paper may prove helpful in showing the path towards sustainable development.

REFERENCES

1. Buckley,R.and J.Pannell(1992), "Environmental Impacts of Tourism and Recreation in National Parks and Conservation Reserves", The Journal of Tourism Studies, Vol.3, School of Business, James Cook University.
2. Cater,Eriet A. and Cwen A. Lawman (Eds).(1993), "Ecotourism-a Sustainable Option", Royal Geographical Society and Belhaven Press, London
3. Romerill, Michael(1989), "Tourism and the Environment- Accord or Discord", Tourism Management, Vol.10(5), Elsevier, New York
4. Hyman, David(1983), "Public Finance- A Contemporary Application of Theory to Policy", The Dryden Press, USA
5. FHRAI Magagine, Jan-Feb. 2004, Vol.4, Issue 4, P-27

Section IV
Information Technology and Tourism

23

Eco-tourism Development in Uttaranchal: An opportunity but challenge!

Strategic analysis of a case study on eco-tourism opportunity in Uttaranchal based on extensive field survey and tourism data
by
Tarun K. Roy

Author is a naturalist, nature educationist, conservationist, eco-adventure tourism consultant, Nature photographer, freelance travel & tourism writer and working as Nature Education Officer (NEO) in CEMDE, School of Environmental Studies, University of Delhi. He extensively travels throughout the country.

He has attended several national and international tourism conferences/seminars in the past and contributed several papers. More than 35 articles on travel & tourism, adventure sports and nature already been published in several travel & tourism magazines and journals.

Communication Address
3/3-A, Street No. 2, K - Block,
Gangotri Vihar, (W. Ghonda), Delhi - 110053
Tel: 011-22183508 **Mob:** 9868831869 **E-mail:** tarunkroy@rediffmail.com

ABSTRACT

Eco-tourism is distinguished than other forms of tourism that provides multi-dimensional benefits. It is a combination of multi-faceted activities those accelerates economic growth, creates large-scale employment, alleviates poverty, generates revenue, earns foreign exchange, educates people, supports conservation and preserves cultural & natural heritage.

After recognized its separate entity in the implementation plan of the "world summit on sustainable development' 2002" as a segment of sustainable development, and after the "world eco-tourism summit' 2002", eco-tourism has got a new dimension in the 21st century and it took a new shape in the country.

Global tourist trends have also been changing fast towards eco-tourism products. Eco-tourism has been greatly emphasized for its promotion in the national tourism policy 2001 and in uttaranchal tourism policy 2001. In the uttaranchal forest policy 2001, it has been identified as the instrument for self-employment and poverty alleviation in the state.

Uttaranchal, ranks 6th amongst the states/uts in terms of percentage of forest areas, which is 64.81% of the state's geographical area and 18.70% of forest area, and 4.5% of the country's forest area. Uttaranchal is truly unsurpassed and fabulous mountain state in india, known as "devbhumi' - the "land of gods" having its enormous bio-geographical diversity. Uttaranchal has 12 distinguished protected areas (pas) and additionally 03 more natural reserves are the impetus of eco-tourism.

Considering the magnitude of eco-tourism and its tremendous resources, there is enormous possibility of eco-tourism development in uttaranchal. But infrastructure development and other supporting facilities are the main issues and challenges to promote eco-tourism. The new revenue tariff for trekking and mountaineering in uttarnachal became another issue of challenge for eco-tourism. It is imperative of infrastructure development with other supporting facilities, and offer of a revised and affordable revenue tariff for overall eco-tourism growth in the state.

Key words: *Eco-tourism opportunity in uttaranchal, eco-tourism promotion, socio-economic development, sustainable tourism, ecological conservation.*

INTRODUCTION:

Uttaranchal

Uttaranchal is located in the north of India in the Himalayan ranges, ranks 6th amongst the State/UTs in terms of percentage of forest areas. Uttaranchal has total geographical area of 53,483 sq. km. includes 34,662 sq. km. of forest area (includes 6,478 sq. km. protected area), which is 64.81% of the state's geographical area, and 18.70% of forest area, and 4.5% of the country's forest area. The human population of the state is 8.48 million i.e. 0.8% of country's population of which 25.6% is urban and 74.4% is rural. Truely, Uttaranchal is unsurpassed and fabulous mountain state in India, known as "Devbhumi' - *the "Land of Gods"* having its varied bio-geographical and rich biological diversity.

Eco-tourism

Eco-tourism is distinguished than other forms of tourism that has multi-dimensional benefits. The key elements of eco-tourism include a natural environment as the prime attraction, an optimum number of environment-friendly visitors, activities that do not have any serious impact on the ecosystem and the positive involvement of the local community in maintaining the ecological balance and gains socio-economic benefits.

Eco-tourism, unlike its conventional counterpart, promotes environmentally responsible travel and seeks to ensure that visitors take nothing but photographs and leave nothing behind but footprints. Eco-tourism is a combination of positive activities those accelerates country's economic growth, creates large-scale employment, alleviates poverty, generates revenue, earns foreign exchange, educates people, supports conservation and preserves cultural & natural heritage.

After recognized its separate entity in the Implementation Plan of the "World Summit on Sustainable Development' 2002" as a component for sustainable development, and after the "World Eco-tourism Summit' 2002", eco-tourism has turned to a new dimension in the 21st century and it took a new shape in the country.

NATIONAL POLICIES

Tourism Policy 2002

Greater emphasis has been given on promotion of Eco-tourism in the National Tourism Policy 2002. The Department of Tourism, Govt. of India has formulated the Eco-tourism Policy and Guidelines in 1998 for its optimum growth in the country. A National Committee on Eco-Tourism & Mountains was also set up by the Central Tourism Ministry for managing the fragile ecosystem and to consider projects/programmes for development of eco-tourism in the country.

Forest and Wildlife Policy and Action Plan

The Ministry of Environment & Forests, Govt. of India has identified eco-tourism as one among the 15 thrust areas in the country. In the National Wildlife Action Plan' 2002-1016, wildlife/eco-tourism promotion was specially emphasized for effective wildlife conservation and management in the country with involvement and benefit of the local communities.

STATE POLICIES

Uttranchal Tourism Policy 2001

In Uttaranchal Tourism Policy' 2001, tourism was considered as the mainstay of Uttaranchal's economy. Nature & Eco-tourism including pilgrimage tourism, cultural tourism, and adventure tourism were given emphasis in its action plan for optimal development and infrastructure development.

Uttaranchal Forest Policy 2001

In Uttaranchal Forest Policy' 2001, eco-tourism was identified as an important instrument for self-employment and poverty alleviation. With the importance of eco-tourism development, Uttaranchal Forest Department has drawn up an eco-tourism policy and guidelines and established a Centre for Eco-tourism.

ECO-TOURISM POTENTIAL

Uttaranchal with its geographical variation and biological diversity has been endowed with a wealth of eco-systems comprising of biosphere reserves with lush green luxuriant forests, national parks & wildlife sanctuaries has rich plethora of flora & fauna, finest tiger reserve, extensive elephant reserve, majestic snowy mountains with lofty peaks, verdant valleys, alpine meadows, sacred rivers, magnificent lakes, white frozen glaciers. The spectacular and typical Himalayan eco-systems include all these are the hub for eco-tourism.

Table 1
List of the pas in Uttaranchal

S. N.	Name of Protected Area (PA)	Area of PA (KM^2)	Date of ESTD.	District
1.	Corbett National Park	520.82	11.05.1936	Nainital, Pauri
2.	Gangotri National Park	1,552,00	16.09.1989	Uttarkashi
3.	Govind National Park	472.08	26.02.1990	Uttarkashi
4.	Nanda Devi National Park	630.00	18.08.1982	Chamoli
5.	Rajaji National Park	820.00	12.08.1983	Dehradun, Hardwar, Pauri
6.	Valley of Flowers National Park	87.50	01.01.1982	Chamol
7.	Askot Must Deer WL Sanctuary	593.93	30.07.1986	Pithoragarh
8.	Binsar Wildlife Sanctuary	45.59	25.05.1988	Almora
9.	Govind Pashu Vihar WL Sanctuary	481.00	22.03.1955	Uttarkash
10.	Kedarnath Wildlife Sanctuary	957.00	21.01.1092	Chamoli, Rudraprayag
11.	Mussoorie Wildlife Sanctuary	10.82	02.09.1993	Dehradun
12.	Sonanadi Wildlife Sanctuary	301.76	09.01.1987	Pauri
	list of other pas in uttaranchal			
1.	Corbett Tiger Reserve	1134.00	1973-74	Nainital, Pauri
2.	Nanda Devi Biosphere Reserve	5860.00	18.01.1988	Chamoli, Almora, Pithoragarh
3.	Shivalik Elephant Reserve	5405.00	28.10.2002	Dehradun, Pauri, Haridwar

Source: wildlife institute of india, uttaranchal forest department, Project tiger and project elephant

Uttaranchal is the 4th largest Himalayan state in the country, has 12 distinguished protected areas, covering 6,472.5 sq km which comprised of 6 wildlife sanctuaries as Askot Musk Deer Wildlife Sanctuary, Binsar Wildlife Sanctuary, Govind Pashu Vihar Wildlife Sanctuary, Kedarnath Wildlife Sanctuary, Mussoorie Wildlife Sanctuary, Sonanadi Wildlife Sanctuary; 6 National Parks as Corbett National Park, Gangotri National Park, Rajaji National Park, Govind National Park, Nandadevi National Park, Valley of Flowers National Park; and additionally, 1 Tiger Reserve as Corbett Tiger Reserve; 1 Elephant Reserve as Siwalik Elephant Reserve; and the Nandadevi Biosphere Reserve - a World Heritage Site. All these can make Uttaranchal an outstandingly year-round eco-tourism destination. A list of the PAs in Uttaranchal is shown in Table No. 1 and potential resources of those PAs are shown in Table No. 2.

TOURIST TRENDS

Towards Eco-tourism Products

In the 21st century, consumer trends have been changing fast towards new products and choice. The modern tourists seek a diversity of new and interesting experiences, resulted in increasing popularity of off-the-beaten-tracks and peaceful natural destinations that are remote and lesser known. It demands the market of special interest tourism - ecology, diving, trekking, nature camping, river rafting, wild safaris, bird watching, flora & fauna, etc which are the multiple components of eco-tourism. Uttaranchal has enormous opportunity & prosperity of eco-tourism, to meet the growing demands in the tourism market.

Tourist Inflow

The tourist inflow in the PAs has also been increasing in the state as shown in the Tourist Arrivals Statistical Data in Table No. 3. But no tourist arrivals data of the other PAs/eco-tourism destinations in the state except a few well-maintained PAs are being maintained so far.

Table 3 Tourist Arrivals in the Pas in Uttaranchal

Name of Protected Area (PA)	2002	2003	2004	2005	2006
Corbett National Park	65,390	91,056	99,675	1,22,822	DNC
Gangotri National Park	DNA	686 (Oct-Nov)	42,404 Pilgrims↓ DNA	4,842 Pilgrims↓ 42,156	6,419 Pilgrims↓ 31,756
Valley of Flowers National Park	1,515	4,457	4,951	5,211	DNC

DNC = DATA NOT COMPILED *DNA = DATA NOT AVAILABLE

Source: Uttaranchal tourism development board, and Uttaranchal forest department

TOURISM IMPACTS

With the momentum of tourism growth in the country, it has been observed that mass tourism has always-negative impact on the environment except economic benefits, and especially at the fragile mountain destinations that is destructive in nature. But eco-tourism is distinguished from mass tourism by having a lower impact on the environment if it is maintained by eco-friendly way & guidelines, by requiring less infrastructure development as well it has socio-economic benefits.

The Himalayas has its own ecosystem with delicate and fragile ecological habitat with meager tolerance for human artifacts, and its variable carrying capacity, which support particular livelihoods and include significant watershed resources, biological diversity and unique flora and fauna. Carrying capacity is a crucial factor for sustainable eco-tourism development - the optimum density of visitors, which a given environment is capable of sustaining permanently, and anything beyond its carrying capacity it adversely affects on the environment and very specifically for Himalayan eco-tourism.

Environmental Effects

Infrastructure development is a major factor of environmental impacts – the amount of water consumption, wastes generates and energy uses – can have severe impacts on the local environment if not properly managed. Unplanned and unscientific tourism development creates serious environmental problem.

Over exploitation of natural resources (includes fuel wood, timber, non-wood forest products & other forms of utilization for human benefits) by unregulated tourism is another factor of environmental impacts that causes environmental threats resulting global warming i.e. average global temperature has risen 0.8^0 C where devastating impacts would be the result, climatic changes, natural disasters, receding forests & water sources, and overall environmental degradation.

Socio-Economic Benefits

Sustainable eco-tourism has positive impacts on social and economic benefits to the local communities as they are the host as well preserver of the local environment, so local communities are the first target group in the tourism sector towards sustainable eco-tourism growth.

INDIA TOURISM FORECAST

The World Tourism & Travel Council (WTTC) has already forecasted in its status paper "The India Imperatives" that India will be one of the foremost growth centres in the world in the coming decade, and by the year 2010, Indian Travel & Tourism will generate the same level of employment as the world Travel & Tourism will generate 24.8 million jobs, accounting for 6.5% of the total employment world-wide, and then further 25 million jobs would be created over the next decade.

ECO-TOURISM IMPERATIVE

Considering the multi-faceted positive activities as well multi-dimensional benefits of eco-tourism and its vast potential in the state, it is imperative to develop sustainable eco-tourism in Uttaranchal, which would be instrumental for socio-economic development, employment generator, poverty alleviator, environment educator and conservation of the natural resources as it supports the state tourism and forest policies 2001.

SUSTAINABLE ECO- TOURISM DEVELOPMENT:

"Conservation" is the key factor for preservation of environment and natural resources and basic instrument for the growth of sustainable eco-tourism. Management of protected areas and natural resources ensures conservation. At the same time, "carrying capacity" of a destination is another vital factor for eco-tourism development. Conservation and carrying capacity are co-related to each other, and sustainability is the central guiding factor in tourism industry. It requires conservation and sustainable development includes socio-economic benefits to the local communities simultaneously which depends on a dynamic & strategic National Tourism Policy based on scientific planning and effective management.

Sustainable eco-tourism development is a continuous exercise of resource management as well socio-economic development of the local communities that would ensure environmental stability, self-generation/regeneration of naturalness, self-employment, economic stability, and avoid any other forms of development that may results in irreversible changes in the ecosystem especially in the fragile Himalayas that may be disastrous.

Issues and Challenges

After strategic analysis and studies, it has been found there is immense opportunity for eco-tourism but infrastructure development & other supporting facilities and high revenue tariffs could be the main issues and challenges for eco-tourism development in the state.

Various initiatives for infrastructure development with participation of the private sector have been taken. On the vision of infrastructure development with active participation of the private sector and the local host communities, Uttaranchal Tourism Development Board (UTDB) and Confederation of Indian Industries (CII) jointly organized "Uttaranchal Tourism Conclave" from 22nd to 24th February, 2004 at Mussoorie. As per the decision of the conclave, few major tourism projects include a mega eco-tourism project i.e. a 500 crore rupees eco-tourism project at Hempur near Ramnagar has been approved.

Uniform and affordable revenue tariff is important in the initial stage of eco-tourism promotion in Uttaranchal without having proper infrastructure yet. The present revenue tariff for entry, trekking, camping in the forestlands and PAs (only Indian pilgrims are exempted from entry fees for trekking along pilgrimage routes), and recently announced revenue tariff for mountaineering expeditions in Uttaranchal by the forest department is a superimpose of higher tariff and it became a contradiction to the adventure tour operators associations/adventure & mountaineering associations/federations/clubs which may results reversible tourist trends and already number of mountaineering expeditions started reducing in the state. The present revenue tariff for trekking, camping in forestlands & protected areas in Uttaranchal is shown in Table No. 4.

Table 4. Revenue Tariff for Trekking in Forest Lands and PAs in Uttaranchal

1. RESERVE FORESTS (RFs):

Entry fee (per head/day)	Camping fee (per day/tent)	Trail management	fee(per head)	Porter fee (per head/day)	Garbage fee (per head)	Camera fee (per day)
Rs. 10/- (General)	Rs. 20/-	Free	Rs. 20/-	Free	Free: Still/Video (Non-Professional) Rs. 25/- (Still -	
	Professional).			Rs. 100/- (Video -		
	Professional).					
Rs. 50/- (Foreigner)	Rs. 20/-	Free	Rs. 20/-	Free	- Do -	
Rs. 10/- (Student)	Rs. 20/-	Free	Rs. 20/-	Free	Free	

2. PROTECTED AREAS (PAs):

Entry fee per head (for 03 days)	Camping fee (per day/tent)	Trail management for 3 days)	fee (per head	Porter fee (per head/ day)	Garbage fee (per head)	Camera fee (per day)
Rs. 40/- (General)	Rs. 50/- (small tent)		Rs. 60/- (Gen)	Rs. 40/-	Rs. 20/-	Free Still/Video
Rs. 25/-(add. days)	Rs. 100/-(Big Tent)		Rs. 100/-(Add. Days)	Rs. 25/- (A.D.)	Rs. 20/- Gen/	(Non Professional)
		Rs. 20/- (Porter)		porter appli.	Rs. 100/- (Still/	
		Rs. 40/- (A.D.)		to NDNP	Video Professional	
Rs. 150/-(Foreigner)	Rs. 50/- (Small T.)		-Do-	-Do-	-Do-	-Do-
Rs.150/- (A.D.)	-Do-	Rs. 30/- (A.D.)	-Do-	-Do-	-Do-	

Tourism Technologies

The prime strategy for achieving environmentally sustainable eco-tourism is the choice of appropriate technology, which should determine nature magnitude, and scope of tourism. Such technology should match financial, operational and maintenance requirements with the local capabilities. The key to success lies in selecting methods and models that benefit and minimize costs from economic, social and environmental perspectives. The more the local people benefit from eco-tourism, the more they will benefit from a commitment to preserve the environmental tourism planning technology.

RECOMMENDATIONS

Infrastructure Development

The existing infrastructure facilities in the state are poor and insufficient which needs to develop for eco-tourism promotion. World-class infrastructure development for tourism has already been focused in the National Tourism Policy 2001 as well in the Uttaranchal Tourism Policy and Action Plan 2001. The Ministry of Tourism, Govt. of India has offered new scheme for financial assistance to the states for Development of Integrated Tourism Circuits that include all infrastructure tourism facilities as international standard destinations. The state government may take benefits of this scheme by creating such any integrated eco-tourism circuits in the state.

A. ROAD

Most of the tourist circuits in Uttaranchal are entirely dependent on road. Most of the eco-tourism destinations in the state do not have easy access by good roads. It needs to develop the road linkages with connectivity to all the PAs and to develop jeepable tracks/ paths, trails inside the PAs for safari/treks. Transportation facilities in the private sector with regular tourist bus service need to initiate for domestic budget tourists. Trekking routes and trails are needed to develop in the lesser-known and new destinations.

B. RAILWAY

Uttaranchal is connected by Railway to different cities and towns but the existing Rly. Stations need to upgrade, and to connect to other major cities with introduction of more number of super fast and important trains like Shatabdi Express, Janshatabdi Express and Rajdhani Express.

C. AIR

Jolly Grant Airport and other two small airstrips - Naini Saini near Pithoragarh and Pantnagar near Kotdwar need to upgrade and to make operational regularly as well need to link them to major airports in the country with regular flights, to attract the high spender international and domestic tourists. Even private helicopter service to the remote destinations need to encourage.

D. ACCOMMODATION

It needs to upgrade the existing tourist accommodations include the Forest Rest Houses, PWD Rest Houses in and around the PAs/eco-tourism destinations with modern facilities as most of those are substandard, poorly managed and inadequate. Also need to develop new accommodations with modern tourist facilities both at existing and new destinations (as per the environmental parameters), to cater the needs of all categories of tourists. In the remote destinations of the Protected Areas and forestlands as per eco-tourism potential, especially along the trekking routes, need to develop eco-friendly and all-weatherproof cottages or mountain huts with the basic facilities for eco tourists. A list of the existing accommodations in and around the Protected Areas (PAs) is shown in Table No. 5.

Sl.	Name of pas (wls/np)	Existing accommodations	
1.	Corbett National Park	**FRH:** At Dhikala, Khinianauli, Surpduli, Garjia, Gairal, Sultan, Bijrani, Paterpani, Jhirna, Mohan, Kalagarh, Lohachaur, Dhela Kanda, Jamlagwar and Ramnagar.	**PGH/HOTELS/ RESORTS:** at Ramnagar **KMVN TRH:** At Ramnagar **KMVN CAMPS:** At Laldhang and Sigri.
2.	Gangotri National Park	**FRH:** At Gangotri, Bhojbasa. **GMVN TRH:** At Gangotri and Bhojbasa	**PGH/HOTELS:** At Gangotri and Bhojbasa **ASHRAMS:** At Gangotri, Bhojbasa and Tapovan.
3.	Govind National Park	**FRH:** At Netwar.	
4.	Nanda Devi National Park	**FH:** At Lata Kharak.	**PAGH:** At Lata and Tolma village.
5.	Rajaji National Park	**FRH:** At Chilla, Motichur, Beribara, Dholkhand, Asarodi, Ranipur, Kansrao, Kunnao, Phandowala, Satyanarain,.	**GMVN TRH:** At Chilla. **NATURE CAMPS:** At Chilla.
6.	Valley of Flowers National Park	**FRH:** At Ghangaria. At Ghangaria.	**GMVN TRH:** At Ghangaria. **PGH/HOTELS: GURUDWARA:** At Ghangaria
7.	Askot Wildlife Sanctuary	**FRH:** At Askot, Rungling and Patijam.	
8.	Binsar Wildlife Sanctuary	**FRH:** At Binsar. **GMVN TRH:** At Binsar.	**Holiday Resort:** At Binsar.
9.	Govind Pashu Vihar Wildlife Sanctuary	**FRH:** At Netwar, Taluka, Seema, Jakhol, Satta, Istargarh and Har-ki-Dun.	**GMVN TRH:** At Sankri, Taluka, Seema and Har-ki-Dun.

10. Kedarnath Wildlife Sanctuary	**FRH**: At Triyginarayan, Kedarnath, Kalimath, Madmaheswar, Bisurital and Deoriatal. **GMVN TRH**: At Gourikund, Triyuginarayan, Sonprayag, Rambara, Kedarnath. **DHARAMSHALA/MGH:** At Triyuginarayan, Gourikund, Rambara, Kedarnath, Tungnath, Rudranath, Ansuyadevi, Kalpeshwar and Panwalikanta,	**PWDRH**: At Mandal, Sonprayag, Dugalvita, Gourikund. **PGH/Hotels**: At Sonpprayag, Triyuginarayan, Rambara, Kedarnath, Ransi, Madmaheshwar, Gondar, Sari, Chopta, Tungnath, Mandal, Ansuyadevi, Dumak and Devgram.
11. Mussoorie Wildlife Sanctuary	**GMVN TRH**: At Mussorie.	**PGH/ HOTELS/** At Mussoorie
RESORTS:		
12. Sonanadi Wildlife Sanctuary	**FRH**: At Haldu Parao, Sindhikhal, Mundiyapani and Rathuadhab.	

Forest rest house=frh gmvn=garwal mandal vikas nigam ltd kmvn = kumaon mandal vikas nigam ltd trh = tourist rest house pgh= guest house pagh=paying guest house mgh = mandir samiti guest house fh =forest hut

Source: *Uttaranchal.Tourism & Forest Department, Kmvn, Gmvn And Compiled By The Author*

Other Supporting Facilities

A. TELECOMMUNICATION FACILITY

Most of the PAs/eco-tourism destinations do not have telecommunication facility those need to develop with modern technologies include Internet facility.

B. HYGIENIC/ SANITARY CONDITIONS

Most of the eco-tourism destinations have either lack of toilet facilities or do not have proper toilet facilities. It needs to develop healthy sanitary facilities, safe drinking water and hygienic foods & medical facilities at every destination includes trekking/camping destinations.

Tourism Products Development

It needs to improve the eco-tourism products as well need to develop innovative new products with focus to various eco-package tours, especially on the brand of Garwal/

Kumaon Himalayas; as well distinguished Protected Areas need to integrate as an integral part of eco-tourism products, which would be the special attraction, and choice of products to the eco tourists.

Destination Development

The tourist spots of the PAs/eco-tourism destinations need to develop with tourist facilities & special attractions, and also need to emphasize to promote new destinations, to cater the needs of all categories of tourists with option of choice of destinations.

Publicity and Tourism Markeitng

Effective publicity and tourism marketing is vital for eco-tourism promotion. Uttaranchal tourism needs to take such any similar initiative for innovative way of publicity and tourism marketing like the department of tourism, Govt. of India has been successfully promoting 'India' through the byline "Incredible India" as a centralized campaign since 2001 onwards.

Awareness and Conservation

It needs to promote mass environmental awareness for conservation of biodiversity through sustainable use for economic benefits, aesthetic, ethical, cultural and social benefits amongst the locals and host communities. Eco-friendly tourism activities like jungle safari, bird watching, nature walks, nature trekking, nature camping, adventure sports, etc need to encourage and promote in such a manner so that simultaneously promotes awareness and sensitivity towards environmental & biodiversity conservation.

Human Resources Development

Various specialization courses related to travel & tourism industry needs to introduce in the universities/institutions/colleges in the state, and various training programs for skill development of local women, youth and tourism service providers need to organize from time to time. New training institutes for specialized activities may need to establish in the state as per needs and demands of eco-tourism.

Revenue Generation

The present revenue tariffs for trekking, camping and mountaineering expeditions in Uttaranchal need to reduce reasonably, so that the adventure and eco tour operator associations/ adventure sports and mountaineering associations/ federations/ clubs and individual tourists do not feel burden, expensive, and support eco-tourism promotion in the state. Also it requires uniform reasonable revenue tariffs throughout the state whereas peak fee is charged two times from mountaineering expedition teams, once by the Indian Mountaineering Foundation for booking of the respective peaks and again by Uttaranchal Forest Department. The present high revenue tariff for mountaineering expeditions in Uttaranchal is shown in Table No. 6.

TABTable 6
Revenue tariff for mountaineering expeditions in uttaranchal

INDIAN EXPEDITION:		REVENUE TARIFF		
Peak fee (in Rs.)	**Camping site fee & trail management fee (in Rs.)**	**Environ mental levy (in Rs.)**	**Service charge/ handling charge to state govt.**	**Total amount (in Rs.)**
(a) Above 7000 m. Rs.6,000/-	Rs. 3,000/-	Rs. 2000/-	Rs. 3000/-	Rs. 14,000/-
(b) Between 6501 – 7000 m. Rs.4000/-	Rs. 3,000/-	Rs. 1500/-	Rs. 3000/-	Rs. 11,500/-
(c) Below 6500 m. Rs. 000/-	Rs. 3,000/-	Rs. 1500/-	Rs. 3000/-	Rs. 10,500/-
FOREIGN EXPEDITION:		**REVENUE TARIFF**		
Peak fee (in Rs.)	**Camping site fee & trail Management fee (in Rs.)**	**Environ mental levy (in Rs.)**	**Service charge/ handling charge to state govt.**	**Total amount (in Rs.)**
(a) Above 7000 m. Rs. 40,000/-	Rs. 10,000/-	Rs. 20,000/-	Rs. 10,000/-	Rs. 80,000/-
(b) Between 6501 – 7000 m. Rs. 25,000/-	Rs. 10,000/-	Rs. 20,000/-	Rs. 10,000/-	Rs. 65,000/-
(c) Below 6500 m. Rs. 20,000/-	Rs. 10000/-	Rs. 20,000/-	Rs. 10,000/-	Rs. 55,000/-

Source: Uttaranchal Forest Department

Tourism Research and Analysis

It needs regular tourism survey, studies, scientific research and analysis of tourism data, which will help to formulate scientific and strategic action plan and implementation of tourism and forest policies from time to time, for sustainable growth of eco-tourism in the state.

Coordination and Linkages

Tourism is a complex industry where other ministry/departments are also involved such as ministry of civil aviation, ministry of home affairs, ministry of forest & environment, ministry of railway, ministry of transport, ministry of communication, etc. Therefore, good coordination networks need to develop among the other ministries/departments for sustainable eco-tourism development in the state.

REFERENCES:

1. Forest Dept, Govt. of Uttaranchal (2001), Uttaranchal Forest Policy 2001, Dehradun.
2. Dept. of Tourism, Govt. of Uttaranchal (2001), Uttaranchal Tourism Policy 2001, Dehradun.
3. Dept. of Tourism, Govt. of India (2001), National Tourism Policy 2002, New Delhi.
4. Min. of Env. & Forests, Govt. of India (2002), National Wildlife Action Plan 2002-2016, New Delhi.
5. Dept. of Tourism, Govt. of India (1998), Eco-tourism Policy & Guidelines 1998, New Delhi.
6. Forest Department, Govt. of Uttaranchal (2003), Eco-tourism Guidelines 2003, Dehradun.
7. Forest Department, Govt. of Uttaranchal (2001), Biodiversity Conservation in Uttaranchal 2001, Dehradun.
8. Wildlife Institute of India (2000), Envis Bulletin Vol. 3, No. 1, June, 2000, Dehradun.
9. Ministry of Environment & Forests, Govt. of India (2001), Project Tiger Status Report 2001, New Delhi.
10. Ministry of Environment & Forests, Govt. of India (2003), Report of the Project Elephant, New Delhi.
11. Roshni Kutty, and Ashish Kothari (2001), Protected Areas in India - A Profile, Kalpavriksh, Pune.
12. Forest Department, Govt. of U. P, Kedarnath WL Sanctuary Brochure, Lucknow.
13. Forest Department, Govt. of U. P (1999), Rajaji National Park Brochure, Lucknow.
14. Forest Dept, Govt. of U. P. (2000), Wildlife Technical Bulletin No. 2, March, 2000, Lucknow.
15. Kumaon Mandal Vikas Nigam Ltd (2001), Tourism Brochure, Nainital.

16. Forest Survey of India, Govt. of India (2001), State of Forest Report 2001, Dehradun.
17. United Nations (2003), Political Declaration and Plan of Implementation of the World Summit on Sustainable Development' 2002.
18. Department of Tourism, Govt. of India (2004), Annual Report 2003-04, New Delhi.
19. Ministry of Environment & Forests, Govt. of India (2004), Annual Report 2003-04, New Delhi.
20. Uttaranchal Tourism Development Board and Uttaranchal Forest Department (2004), Tourist Arrivals Data 2003-04, Dehradun.
21. Zoological Survey of India (1999), National Policy and Macrolevel Action Strategy on Biodiversity, Calcutta.
22. WWF International, Climate Change - impacts at 2^0 C and 3^0 C: A Press Release.

24

Search Engine as a Tool for Destination Choice: A Paradigm shift

Rakesh Kumar
Department of Computer Sc. & Applications,
K.U. Kurukshetra, Haryana, India,
E-mail: rsagwal@rediffmail.com
Sanjeev Dhawan
University Institute of Engineering & TechnologyK.U. Kurukshetra, Haryana, India,Email: rsdhawan@rediffmail.com

ABSTRACT

In this paper, we present the different scenarios of search engine optimization, a paradigm shift in the market of tourism science & management. Promoting websites online can acquire various form. Nevertheless, the most popular ways to advertise the tourism based websites are through search engine optimisation pay per click, pay per impression, & pay per percentage advertising techniques. However, each of these methods has one aim; to catch the people searching for your product onto your website in an optimised way. In correct optimisation the chances of getting a website found under its key phrases should be significantly increase. If your website can't be found in the web space priorities then potential customers will visit a competitor's site & you could lose out on a faith & sale. A thoughtful SEO strategy requires more than an automated service promising submission to "10000" search engines available today. This paper addresses the function & design prediction of SEO techniques, which will be used to increase the web page ranking among the customers, presents the implementation of a practical web based information system, by using the PPC, PPI, & PPP design techniques, & discusses the implications & results of SEO techniques with the use of above mentioned approaches.

Keywords: Function & design prediction of SEO, implementation of web based system, implications of SEO techniques, & search engine algorithms

INTRODUCTION

Conde Nast Traveller ranked India as the fourth most preferred travel destination & Lonely Planet selecting the country among the top five destinations from 167 countries this year, India has finally made its mark on the world travel map. Global recognition is evident from the rising number of India-bound tourists. From just 17,000 international arrivals in 1951, the number has grown to 39 lakh in 2005. According to the Ministry of Tourism, we have already clocked almost 30 lakh foreign tourists between January & September, as compared with 27 lakh during the same period last year. The tourist arrivals, pushing India's foreign-exchange earnings from $3.5 billion in 2003 to $5.7 billion in 2005. Much of the credit goes to the Ministry of Tourism's 'Incredible India' campaign launched towards the end of 2002 [Saikat Neogi 2006]. The campaign built a combined effort in international print, electronic, & most importantly in Internet media to showcase the country's tourism-friendly aspects. Earlier, the ministry was solely dependent on its overseas offices to promote India as a tourist destination. But now we have one of the top-most mediums for promoting the tourism i.e. through user-friendly Websites techniques, which have been discussed in this paper.

The volume of information on World Wide Web is increasing enormously everyday. The primary tool to locate any information on the web is search engine. The goal of search engine is to locate relevant documents in response to a user's query. Documents are typically retrieved as a ranked list, where the ranking is based on estimation of relevance [Belkin, N., & Croft, W.B. 87]. There may be millions of the sites pertaining in some manner to user's queries, search engine will retrieve them, rank them on the basis of their relevance using some criteria, & present a huge list of documents. But studies show that approximately 80% of Web searchers never view more than first 10 results in a result's list [Holscher C. & Strube G. 2000, Silverstein C., Henzinger M., Marais H., & Moricz M. 1999, Jansen B.J., Spink A., & Saracevic T. 2000]. A search engine typically displays results page by page, perhaps 10 hits at a time. Many users tend to look at only the first page of results they get from a search engine, rather than scrolling through pages & pages of hits. Some users scan additional result pages, usually in the natural ordering. A search session implicitly terminates when the user decides not to browse additional result pages on the topic that initiated the session.

Several studies have analyzed the queries that users submit to search engines, & the length of search sessions [Markatos, E. P. 2000, Lempel, R., & Moran, S. 2003]. Three findings that these studies share are particularly relevant to this work (1)The queries submitted to WWW search engines are very short, averaging less than 2.4 terms per query, with over half of the queries containing just one or two terms. These results were reported by [Croft, W. B., Cook, R., & Wilder, D. 1995] & [Wen, J.R., Nie, J.Y. & Zhang, H.J. 2002]. While the two studies define query terms somewhat differently, the reported term counts may be loosely interpreted as the number of words per query, (2) Users browse through very few result pages. These studies differ in the reported distribution of page views, but agree that at least 58% of the users view only the first page (the top-10 results), & that no more than 12% of users browse through more than 3 result pages. While the above describes the behavior of users as they browse through multiple result pages, statistics have also been gathered on the browsing patterns of users as they view a single page of results. It has been observed that users are reluctant to scroll beyond the visible part of the page, & so search results that are "above the fold" are viewed (and clicked on) by more users than results at the bottom of the page [Broder, A. 2000], (3) The number of distinct information needs of users is very large, as can be seen from the huge variety of queries submitted to search engines. However, popular queries are repeated many times, & the 25 most popular queries account for over 1% of all queries submitted to the engines

With the growing economic impact of the WWW, & the growth of e-commerce, it is crucial for businesses to have their sites ranked high by the major search engines. In the increasingly market-driven environment that is the web, it is becoming even more important to ensure that, as many people should see the site as possible. In particular, corporate & organizations who are trying to attract advertising revenue to their web sites need to ensure that they can show potential advertisers that placing an advertisement on their pages is likely to achieve maximum exposure. There are quite a few companies who sell this kind of expertise; they design web sites, which are tailored to rank high with specific queries on the major search engines. Under such competitive circumstances, web authors are increasingly beginning to rely on underhand techniques to ensure their sites get seen. Emerging practices are popularly known as keyword spamming (Keyword spamming is doctoring the content of a web site to ensure that it hits the top of a list of results retrieved from a web search engine. It is writing keywords multiple times so that one will be on top of a search results) & site optimization. These companies (which call their business "search engine optimization/positioning") research the ranking algorithms & heuristics of term-based search engines & know how many keywords to place (and where) in a web page so as to improve the page's ranking (which directly impacts the page's visibility) [Lempel R. & Moran S., Salsa 2001]. A less sophisticated techniques used by some site creators, is called keyword spamming [Chakrabarti, S., Dom, B., Gibson, D., Kumar, S.R., Raghavan, P., Rajgopalan, S., & Tomkins A. 1999]. Here the author repeats certain terms (some of which are remotely connected to their site's context), in order to lure search engines into ranking them highly for many queries.

So it has become all-important to be ranked in top-10. To design user friendly & high-quality Websites require lot of efforts. So lot of concentration will be given to design a precise & reliable Website depending upon the Search Engine Optimisation (SEO), Pay per Click (PPC), Pay per Impression (PPI), & Pay Per Page (PPP) techniques.

Search Engines

It is a well known truth that maximum users use search engines to locate the information on the web. Three components of search engine are – catalogue engine, spider, and query processor. The Boolean search engine uses exact matching to match documents to a user query by finding documents that are "relevant" in terms of matching the words in the query. The adjective "Boolean" refers to the use of Boolean operators AND, OR, & NOT to logically combine the query words. The Boolean information retrieval model considers which keywords are present or absent in a document or title. Thus, a document is judged as relevant or irrelevant – there is no concept of a "partial match" between documents & queries. The inability to identify partial matches can lead to poor performance [Baeza-Yates, R., & B. Ribeiro-Neto 1999]. Other more advanced set theoretic techniques, such as the so-called "fuzzy sets", try to remedy this black-white Boolean logic by introducing shades of gray. For example, a title search for Tourism AND Hotels on a Boolean engine causes the virtual machine to return all documents that have both words in the title. As a result, a relevant document entitled "Tourism" will not be returned. Fuzzy Boolean engines use fuzzy logic to categorize this document as somewhat relevant & return it to the user. Fuzzy engines, on the pattern of human reasoning, use approximate information & uncertainty to generate decisions. The main limitation of Boolean search engines is observed in dealing with the problems of synonymy (multiple words have the same meaning) & polysemy (word has multiple meanings). Boolean search engines also require the user to be familiar with Boolean operators. E.g., to find information about the phrase Taj Mahal Fort, many engines require quotation marks around the phrase, which tell the search engine that the entire phrase should be searched as if it were just one keyword. A user who forgets this syntax requirement would be surprised to find retrieved documents about Taj Mahal tea or Taj Mahal mineral water for actual Taj Mahal fort. Nevertheless, Boolean model form the basis for many search engines. There are several reasons for their popularity: (i) Creating & programming a Boolean engine is straightforward. (ii) Queries can be processed quickly - a quick scan through the keyword files for the documents can be executed in parallel.

Search Engine Optimization vs. Pay Per Click

Promoting Websites online can take many forms, such as SEO, PPC, PPP, & PPI. Each of these methods has one aim: to catch the people searching for your product onto your Website. Although how they achieve this goal differs slightly.

Traditional SEO

SEO is the process of optimizing your Web site to reflect specific keywords & phrases that are relevant to your business & for which you want to attract visitors to your site who are searching for such words. This optimization relates to a variety of elements like title tags, meta tags, alt tags, link structure, link popularity & the content of the site itself, not only on your web site's home page, but its sub pages as well. Once your Web site is properly optimized, the goal then is to make sure that each of the top search engines find your site & add as many pages as possible in their indices. These engines will usually start with your home page & then work their way to other pages of the site. The important aspects of SEO are as follows: (a) Make sure that the sub pages or the main areas of your site are accessible from the home page, (b) It can be assumed that if many of your pages are optimized for different keywords & can be found in the search engines, they will draw traffic to your site, (c) SEO also involves making sure your site is listed in the major directories such as Yahoo & Open Directory to name a few. It is important to make sure you are listed in the right category & have the reflective keywords in title & description that user is trying to target. Other elements of SEO include monitoring your positioning in the search engines, making adjustments as necessary to your site to stay in top position & submitting to new engines that come along as well.

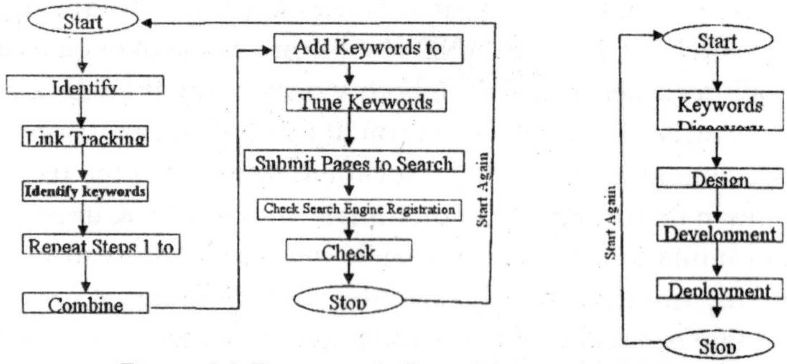

Figure 2.2 Framework flow diagram for PPC

Figure 2.1 shows the framework flow diagram for SEO in which one should identify competition to select keywords that you expect surfers to use to locate your site, submit your obvious keyword terms & use the online freeware research tools to locate top ranked competing sites. The purpose of link tracking allows you to identify & choose possible sites that you will want as link partners once your site is content-rich & optimized. If these sites link to your competition, then you want them to also link to you. This is also done so that these potential link partners can be checked for meta keywords that might be related to your site that were missed by your competition. The purpose to identify keywords is to understand the search terms & keywords used to locate your site as a part of a search engine query. To help in this keyword analysis effort we offer advice to research the competition & query history information available through several sources. Repeat steps 1 through 3 until you have finished all your keyword searches. The purpose of combine keywords is based upon frequency of use & applicability. It is also important that you add words to help clarify the use of your keywords. For instance "Bank" might have very different meanings — such as River Bank, Blood Bank, State Bank, Reserve Bank, etc. To add your keywords to the content is very much important to discover your real issue. Also, most sites use images to relay their message to humans, but are now discovering that search engines are blind & do not see images. The aim to tune keyword list will allow you to submit (to replace or add a page to the index) a URL once every day & changes are usually live quickly (faster than other search engines), so use the search engine with the fastest indexing process to 'debug' your keywords & SEO tactics. Once the same words are in your meta title, description & keywords, & also in other text & displayed content, & you are satisfied with your results, & only then, is it appropriate to submit your URLs to each major search engine. Furthermore, the Web site submission to search engine is done by making registration at search engine server & moreover time-by-time Web site checking has to be done. Finally, go to step 1 again & again for better search optimized results.

Pay Per click Search Engine Advertising

PPC is a service in which an advertiser selects specific keywords or phrases & then creates a listing that will show up when someone searches for that phrase. The advertiser selects an amount they are willing to pay for each click on their listing, which results in a visit to their site. They are the sponsored links you might see when you perform a search in a search engine. They usually appear at the top, bottom or right side of the search engine results page & are identified as sponsored links. At Overture, you can bid anywhere from $0.10 up to $50.00 for each click. If other advertisers have selected the same keyword or phrase as yours, you are competing against them for the highest position. Whosoever is interested to spend the most shows up first & the others following in order. What makes PPC attractive in the case of Overture is that they distribute their paid listings to other partner sites. In fact, if you bid in one of the top three positions at Overture, your listings will also show up at some of the leading search engines including AltaVista, HotBot, InfoSpace, iWon, Lycos, MSN, Yahoo & others. They also show up in several meta crawlers & other minor search engines. There are many other PPC programs including Google AdWords, Altavista, ah-ha.com, Sprinks & Looksmart to name a few. All function in a similar manner.

Figure 2.2 shows the framework flow diagram for PPC in which a discovery phase searches a word or phrase that people would employ to locate information on the products or services or topic that they are interested learning more about or purchasing. The core idea behind discovery phase is to identify the words or phrases that are important to your target audience & therefore will be the most effective to use on your Web site. The purpose of the design phase is to design the PPC Campaign based on the strategy & short or long-term needs identified in the discovery phase & help develop your bidding strategy. This phase could include: modeling the keywords in terms of monthly counts, estimated click-thru rates, & conversion rates, identifying which PPC engines will be used for the campaign, identifying site landing pages & destination pages for conversion purposes, & identifying any tracking & reporting tools. The purpose of the development phase is to develop the PPC strategies & campaign design produced in the first two phases. This phase includes converting the audience issues into "creative content statements." once the creative content statements are finalized, the ads are customized for each PPC engine to adjust for each engine's constraints, such as the length of the ad, the reach & demographics of the engine, etc., & bidding strategies are developed. At the conclusion of the development phase, you should have: development of title & description by PPC Engine for each keyword, application of tracking URLs & reporting tools, development of new destination pages or editing existing pages, & implemented tracking & reporting tools. Finally, the purpose of the deployment phase is to "launch" & monitor the PPC Campaign as a result of the short & long-term needs. The deployment phase begins by uploading the PPC advertisements to the PPC search engines. Some PPC Engines allow advertisements to "go live" almost immediately & others require editorial approval. Finally, go to step 1 again for making sufficient changes to Web site depending upon the Web server statistics in term of their log files. The biggest benefit of PPC is the fact that it will provide you with an immediate boost of qualified visitors, lead & sales giving you fast results within just hours or days. In fact, a PPC advertising program is your best option if you seek fast results & a good return on investment while you are waiting for your SEO program to "ramp up". PPC search engines also give you the added benefits of being able to quickly test your web site & track your alteration rates (leads, opt-ins, & sales) & turning keywords (visitors) on & off easily. So, as a short-term strategy PPC gives you the clear advantage over SEO. But, the disadvantage is the cost involved. Depending on the market demand for your keywords & clicks, your PPCSE campaign can generate tons of traffic & can cost hundreds, even thousands per day. With various optimization strategies you can lower your costs, but over the long term natural search engine optimization will give you a higher return on your marketing dollar. The screen shot below shows the SEO, & PPC areas from Google using the example phrase 'India Tourism Perspective'.

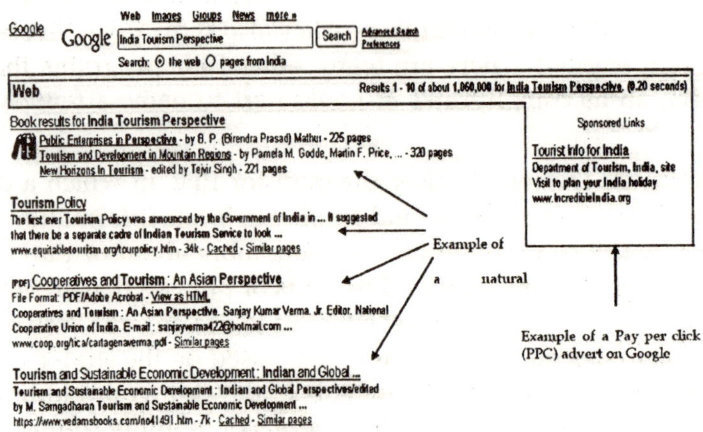

Figure 4: Screen snapshot of the SEO & PPC areas from Google.

Google Pay Per Click Advertising

Google is the best-known PPC provider. With Google the PPC adverts, labeled 'sponsored links', appear on the right of the page, & sometimes also at the very top. You only pay when someone clicks on your advert. The minimum cost per click is five pence. Most of the time you will find that others also want their advert to show up for your keywords. That's where the bidding comes in. The more you are prepared to pay per click, the higher in the list of adverts you will appear. You can sign up to Google Adwords & within an hour you can start getting traffic to your Website. In designing a Website be specific. Don't use vague or general terms. The more precise & targeted your keywords, the less you will pay per click & the better quality of visitor you will welcome to your Website. Getting lots of traffic is not the objective. You only want traffic that is likely to turn into sales. If your company sells to the local area, make sure to include your town or county in the keywords. There is no point getting lots of people in New Delhi to your Website, if you only deliver to Chandigarh. For feed back mechanism for your Website, run two adverts & compare their results. The same can be done for e-commerce sites to measure, which adverts resulted in a sale by checking the log files from the respective Web servers.

Importance of SEO

With the current rise of pay PPC advertising services, professional SEO companies have to deal more & more with the issue of why their clients should spend money on traditional SEO when they can simply "buy their way to the top." Natural search engine optimization usually gives you a much higher return on investment than pay per click. This is true for two main reasons: (a) More searchers click the natural search engine results versus the PPC ads, so you'll get much more traffic for less, (b) One of the biggest factors to improve your rankings with natural search engine optimization is by boosting your "Link Popularity" by acquiring or paying for links that point to your Website. These links give you lasting results by giving you top rankings & traffic from the search engines. Plus, the links themselves will provide a significant boost in long-term traffic. It is also observed that more than 80% of all search engine traffic in July, 2006 came from the top 3 engines Google, Yahoo, & MSN . We have considerable reason to believe that your appearance in relevant search engines will boost your rankings in the 'Big 3' as well as gaining additional traffic from the smaller engines. The figure 3 shows the search engine relation ship chart between top search engines, which has been designed virtually after carried out an empirical study with different people including students of the advances university classes, industry person, & facilitators.

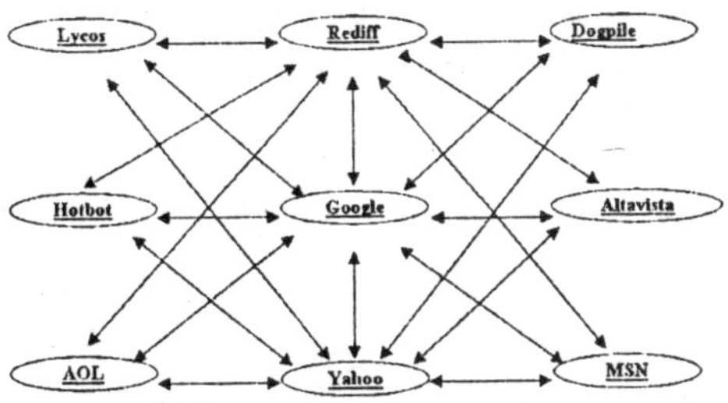

Figure 3. *Shows the Search Engine Relationship Chart between Top Search Engines*

When a Website is implemented correctly, search engine optimisation can have a dramatic effect on a business. Many companies purchase a Website in hope that it will bring business without actively promoting it. Alternatively many companies are offering 'Web promotion' businesses for submitting your site to thousands of search engines in the hope it will make their site easier to find. In reality there are only half a dozen search engines worth spending time over, with. Google, Yahoo & MSN being the biggest of these.

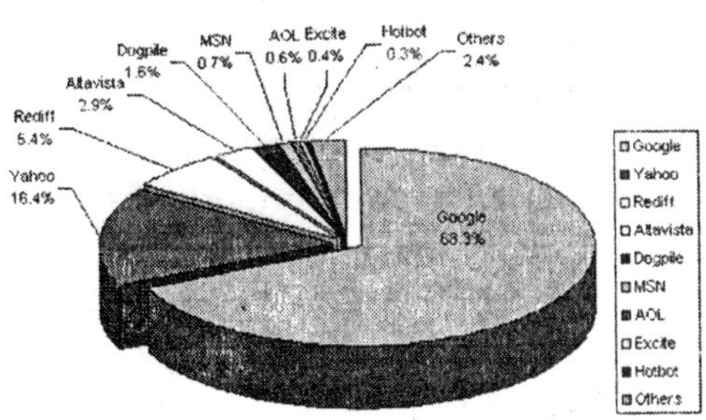

***Figure 4** shows the statistics of relative usage of popular search engines*

We carried out an empirical study with the students of the advanced university classes that used various search engines & client-server based Web technologies for measuring & predicting the search behavior of the information retrieval systems. Our first goal was to compare the relative importance of each design activity. These students have Web log files on their computers, which monitor the sites they visit. These informations are compiled to produce results. Figure 4 shows are statistics about the relative usage & importance of popular search engines.

In order to assess the relative usage of popular search engines using the Internet services, it has been found (figure 4) that academic community use Google (68.3%), Yahoo (16.4%), Rediff (6.4%), Altavista (2.9%), Dogpile (1.6%), MSN (0.7%), AOL (0.6%), Excite (0.4%), Hotbot (0.3%), & remaining respondents use 2.4% of other search engines. Our first goal was to compare the relative usage & importance of major search engines. Second, we tried to assess the accuracy of the top search engines for optimized results in context to user queries. Third, we also discussed the implications & results of SEO techniques by capturing the dynamics involved in user behavior. The results obtained from the user assessment can help us to systematically identify the designing of tourism based Websites for evaluating priority levels, reliability, compatibility, usability, maintainability, complexity, cost, configuration, time requirements, types of interfaces, & type of nature of Website design.

Ethical SEO

Suppose there are 300 hotels in New Delhi, each of which has a Website. Against a query "New Delhi hotels", all 300 Websites are equally relevant. But Google & other engines have been designed to display the 10 results at a time. But which of the 300 hotel sites will be displayed in the first 10, in the second 10, & so on. It is well known that the sites that are nearer the top will take all the business, & those that are further down will get none. It is patently obvious that all 300 equally relevant Websites will not be displayed on the first results page. It is also obvious that equally relevant sites cannot be displayed where they belong. The site is just as relevant as the top ones; it's just that Google cannot satisfy all the relevant sites. So there is noting wrong by the owner of one of the Websites to try & push their sites to the top. This is where ethical SEO comes. SEO allows the pages of relevant Websites to be displayed at or near the top of relevant search results. SEOs have exactly the same aim as the engines – 'relevant search results'. The difference is that search engines don't care about individual Websites, whereas search engine optimizers & Website owners do. Engines don't care if a particular Website is in the top 10; SEOs care very much that a particular Website is in the top 10. But they can't get an off-topic site there because the search engine algorithms see to that. & that's an important point - search engine optimization can only get pages to the top of relevant results. The search engines own algorithms keep off-topic pages out. As a search engine optimizer, we give Search Engines a choice & adjust things according to our Website design so that our relevant pages are at the top of the relevant results & that's why PPC, PPI, & PPP come into the existence.

PPC, PPI, & PPP

Pay per click (or PPC), pay per impression (or PPI), & pay per percentage (PPP) are three distinct approaches to online advertising. PPC tools bring targeted traffic to a web site quickly & efficiently, whereas PPI tools can help to build brand recognition & PPP tools can help to build company's revenue The PPC charge advertisers for web site visitors; the PPI charge advertisers for message displays; & PPP charge advertisers for percentage of genuine message displays. The following table 1.1 summarizes the key differences between the three advertising approaches:

Table 1.1 summarizes the key differences between the three advertising approaches

	PPC	PPI	PPP
Primary Objective	Build Web Site Traffic	Build Brand Name	Build Company Revenue
Media Exposure	Search Engine Results	Web Page Banners	Online advertising
Cost per visitor	Low to medium	High	High
Cost per impression	Medium to high	Low	Low to medium
Pros	Predictable cost per visitor	Predictable cost per impression	Predictable cost per percentage
Cons	Time-consuming bid management	Costly for targeted products & services	Cost effective for targeted products & services

PPC advertising is, of course, one of the alternatives in the increasingly popular 'pay per action' marketing field. As visitor tracking systems become more sophisticated, two other online advertising models have been developed: 'pay per lead' & 'pay per sale'. These models are called affiliate marketing, can offer advertisers valuable exposure on a range of relevant websites & offer website publishers an opportunity to generate revenue from their resource sites. PPI & PPP are the examples of online advertisements & images or impression, which generally come while we browse our e-mail accounts (like Rediff, Yahoo, Gmail, hotmail etc.).

Click and impression frauds

One way to prevent click fraud is to revert to a PPI model. In this way, clicking on an ad does not defraud the advertiser. Click fraud is the biggest threat to the Internet economy. It has been shown that a simple system, PPP of impressions, is immune to both click fraud

& impression fraud. In this system, an advertiser picks a keyword, e.g. "star hotel" & purchases, perhaps through bidding, a certain percentage of all impressions for that keyword. For instance, an advertiser might pay $1.00 to Google search. In return, the advertiser might receive 10% of all impressions for "star hotel" for 1 week. What does this mean? It means that for 1 week, one out of ten times that someone searches for the word "star hotel", they will see the ad. If someone clicks on the ad, the advertiser is not charged any extra money. It might seem that this method is subject to impression fraud: someone could create fake searches for the word "star hotel" causing fake impressions. A common variation on the PPC model adjusts the pricing or the positioning based in part on click through rate. Some services, like Google, also have a minimum click through rate. This creates its own additional motivations for impression fraud. Since click through rate is roughly the ratio of number of clicks to the number of impressions. With weighted-pay-per-percentage, we first choose at random which word in a phrase to target, & then select it based on the percentage of volume purchased. For instance, if an advertiser purchases a weighted 10% share of the broad matches for "star hotel," he will receive the following: 10% of exact match searches for "star hotel", 5% of the searches for two word phrases that include star hotel, 3.33% of the searches for three word phrases that include star hotel, etc. So, in order to prevent fraud, we still must respect certain constraints. For instance, if we sell 70% of matches for "star hotel", & 80% of matches for "seven star hotel", then for a phrase like "seven star hotel", we can sell no more than 25% of the traffic (100% - (70%/2 + 80%/2) = 25%). Notice that weighted-pay-per-percentage is immune to fraud, because it preserves all independence assumptions. Our preferred method simply always chooses the first word, or always chooses the last word. We'll call this "Prefix or Suffix PPC". In this system, rather than selling a full broad match, we sell only prefixes or suffixes. For instance, "star hotel *" would match "star hotel Delhi" & "star hotel Bombay" but not "wanted star hotel. For instance, "* star hotel Delhi" would match "seven star hotel Delhi".

Designing a high-quality Website

Designing a search engine friendly Web site is not complicated, but it requires dedication & constant communication between the graphic designer, content developer & SEO analyst, as well as special attention to the site's architecture. Site architecture should not be an afterthought, nor should SEO. Your site must be both visually appealing to visitors & contextually appealing to the search engines. In order to attain both of these goals, we recommend enlisting a graphic designer to design the look & feel of the site, & a content developer to create a clear message for your site. This will cause the search engines to rank your site higher & will increase your visibility for visitors. Creating a site that is easily navigable, visually appealing, & gives your visitors what they are looking for, will encourage visitors to stay longer & come back often. We recommend that in at least 200 words as close to the top of your HTML code as possible, you need to make sure that you are using keywords in a manner that makes sense to a visitor & will allow the search engines to see your site as a subject matter expert. Never stuff your pages with keywords; the engines will penalize you for spamming. Keyword research can be time consuming & even daunting, but it is an important step in getting your site ranked. Once you have completed your keyword research, created your keyword list, & constructed your meta tags, check that you have at least 200 words of succinctly written, grammatically correct content that tells your visitors what your page/ site is about. When this is finished, your site is ready for submission to the search engines. Designing a search engine friendly web site is not difficult, but it is time consuming. To optimize a site, we must have the idea of search engine algorithms.

Search Engine Algorithms

Each search engine employs different algorithms for determining page rank & these algorithms are subject to change over time. Page Rank has been defined by [Sergey Brin & Lawrence Page]: We assume page 'A' has pages T1,T2, T3,.............,Tn which point to it (i.e., are citations). The parameter 'd' is a damping factor, which can be set between 0 & 1. We usually set d to 0.85. Also C(A) is defined as the number of links going out of page 'A'. The PageRank of a page 'A' is given as follows: PR(A) = (1-d) + d (PR(T1)/C(T1) + ... + PR(Tn)/C(Tn)) ––––––– (3). Page Rank can be thought of as a model of user behavior. We assume there is a "random surfer" who is given a Web page at random & keeps clicking on links, never hitting "back" but eventually gets bored & starts on another random page. The probability that the random surfer visits a page is its Page Rank & the d damping factor is the probability at each page the "random surfer" will get bored & request another random page. So it is very much important to add the damping factor d to a single page, or a group of pages to check Page Rank. This allows for personalization & can make it nearly impossible to deliberately mislead the system in order to get a higher ranking. The parameters C(A) is defined as the number of links going out of page 'A'. So on the basis of these an another intuitive justification is that a page can have a high Page Rank if there are many pages that point to it, or if there are some pages that points to it & have a less Page Rank. As damping factor approaches to'0' the PR(A) from equation (1) becomes '0'. So Page Rank will be zero & Page ranking priority of that Web page will be at lowest level of hierarchy of WWW. Generally, the Page Ranks form a probability distribution over Web pages, so the sum of all Web pages' Page Ranks will be one. A compromise between the two extremes of uniform [damping factor] & single page [damping factor] is to let [the damping factor apply from] all the root level pages of all Web servers. Aside from the Page Rank algorithm, Google also indexes anchor text (i.e. the text of a link), text proximity, & visual presentation details such as font size of words. These factors have several implications: Internal links on a site contribute to Page Rank, as well as links from other sites; a link from a home page is likely to contribute more to Page Rank than a link from other pages; the more links on a page, the less contribution each link will make to Page Rank; & the link text is significant.

There are two broad generalizations that can be made about search engine positioning: (1) word frequency in a page is important, particularly in the page title & near the top of the page. (2) The number of links to a page is important, particularly from sites that are in some way recognized as being authoritative & relevant. Of course, the question of what it is that makes a site authoritative or relevant, from the point of view of a search engine, is an interesting one. Different search engines address this issue in different ways. Other criteria that may be significant, include: text used in description & keywords meta tags; text used in links that point to a page; the proximity of words in the text for searches on phrases of two words or more; the size (and color) of font used for text; the use of H1-H6 tags; & whether a page is the root page of a domain. The generalized scripting codes for description, keywords, title, robots meta tags have been used for tourism based Website are as follows:

<head><meta name="title" content="Department of Tourism"><meta name="description" content="An national tourism congress will be held in the month of Feb., 2006 at the Department of Tourism, Kurukshetra University, Kurukshetra, Haryana"><meta name="keywords" content="PPI, PPC, PPP & SEOs"><meta name="robots" content="ALL"><meta name="revisit-after" content="1 days"><meta http-equiv="refresh" content="8;URL=http://kuk.ernet.in"></head>.

Design Criteria

There are many, but some important one are discussed here.

Usage of Meta-tag

Meta tags are used to define meta data. A meta tag carries information about a document & is placed in the HEAD of the HTML page. Meta tags are easy to implement on your Web pages. They look just like regular HTML tags, but they follow a few rules: (1) All begin with the word META, the element name, (2) All are located within the HEAD element, (3) No closing tag is used; the META element is an empty element. When you use a meta tag, you define attribute/value sets. For each attribute, you assign a value. If you look back at the element declaration, you'll see there are several available attributes, only one of which is required. So, the format might be diagrammed as: <META attributeName="value" attributeName="value">.

Significance of Meta tags in SEO

Although there are no concrete rules defining what information a search engine spider pulls from your page, many search engines do make use of two primary meta tags: description & keywords. Both of these meta tags let you further define your site's content & function so that those searching for your site's content have a better chance of finding you & can get an accurate sense of what your site offers. Although some search engines index all the words on a Web page, often the first few words get the most exposure. For example, in the absence of a description meta tag, AltaVista uses the first few words on the page when it returns a set of search results. Using the description tag, you'll enter a sentence or two describing the page. Many search engines use this information when a list of search results is returned. The description tag for our gardening site might look like this: <META name="description" content="Tourism Perspective in India: A case study">. WebPromote suggests that you keep your description at less than 25 words. To get noticed, if you are tempted to put in a whole paragraph or more in description, don't waste the kilobytes. Search engines use a set amount of characters in the descriptions. If characters are too long, it will be cut off abruptly. WebPromote also suggests that you use lowercase keywords, as this is how most users enter search terms. After carefully considering the site's function & audience, the keywords tag for our tourism site might resemble the following: <META name="keywords" content="tourism, hotels, supply chain management, agri products, gardening, garden, mountains">. Not all search engines use all of these meta tags. E.g., Excite does not use meta keywords in indexing sites. It does, however, use the meta description for generating the summary of the site. They should be used to reiterate the words used in the title & description, including synonyms, plurals, regional variations & even common misspellings. In general: use all lower case; don't use commas & don't repeat words.

Use of Indexing and search phrases

The over-enthusiastic use of search terms in your title, description & keywords tags is self-defeating & is likely to dilute the rank of your site; it is usually better for a page to appear near the top of one search query than for it to appear lower down on several. For this reason it is generally not recommended to target more than a single search phrase or, at most, two or three closely related phrases in the same page. Creating a robots text file lets you specify whether robots or spiders will index your site. But, you can also talk to the robots via the robots meta tag. This tag uses the name value robots & has two properties for content: index & follow. The following sample robots tag tells a) to not index this page, & b) to not follow links from this page to other pages: <META name="robots" content="noindex, nofollow">. The available values for each pair are: index or noindex; follow or nofollow

Layout of text and links on Web page

The first content that appears on every page should be a heading that reiterates the text of the title. This should be followed by a repeat of the description, & then the text that describes the main theme of the page. When linking to a page on your site, use the title of the page as the link text. For search engines that measure the relevance of links, this is likely to help reinforce the relevance of the page to the search terms used in the title. Try to avoid representing any of your link text as images. If you insist on it, then use Alt tags, so that engines can identify the text.

Use of Grammatical aspects, frames and presentation elements on Web page

Some search engines distinguish between singular & plural versions of a word, while some don't, so, particular care needs to be taken where both versions are likely to be used in search terms. If both singular & plural versions of words are to be targeted, then there are two options: either creates two different pages that target the words separately; or, include both versions in the same page, which means including them both in the title & description of the page & using them both in your page copy. Be very careful when using frames. Some indexing agents will ignore your frameset & go straight to any text that has been placed outside the frameset. It is important to ensure that relevant text & links are placed here. These will need to be maintained & updated in tandem with the visible content on a site. Remember, even if you do manage to get your pages indexed, visitors to your site are likely to be referred to an orphaned frame lacking the navigational structure carefully constructed for it. Text contained in a Flash presentation will not be indexed by search engines. Flash should not be used for pages that you want to appear in search engines. Also, avoid excessive use of JavaScript. It makes a page harder to maintain & harder for search engines to decipher. Put any JavaScript functions in a separate file & link it from the page header

Submission of Web page to directories & search engines

Before submitting your site to any directories, you should be satisfied that the title & description of your home page reflect your most important search terms & that they convey the right impression of your site. This should be the text that is submitted. By a wide & apparently increasing margin, Yahoo & Google are likely to be the most important in terms of generating traffic to your site. You should submit your home page to the major search engines. This should include, as a minimum: AltaVista, Excite, Fast, Google, HotBot, Lycos, & Northern Light.

Web Site architecture

While the keyword research is being done, your designer should be working on site templates & site architecture. Using Cascading Style Sheets (CSS), Frames, table tricks & external JavaScript will ensure that the search engine spiders are able to crawl your site without getting bogged down within the html code. You want them to be able to go to the page & quickly establish what your site is about. This will determine whether or not you get ranked. The content developer should work closely with your SEO analyst to make sure that the keywords are being used properly throughout the site. This means using heading (h1, h2, h3) tags, & links within the content using keywords, anchor text, etc. Finally, to make an effective web site, follow the basic ideas on web design techniques given in the web site of each engine's specific design guidelines. The some of the top most engines guidelines are as follows:

Google says: (1) Make a site with a clear hierarchy & text links, (2) Offer a site map to your users with links that point to the important parts of your site, (3) Create a useful, information-rich site, & write pages that clearly & accurately describe your content (4) Think about the words users would type to find your pages, & make sure that your site actually includes those words within it (5) Try to use text instead of images to display important names, content, or links (6) Make sure that your Title & Alt tags are descriptive & accurate (7) Check for broken links & correct HTML,(8) If you decide to use dynamic pages, be aware that not every search engine spider crawls dynamic pages as well as static pages, (9) Keep the links on a given page to a reasonable number (fewer than 100).

Yahoo! suggests: (1) Build a quality site, (2) Get big-sites with over 100 pages will attract more attention from search engines looking for sites with quality content, (3) Say something-sites with frequently updated & new content rank higher in search engines typically, (4) Use keywords not only as a tag, (5) Exchange links, (6) Get involved & get your name out there.

Clickthrough Data in Search Engines

Clickthrough data in search engines can be thought of as triplets (q,r,c) consisting of query q, the ranking r, & the set c of links user clicked on. E.g. the user asked query "India Tourism Perspective", received the ranking shown in figure 5, & then clicked on the links ranked 1, 4, & 8 (marked in bold).

1. **Tourism Policy**
   www.equitabletourism.org/tourpolicy.htm - 34k - Cached - Similar pages
2. **Cooperatives and Tourism : An Asian Perspective**
   www.coop.org/tica/cartagenaverma.pdf - Similar pages
3. **Tourism and Sustainable Economic Development : Indian and Global ...**
   https://www.vedamsbooks.com/no41491.htm - 7k - Cached - Similar pages
4. **Development of Tourism and Travel Industry : An Indian Perspective ...**
   https://www.vedamsbooks.com/no43170.htm - 3k - Cached - Similar pages
5. **Indian Tourism in Perspective**
   www.ficci.com/media-room/speeches-presentations/2001/Dec/dec-newzea-tourism.ppt - Similar pages
6. **Tourism of India - Special Feature - India Tourism Launches ...**
   www.tourismofindia.com/misc/marketing.htm - 16k - Cached - Similar pages
7. **Visa Southeast Asia | Travel and Tourism Reports**
   www.visa-asia.com/ap/sea/valueofvisa/industrywatch/vov_travel_and_tourism.shtml - 35k - Similar pages
8. **Indian Tourism Industry Outlook (2006) - Market Research Reports ...**
   www.researchandmarkets.com/reportinfo.asp?report_id=338113 - 42k - Cached - Similar pages
9. **India Tourism | East India - Excitement and Tranquillity**
   www.india-tourism.com/EN/east_india_excitement_and_tranquillity.html - 27k - Cached - Similar pages
10. **The Hindu : Tourism in social perspective**
    www.hinduonnet.com/2001/10/16/stories/1316017g.htm - 8k - Cached - Similar pages

Figure 5: ranking obtained for the query "India Tourism Perspective".

Since every query corresponds to one triplet, the amount of data that is potentially available is virtually unlimited. However, each query is assigned a unique ID, which is stored in the query log file of the server with the query words & the presented ranking. The links on the results page presented to the user do not directly suggest document, but point to a proxy server on which this document is stored. From the example of figure 5, it is not possible to infer that links 1, 4, & 8 are relevant on an absolute scale. Furthermore, it is much more probable to conclude that link 4 is more relevant than link 3 with probability higher than random [N. Fuhr 1989]. Assuming that the user scanned the ranking from top to bottom, he/she must have observed link 3 before clicking on 4, making a decision to not click on it. Given that the abstracts presented with the links are sufficiently informative, this gives some indication of the user's preferences. Similarly, it is not possible to infer that link 8 is more relevant than link 2, 3, 5, 6, & 7. This means clickthrough data does not convey absolute relevance judgements, but partial relative judgements for the links the user browsed through. A search engine ranks the returned links according to their relevance to user's query q, which ranked link 4 ahead of 3, & link 8 ahead of 2, 3, 5, 6, & 7. Denoting the ranking preferred by the user with r*, we get partial relative information as follows:

$link_4 < r^* \, link_3$ -------(1)

$link_8 < r^* \, link_{2,}$ $link_8 < r^* \, link_{3,}$ $link_8 < r^* \, link_{5,}$ $link_8 < r^* \, link_{6,}$ $link_8 < r^* \, link_7$ ------(2. Therfore, for a ranking (link1, link2, ...linkn) & a set c containing the ranks of the clicked on links. We extract a preference equation: $Link_i < r^* \, link_j$ for all pairs 1d"j<i.

Future Predictions & Challenges

For making the desired search of tourism information we are looking for non textual informations more heavily i.e. each & every user wants to look images, sounds, video etc. At present it is very difficult to search these informations efficiently by search engines. Because the non-textual information requires Tera or Peta bytes of databases. In tourism based Websites the existence of non-textual information is more & therefore search engines should also handle the queries based on non-textual informations in a precise & controlled manner. Near future will see the designing of non-text based information retrieval system of tourism. Web search engines processed a user query on the basis of textual information. As far as tourism perspective is concerned, one should maintain the Websites with much more graphical coverage (such as images, program, & databases). So, the existence of images, programs & databases can't be in cooperated by text-based search engines. Most search engines associate the text of a link with the pages that the link is on. In addition, we associate it with the page the link points to.

There are many information retrieval challenges in addition to those briefly mentioned already in this paper, such as polysemy, synonymy, query language, & speed. The Web presents its own unique challenges— it can be viewed as one huge database with unique properties: large amounts of volatile data (rapid updates, broken links, file disappearances); heterogeneous data (multiple formats, languages, alphabets); an exponentially growing number of pages; redundant data; lack of structure; & a lack of an editorial review publication process, which leads to numerous information errors, a falsehoods, & invalid statements. Many search engines are beginning to incorporate structured text retrieval, meaning that users can search for text in italics, capitals, or boldface print. Google currently incorporates some structured retrieval. Users can choose to search for keywords located in the title, body, or hyperlinks of documents. Google's advanced features include searching for HTML documents, images, language filters, PostScript documents, or Excel documents, among other choices. Hotbot allows users to search for video, MP3-formatted data, or images, in addition to ordinary text. Its advanced features also include date information.

E.g. users can choose to retrieve only recent documents, those updated in the last two weeks, two months, or two years. Another recent trend in search engine research is to use syntactic clues & query structure to improve retrieval results. These methods incorporate the location of the keywords in the query, the use of prepositions, verbs, & adjectives, hyperlink structure on document pages, & citation links to enhance retrieval. The futuristic efforts will include the concepts of non-textual information system, pattern matching, fuzzy logic, & edit distance to eliminate & enhance the query results. In upcoming future, one of the most exciting applications of information retrieval will be an image retrieval system. True image retrieval uses mathematical models to capture how similar images are to an original image without using text hints, such as HTML image tags. Soon users will be able to retrieve images in addition to text documents. One application of image retrieval will be applicable for locating suspected criminals through a criminal photo Ids database electronically to find those criminals whose photo profiles most completely match the sketch rendered by the crime scene artist. But there are many parameters, which will be involved to search such type of non-textual information on the WWW. This can be further extended to sound retrieval systems, fingerprint information retrieval systems, & eye retina information retrieval systems. Searching through audio files is as challenging as image retrieval, but may be possible in the near future.

REFERENCES

1. Baeza-Yates, R., & B. Ribeiro-Neto, Modern Information Retrieval.: ACM Press, New York 1999.
2. Belkin, N., & Croft, W.B. Retrieval techniques, Ann. Rev. Inf. Sci. & Tech. (ARIST), 22, 109-145, (1987).
3. Broder, A., "Web search", Invited talk at the 9th Text Retrieval Conference (TREC-9), Gaithersburg, Maryland, November 2000.
4. Chakrabarti, S., Dom, B., Gibson, D., Kumar, S.R., Raghavan, P., Rajgopalan, S., & Tomkins A., Hypersearching the web Sci Am 1999.
5. Croft, W. B., Cook, R., & Wilder, D., Providing government information on the Internet: Experiences with THOMAS, In Proceedings of the 2nd International Conference on Theory and Practice of Digital Libraries, Austin, TX, pp. 19-24, June 1995.
6. Holscher C. & Strube G., "Web Search Behaviour of Internet Experts & Newbies" International Journal of Computer and Telecommunication Networking, Vol. 33, pp. 337-346, 2000.
7. Jansen B.J., Spink A., & Saracevic T.,"Real Life, Real Users, & Real Needs: A Study & Analysis of User Queries on the Web," Information Processing and Management, vol. 36,pp.207-227, 2000.
8. Lempel R. & Moran S., Salsa: The Stochastic Approach for Link Structure Analysis, ACM Transactions on Information Systems, Vol. 19, No. 2, April 2001, pages 131-160 (2001)

9. Lempel, R., & Moran, S., "Predictive caching and prefetching of query results in search engines", In Proceedings of the 12th World Wide Web Conference (WWW2003), Budapest, Hungary, 2003.

10. Markatos, E. P., On caching search engine query results. In Proceedings of the 5th Inter-national Web Caching and Content Delivery Workshop, May 2000.

11. N. Fuhr, Optimum polynomial retrieval functions based on the probability ranking principle. ACM Transactions on Information Systems, 7(3): 183-204, 1989.

12. Saikat Neogi, India's incredible tourism story only gets better, October 16, 2006, http://www.hindustantimes.com/

13. Sergey Brin & Lawrence Page, Computer Science Department, Stanford University, Stanford, CA 94305, USA, http://www7.scu.edu.au/programme/fullpapers/1921/com1921.htm

14. Silverstein C., Henzinger M., Marais H., & Moricz M., "Analysis of a Very Large Web Search Engine Query Log, "SIGIR Forum, vol.33, pp.6-12, 1999.

15. Wen, J.R., Nie, J.Y. & Zhang, H.J., Query Clustering Using User Logs, ACM Transactions on Information Systems (ACM TOIS), 20(1), pp. 59-81, 2002.

25

Issues in Web-based Tourism Marketing

Vikram Singh, Dean,
Engineering & Technology,
Ch. Devi Lal University, Sirsa.
Email – *vikramsinghkuk@yahoo.com*

Dalbir Singh, Lecturer,
Department of Management,
Guru Jambheshwar University, Hisar
Email – *dalbirkuk@yahoo.com*

ABSTRACT

The exponential growth of the Internet, especially the WWW, in 1990s has attracted a great deal of interest among both academic researchers and entrepreneurs, especially in the field of use of Information Technology for marketing. Of lately, enterprises have started using the Web a medium for marketing and promoting products and services. Travel and tourism sector has also fallen in the line. Through an examination of various aspects of Web and the characteristics of the tourism industry, it has been found that the Web, as a marketing tool, is indispensable for tourism sector. This paper discusses the vital issues in realizing the potential of Web as a promotional tool for tourism industry.

INTRODUCTION

The Internet originated in the mid sixties, yet it is only in the 1990s that it became hugely popular. Since 1993, the Internet has been transformed completely by the World Wide Web. The Web allows the users to access data that has been made available by other users. Through a Web browser, a user can link to any website and may explore the Web resources in an unprecedented way for both leisure and commercial purposes. Moreover, the Net's capability to blend text, pictures, sounds and video clips into multimedia documents played the key role in popularizing the Web beyond its traditionally academic boundaries and become an effective communication means in business and everyday life.

The strength of using the Web for marketing activities is derived from its general use as an information exchange system in the cyber age. The information can be stored, indexed, retrieved, restructured and redistributed automatically by software. This paper is aimed at investigating potential and constraints of Web as a tourism-marketing device.

WEB-BASED TOURISM MARKETING

As a marketing device, the Web can be of help in almost all areas of marketing, viz. marketing research, market segmentation, targeting and positioning, marketing mix, and marketing the product/service.

Marketing Research: Marketing is essentially an information-processing activity that links an organization to the external environment in which it operates. The Web is an invaluable source of low cost but up-to-date marketing intelligence, which can be sourced through a company's own site. The Web is extremely useful in building a customer information database. This information can be used to identify prospects customers, understand customer needs and customize resources to give better service to customers. A database of online transaction histories can be the primary marketing resource of tourism companies for determining: 1) what kind of travel products they can deliver, 2) what market segments they serve best, and 3) what is the lifetime value of each customer to the firm?

Market Targeting: The online consumers can provide instantaneous feedback to the marketer. Indeed, the web server can memorize every "click or hit" the user makes. Through the application of the IT data mining technique, companies can find patterns within their internal customer data and transform it into meaningful marketing information.

Product: Tourists can provide individual preferences or specifications of holiday packages through feedback using web forms, email messages or simply the 'clicking' patterns, which the tourism marketer can use to develop new products or tailor existing products to suit the needs of particular consumer(s).

Pricing: Information exchange capacity of the Web enables enterprises to set and change prices in real time and also facilitates online bidding and flexible pricing. With the help of a web-based reservation system, a tour operator can make real-time adjustment to its thousands of holiday prices at the touch of a button in response to competition moves and demand changes. A special late-booking section can also be included in the main web site to promote leftover holidays at the last minute to solve the problems of over-supply or under-demand in the package tour industry.

Distribution: The uniqueness of the Web as a means of distribution is based on the fact that it exists in "cyberspace." Physical phenomena such as location and distance are less significant or even irrelevant. The foremost role of the Web in tourism distribution is the direct electronic reservation and transactions between tourism product supplier and consumers. The biggest change to tourism distribution brought by the Web could be the noticeable shrinking of the travel agent sector. Agents are squeezed by both: 1) a decreasing market as more and more consumers go online and book directly from airlines and operators and 2) by airlines' declining commission levels.

Promotion: The Web provides a labor-efficient and cost-effective way of distributing information almost instantaneously to millions of potential clients in the global markets. Web promotion combines mass media's reach with the personalization inherent in two-way dialogue - previously only possible in personal selling. The Web enables more information to be transmitted to more people at a cheaper rate. Followings are the key features to achieve these benefits:

- Well designed and maintained website
- Memorable Web address
- Links "from" other web sites
- Promoting the website through the traditional media

POTENTIAL AREAS OF BENEFIT

It is widely recognized that the Web offers substantial advantages over traditional means of communication, namely, 1) reduced costs of information exchange; 2) increased speed of information transfer and retrieval; 3) increased customer involvement in control of transactions; and 4) greater flexibility of using the marketing mix. Following are the main features of the Web tourism marketing.

Customized marketing: The Web has the unique quality that transforms the marketing communication paradigm from one-to-many to one-to-one. The traditional media, such as print, radio and television, follow a one-to-many communication model. In contrast, the Web enables a company to individually address consumers in its marketing communications by having a record of the user's individual habits and needs. As a matter of fact, it represents the opportunity to customize and tailor the product/service/marketing effort to one consumer at a time.

Customer oriented: In contrast to traditional communication media like print or television, the cyber media allows customers to actively participate and be in greater control of making choices. It is the customer - and not the marketer - who decides with whom to interact and how to interact. In other words, it is entirely in the customer's power to decide which web site to visit, which web page to browse, for how long, how often and how much information to obtain.

Interactivity: Another aspect of the Web that comes in contrast with the traditional media is its interactivity – its ability to respond to users' queries. This two-way dialogue forms an important component of relationship marketing, and is an important factor in building customer loyalty. Customers effortlessly communicate with companies to find product information and conduct transactions with a few keystrokes while companies can easily contact customers to clarify their needs or inform them of new products.

Flexibility: The Web is a much more flexible marketing medium than the traditional mass media. A website acts as an electronic advertisement or an electronic catalogue that provides information on products, services and contact information to interested consumers. A web-ad is much flexible than a physical advertisement. It can gather fresh and updated information based on the direct feedback received from consumers. A web catalogue can be organized and indexed based on the actual interest of consumers.

Instant Global Reach: As a communication medium the Web has an instant and global market reach. With an effective web site, a company is on business on a global spectrum 24 hours a day, 365 days a year. Any web user in the world can access its marketing information anywhere any time. The round the clock accessibility is extremely important especially in international trade where business is conducted across different time zones.

Service Quality: Tourists' satisfaction depends on the accuracy and relevance of tourism information as well as the promptness of responding to consumers' requests. In tourism the web-based distribution systems can satisfy consumer needs by providing easy access to transparent and easy to compare information on a wide variety of choices of destinations, holiday packages, flights, lodging and leisure services. They also provide immediate confirmation and speedy documentation of reservations providing a greater degree of flexibility and enabling prospective travelers to book at the "last minute."

Reduced Costs: Using the Web for marketing results into substantial cost reduction in spending of enterprises. The cost of setting up a promotional website is relatively low. An average user can build such a website in a couple of days. Comprehensive and powerful web sites cost somewhat more and take longer to develop. However, compared with spending of airlines, tour operators and hotel chains on TV and magazine ads, the Web is a low cost medium for promotion. Cost savings from the Web are derived mainly from following:

- e-Booking and e-Payments cuts down sales cost
- Automation reduces the labor/training cost
- Direct links between the producer and the consumer helps the producer to save distribution costs
- Reduced office and sales space, furniture and decoration outlay

THE CONSTRAINTS

The comparative advantages of using the Web in tourism marketing is compelling but at present its full potential as a marketing tool has not been realized due to several constraints. Authors visualize such realization if following issues are successfully addressed.

Online Demand: Consumer demand is the fundamental determinant of all forms of businesses. Whether an industry is initially supply-led or demand-driven, consumers are the key force in deciding the scale, structure, style and speed of its development. Although people with Web access are more affluent, better educated and younger than the average consumer, yet globally it is a smaller market. Furthermore, not all the web users are online customers. At the well-known travel website - *lastminute.com* - only 6% of its 15 lac registered users have ever purchased anything there. Cost and unreliable connectivity are reasons for low frequency of web surfing. Privacy, information abuse, web crime, payment security and non-delivery/late delivery are detrimental for online shoppers. A web users has to trust that he receives the product he orders as well as trust its quality to be as described. He is also scary about his private information such as address and credit card numbers. Moreover, consumers' fear about safety and security in online shopping is further multiplied by frequent media reports about web security breaches and frauds.

Technology: Several of the existing problems faced by web-based business are caused by the underlying technology - hardware, software and networks that enable individuals and organizations to come online. Slow speed of the Web hampers the growth of the web-based businesses as users are often not prepared to wait for too long to see the information appears on the screen. The slow speed of the Web is a combined result of three factors:

1) The increasing number of Web users,
2) The increasing frequency of use, and
3) The increasing richness of the information.

Technology itself will help expand the Web's capacity for accommodating the increasing demand. 'Cyber crime' is another technology related issue that includes hacking and virus attacks etc. Web technology does not cause the web crimes but these crimes are more difficult to prevent and detect as they are committed in a virtual space. Unless the IT industry can come up with some effective solutions to the security problems in web-commerce, consumers will have to either take a high risk or stay away from eShopping.

Organizational issues: The low level of web-based business is also attributable to the failure of business organizations in implementing the Web technologies in operation and marketing. Most business leaders did not realize the potential impacts of the Web on commerce until very recently (some still do not).

As a result, not all tourism companies are on the Web. When they are on the Web, most of their web sites are public relations or promotion sites that provide merely the companies a presence on the Net or little more than advertisements for their products and services. With the few comprehensive sales and transactions web sites, users were often asked to phone an operator or offered a brochure in the post. Even when web sites are fully operational in real-time transactions, they often offer limited choice. Another problem is that the Web does not always offer the lowest prices compared with the traditional distribution outlets.

Government issues: No one controls the Internet and every one controls the Internet. Some of the aforementioned problems are partly caused by the lack of effective centralized control and government involvement in promoting, facilitating and regulating e-commerce on the Web.

Governments across the world have been slow in realizing the potential of the Web for economic growth and even slower in providing the necessary regulatory framework appropriate for conducting eBusiness. Although existing business laws and regulations are applicable to e-commerce, the particular nature of Web-based business does require special treatment, especially in the areas of security, fraud, sabotage, and data and consumer protection. Without the confidence and trust of those participating in the process, it will be impossible to achieve sustainable growth in e-commerce.

CONCLUSIONS

Some of the key issues related to the marketing of tourism on the Web were discussed. Main features of the Web as an effective and efficient communication medium, including its customizability, interactivity, flexibility and instant global reach, and its role in improving customer service and reducing costs were highlighted. Four broad categories of factors: demand, organizational, technological and governmental - could enable as well as restrict the application of the Web in tourism marketing.

With regard to the future of Web tourism marketing, there appears to be little question that the Web will filter through every aspect of tourism business and every area of marketing activities. Indeed, the Web/Net could become the dominant platform and instrument for tourism promotion and distribution in near future. The increasing power of computers, decreasing surfing cost, and higher level of computer literary and web skills will make web surfing as a necessity in everyday life to an increasingly large population. Many of the current technological constraints could also be overcome in the next few years with: 1) the high quality broadband access via optical fiber or satellites to improve speed; 2) the wide application of constantly improving firewalls, encryption and digital signature software to enhance security; 3) the development of more sophisticated search engines and intelligent search agents to simplify web search task; and 4) the Wireless Application Protocol (WAP) technology linking mobiles to the Web to extend the range of services available to the public. At the same time, governments are increasingly involved in the expanding e-commerce by providing incentives to small businesses, facilitating infrastructure development and establishing the regulatory framework which supports and protects all those concerned.

In order to market tourism products successfully on the Web, a tourism organization must first of all have a strategic vision whereby it can fully comprehend the changing market space, from physical to both physical and virtual, and the underlying forces shaping this new marketing space. The Web has altered forever the tourism marketing system and its environment. No tourism business can escape its impacts but companies willing to become engaged in Web should find more opportunities while those who still pretend that the Web is a bad dream, will be left with all the threats. Whether an organization likes it or not, the Web is here to stay and is going to dominate tourism marketing. The Web must not be treated as just a promotion aid or distribution device, but be seen as a major force in itself that profoundly changes the way tourism business is conducted. Marketers will need to rethink fundamentally the processes by which they identify, communicate, and deliver customer value.

REFERENCES

- Aldridge A., Forcht K. and Pierson J., Get Linked Or Get Lost: Marketing Strategy For The Web. Web Research, Vol.7, No.3, pp.161-169, 1997.
- Banerjee T. and Mayling S., Growth In Web Cannot Be Ignored, TTG (UK & Ireland), 24 April, p.2, 2000.

- Bender, D., Marketing On The Web: Web Strategies For Hospitality Travel And Tourism. Washington, DC: Hospitality Sales and Marketing Association, 1997.
- Benhow S.M., A View Through The Glass: Aquariums On The Web. Web Research, Vol. 7, No.1, pp.27-31, 1997.
- Buhalis D., Information Technology As A Strategic Tool For Tourism And Hospitality Management In The New Millennium. Tourism Review Magazine, No.2, pp.34-36, 1996.
- Buhalis D. and Schertler W. (eds), Information and Communication Technologies in Tourism, New York: Springer Wien, 1999.
- De R. and Mathew B., Issues In The Management Of Web Technologies: A Conceptual Framework. International Journal of Information Management, Vol.19, No.6, pp.427-447, 1999.
- Dellaert, B.G.C., The Tourist As Value Creator On The Web. In D. Buhalis and W. Schertler (editors), Information and Communication Technologies in Tourism, New York: Springer Wien. pp.66-76, 1999.
- Ellsworth J.H. and Ellsworth M.V., Marketing On The Web: Multimedia Strategies For The WWW, New York: John Wiley, 1996.
- Furnell S.M. and Karweni T., Security Implications Of Electronic Commerce, Web Research, Vol.9, No.5, pp.372-382, 1996.
- Purnell S.M. and Warren M.J., Computer Abuse: Vandalizing the Information Society, Web Research, Vol.7. No.1. pp.61-66, 1997.
- Hafner K. and Lyon M., When Wizards Stay Up, Late: The Origins of the Web, New York: Simon and Schuster, 1998.
- Helnen J., Web Marketing Practices. Information Management and Computer Security, Vol.4, No.5, pp.7-14, 1996.

26

Information Technology: A Tool for Promotion of Tourism in Andhra Pradesh

Hemant Kumar Sastry
Faculty, National Institute of Tourism & Hospitality Management,
Telecom Nagar, Gachibowli, Hyderabad – 500 032.
Email :hk_shastry@yahoo.com

ABSTRACT

Tourism is recognized as an important economic and social activity, generating a large amount of income, employment and foreign currency along with investment opportunities Information and communication technologies are prominently in use in the tourism sector around the world. IT is used for tourism product development, marketing, distribution and training of tourism sector personnel. The technologies have become indispensable in order to find out and satisfy the ever-changing demands for tourism products. Information technology has during the last decade evolved in a dramatic way and has become a part of everyday life for most people in the modern society. IT has a significant impact on industries as well. With markets becoming faster, bigger, more standardized as well as segmented, and more competitive, importance of IT in the day to day business of organizations growth would have opportunities or face threats. The article looks at the use of information and communication technologies in tourism across various destinations in India. Further, a comparison is drawn of usage in Andhra Pradesh with indicative areas of improvement.

Keywords: *Tourism, Information Technology*

INTRODUCTION

Information Technology (IT) may be defined as electronic means of capturing, processing, storing and communicating information, as well as the products and services that provide or support such activities. IT encompasses computer hardware and software, telecommunications equipment, and electronically-based industries, as well as information applications in all economic sectors. ITs include not only hardware and software but also the groupware, NetWare, as well as the intellectual capacity to develop, program and maintain the equipment (Buhalis 2000).

Poon (1993, pp 424.) defines Information Technology as a collective term given to the most recent developments in the electronic mode and the mechanisms (Computers and communication technologies) used for the acquisition, processing, analysis, storage, retrieval, dissemination and application of information. Here, IT may be considered as the entire range of electronic tools that facilitate the operational and strategic management of organizations such as: Computers, Multimedia, Computer Networks, Internet, Intranet and Extranet, Satellites, Teleconferencing, Management Information Systems, Wireless communication systems, Telephones, fax, telex and Modems. Therefore, Information Technology has the potential to be a major driving force behind economic growth through two paths: first, by generating new economic activity, notably through the production of IT goods and services; and second, through its potentially strong restructuring impact on existing economic activities. Thus, IT may affect economic activities in a variety of ways: improving the quality of existing services; creating new services; raising labour productivity; increasing capital intensity; enhancing economies of scale; and creating new economic structures.

INFORMATION TECHNOLOGY AND TOURISM INDUSTRY

Information Technologies (ICTs) and tourism are two of the most dynamic drivers of global economy. Tourism should be treated as an information-intensive industry. Travel and tourism can be defined in simple terms as an information business, since information is one of the most important quality parameters to support actions for the tourism area as a service industry. Therefore, IT is important for day-to-day operations of travel and tourism industry through generation, gathering, processing, application and communication of information.

The Internet as an information technology is a perfect platform for companies within the industry to bring information about their products to the customers, in a direct, cost-minimizing and time-effective way. The tourism industry has always been one of the pioneers by using new communication and information technologies. The Internet is a possible instrument to change the structures and processes within the tourism industry. New value chains and value systems are emerging and the players within the industry have to redesign their strategy under the power of IT. A competitive strategy is based on the defense or creation of competitive advantage.

INFORMATION TECHNOLOGY ACROSS VARIOUS STATES IN INDIA

Information Technology is an engine of global economic growth. IT equipment appears to be almost everywhere, in the office, on the factory floor, in the classroom, at home, and even in people's pockets. By all accounts, IT appears to be rapidly changing the way many enterprises conduct business and communicate. The proliferation of IT has made the world seem much a smaller, as computer-related innovations, such as the Internet, let individuals on opposite sides of the world interacts in ways that were unimagined 20 years ago. The explosion of IT spending over the last few decades has sparked renewed interest in the growth. Use of Information and Communication Technology for Tourism Promotion across 08 Indian States is listed is Table 1. Usage of ICTs for the State of Andhra Pradesh is limited to Mass Mailing and System Administration, and Single Point – Universal Access Number. On comparison with practices across the States, the following recommendations emerge for the State of Andhra Pradesh:

- Production of Multimedia and CD-ROMS & DVDs on *'Andhra Pradesh'* and its USP
- Print Media: Picture book on Andhra Pradesh
- Theme-based Advertisement on TV commercials
- Short documentaries in satellite TV Channels
- Toll Free phone service
- Installing close circuit television (CTV) at railway stations, airports, bus terminals
- Installation of Touch screen kiosks
- Interactive websites
- Digital tourist guide in multiple language
- Formation of e-mail fan club
- Online reservation with payment facility
- Wide area Network dedicated
- Tourism database management System with GIS facility
- Digital Library provides information about destinations
- Corporate film for presentations

Table 1: Use of ICTs across 08 Indian States

STATE	Use of ICT
KERALA	1. Multimedia and CD-ROMS on *'Ayurveda'* 2. *'The Kerala'* CD-ROMS in Foreign Languages (French and German) 3. Set of Seven CD-ROMs on different attractions of the state 4. A series of DVDs on classical dances of India 5. Print Media: Picture book on Kerala 6. Advertisement on TV commercials: *'Water Colours by God'* 7. Short documentaries in satellite TV Channels 8. Connectivity with BBC world TV channel 9. Toll Free phone service
TAMILNADU	1. Producing regular CD-ROM's DVD's Films and TV 2. Telecasting of short documentaries in satellite TV channels. 3. Installing close circuit television (CTV) at railway stations, airports, bus terminals 4. Commercials in various TV channels 5. Installation of Touch screen kiosks 6. Interactive websites 7. Digital tourist guide in multiple language 8. Formation of e-mail fan club 9. A Part of Global Toll free services for US and International Telephone conference service, International data transmission service and International digital leased line service 10. Online reservation with payment facility
KARNATAKA	1. Call centre with national Toll free number 2. Touch screen kiosks
WEST BENGAL	1. Wide area Network dedicated 2. Tourism database management System with GIS facility 3. Interactive Touch screen kiosks
GUJRAT	1. Preparation of Digital Tourist guide 2. Digital Library provides information about destinations

GOA	1. Touch screen kiosks about 11 are installed at prominent places with 30 minute video screening 2. 8 minute corporate film for presentation 3. New web site with 24 hours monitoring is about for implementation
SIKKIM	1. Information Technology training for its officials 2. Making an employee computer literate
UTTARANCHAL	1. Touch screens kiosks have installed for information 2. Hotels are also computerized

(Source: Ministry of Tourism, Government of India, 2005)

Table 2: Effectiveness of Tourism Websites of 11 Indian States

Parameters	Orissa	WestBengal	Maharastra	Gujrat	Goa	Rajashtan	Uttaranchal	Kerala	Tamilnadu	Karnataka	sikkim
User friendliness	2	2	2	2	2	2	1	1	2	2	3
Graphic design	4	3	2	2	2	2	2	2	3	3	4
Aesthetics and beauty	4	3	3	3	3	2	3	1	3	2	4
Functionality	2	3	3	3	3	2	2	2	3	3	4
Navigation and links	3	3	2	2	2	2	3	2	3	3	4
Search facilities	2	4	3	4	4	2	2	2	5	2	5
Interactivity	1	5	4	5	5	2	2	2	5	4	4
updation of site	2	4	4	1	1	2	1	1	3	4	4
relevance of content	2	3	3	3	3	2	2	1	3	2	3
Innovation	2	4	2	4	4	3	1	2	4	4	4
Creativity	2	4	3	3	3	3	2	2	3	3	4
Integration	4	5	2	3	3	3	3	2	4	4	5
Sum	30	43	33	35	34	27	24	20	41	36	48
Average	2.5	3.6	2.8	2.9	2.8	2.3	2.0	1.7	3.4	3.0	4.0

(Source: Ministry of Tourism, Government of India, 2005)

1-Strongly Agree 2-Agree 3.Neither Agree nor Disagree 4.Disagree 5-Strongly Disagree

Further, Internet presents a great possibility for the tourism industry to sell and market their services online. Effectiveness of a web site may be measured from its user friendliness, graphic design and its accessibility. An effective web site should provide significant value added to visitors through its features. Web sites of 11 Indian states were judged (Ministry of Tourism, Government of India, 2005) on various parameters: user friendliness, graphic design, aesthetics and beauty, functionality, navigation and links, search facilities, interactivity, updating of site, relevance of content, innovation, creativity and integration, as listed in Table 2.

Kerala has scored 1.7 as average and for all the parameters it has scored weight age between 1 and 2, which indicates that Kerala website is an effective website. For the website of Andhra Pradesh, the rating of parameters is shown in Table 3.

Table 3: Andhra Pradesh Tourism Website: Ratings

Parameters	ANDHRA PRADESH
User friendliness	1
Graphic design	2
Aesthetics and beauty	2
Functionality	3
Navigation and links	3
search facilities	2
Interactivity	1
Updation of site	3
relevance of content	2
Innovation	3
Creativity	3
Integration	3
Sum	28
Average	2.3

(Source: Ministry of Tourism, Government of India, 2005)

Recommendations

Comparatively, Andhra Pradesh has to improve its website on the Graphic design, Aesthetics and beauty Functionality, Navigation and links, search facilities, updation of site, relevance of content, Innovation, Creativity and Integration.

Conclusion

In today's society information technology has become an important part to simplify peoples' everyday life. Speed and flexibility are factors which both the tourists and companies demand and information technology can help to provide. The Tourism Industry is a growing and very important industry. The tourism and information technology are two of the largest industries in the world and the dynamic relationship between the two changes the way society operates. The use of IT will enhance the Tourism sector significantly. The usage of IT across various states on its tools such as Multimedia and CD-ROMS , DVDs , Print Media: Picture book's, Advertisement on TV commercials, Short documentaries in satellite TV Channels and Toll Free phone service will promote tourism in a big way.. Recommendations are suggested on using various IT tools for the promotion of Andhra Pradesh. Of the ICT application and specific reference of web sites for certain States of India were judged by Ministry of Tourism, Government of India (2005) on parameters listed. A comparative analysis was drawn for the State of Andhra Pradesh for enhancing ICT applications for better promotion of tourism along with improving offering through website by enhancing design, aesthetics and functionality, navigation and links, search facilities, updation of site, relevance of content, innovation, creativity and integration.

REFERENCE

- Buhalis, D. (2000) Tourism in an Era of Information Technology in Faulkner, B. Moscardo, G and Laws, E (Eds.). *Tourism in the 21st Century- Reflections on experience.* New York, Continuum.
- Cooper, C. (1993). The future of Tourism - Information Technology in *Tourism Principles and Practice.* Singapore, Prentice Hall.
- Ministry of Tourism, Government of India. (2005). Documentation of best practices adopted by State Governments in *State Profile and Tourism Development*, Final Report, Vol- II. New Delhi, MOT (MR Division).

27

Need of Networking and Coordination Among Government Departments in Public Private Partnership, A study of the Tourism Policy of Andhra Pradesh Tourism

P. J. Shyju

INTRODUCTION

The diffuse and fragmented nature of tourism development has paved the way to think the governments to redifine the nature of planning of tourism development. Like many modern industries," tourism is an assembly process. Over the past few years the centralised system of tourism administration has witnessed both positive and negative impacts. In many countries the concept of intra-industry cooperation have been promoted by the stake holders and the need of cross border tourism alliances have been established to maximise the benefits from tourism. The importance of involving diverse stake holders in tourism planning and management is gaining momentum. Collaborative arrangements ror tourism planning involve the direct interaction between the industry representatives and governments. This is aimed to improve the networking and cooperative endeavour from the state's side. The biggest bottleneck for tourism development in any state is lack of coordination among the implementing agencies. In certain cases the role of investors are confined to the construction and management of the tourism infrastructure and latter the changing policies of governments create hassles in the way ahead.

Partnerships involved in tourism planning bring together interests in the same destination but in different sectors or else parties in different destinations but with mutual interests in one issue or related issues. A key reason for the growing interest in partnerships in tourism development is that tourist destinations and organisations may be able to gain competitive advantage by bringing together knowledge, expertise and other resources of several stake holders (Kotler et.al 1993). Some experts claim that the broadly based ownership of tourism policies can bring democratic empowerment and equity, operational advantage and an enhanced tourism product (Jamal and Getz 1995).

Partnership approaches to tourism planning are widely endorscd by government and public agencies in many developed nations. A variety of terms used to describe different collaborative arrangements in tourism including coalitions, forums, alliances, task forces, and public private partnerships. The term 'partnership' label is widely used to show the commitment and concerned towards environmental quality, resource management and sustainable development.

Objectives

1. To find out the critical gaps in tourism administration of Andhra Pradesh, to coordinate various departments and other agencies who are functioning in the state.
2. Role of state in attracting private investment for tourism development and requirement of networking and coordination at higher level to lower level of administrative mechanism.
3. Suggest a possjble working model for the betterment of communication and coordination among various levels.

Methodology

This paper is an attempt to bring out the major issues involved in Public Private Participation Policy of the Government. The major issue is the term Public Private. Participation is not defined properly. It gives different meanings like the participation of public in tourism projects, or investment by the public sector only. Then the question naturally comes like what is the role of government. Here the interpretation of Public Private Participation is the joint venture of Government and the Private sector to establish tourism projects. The report of National Committee on Tourism, National Action Plan of Government of India has clearly defined the role of government as a catalyst to speed up the tourism promotion activities in the country.

The need of coordination among stake holders for sustainable development is studied in the beginning part of the paper. A detailed study of the investment strategy of the state is presented and the issues are also analysed in the second part. As a major role player, the role of state, different functionaries, line departments, categorisation of areas required, coordination and networking, a working model are the discussion points in the later part. The tourism policy of Andhra Pradesh mentioned here is for the time period of 2000-2005. Secondary data sources are gathered from the brochures and other published materials hrought out hy the Government of Andhra Pradesh time to time. Interaction with the state government officials and personal experience in the capacity of Tourism Officer are also utilised here to present the information related to investment patterns.

Need of coordination among stake holders for sustainable development.

The question of sustainability is based on the use of available resources. Tourism makes extensive use of natural resources, thereby affecting the long term viability of tourism projects. The Bruntland Commissions defined sustainable development is development that meets the need of the present without compromising the ability of future generations to meet their needs (WECO 1987). This definition underlines needs of usage of resources with proper care on future generation. Problem always arises when there is a competition for the scarce resources. This is particularly relevant in developing countries where tbe need to generate income is more likely to lead to a rapid exploitation of the resource base and an uneven distribution of the related profits between foreign investors and host populations and governments directly involved in the shaping of tourism development activities in the shaping of tourism development.

Developing Sustainable Partnerships

It is proved that collaborative actions lead to the efficient use of resources.

Integration is taking place in between governments, regional planning authorities, local go\"crmm:ms and the community. This results in new inter organisalional forms, mutual agreements coalitions and joint management of tourism resources. A majority of tourism partnerships described in the sustainable development literature are cross sector initiatives that often representatives from industry, government, and the voluntary secto.rs (Sitarz, 1998). Selin and Chavez (1995) suggest that tourism collaborations may be highly structured characterized by legally binding agreements or may be quite unstructured verbal agreements between participating organisations. The intended outcomes of collaborative agreements can also differ. with the objectives sometimes being to develop a strategic vision or a plan for a destination. There are often complex relational webs between stake holders that are structured around diverse economic, political and cultural forces, with some linkages in these networks being relatively more structured than others. Wood and Gray define collaborative arrangements related to formal institutional or policy networks and their associated stake holder relations.

Lack of information about returns on private investment may lead firms to select alternatives that directly increase the revenue, rather than environmental amenities, that indirectly contribute revenue through increased customer satisfaction. From an economic perspective, an investment's cost and revenues are used to judge its desirability. /(n investment in product characteristics like any other although estimates of the revenues and costs associated with the investment is difficult to obtain. An investment is acceptable if the revenues it generates are greater than its total cost, and not an acceptable if they are less than the total cost. However the calculation of the revenues and costs associated with an investment is difficult because it happened at different times. The revenues and costs are realised incrementally over time.

Role of the State

Various state governments have a greater role to promote tourism in the states. To motivate private sector in tourism by providing basic infrastructural support and an investor friendly policy in the state Public Private Participation is highly appreciated. The Government will identify land for various tourism projects and the agreement will be signed for a longer period depends on the investment. Availability of land at a moderate rate is the pressing issue. By solving the issue the of identification of vacant land for establishing *hotels.* amusement parks and related establishments basic step is laid down to attract investors.

The Government plays a crucial role here to identify and take over land from other departments municipalities gramapanchayats and public land. Rules have to be amended in many cases in order to taking up land, conversion of land located near to the lakebeds, riverside and the beachfront. Negotiations and entering in to agreement with investors and the monitoring progress of the work, approval of various phases of the projects are the steps ahead. In order to ground the project coordination and a cooperative endeavor is necessary among various departments, unless all the efforts will be like any other projects only.

The above mentioned information emphasize the effort on the side of government to attract investment to the state. A pro-investment approach is necessary to create a platform to encourage the investors. Andhra Pradesh is second only to Uttar Pradesh in terms of domestic tourist arrivals. Although Tirupathi and other pilgrim centres have become the centre of attractions, natural attractions like Vishakpatnam, Godavari Districts attracts lot of tourists. The tourism policy announced by the government in the year ::WOO. special tourism areas were formed and the attention is diverted in to Public Private Participation Programme. The vision 2020 of Andhra Pradesh Tourism says

Tourism is recognised the world over as a growth engine as it is an income multiplier. employment generator and foreign exchange earner. By 2020 Andhra Pradesh will be a leading tourism destination in India offering a variety of experiences 10 its visitor.

Major initiatives by the sate government to promote tourism

1. State Tourism Promotion Committee—Chief Secretary as chairman has been set up for decision making, and improves coordination among different departments.
2. At the district level District Tourism Promotion Councils have been formed with District Magistrates as Chairpersons, to speed up the tourism promotion activities at district level.
3. A State Tourism Promotion Board is the policy making body under the (Chairmanship of the (Chief Minister It has the representation of the membership *like* F *APCCI, ClI,* Airlines, and Hoteliers.
4. *District* Tourism Promotion Councils are empowered to take decisions concerning private investment with the value of the project cost for plant and machinery cost not more than 100 Lakhs.
5. The Empowered Committee may review the rejected or conditional sanctions, permits etc. and pass appropriate orders.
6. The State Board, the highest committee under the Chairmanship of the Chief Minister may review any cases referred to it and take appropriate decisions.

7. The decisions of these committees are binding on the Committees below them and on all the concerned competent agencies like municipalities, Grampanchayats, and factories inspectorates, etc
8. The Andhra Pradesh Single Window Clearance Act 2002 has been legislated to enable the entrepreneurs to submit and obtain their licenses, No Objection Certificates, Permits etc.
9. Every committee has representation from the stakeholder agencies like hoteliers, representatives from tour operators, travel agencies etc.
10. The state government will act as a catalyst and adopt a pro-active, investor friendly, open door policy for investors.

Public Private Participation

Under this policy the vacant government lands will be offered for private investment through advertisement, inviting private entrepreneurs. The entrepreneurs will .be supplied with the Reqpest for Proposals documents which need to be submitted back with complete information and supporting documents. The land will he leased for a maximum period of 33 years and actual period depends on the project cost, components and economics of the project. Towards leasing of the land, the entrepreneur has to pay a lease rent at 5% of market value with 5% annual escalation over the previous year's amount.

For private entrepreneurs who wish to set up tourism projects on their lands, necessary guidance and assistance will be extended by the department.

For preparation of feasibility report or architectural concepts and drawings, services of em panelled consultants may be empanelled on payment of their fees.

For small projects, the architect's services from the department will be provided. The government has catagorised tourism units as ·

- ✓ Special Tourism Units—Fixed capital investment of Rs 10 Crores or more
- ✓ Large scale Tourism Units -Fixed capital investment of more than Rs 90 lakh
- ✓ Small scale Tourism llnits – Fixed capital investment of more than Rs 10 lakh 90 lakhs
- ✓ Tiny Tourism Units – Fixed capital investment of less than Rs 10 lakh

Incentives Concession and Cooperation

Sales Tax-Fully exempted for Five years for new units and special projeds limited to three star hotels and above. Exemption is limited to 100% of the fixed capital costs to the amusement and theme parks coming up in Special Tourism Areas and Notified areas.

Luxury Tax: Five year exemption of luxury tax for new hotels. No luxury tax for room tariff up to Rs. 300 per day.

Entertainment Tax: Exemption is given 5 years for IMAX and for multiplexes on case by cases.

Special Incentives: A large project above Rs 10 crore investments in the state is given the status of special Projects. Special incentives will be given case by case.

Automatic conversion of Land use: Exemption from zoning regulations of the Urban Development Authorities and Municipalities for the purpose of local approvals subject to pollution checks. Provision is made to convert land to tourism projects from Industrial. Commercial. R,esidential. and Public.

Other than, the above mentioned concessions are available under the central govt. policy. deductions are also available under central excise. income tax. other laws for hotels, multiplexes, ropeways etc.

List of Major Projects Awarded by Projects Monitoring Unit, Dept. of Tourism, Govt. of Andhra Pradesh .

1. IMAX Theatre, Hyderabad Rs. 61.00 Crores
2. Beach Resort, Visakhpatnam Rs. 38.00 Crores
3. Rock Garden, Hyderabad Rs. 27.00 Crores
4. Beach Resort, Manginapudi Rs. 4.75 Crores
5. Maya Bazar, Snow Theme Park Rs. 20.80 Crores
6. Botanical Garden at Kothaguda Rs. 21.40 Crores
7. Theme Park at Shamcerpet. Rangareddy Rs. 57.00 Crores

Other than the above said projects a number of small units were also initiated by the government in various districts with Private Public Participation.

Need of coordination and integration among departments.

There are approximately 70 departments functioning under the government in Andhra Pradesh. These departments are directly or indirectly associated with departments. The following chart explains the related departments associated with tourism development activities.

Departments directly associated with tourism development

- ✓ Forests and Wildlife
- ✓ Sporls and Youth Welfare
- ✓ Endowment
- ✓ Archeology and Museums
- ✓ Culture

Departments indirectly associated with Tourism Development

- ✓ Revenue
- ✓ Social Welfare
- ✓ Rural Development
- ✓ Industries

- ✓ Education
- ✓ Agriculture
- ✓ Irrigation
- ✓ Roads and Buildings
- ✓ Home Affairs
- ✓ Finance
- ✓ Tribal Welfare
- ✓ Electricity
- ✓ Panchayati Raj
- ✓ Health
- ✓ Transport
- ✓ Planning
- ✓ *Pollution control*
- ✓ General Administration, and Urban Development
- ✓ Public Relations

Govt. Agencies involved in Tourism Development in Andhra Pradesh

1. Department of Tourism
2. Andhra Pradesh Tourism Development Corporation
3. Urban Development Authorities (Hyderabad Urban Development Authority,(HUDA), Vijayavada Urban Development Authority,(VUDA), Vizag Urban Development Authority, Tirupathi Urban Development Authority (TUDA) etc.
4. Municipal Administration, Hyderabad, Warrangal, Tirumala- Tirupathi, Vizag, Vijayavada
5. Religious. i.e. Tirumala Tirupati Devasthanam, (TTD), Basar, Srisailam, Lepakshi, Kanaka Durga Temple, Vijayavada, Puttaparthi Sri Sai Baba Trust, Vaqf Board etc.
6. AP Khadi Village Industries Corporation, AP Productivity Council
7. AP Velugu and Self Help Groups

The structure of Tourism Department in terms of implementing Tourism Plan

State Tourism Promotion Committee

↓

Department of Tourism

↓

District Tourism Promotion Councils

Andhra Pradesh Tourism Development Corporation a) Accommodation units (Hotels & Guest houses), b) Water fleet, c) Adventure Tourism Unit d)Ecotourism unit e)Engineering Unit t) New Projects & Investment, g)Marketing, h) Planning. i) Administration j) Booking and Information k) Accounts

Department of Tourism

a) planning and budgeting, b)Public Relations & Marketing, c) District Tourism, d) Tourism Information. e) Gnapika (Souvenir shops). t) Projects, g) Administration, h) Accounts. i) Promotional programme (fairs, festivals etc) Competition than coordination

The following areas are where the Department of Tourism and Andhra Pradesh Tourism functions as competitors

- ✓ New investments,
- ✓ Marketing
- ✓ Tourism information
- ✓ Creating tourism infrastructure

Inter Departmental Issues

Lack or coordination among. various departments like Archeology and Museums, Irrigation etc. orten results in unnecessary delays in taking decisions, grounding projects, completion and even in operational levels. Many tourists' spots are located in the premises of the Department of Irrigation. Insufficient allocation of fund for proper maintenance and human resources resulted in degradation of facilities available in many destinations. The land can'(he easily handed over to the Dept. of Tourism. hecause of no. or hurdks ahead. Lven if all) reply eomes from the higher levels it always takes a cautious approach to keep the project in pending. Many departments are running with insufficient funds and which results in the poor maintenance of facilities. Normally the time duration taking place for transferring the properties through PPP mode is high, its become difficult to manage the properties it has taken over.

The behavjour of top officials also play a key role in the decision making part, where its understood that unless there is pressure from the Chief Ministers office level the movement of files in a slow manner. Ego clashes, communication gaps, official conflicts and political interference are further delaying projects from its implementation. Lack of proper support form the subordinates, communicating information late to the Senior officials, confusions over the official jargons and wrong interpretation of Government orders further make things in typical bureaucratic manner. The escort services provided by the Department of Tourism could sort out such issues up to certain extend. Proper communication from the district level and the revenue department is the prerequisite to identify vacant lands in the state. The valuation process also need to be highlighted here because always protests are taking place due to allegations that the price of the land value is under estimated.

Issues and Problems Facing by Investors

Government departments are often blamed of delay in processing and lack of integrity of officials. Redtapism, laxity, lack of efficiency from the part of officials are the major concerns, which create a negative attitude among the investors. The ignorant approach of the lower level functionaries also a matter of serious concern because the higher officials are sometimes. directed, or influenced by the lower level staff.

Political motives, vested interests keep the investors always away. Problems arise when there are no unanimous decisions among the political leaders on issues like foreign Direct

Investment, inviting private investment etc. Many issues are also drawn to court and the long time required sorting out the legal disputes, investors are discouraged and the smooth coordination of departments also curtailed in a certain extent.

Model of Communication network in State administration

Horizontal Integration Among Line Departments

Here the role of Department of tourism is a coordinator. Other function is monitoring the progress and reminding other department heads about the activities in completion, pipeline and grounding etc. Priority should be given to those departments which are directly associated with tourism development. Departments such as Forests, Revenue, Culture, Archeology etc.

Vertical Integration within the Department

Its important to look in to the intra departmental coordination. Communication should be promoted in the top-down and vice versa. It has been observed in many times that lack of good communication within the department results in unnecessary delays. Many officers who are working in tourism are either deputed from other departments or appointed on contract basis. This prevents them to deliver the work at the desired level. Decentralisation of power, raising the funds to the district, organised effort to promote tourism at district level, support to investors etc are essential to improve the performance of the department.

Communication Network in State Tourism Administration

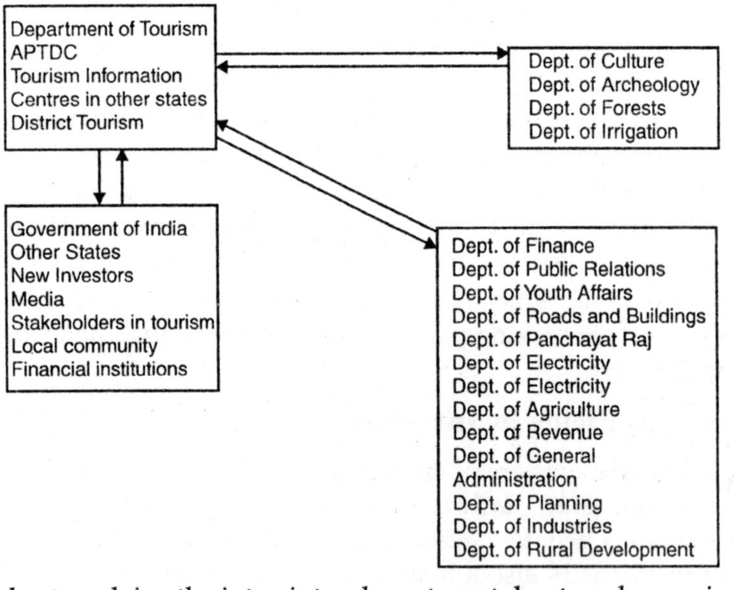

The above chart explains the intra-inter departmental network, required for the better coordination among the administrative level. The proposed system will bring out the best output and organised frame work for tourism development in the state. Regular meetings at higher level to the lower level are essential to coordinate the development activities in the state, Overlapping of works. duplication of documents. interdepartmental issues etc, can be sorted out without any administrative hassles.

The cooperative endeavour from the line departments is as important as the role of major departments. The primary objective of any government is welfare of the people and the state; hence than an individual identity, achievement of the state should be the main concern of any departments. The role of private sector is crucial for the development of tourism infrastructure in the state. In order to develop tourism, the joi,!1t venture state, private sector and the community.

South Indian Tourism Conference

This was an innovative step to unite the southern states of India (Kerala, Tamil Nadu, Karnataka and Andhra Pradesh) to coordinate the tourism development programme. The first meeting of the four states was held in Hyderabad in 2003. Tfie conference of top officials and ministers of these states agreed to work together in the following areas.

1. Promotion of tourism in South India
2. Aggressive marketing, instead of competing each other the states will work together tl1.ereby share the benefits.
3. Conducting joint exercises like organising and participating promotional programmcs in I ndia and ahroad.
4. Reducing road tax, entry fees etc.
5. Protecting the rights of the states, attracting investors
6. Tour packages to cover the untapped potentials of the states.

The thrust was given to marketing and promotion of tourism, where every state can mutually share the benefits. There are many attractions which are unexploited, or tourists are unaware. Reducing taxes and entry fee will help tourists to visit the neighbouring states without incurring additional costs.

CONCLUSION

This paper analysed the need of coordination among the stakeholders in tourism and various government departments. Governments are seeking means to increase the private investment in the states, its imperative to channelise the efforts in to a better output. The ultimate aim of the state is to increase the employment opportunities, and economic prosperity. The preferred model suggest the vertical integration within the department and better interaction among the related departments which are directly or indirectly associated with tourism.

Within the framework of the individual departments, each functionary has a single goal, which depends on the flow of communication and effective networking among the participants. In the context of investment in physical capital, it has an important role in upgrading the infrastructure that underpins the industry. Small investments also has a dominant role, were the participation of the local community is ensured. Here the invest offers like interest subsidies, tax holidays has a greater role.

During the period of 2000-2005, Andhra Pradesh could attract investments approximately of Rs. 360 crorcs in tourism. As the tourism policy of the states, the role of tourism as an engine of economic growth and the state functions as a facilitator to bring in to effect the a cooperative endeavour of both private and public sector on one hand and among di flerent sectors of the government of the on the other for orderly utilisation of the above mentioned resources for sustainable development.

The Andhra Pradesh *model* of investment policy is well appreciated and many states had followed the same approach. Still there are bottlenecks at the time of grounding of the projects and various stages of implementation. The only possible solution to overtake this issue is, a well coordinated administration, where the bureaucracy and the representatives of the public functions as the tools of a same machine. Thereby solving the issues of unemployment, poverty, under-utilisation of resources and driving the nation to a developed and advanced country.

REFERENCES

- A Blake, Sinclair and J A C Soria (2006), Tourism Productivity Evidence from the U K, *Annals of Tourism Research,* Vol. 33, No 4, pp 1099-1120.
- B. Bramwell and B.Lane (2006) 'Collaborative Tourism Planning', Tourism Collaboration and Partnerships, Politics, Practice and Sustainability, Viva Books, New Delhi.
- Claudia A.G, (2006), Territorial Planning and Tourism Development Tax, *Annals of Tourism Research,* Vol. 30, No 4, pp 886-905.
- Kotler. P, Haider,D.H. Rein (1993), Marketing Places, Attracting Investment, Industry and Tourism and Tourism Cities.
- LJ Cox and G R Veith, (2003), Hotel Investment in Open Area, *Annals of Tourism Research,* Vol. 30, No 2, pp 342-352.
- P Teo. and L.H Li 2003. Global and Local interactions in Tourism. *Annals of Tourism Research,* Vol. 30. No 2. pp 287-306.
- Maureen G. Reed 'Collaborative Tourism Planning as Adaptive Experiment in Emergent Tourism Settings', in B. Bramwell and B. Lane, (eds) *Tourism collaboration and Partnerships, Politics, Practice and Sustainability,* Viva Books, New Delhi.

- Steve Selin, 'Developing a Typology of Sustainable Tourism Partnerships' in B. Bramwell and B. Lane, (eds) *Tourism Collaboration and Partnerships, Politics, Practice and Sustainability*, Viva Books, New Delhi.
- Selm and Chavez D (1995), Developing an Evolutionary Tourism Partnership Model, *Annals of Tourism Research*, Vol. 22, No 4, pp 844-856.
- The Hindu- Business Linc. July 09. 2004.
- www.aptourism.com
- Tourism Projects Profile, Youth Advancement and Culture Department, 2003 Andhra Pradesh Celebrations, *Indian Express Group*, 2001, pp 30-35.